T0391850

Gender Equality and Policy Implementation in the Corporate World

Gender Equality and Policy Implementation in the Corporate World

Making Democracy Work in Business

Edited by

ISABELLE ENGELI
AMY G. MAZUR

OXFORD
UNIVERSITY PRESS

Great Clarendon Street, Oxford, OX2 6DP,
United Kingdom

Oxford University Press is a department of the University of Oxford.
It furthers the University's objective of excellence in research, scholarship,
and education by publishing worldwide. Oxford is a registered trade mark of
Oxford University Press in the UK and in certain other countries

Published in the United States of America by Oxford University Press
198 Madison Avenue, New York, NY 10016, United States of America

British Library Cataloguing in Publication Data
Data available

Library of Congress Control Number: 2021951446

ISBN 978–0–19–886521–6

DOI: 10.1093/oso/9780198865216.001.0001

Printed and bound by
CPI Group (UK) Ltd, Croydon, CR0 4YY

To Hege Skjeie for her pioneering scholarship, her engagement toward making equality work on the ground, and her zest for life

Acknowledgments

This book is the outcome of a collective effort to conduct research that matters on the ground despite limited funding. Many scholars and institutions have stepped in all along this adventure to keep it running. Their dedication, support, and generosity drove this book home.

First and foremost, we would like to express our appreciation and gratitude to all of the chapter contributors who have ridden out the wave of slow science with us in challenging times for gender-related research funding and, later on, in the midst of a global pandemic. They have worked tirelessly through the iterative process between their country-based fieldwork and the application of the Gender Equality Policy in Practice (GEPP) approach. Without their engagement, the project would neither have seen the light of day nor come to such successful fruition.

We are very grateful to CORE-Center for Research on Gender Equality at the Institute for Social Research in Oslo and its director, Mari Teigen, for hosting the first GEPP-Board workshop in June 2018. The world-class organizational support from CORE, the tireless efforts of Mari Teigen, and the funding secured by her from the Norwegian Ministry of Gender Equality for this workshop were instrumental to our research, also for providing the financial support necessary for our contributors to come from far and wide—Western, Central and Eastern Europe, North America, and Australia. Our appreciation also goes to the Amsterdam Research Centre for Gender and Sexuality (ARC-GS), Liza Mügge, and Sanne van Oosten, for hosting and supporting the organization of our GEPP-Board mid-point workshop in Amsterdam in July 2019.

We are extremely thankful to Joni Lovenduski who co-founded the GEPP International Network. She went above and beyond for GEPP and provided way more than "just" core leadership and an administrative home at Birkbeck, University of London. We greatly appreciate Birkbeck, University of London for financial support for GEPP between 2013 and 2018 and the large-scale workshop in May 2016 with over fifty participants from Europe and North America. Our heartfelt thanks go to the Laboratory for Interdisciplinary Evaluation of Public Policies (LIEPP) at Sciences Po Paris and its past and present directors, Cornelia Woll, Bruno Palier, and Anne Revillard. LIEPP has been instrumental in supporting GEPP since its very beginning, notably, through funding and hosting the inaugural GEPP research workshop held in 2014. Many thanks also go the Department of Government at Uppsala University, Elin Bjarnegård, Christina Bergqvist, and Pär Zetterberg, and to the Center for Gender Studies (CEG) at the University of Lausanne and Eléonore Lépinard for hosting our first large-scale GEPP workshop in June 2015 in Uppsala and our third large-scale workshop in June 2017 in Lausanne.

Without the enthusiasm of Dominic Byatt at Oxford University Press for the original proposal when we first pitched it to him in 2018 and his continued faith that we would submit a high-quality final manuscript, we would not have been able to navigate through the shoals of COVID-19. We would also like to thank our institutions, the University of Exeter and Washington State University, for providing our home bases and key financial resources, with special recognition to the CO Johnson Professorship at WSU. Finally, and last but not least, our colleagues, friends, and families have provided essential unwavering support throughout the project and at crucial times when the light of the tunnel was only a flicker.

This book is dedicated to Hege Skjeie whose imprint has been fundamental to the GEPP project and this book. Hege was a pioneer of gender research in political science, a hugely influential figure in the field of gender equality policy, and a vibrant and generous presence in our GEPP research community. Throughout her path-breaking career, Hege unremittingly demonstrated how excellence in academic research can promote gender equality on the ground and will remain a long-lasting inspiration for gender equality research.

Isabelle Engeli, Bristol, UK
Amy G. Mazur, Moscow, ID, USA

Contents

List of Figures

List of Tables

Contributors Biographies

Petra Ahrens is Senior Researcher on the ERC-funded research project EUGenDem at Tampere University. She was Assistant Professor at Humboldt-Universität zu Berlin (2014–2016), Marie-Curie-Sklodowska-Fellow, and Guest Professor at the University of Antwerp (2017–2019). Her research focuses on gender policy and politics in the European Union, transnational civil society organizations, as well as gender equality in Germany. Petra is the Co-Chair of the ECPR Standing Group on Gender and Politics and is Co-Editor of *Femina Politica*. She is the author of *Actors, Institutions, and the Making of EU Gender Equality Programs* (Palgrave Macmillan, 2018), co-author of *Gender Equality in Politics—Implementing Party Quotas in Germany and Austria* (Springer 2020, with Katja Chmilewski, Sabine Lang, and Birgit Sauer), and co-editor of *Gendering the European Parliament* (Rowman & Littlefield/ECPR Press 2019, with Lise Rolandsen Agustín).

Soline Blanchard is Associate Professor in Sociology at the Université Lumière Lyon 2 and a member at the Max Weber Centre. Her research explores multiple inequalities in the workplace (gender, class, and age) at all levels of the organizational hierarchy, including corporate governance. She is the author of *Qualifier l'égalité: Outil politiques et enjeux scientifiques* (Presse Universitaires de Rennes 2021, with Sophie Pochic) and has published articles in *French Politics*, *Nouvelles Question Féministes* and *European Journal of Politics and Gender*.

Isabelle Engeli is Professor of Public Policy and Head of the Politics Department at the University of Exeter. Her research focuses on gendering policy attention and implementation, party competition, and morality politics, as well as comparative research strategies for policy analysis. She leads, with Amy G. Mazur, the Gender Equality Policy in Practice (GEPP) International Network. Her research appears in journals such as *European Journal of Political Research*, *European Journal of Politics and Gender*, *Journal of European Public Policy*, *Regulation & Governance*, *Revue Française de Science Politics*, and *West European Politics*. She is Editor-in-Chief of the *European Journal of Political Research*, and Founding Editor of the *European Journal of Politics and Gender*. She currently serves as the Vice-President of the International Public Policy Association and is on the Advisory Board of the European Politics and Society Section of the APSA.

Lenita Freidenvall is Associate Professor in Political Science at Stockholm University. She specializes in political representation, candidate selection, and gender equality policies, including gender quotas. Her most recent articles include "The speaker's gender equality group in the Swedish parliament—a toothless tiger?" (*Politics, Groups and Identities* 2020, with Josefina Erikson) and "Implementing Gender Mainstreaming in Swedish Model Municipalities" (*Politics & Gender* 2019, with Madeleine Ramberg).

Joan Grace is Professor in the Department of Political Science at the University of Winnipeg. Her research examines the Manitoba public policy environment, how institutions of the state structure women's policy advocacy and how Canadian governments, through gender-based analysis, influence women's achievements in organizations and workplaces. Joan has also contributed significant Canadian experiential insights to feminist institutionalism. Recent publications have appeared in *Parliamentary Affairs* and the *Manitoba Law Journal*.

Nora Gresch studied sociology at the University of Bielefeld and holds a PhD from the Department of Political Sciences, University of Vienna. She was Visiting Scholar at the Women's Studies Program and the Carrie Chapman Catt Center for Women and Politics at the Iowa State University in the United States. Her research interests include citizenship studies, body studies, and gender and politics. She has taken part in several research projects, including the EU-funded project, "VEIL. Values, Equality and Differences in Liberal Democracies Debates about Muslim Headscarves in Europe" (2006–2009) and "Changing Identities of Ethnic Minority Groups—the Comparative Study of Autochthonous and Immigrant Groups in Austria, Croatia, Kosovo, Slovenia and Serbia" (2010–2011) funded by the Austrian Science and Research Liaison Office.

Season Hoard is Associate Professor jointly appointed in the School of Politics, Philosophy and Public Affairs and the Division of Governmental Studies and Services (DGSS) at Washington State University. She received her PhD in political science from Washington State University, and her areas of expertise include gender and politics, comparative politics, public policy, and applied social science research methods. As the Project Manager at DGSS, she provides applied research, program evaluation, and technical assistance for governmental agencies and non-profit organizations in the USA. She has published on research methods and public policy, including recent publications in *Community Development*, *Politics and Life Sciences*, *Politics, Groups and Identities*, *Biomass and Bioenergy*, and the *International Journal of Aviation Management* and *American Political Science Review*.

Ewa Lisowska is Professor of Economy at the GBH Warsaw School of Economics. She conducts research on women in the labor market, women managers and entrepreneurs. Her teaching focuses on gender equality in society. She is the author of the books: *Kobiecy styl zarządzania* (2009, [Feminine style of management]) and *Równouprawnienie kobiet i mężczyzn w społeczeństwie* (2010, [Equality between women and men in a society]).

Emanuela Lombardo is Associate Professor at the Department of Political Science and Administration of Madrid Complutense University. Her main research areas include gender equality policy adoption and implementation and Europeanization, with a recent focus on issues related to populism and democratic backsliding. Her latest monographs are *Gender and Political Analysis* (Palgrave 2017, with Johanna Kantola) and *The Symbolic Representation of Gender* (Ashgate 2014, with Petra Meier). Her latest articles appear in *European Journal of Political Research*, *Journal of Common Market Studies*, *Social Politics*, and *Policy and Society*.

Amy G. Mazur is CO Johnson Distinguished Professor of Political Science at Washington State University and Associate Researcher at LIEPP at Sciences Po Paris. Her research interests focus on comparative feminist policy issues with a particular emphasis on France and comparative methodology. Some of her books include *Theorizing Feminist Policy* (Oxford 2002), *Politics, Gender and Concepts* (Cambridge University Press 2008, edited with

Gary Goertz), *The OUP Handbook of French Politics* (2015 and 2020 paperback, edited with Robert Elgie and Emiliano Grossman), and *The Politics of State Feminism: Innovation in Comparative Research* (Temple University Press 2010, with Dorothy McBride). Her work appears notably in *French Politics, European Journal of Politics and Gender, Comparative European Politics, Revue Française de Science Politique, Politics and Gender, Political Research Quarterly, Journal of Women, Politics and Policy, PS: Political Science, Politics, Groups and Identities* and *American Political Science Review*. She convenes, with Isabelle Engeli, the Gender Equality Policy in Practice Network (GEPP). She is Lead Editor of *French Politics* and is Fellow-in-Residence for the Global Contestations of Gender and Women's Rights ZiF Research Group at Bielefeld University.

Susan Milner is Professor of European Politics and Society at the University of Bath. She has researched and published on gender equality in the workplace in Britain, France, and the European Union. She is currently engaged in a Leverhulme Major Research Fellowship (2020–2022) on equal pay policies under Labour governments (1997–2019) and leads the GW4 research consortium on equal pay.

Beáta Nagy is Professor at the Institute of Communication and Sociology at Corvinus University of Budapest and co-directs the Gender and Cultural Centre. Her latest research deals with the work-life balance of managers with a focus on the time teenagers and their parents spend together through digital technology. She has recently published a book on the lack of female students in IT and technology and has co-edited a special issue on "Work-life balance/imbalance: individual, organizational and social experiences" for *Intersections*. Other recent contributions appear in *East European Journal of Society and Politics, Gender Management*, and in a special issue on "Leveraging cooperation for gender equality in management" for *European Management Review*. She also serves as an elected board member of the European Consortium for Sociological Research (ECSR).

Lucie Newsome is Lecturer in Management and Economics at the University of New England. She has published research on gender and politics, policy, and business. Formerly, Dr Newsome has held senior policy and project roles in the New South Wales and Queensland governments.

Marion Rabier is Associate Professor in Political Science at the University of Haute Alsace and a member of the SAGE research lab in Strasbourg. Her work focuses on women entrepreneurs and CEOs and their mobilizations toward a more gender-balanced representation in executive positions and the business world.

Hannelore Roos is Research Fellow at Hasselt University and an affiliate member at the Policy Research Centre of Equality Policies, an inter-university consortium of the universities of Antwerp, Hasselt, Brussels, Ghent, and Leuven. She completed her PhD in social and cultural anthropology from KU Leuven and has taught several qualitative research methods courses in the Faculty of Business Economics at Hasselt University. She recently carried out a policy-oriented study on gender imbalances and diversity on corporate boards of publicly listed companies in Belgium.

Ewa Rumińska-Zimny is an economist and is currently Lecturer at the Polish Academy of Science, Gender Studies. She is the president of the International Forum of Women in

Science and Business at the Warsaw School of Economics, a board member of the Congress of Polish Women, and a member of the Experts' Forum of the European Institute for Gender Equality. She was Visiting Professor at Georgetown University, worked as Senior Economist at the Human Development Report Office of the United Nations, and as Gender Focal Point Administrator at the United Nations. She is the author of reports and publications to the United Nations, the European Parliament, the European Commission, and the Council of Europe.

Birgit Sauer is Professor of Political Science at the University of Vienna. From 2014 to 2018 she was Speaker of the Research Network "Gender and Agency" at the University of Vienna. Her research fields include comparative gender equality policies, right-wing populism and racism, democracy, and politics of emotions and affects. She was a member of the Research Network on Gender and the State as well as a member of several EU research projects, including projects on violence against women, gender, migration and religion, gender and right-wing populism, and right-wing populism and the media. She has also conducted research projects on affective state transformation. Recent publications include *Governing Affects: Neoliberalism, Neo-Bureaucracies, and Service Work* (Routledge 2020, with Otto Penz).

Alexandra Scheele is Senior Lecturer for Economic Sociology and Sociology of Work at the University of Bielefeld and Visiting Associate Professor at the University of Bielefeld (2020–2021). She is the convenor of the interdisciplinary research group "Global Contestations of Women's and Gender Rights" at the Centre for Interdisciplinary Research (ZIF) at the University of Bielefeld and Co-Editor of *Femina Politica*. She co-edited the special issue "New Research on Gender Pay Gap(s) in Organizations and Occupations" (*Gender, Work & Organization* 2019, with Susan Milner, Sophie Pochic, and Sue Williamson) and co-edited *Feminismus—Marxismus* (Beltz Juventa 2018, with Stefanie Wöhl).

Alison Sheridan is Professor of Management at the University of New England. She has been teaching and researching women's experiences in paid work, including their representation on boards, for more than two decades.

Andrea Spehar is Associate Professor in Political Science and Director of the Centre on Global Migration (CGM) at the University of Gothenburg, Sweden. Spehar's broad research interest is comparative public policy, particularly with regards to gender policy and immigrant integration policy in a European context. Her work has appeared, among others, in the *Journal of European Public Policy, Comparative European Politics, Journal of Women, Politics & Policy, Eastern European Politics & Societies, and International Feminist Journal of Politics.*

Mari Teigen is Research Professor at the Institute for Social Research in Oslo and Director of CORE—Centre for Research on Gender Equality and NORDICORE—Centre for Research on Gender Equality in Research and Innovation. Her research engages with change and stability in gender relations, through the analysis of gender equality policy, social elites, and gender segregation in the labor market and academia. Teigen is Editor of the *Norwegian Journal of Gender Research*, Co-Editor of *Comparative Social Research*, and Co-Editor of *Nordic Journal of Working-Life Studies*. She holds various board and committee positions in the Norwegian Research Council and other research policy organizations as well.

Tània Verge is Associate Professor at the Department of Political and Social Sciences, Universitat Pompeu Fabra. Her main areas of research are political representation and political parties, with a focus on the gendered informal institutions underpinning party politics and parliaments and on the resistance to the adoption and implementation of gender equality policy. Her most recent publications have appeared in the *European Journal of Political Research, Politics & Gender, Party Politics*, and the *European Journal of Politics & Gender*.

Patrizia Zanoni is a Full Professor at the Faculty of Business Economics at Hasselt University where she leads the Research Center SEIN—Identity, Diversity & Inequality Research, and Chair in Organization Studies at the Utrecht School of Governance at Utrecht University. Drawing on critical theories, her research investigates the relation between diversity (gender, ethnicity, disability, and age) and the dynamics of control and resistance, the processes of unequal valuation, and the possibility of alternative economies. Her work has appeared widely in international organization studies and educational journals. Together with Raza Mir, she is currently Editor-in-Chief of *Organization: The Critical Journal of Organization, Theory & Society*.

1

Introduction

Negotiating Gender Equality in the Corporate World

Isabelle Engeli and Amy G. Mazur

How to Make Equality Work in the Corporate World?

This book places the practices pursued by business and government to promote women's representation on corporate boards under the policy microscope. Access to corporate boards is limited to a privileged minority. Indeed, promoting gender balance on boards is more likely to directly benefit women who are already in a situation of privilege than women who must jump through the intersectional hurdles of race, class, ethnicity, sexual identity, and disability, among others. Gender balance on corporate boards is nevertheless a central issue for gender equality.

> Because corporate boards are at the top apex of the corporate world, controlling—along with the top management They hire—all aspects of corporate behavior, getting more women on corporate boards is seen as an important way to advance all women.
>
> (Burk and Hartmann, 2017, p. 128)

Attention to gender balance on corporate boards is more often than not framed in terms of "the business case" (Elomäki, 2018) where a higher presence of women on boards is seen to improve the governance, performance, and sustainability of business (e.g., Lewellyn and Muller-Kahle, 2020; Fernandez-Feijooo et al, 2013; Comi et al, 2020; Adams and Ferreira, 2009; Ferreira, 2015; Pande and Ford, 2011). In the words of the "chairman" of the World Economic Forum,

> Business leaders and policymakers must remove barriers to women's entry to the workforce and provide equal opportunities for rising to positions of leadership to ensure that all existing resources are used in the most efficient manner.
>
> (Klaus Schwab, 2010, p. v)

We argue that the issue of women's presence on corporate boards is ultimately a litmus test for whether and, if so, how democracies are up to the task of advancing women's rights and taking the gender equality agenda to the next level. Given

Isabelle Engeli and Amy G. Mazur, *Introduction*. In: *Gender Equality and Policy Implementation in the Corporate World*. Edited by Isabelle Engeli and Amy G. Mazur, Oxford University Press. © Oxford Unversity Press (2022). DOI: 10.1093/oso/9780198865216.003.0001

persistent resistance to gender transformation, the top echelon of the corporate world is acknowledged to be one of the remaining bastions of male dominance. As more and more governments across postindustrial democracies have given increasing latitude to corporations to pursue unfettered competition in the global economy through neoliberal policies that downsize the public in favor of the private, core principles of representation and gender equality become even harder to enforce in the corporate world. While corporations tend to be driven by the economic bottom line rather than social justice and equality, the corporate board room is where a large share of power and control lie.

Thus, the question of who is in control of the world's corporations leads to larger thorny issues of national economic health and the global balance of power, as well as social and economic justice. As with gender equality policy more broadly speaking (Verloo, 2018; Krizsan and Lombardo, 2013; Engeli and Mazur, 2018), pursuing concrete action that not only boosts women's numbers on boards but also empowers their voices in corporate decision-making as well as pushing inclusivity forward to open up to other underrepresented groups, makes stable democracies even more democratic and representative.

This gender diversity deficit in leadership is by no means specific to the corporate boardroom and the business arena. Policy actors on the world stage have continued to lament that gender equality remains an "uphill battle" (OECD, 2017). The persistence of large gaps between men and women regarding status, resources, and power, even in the wealthiest democracies, remains one of the most serious challenges of our times. It endangers girls and women's safety and well-being, undermines sustainable economic productivity and growth, and arguably weakens democracies. The multiple ways in which the COVID-19 pandemic has hit women harder than men sounds the alarm about the resistance to and back pedaling from the gender equality agenda (World Economic Forum, 2021). More fundamentally, it raises the question to understand why, after over forty years of policy action, gender equality advances have remained so fragile and vulnerable to attacks of all kinds. Two core questions need to be answered: How and why are the current public policies in action across the globe not up to the task? What can be done to make policy action more resilient on the ground?

We contend a large part of the answer lies in the policy implementation process and how policy action is negotiated, adjusted, or even radically shifted from words to deeds. Scholarship is behind the curve in conducting the time-consuming and evidence-based research on the implementation and impact of policies that formally address these persistent and pernicious gaps and to link the findings of this necessarily slow science to the design and practice of innovative policy solutions. The comparative study of the implementation of corporate gender equality policy in western democracies presented in this book is a part of a new generation of equality policy studies that is taking on this crucial yet challenging project (Blofield and Hass, 2013; Mazur, 2017; Bustelo, 2017; Krizsan and Lombardo, 2013; Engeli and Mazur, 2018; Verloo and Walby 2012; Seirstad et al. 2017).

Whereas a growing body of research has begun to tackle understanding the resistance of corporate governance to demands for equality and inclusion, this book conducts a systematic and thorough study of the adoption, implementation, and outcomes of discrete corporate board equality actions within and across Western (Austria, Belgium, France, Germany, Norway, Spain, Sweden, and the UK) and Central Eastern Europe (Croatia, Hungary, Poland, and Serbia), North America (Canada and the USA), and Australasia (Australia). A two-fold comparative perspective is adopted. First, similarities and divergences across a diverse sample of democratic settings, state-business relationships, and political dynamics are examined in rich country-based case analyses in Chapters 3 through 15. Second, the book conducts a cross-national analysis of the dynamics and determinants of the national policy trajectories across the fifteen countries in the last section through a comparative lens. The book also goes beyond a sole focus on countries that have seen the introduction of legal quotas for corporate boards, taking the analysis to the next level in comparing policy practices and their outcomes across the full spectrum of existing actions toward corporate equality: legislated quotas as legal framework, corporate self-regulatory frameworks without quotas, and a hybrid combination of state and corporate action frameworks that are piecemeal and fragmented, at best, often with little ambition to change the existing state of affairs.

This book is much more than an edited collection of various contributions on a common theme. It is the result of a collective enterprise that took us on a four-year research journey, fueled by a far-reaching scholarly curiosity and collective drive to seek explanations and solutions to the fragility of policy action toward equality in the corporate world. By its analytical and methodological rigor, this book is the output of a research project like no other. By its moments of challenges and joy of conducting research collectively, this book is also the output of a human adventure. We are very grateful to our chapter authors to have accepted to be our partners in crime in this deep dive into the challenges and opportunities for the promotion of equality in the corporate world.

Each of the fifteen country-based analyses presented in the book have applied and followed the Gender Equality Policy in Practice (GEPP) approach (Engeli and Mazur, 2018; Mazur and Engeli, 2020). The GEPP approach seeks to study comparatively the gender equality policy implementation puzzle—whether, how, and why the broad range and large number of government policies explicitly designed to promote women's rights and strike down gender-based hierarchies that were put on the books starting in the early 1970s have been put into action to generate meaningful change. More simply put, does gender equality policy implementation matter, and, if so, how, why, and to what end? The GEPP approach provides a systematic roadmap for the country-level analyses in the book and frames the comparative discussion of the politics, processes, and outcomes of corporate equality policy implementation in the fifteen countries in the last two chapters. The last chapter concludes with the theoretical lessons learned from the study for the scholarly community and evidence-based recommendations for practitioners and policy makers for the design of better policy, returning to the larger question of whether, how, and why gender equality policy implementation matters.

As such, this book and the GEPP approach contribute to the ever-growing body of research that investigates gender equality policies in action across the globe (Lombardo and Meier, 2022). The approach has been applied to other areas of policy that address gender equality issues in care (Ciccia and Lombardo, 2019) and political representation (Lange, Meier, and Sauer, forthcoming) as well as across different sectors of gender equality policy in France (Mazur and Engeli, 2020). This book is thus firmly anchored to the larger research agenda on gender equality policy that has at its core the pursuit of the "elusive recipe" for successful gender equality policy. As we put it elsewhere, "While a rich scholarship examines gender policy and the state, the recipe for successful policies still remains as elusive as the formula to turn lead into gold" (Engeli and Mazur, 2018, p. 112).

Given the importance of explaining not only just the goals of the book but also how the GEPP approach is used in the comparative analysis of corporate board equality policy in action in the fifteen countries included in the study, this introductory chapter provides an overview of first the GEPP approach and then a preview of the findings of the thirteen country-based chapters through the lens of a two-way categorization of policy approaches, self-regulation, and state-regulation, which provides the organization for the country analyses in the rest of the book. In the next chapter, we turn to the nuts and bolts of how policies that seek to promote gender balance on corporate boards are assessed through the GEPP approach in the country chapters, first, starting with an in-depth foray into how and why the corporate boardroom serves as an ideal arena for studying the politics and outcomes of gender equality policies in action. Chapter 2, therefore, serves as a road map for the rest of the book. The cross-national analysis in the last two chapters of the book places the rich process-tracing, country-based studies conducted by the chapter authors in a comparative perspective by first examining what did and did not work in achieving numerical success "by the numbers" in Chapter 16 and then in Chapter 17, in terms of the more qualitative GEPP measures of "policy empowerment" and "gender transformation."

The GEPP Approach: Gendering Equality Implementation in Practice

The GEPP approach has been developed as a response to calls to shift the lens of analysis from the politics of how gender equality policies are placed on government agendas and formalized to what takes places following the adoption stage in the crucial yet messy processes of implementation and evaluation. These "post-adoption" stages present key features leading to the success or failure of gender equality policies (Engeli and Mazur, 2018). First, as the approach posits, the post-adoption processes are more likely to be multilevel. Multilevel action involves the participation and coordination of actors between and across levels, and—in the case of corporate equality—between the corporate world and the state. Second, it is unlikely that the constellation of actors remains identical across the entire policy process. While some actors are already present in the pre-adoption stages of problem definition and agenda-setting and at the time of the adoption of the policy, the implementation process offers a new venue for pushing for and pulling away from gender equality through passive resistance and active opposition. New constellations of actors actually emerge around these processes—government bureaucrats, as well as representatives of target and implementer groups. As a result, the way the post-adoption process unfolds is likely to significantly impact the success or failure of gender equality politics. Moreover, the very meaning of gender equality becomes the object of debate at each phase of the policy process and even beyond the specific policy. A third feature of the GEPP approach, therefore, is the operating premise that notions of gender are negotiated, adapted, and contested in the practice of policy implementation (Engeli and Mazur, 2018; Lombardo et al, 2009; Krizsan and Lombardo, 2013; Verloo and Walby, 2012).

Opening the Black Box of Policy Implementation

The analytical "turn to implementation" has been the logical next step in the research cycle on gender equality policy for a new generation of comparative gender policy scholars (Mazur, 2017). On one hand, democratic governments have responded to equality demands since the late 1960s in an ever-increasing number of policy actions that explicitly target gender equality across a wide range of sectors of government action with the potential, at least on paper, to significantly improve women's rights and status and to mitigate, if not dismantle, gendered hierarchies of privilege. On the other, the reality shows otherwise; many policies have not resulted in significant major progress toward the realization of gender equality and have fallen short of transformative change. The moment is thus ripe to take stock in this broad array of policies and to assess the reasons for their disappointing results in the ongoing struggle to achieve meaningful transformative change.

Until recently, gender and policy scholarship had not focused systematically on policy success and failure in terms of post-adoption and impact. Nor had it developed a comprehensive range of tools to take on this challenging analytical task. Indeed, given the difficulty of identifying causality in long-term social change and what constitutes a successful outcome of gender equality policies, this daunting project had tended to be put on the back burner (Mazur, 2017). Implementation was usually mentioned, but not studied in its full and often non-linear complexity. In addition, a growing number of critics assert that the plethora of quantitative indices developed at the international level to measure gender equality across the world are insufficient to capture the complex reality of gender inequalities in practice (e.g., Lombardo et al, 2009; Liebowitz and Zwingel, 2014; Engeli et al, 2015).

The GEPP approach represents a fresh way to assess policy success and failure that addresses the insufficiencies of research on gender policy and the international gender equality indices with two main aims (Engeli and Mazur, 2018, p. 112). The first aim is to open and unpack the black box of government once policy is adopted, and the second is to assess whether, how, and under what conditions some policy tools and actions are successful in promoting gender equality and achieving gender transformation while others are not. The approach conceives the post-adoption stages as an arena for the policy struggle over the control of the meaning and content of gender equality where vested interests organize into configurations of power for and against gender equality. The outcome of this power struggle has an impact on the capacity of policy to progress toward gender equality and transformation. What is important to note about research that follows the GEPP approach, unlike other studies that apply similar standards across all outcomes, is that it assesses policy progress and success in the context of a given policy implementation case within a country context rather than only gauging policy successes in terms of a perceived and often politically constructed gold standard derived from international best practice.

The GEPP Framework: Negotiating Equality in Practice

Figure 1.1 maps out the different analytical components of the post-adoption process in the GEPP framework (Engeli and Mazur, 2018). Post-adoption entails all of

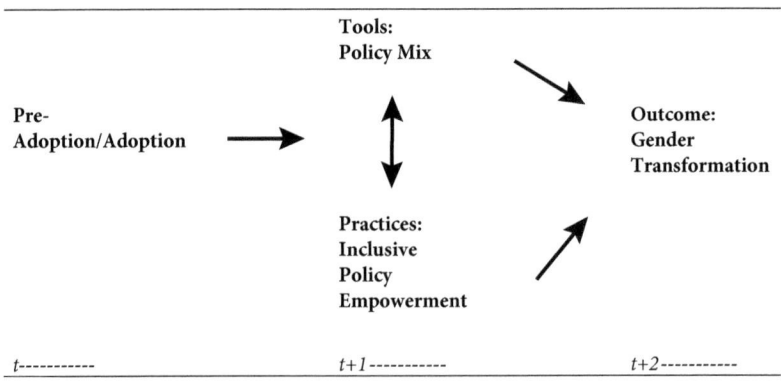

Fig. 1.1 The Gender Equality Policy in Practice Framework
*t = Time.
Source: Engeli and Mazur (2018)

the processes that follow after a formal policy decision is made; in reality, they are complex and intertwined in the practice of implementation, monitoring, and evaluation. The framework indicates the way in which the dynamics and determinants of policy implementation are conceptualized for this study. On a more practical level, it also provides a guide for data collection and analysis for the country and comparative analyses in the book. How each component of the framework is used in the study of corporate gender equality policy in action in the remainder of the book is the focus of the next chapter.

The pre-adoption stages include issue attention, problem definition, agenda-setting, and the policy decision process. The adoption stage produces "policy outputs" (Dye, 1992), the policy instruments that are formally established to implement, monitor, and evaluate the policy. The model then focuses on the post-adoption stage to investigate the use of those instruments "in practice" (Montoya, 2013 and Bacchi, 2017) and then, most importantly, the policy outcomes and their eventual impacts. It provides a guide for tracing the unfolding of a given policy over time as it moves through the necessarily messy and seldom stepwise process of policy formation in democracies where the lines between pre-adoption, adoption and post-adoption are often blurred (Gains and Lowndes, 2015). The approach focuses attention on three main components at the post-adoption stage: the Policy Mix (tools), practices in terms of Inclusive Policy Empowerment, and outcomes in terms of Gender Transformation, which together cover the complex parameters of gender equality policy implementation (Engeli and Mazur, 2018).

The first component, the **Policy Mix**, accounts for the full range of "identifiable methods through which collective action is structured to address a public problem" (Salomon, 2002, p. 9). Ingram and Schneider (1990) and Capano and Engeli (2021) identify four types of instruments that can be potentially included in the mix. The first type covers command-and-control instruments that define, prescribe, or ban specific behaviors. The legal prohibition of gender-based discrimination is a classic example of an authority-based instrument. The second type includes tools that aim at inducing or reducing a behavior without formally commending or banning it. For example, the comply-or-explain instrument, which requires companies to either achieve equal pay or to publicly explain gaps in gender balance on boards, is an incentive-based instrument. While employers are not required to eradicate the gender gap on their boards, if they fail to do so, they then have to provide the reason for non-compliance, potentially exposed to the scrutiny of public opinion and consumers. This second type of instrument is the major tool used in corporate board policy. Tools providing resources, knowledge, and skills are part of the third category of instruments. They aim to enable and provide capacity for action. In the corporate world, training programs have been developed, often by feminist-oriented business NGOs, to help women business leaders to be better prepared for getting access to corporate boards. Communication tools are the fourth type of policy instruments, designed to promote good behaviors and expose bad ones. Information campaigns on micro-aggressions at work are examples of communication-based instruments as well as campaigns on why promoting women on boards is a good idea.

Instruments usually do not work in isolation. They are assembled in a "policy mix" (Howlett and Rayner, 2007). It is the specific combination of instruments that is the focus of analysis and how that combination is used in practice and whether it leads to any successful outcomes. While one can identify the specific mix of instruments, the notion of regulatory approach captures how those tools generally operate—that is, whether the action is entirely designed by the state, is co-designed by the state and a private partner, or is entirely delegated to the private partner. The GEPP framework also allows for the assessment of the extent of comprehensiveness of policies and their level of authority.

The second component of the GEPP approach addresses the representation potential of policy implementation—**Inclusive Policy Empowerment**. Representation is conceptualized as the practices through which the policy process strengthens and weakens women's empowerment. Drawing on Krizsan and Lombardo (2013), policy empowerment allows for the potential of excluded groups of women to be given a seat at the implementation table and to bring in ideas and actors that had been largely ignored or excluded in pre-implementation stages. Alternatively, disempowerment can occur when groups who had a voice, however minor, in the pre-implementation stages can be further marginalized or even excluded after a policy is adopted. In the corporate world, the issue of policy empowerment has been problematic given that women from underrepresented groups and any expression of their interests are rarely included in policy discussions and implementation.

The third component of the model addresses the **outcomes** of policy implementation. It tackles the thorny problem of how to measure success and goes beyond the "score card" approach of quantitative national and international level gender equality indices often designed more to show which country is on top, rather to disentangle the complex reality of the different ways gender equality policies can affect and change gender relations and norms as well as the attitudes of gatekeepers and even citizens more generally. Potential policy outcomes include both direct and indirect (spill over) effects of the policy with three different discrete indicators: the extent to which the problem originally identified in the policy is solved; whether the policy has resulted in a long-lasting change in the practices and frames of the actors that are charged with implementation, e.g., bureaucrats, gatekeepers, judges, etc.; and whether implementation has triggered a larger-scale shift in public attitudes. The overall measurement of **gender transformation** aggregates the three indicators to gage the extent to which policy has successfully induced transformative change.

Corporate Board Gender Equality Policy in Action: Telling the Stories of the Fifteen Countries

Each country case analysis in Chapters 3 through 15 tells the story of implementation over time in terms of the different components of the GEPP approach. The story opens with the pre-adoption and adoption processes, moving to the mix of policy instruments and outputs that were adopted and then how and, for most countries, if they were put into practice. The end of the story is about whether implementation actually mattered in the outcomes: Was there policy empowerment and gender transformation? And what were the major drivers for the way the story ended? In GEPP terms, what were the ingredients for the recipe for policy success in corporate board gender equality? The outline of the book is structured in terms of each country's regulatory approach to corporate board gender equality, either the **self-regulation path** covered in Part I in Australia, the UK, Sweden, the USA, Canada (Quebec), Croatia, Serbia, Hungary, and Poland, or the **state-regulation path** covered in Part II in Norway, France, Belgium, Spain, Germany, and Austria. Within each approach two tracks are identified: **flagship** and **alternative**. To understand the larger plot of the corporate gender equality policy story, we now present an overview of each country story in terms of these two approaches.

Path One: The Self-regulation Approach to Corporate Equality

While much attention has been dedicated to state intervention and mandatory quotas, the first measures that were put into place were voluntary, largely designed by corporate actors. Among the countries that have preserved the voluntary approach over time, we distinguish two tracks. Australia, the UK, and Sweden are examples of a **flagship** track for the self-regulation approach. In these three cases, early calls for mandatory quotas were rejected in favor of delegating to the corporate world the mandate to improve the blatant underrepresentation of women in corporate leadership. Corporate leadership in the three countries has stepped up to the task and implemented a number of voluntary measures to promote gender balance on boards with the early calls for state intervention mostly fading away over time to give full preeminence to the self-regulation approach. In contrast, for cases on the **alternative track**, there is no long-term corporate strategy to promote women's access to corporate boards. The cases - of the USA, Canada, Croatia, Serbia, Hungary, and Poland are best characterized by a piecemeal approach of isolated one-off initiatives that have been put forward by various actors in the corporate world without any follow-up or integrated strategy.

Women's underrepresentation in corporate leadership has attracted increased attention in **Australia** since the end of the 2000s and the recommendation by the Sex Discrimination Commissioner and the Human Rights Commission to adopt a mandatory quota system. In Chapter 3, Lucie Newsome and Alison Sheridan emphasize that it was the strong opposition from the corporate sector that persuaded the government to opt for the self-regulatory route. Under the leadership of leading corporate actors, a reporting mechanism was implemented for listed companies in 2011 and a target of 30% of women on boards was set in 2015. The Australian self-regulatory approach has seen some concrete material change in women's empowerment. The proportion of women on the boards of the top-200 companies has significantly increased to reach 30% in 2019. As the authors argue, corporate leadership succeeded in making the sex criteria more salient in board appointments, alongside a number of failures. Smaller companies not covered in the corporate regulation have not yet followed the upward trend, and women are still in the minority in executive teams even among the largest companies. Moreover, the gender transformative effects of this policy are limited by the "golden skirt" phenomenon (the framing of the issue as a supply side problem) and the persistence of the glass ceiling and gender pay gaps.

As Susan Milner shows in Chapter 4, the lack of gender balance on corporate boards reached the policy agenda in the **UK** in a similar timeframe to Australia. In the face of timid calls for direct state intervention, policy in the UK early on gave preference to the voluntary corporate-led pathway. Through two high-profile reviews, a limited number of soft instruments have been implemented. A voluntary target of 25% female board members in the 100 largest companies was set to be reached in 2015 and later increased to 33% by 2020. The effort has paid off and the target has been met. Companies are also nowadays more likely to address issues related to equality and diversity in their annual proceedings. Nevertheless, as Milner emphasizes, the UK approach suffers from similar weaknesses to the Australian one. Women are less likely to serve as executive directors and women's access outside the 100 largest companies has not taken off. In contrast to Australia though, improving diversity on boards has received recent attention.

Sweden already distinguished itself in refusing to implement legislated political quotas in the past. The same is true for the corporate world, Lenita Freidenvall tells us in Chapter 5. She assesses how the corporate sector itself introduced in 2005 and then reasserted in 2016 the voluntary measure of comply-or-explain through the corporate governance code in order to avoid a state-led approach to the promotion of women on boards. The corporate effort has proven successful to a certain extent. In 2020, women's representation on the boards of the largest companies in Sweden has outperformed all the EU member states with the exception of France. This numeric performance has nevertheless not given way to a far-reaching transformation of gender relations in the corporate world.

The case of the **USA** kicks off the story of an **alternative track** within the first approach. Organized self-regulation in the USA has remained very limited and without a gender specific lens, as Season Hoard explains in Chapter 6. The Securities and Exchange Commission implemented a clause on reporting about "diversity" considerations, without even mentioning gender, for the nomination of directors in 2010 but only clarified in 2019 what was meant by diversity. The piece-meal promotion of women's access to corporate boards has thus almost uniquely relied on company actions at the regional or state level, such as the Rooney Rule promoted by the Midwest Investors Diversity Initiative to include women and minority candidates in board recruitment, with some instances of highly symbolic state legislation, according to Hoard.

In Chapter 7, Joan Grace explains how **Canada** has refrained from any state intervention in board appointments across the public and private sectors with the exception of **Quebec**. The province led the way in 2006 through implementing a quota for state-owned companies but stopped short of expanding the quota mandate to private companies due to the lack, until recently, of political will and advocacy for gender equality in the corporate sector.

Andrea Spehar also highlights the impact of the lack of political interest and gender champions in Chapter 8. In **Croatia** and **Serbia** this absence has resulted in a handful of largely symbolic actions focused on the pool of female candidates. Mostly promoted via international channels, gender equality on boards has not found national policy brokers to push it through the corporate and political agendas. As a result, the promotion of corporate equality has largely remained fragmented and ineffective.

The investigation of the cases of **Hungary** and **Poland** in Chapter 9 confirms a post-socialist pattern in low levels of political and corporate engagement toward equality in the private sector. Beáta Nagy, Ewa Lisowska, and Ewa Rumińska-Zimny shed light on how the conservative backlash has severely limited any pursuit of gender equality in Poland since 2015, if not completely stalling it in Hungary. The lion's share of the promotion of corporate equality has been taken up by women's organizations, which have faced a high level of inertia when there is not outright resistance from public and corporate leadership.

Path Two: The State-regulation Approach to Corporate Equality

The second section of the book moves to the investigation of the cases that have expanded—or entirely moved away from—an early self-regulatory to a state-intervention approach that often coexists with the self-regulatory elements. The **flagship** track includes three country cases where the state-led approach has fully replaced self-regulation, as has occurred in Norway, France, and Belgium. In all three political systems, self-regulation remained at the embryonic level and the state-intervention approach quickly superseded it. The **alternative track** covers the mixed-approach cases that share a key feature with the self-regulation approach first being favored, and then in a second stage, sometimes quite a long time after, a more state oriented approach progressively emerges. The cases of Spain,

Germany, and Austria shed light on how opposition to gender equality in the corporate world can be progressively circumvented through convincing neutral actors of the relevance of policy action in the light of early failures in the voluntary approach. A move toward state intervention does not necessarily mean that the policy design becomes fully comprehensive and effective. Here again, early opposition proves to have long-lasting effects in limiting the scope of state action and the potential for gender transformation.

Norway was the first country in the world to adopt mandatory quotas for corporate boards of listed companies (in 2003), Mari Teigen reminds us in Chapter 10. The Norwegian model of a 40% quota with a strong sanction system has since remained one of the most ambitious designs to improve gender balance on boards. As Teigen shows, partisans of the quota mandate built on the legacy of state intervention in favor of gender equality to frame the law as a threat if companies did not improve their gender balance spontaneously. The short deadline effectively sidelined the partisans of the self-regulation alternative. While the initial scope of the mandate was reduced to public limited companies only, its coercive character was strengthened through the decision-making process. Although the quota mandate was quickly fulfilled by the companies covered by the law prior to its formal enforcement, any spillovers or "ripple effects" remained quite limited until the past few years; women's presence at the executive level has been lacking and leadership recruitment practices are still mostly targeted at white men.

Soline Blanchard and Marion Rabier question the French "success story" in the promotion of board equality in Chapter 11. **France** has moved from being a laggard to a leader in the span of a few years through the introduction of a quota mandate in 2011. The quota mandate was championed by femocrats in women's policy agencies and the coalition in favor of political parity. The corporate sector tried to reverse the course of action by recommending a target of 40% women to listed companies, but it came too late in 2010. Facing opposition from the corporate sector, the parity principle was abandoned in favor of a 40% quota. The quota mandate has been better implemented in the larger companies than in smaller ones. Most companies did not go any further than the 40% minimum; the proportion of women in executive positions has not, for example, significantly increased. Nevertheless, additional indicators have been designed to monitor the promotion of corporate equality.

Hannelore Roos and Patrizia Zanoni present evidence in Chapter 12 of how the 2008 economic crisis opened a window of opportunity for putting the issue of gender balance on corporate boards on the agenda in **Belgium** despite strong opposition. It was, nonetheless, the patchy implementation of the comply-or-explain mechanism introduced through the 2009 Corporate Governance Code that gave the impetus to introduce the gender board quota law in 2011. Supported by a sanction mechanism, the law has shown clear numerical success even if many companies waited for the last moment to comply with the mandate. While the quota has not empowered minority women, it has at least contributed to breaking down informal recruitment practices and featuring women business leaders as role models in the media.

Moving to the **alternative track**, Emanuela Lombardo and Tània Verge demonstrate in Chapter 13 why **Spain** has ended up with a mixed approach due to the high level of resistance toward enacting a comprehensive state-sponsored quota mandate that has had long-lasting consequences on implementation. Among the first European countries to take up the issue of board equality, the quota was part of the ambitious agenda of the Spanish Socialist Worker's Party in the early 2000s. This early start triggered far-reaching opposition from the corporate world and the conservative party. At first, the newly launched self-regulatory governance code merely reiterated the content of the draft equality law regarding corporate boards, although it proved to be a significant rallying point to promote corporate equality with its compulsory reporting mandate. Nonetheless, the core of the 2007 equality law, a strong compulsory mandate to reach 40% of female board members within four years, was finally diluted in the adoption of the law with a prolonged eight-year target date for compliance and the absence of reporting requirements for private companies. The victory of the conservatives in 2011 further watered down the legislative mandate in 2014 and the 2015 revision of the governance code followed this downward trend. This opposition has been amplified in post-adoption, resulting in lax implementation and placing Spain's poor performance at the bottom of the EU ranking.

Chapter 14 retraces the long road toward the introduction of the mandatory quota system in **Germany**. Petra Ahrens and Alexandra Scheele emphasize that a generalized debate about the intervention of the state kept pushing the initial self-regulatory solution to the front stage, and this despite the fact that the introduction of a quota system was already proposed at the end of the 1990s. Implemented in 2001, the reporting mandate quickly turned out to be a paper tiger. At the same time, it took another fifteen years to see a quota of 30% women on supervisory boards for large listed companies and an individualized target for the intermediate ones to enter into force. The empty-seat sanction and the reporting and monitoring instruments have, so far, proven to be an efficient combination at the implementation stage for the larger companies, while the policy has less teeth for smaller firms.

In the last country case analysis in Chapter 15, Nora Gresch and Birgit Sauer paint a similar picture of deep aversion to a quota mandate in **Austria**. The conversation about women's representation on corporate boards started in the early 2000s. Opinions became quickly polarized with strong opposition to any coercive measure. The 2009 amendment to the Austrian Corporate Code reflects this state of play; companies were only required to report on the measures taken to advance gender balance on executive and supervisory boards. In 2012, the code was amended a second time to implement a comply-or-explain mechanism. Issues in the governmental coalition in 2017 opened a window for state involvement that eventually led to the 2017 law, which has introduced a 30% gender quota for the supervisory boards of listed companies and large firms. Restricted to a minority of the listed companies, the law has failed so far to trigger a contagion effect to the companies not formally covered by the law or to women's increased presence on the board executives.

Conclusion

Without revealing too much of the plot, this first glimpse into the complex and often protracted stories of corporate board gender equality in action indicates that gender transformation and policy empowerment have been scarce at best, with limited progress made in some countries. With the broad brushstrokes of the analytical questions, approach, and structure of the book laid out, as well as an overview of the country stories, we can now take a deeper dive into the analytical terrain of corporate board policy and the specific measurements and comparative study design for the country-based analyses in Chapters 3 through 15 and the capstone comparative analysis in the last section of the book.

References

Adams, Renée B. and Ferreira, Daniel (2009) "Women in the Boardroom and Their Impact on Governance and Performance," *Journal of Financial Economics*, 94(2), pp. 291–309.

Bacchi, Carol (2017) "Policies as Gendering Practices: Re-Viewing Categorical Distinctions," *Journal of Women, Politics & Policy*, 38(1), pp. 20–41.

Blofield, Merike and Liesl Hass (2013) "Policy Outputs," in G. Waylen, K. Celis, J. Kantola and S.L. Weldon (eds) *The Oxford Handbook of Gender and Politics*. New York, NY: Oxford University Press, pp. 703–726.

Burk, Martha and Heidi Hartmann (2017) "Gender Parity on Corporate Boards: A Path to Women's Equality," in Shannon N. Davis, Sarah Winslow, and David J. Maume (eds) *Gender in the 21st Century: The Stalled Revolution*. Oakland, CA: University of California Press, pp. 127–146.

Bustelo, Maria (2017) "Evaluation from a Gender+ Perspective as a Key Element for (re) Gendering the Policymaking Process," *Journal of Women, Politics & Policy*, 38(1), pp. 84–101.

Capano, Giliberto and Isabelle Engeli (2021) "Using Instrument Typologies in Comparative Research: Conceptual and Methodological Trade-Offs," *Journal of Comparative Policy Analysis*, online first.

Ciccia, Rosella and Emanuela Lombardo (2019) "Care Policies in Practice: How Discourse Matters for Policy Implementation," *Policy and Society*, 38(4), pp. 537–553.

Comi, Simona, Mara Grasseni, Frederica Origo, and Laura Pagani (2020) "Where Women Make a Difference: Gender Quotas and Firms' Performance in Three European Countries," *ILR Review*, 73(3), pp. 768–793.

Dye, Thomas R. (1992) *Understanding Public Policy*. Englewood Cliffs, NJ: Prentice Hall.

Elomäki, Anna (2018) "Gender Quotas for Corporate Boards: Depoliticizing Gender and the Economy," *NORA-Nordic Journal of Feminist and Gender Research*, 26(1), https://doi.org/10.1080/08038740.2017.1388282 (Accessed September 1, 2021).

Engeli, Isabelle, Joni Lovenduski, Amy G. Mazur, and Rosie. Campbell (2015) "Toward a Feminist Measure of Gender Equality: Lessons from the Gender Equality Policy in Practice Project," European Conference on Gender Politics. Uppsala. June.

Engeli, Isabelle and Amy G. Mazur (2018) "Taking Implementation Seriously in Assessing Success: The Politics of Gender Policy in Practice," *European Journal of Gender and Politics*, 1(1), pp. 11–29.

Fernandez-Feijoo, Belen, Silvia Romero, and Silvia Ruiz-Blanco (2013) "Women on Boards: Do They Affect Sustainability Reporting?," *Corporate Social Responsibility and Environmental Management*, 21(6), pp. 351–364.

Ferreira, Daniel (2015) "Board Diversity: Should We Trust Research to Inform Policy Corporate," Governance: An International Review, 23(2), pp. 108–111.

Gains, Francesca and Vivien Lowndes (2015) "Making Violence against Women a Political Priority. The Importance of Sub-National Institutions in Shaping Gender Policy Reform: A Case Study of the New Police and Crime Commissioners in England and Wales," *Working Papers in Gender and Institutional Change*, no. 3.

Howlett, Michael and Jeremy Rayner (2007) "Design Principles for Policy Mixes: Cohesion and Coherence in New Governance Arrangements," *Policy and Society*, 26(4), pp. 1–18.

Ingram, H. et A. Schneider (1990) "Improving Implementation by Framing Smarter Statutes," *Journal of Public Policy*, 10, pp. 67–88.

Krizsan, Andrea and Emanuela Lombardo (2013) "The Quality of Gender Equality Policies: A Discursive Approach," *European Journal of Women's Studies*, 20(2), pp. 77–92.

Lange, Sabine, Petra Meier, and Birgit Sauer (eds) (forthcoming) *Implementing Gender Quotas in Political Representation: Resisting Institutions*. Palgrave/MacMillan

Lewellyn, Krista B. and Maureen I. Muller-Kahle (2020) "The Corporate Board Glass Ceiling. The Role of Empowerment and Culture in Shaping Board Gender Diversity," *Journal of Business Ethics*, 165, pp. 329–346.

Liebowitz, Debra, J. and Susanne Zwingel (2014) "Gender Equality Oversimplified: Using CEDAW to Counter the Measurement Obsession," *International Studies Review*, 16(3), pp. 362–389.

Lombardo, Emanuela and Petra Meier (2022) "Challenging Boundaries to Expand Frontiers in Gender and Policy Studies," *Policy and Politics*, 50(1), pp. 99–115.

Lombardo, Emanuela, Petra Meier, and Mike Verloo (eds) (2009) *The Discursive Politics of Gender Equality. Stretching, Bending and Policymaking*. New York City: Routledge.

Mazur Amy G. (2017) "Does Feminist Policy Matter in Post Industrial Democracies?: A Proposed Analytical Roadmap," *Journal of Women, Politics and Policy*, 38(1), pp. 64–83.

Mazur, Amy G. and Isabelle Engeli (2020) "The Search for the Elusive Recipe for Gender Equality Policy: When Implementation Matters," *French Politics*, 13(1–2), pp. 3–27.

Montoya, Celeste (2013) *From Global to Grassroots: The European Union, Transnational Advocacy and Combating Violence against Women*. Oxford: Oxford University Press.

OECD (2017) *The Pursuit of Gender Equality. An Uphill Battle*, http://www.oecd.org/gender/the-pursuit-of-gender-equality-9789264281318-en.htm (Accessed December 14, 2021).

Pande, Rohini and Deanna Ford (2011) "Gender Quotas and Female Leadership," Background Paper for the World Development Report 2012: Gender Equality and Development, https://openknowledge.worldbank.org/handle/10986/9120

Salamon, L.M. (eds) (2002) *The Tools of Government*. Oxford: Oxford University Press.

Schwab, Klaus (2020) "Preface," in Saadia Zahidi and Herminia Ibarra (eds) *The Corporate Gender Gap Report 2010*. Geneva: World Economic Forum.

Seirstad et al. 2017. the two volumes https://link.springer.com/book/10.1007/978-3-319-57273-4

Verloo, Mieke (ed.) (2018) *Varieties of Opposition to Gender Equality in Europe*. New York: Routledge.

Verloo, Mieke and Sylvia Walby (2012) "Introduction: The Implications for Theory and Practice of Comparing the Treatment of Intersectionality in the Equality Architecture in Europe," *Social Politics*, 19(4), pp. 433–445.

World Economic Forum (2021) *Global Gender Gap Report*. March.

2

The Boardroom as Terrain for Comparative Gender Policy Research

Isabelle Engeli and Amy G. Mazur

Introduction

With a long-lasting legacy of male dominance and gender norms that delegitimate women from gaining significant entry, the terrain of corporate boards provides a new environment in which to pursue the "elusive recipe" for gender equality policy success. The business corporate sub-system is even more closed to outside voices than the highly structured employment policy arena comprised in most settings of only labor, business, and state actors, and it is highly resistant to demands for gender equality and the very actors who forward it (e.g., McBride and Mazur, 2010). Women or other underrepresented groups are excluded on a substantive level in terms of their ideas and demands and descriptively in terms of their presence at the top echelons of corporate power. If progress toward gender equality is to be made in society in general, it is necessary that it should occur in this last bastion of male dominance.

As such, the implementation of gender equality policy in the corporate arena in consolidated and emerging democratic settings provides a laboratory in which to observe whether how and why gender transformation can occur in a setting highly adverse to gender equality. Given that policies were only placed on political agendas in the past fifteen years, the likelihood of success may be even less. Still, the stories of successful corporate board policy told in this book will contribute to further identifying the ingredients for winning gender equality policy more broadly speaking.

The chapter first maps out in detail this fertile terrain for studying and understanding the process and impact of gender equality policy in action then delves into the GEPP measurements that are used by the chapter contributors in their analysis of corporate board policy implementation and our cross-national analysis of the fifteen country cases in the closing chapters of the book. Next, the chapter discusses how the comparative method and the selection of the fifteen country cases

Isabelle Engeli and Amy G. Mazur, *The Boardroom as Terrain for Comparative Gender Policy Research*. In: *Gender Equality and Policy Implementation in the Corporate World*. Edited by Isabelle Engeli and Amy G. Mazur, Oxford University Press.

provide a "most similar systems" (Przeworski and Teune,1970) design to put to the test hypotheses about the combination of factors that allow for authoritative gender equality policy in this highly gender-resistant policy sector, often seen as one of the last holdouts of male dominance.

The Long Road Toward Corporate Equality

The story of equality on corporate boards has long been a story of immobilism, resistance, and opposition. Opposition to equality is not distinct to the corporate world. The state itself has long resisted mainstream equality. At each step of the process, opposition has remained fierce to any attempts to broaden the definition of equality beyond framing core issues only in terms of gender binaries of masculine and feminine to account for the more complex intersectional nature of inequalities (Verloo, 2018; Kantola and Verloo, 2018; Verge and Lombardo, 2021). It is thus worthwhile retracing the long road to corporate equality across its pivotal moments of opposition and rupture.

The first generation of opposition was silent but highly effective. The scrutiny of the numeric underrepresentation of women in politics gained traction in the 1990s. The UN World Conference of Women in Beijing in 1995 firmly anchored women's access to decision-making to the equality agenda. Nevertheless, glaring gender imbalance at the apex of corporate power was put aside and buried in the classic strategy of non-data collection. As Bacchi (1999) and others have noted, mobilization and advocacy are difficult without any numbers to identify the problem at hand and get it on the policy agenda. This was the agenda-denial phase.

The quasi-complete male dominance of the corporate boardroom was the rule up until the early 2010s. Prior to the take-off years for the issue of gender diversity on boards, valid comparable statistics were difficult to come by. The first effort to conduct a systematic study of women on boards was undertaken in 2000 by Burke and Mattis (2000). In their agenda-setting piece, they point out that one of the major barriers to studying the issue was "the lack of availability of data for many companies, especially privately-held firms" (p. 2). A 2012 report by the OECD, *Entrepreneurship at a Glance*, presented comparative figures for women on boards in 2009 while at the same time questioning their accuracy given the uneven coverage of firms in their databases—a business reporting problem as much as a data collection problem.

> The main comparability issue is represented by the fact that the coverage of firms is still uneven across countries in the OECD ORBIS dataset. Large companies are generally over-represented, and this is particularly an issue in non-OECD countries.
>
> (p. 102)

The report's figures on publicly listed companies ranged from a high of 36% in Norway to a low of 0% in Iceland and Austria. Fagan et al, (2012), in the publication of the European Union funded project, "Women on Corporate Boards in Europe," were unable to conduct systematic cross-national analysis of all member states, given that data had not been officially collected. Instead, the project presented its own numbers for the country's covered in the study, France, Hungary, Slovenia, Spain, Sweden, the UK, Finland, and Norway, only going back to the period from 2007 to 2010.

Norway in 2003 was the first country to enact legislated quotas for corporate boards of public limited companies. Spain followed in 2007. In the aftermath of the financial crisis in 2007–2008, the issue gained momentum with a first episode of rupture (Prügl, 2012). International organizations, women's coalitions, some business leader stakeholders, and governments placed the issue on their agendas and slowly began proactive efforts to counter the unchanging "business as usual" practice of keeping white women, as well as men and women from other underrepresented groups, off boards. A handful of governments adopted legislated quotas for privately held companies: Iceland in 2010 as well as Belgium, Italy, and France in 2011. Sector-led initiatives to empower women on boards were launched in the USA with, for example, Women on Boards in 2010—now 50/50 Women on Boards—and the Thirty Percent Coalition in 2011, and in the UK with Women on Boards founded in 2011 and the 30% Club in 2010, which has since become a global initiative. Pioneering companies made commitments to improve women's presence in management, such as Daimler in 2006 and Deutsche Telekom in 2010 (Pande and Ford, 2011). Attention increased at the supranational level as well with the launching of EU effort in 2011, the "Women on Board Pledge for Europe," and the increased attention from international bodies such as the OECD, the World Economic Forum, and the World Bank, starting in 2010–2011 (Armstrong and Walby, 2012 and Elomäki, 2018).

Comparable data began to be produced across Europe, and the exclusion of women from corporate boards started to be exposed quantitatively. More systematic equality tracking was put in place across the European Union and elsewhere. For example, the European Institute for Gender Equality (EIGE) was established in 2006 with the task of collecting and disseminating data on gender equality. Women's representation on corporate boards, meanwhile, made overall progress in Europe from 11.9% in 2010 to 21.2% by 2015 (Aluchna and Aras, 2018, p. 5). Recent EU figures confirm these trends. In 2020, the EU member state average is at 29.5% of women on corporate boards with the member states operating within a legislated quota system leading the way at 37.6% of women (EIGE, 2021). Similar progress was evidenced in an earlier 2017 OECD report on gender equality. Its chapter on "glass ceilings unbroken" presented the "modest" progress of women on corporate boards. From 2016, women held 20% of the seats on boards compared to 16.8% in 2013 across all OECD countries—a 3.2% increase. The report also showed that the overall presence of women on boards continued to lag behind other decision-making arenas. In 2016, women made up 28.7% of national parliaments across the OECD, 35.3% in senior public management, and 54.7% in judgeships. The report concluded, "Gender balance at the top of listed companies is still a distant goal" (p. 177).

The problem might not have had a name yet, or better said, there were still disagreements on the root of the problem and the preferred solution (Humbert et al, 2019 and Elomäki, 2018). At least it had a number. It was now quantified. A second generation of opposition efforts to equality on boards, therefore, had arrived; blocking any policy attempt or diluting policy that went through so much that, at best, impact on the ground would be minimal or, even worse, ineffective. Indeed, at the EU level, opposition from key member states like the UK and Germany prevented a draft directive on gender quotas on corporate boards from moving forwards in 2014 (Chandler, 2016 and Terjesen and Sealy, 2016). As the country chapters that follow show, similar scenarios repeated themselves across North America and most of Europe. Many governments refrained, initially at least, from direct intervention and largely favored the self-regulation approach for companies not owned by the state.

While the issue of gender inequality in corporate decision-making was finally in the spotlight, the definition of equality itself became an issue for debate. As Elomäki (2018) argues, gender inequality on corporate boards was rapidly framed as an "economic problem." For European institutions, resolving the problem in this perspective was seen as a benefit to the economy rather than to address social justice or as a "condition to achieve gender equality." The "economization" of the issue was pushed so far that key EU documents failed to make any mention at all of gender equality. The framing of women as "untapped talent" rather than an "underrepresented group" closed out any consideration of more complex issues that went beyond women's numerical presence on boards—their descriptive representation—to ask the tough questions of who the new women on boards were and whether they had any voice in business decisions.

Yet, as advocates and experts agree, to really understand the deep-seated inequities between men and women in the corporate boardroom, analysis must go beyond the numbers of women on boards at the national level. Aggregate numbers are, at best, snapshots of all businesses lumped into a single monolithic category in a given country or regional collection of countries. More women on boards does not mean that quality representation is being achieved where women are placed in positions of power—in directorships or included on board committees and supervisory levels, depending on the type of corporate board structure found in a given setting. As the most recent EIGE (2021) data shows, any potential spillover effects—called "ripple effects" in the chapter on Norway—of the increase of women on corporate boards in other arenas of business decision-making has remained quite underwhelming: women are only 7.5% of the chief executive officers (CEOs) and 7.1 of the board chairs. In addition, the intersectional blindness of the debate has remained. It is striking to see that in the large majority of reports that quantify the problem of women's underrepresentation on boards, women are presented as a homogeneous group. There is little attention paid to the fact that the women who have accessed board positions are more likely than not to be part of a very specific group of women in situations of privilege.

Measuring Policy Actions Toward Gender Equality on Boards

Before Norway opened up the way for state intervention in 2003, the promotion of equality on corporate boards was entirely left to individual companies and the corporate leadership. Since then, two main regulatory approaches have emerged. A first set of countries has maintained the self-regulatory approach. A second set of countries has followed the Norwegian impulse and designed state-led actions toward gender balance. This divergence in the regulatory approach is often the result of animated political debates where arguments for quotas are strongly opposed in favor of arguments for soft measures such as targets and disclosure mechanisms (Klettner et al, 2013 in Mensi-Klarback and Seierstad, 2020). While quotas are often presented as a "fast track" that leads to a steady pace of change by quota advocates, soft measures are often portrayed to be less effective—a form of self-regulation with a more gradual pace of change. On the contrary, advocates of soft measures highlight the need for flexibility and tailored-made approaches to the specifics of each company. Self-regulation, they argue, is more likely to stimulate innovation among companies who make the issue their own in order to respond to market competition (Maseko, 2015). In the words of the former UK Prime Minister David Cameron: "Coercion can undermine the real talent that is out there" (Milner, p. x).

The growing scholarship on gender representation on corporate boards points to a set of contrasting findings regarding the capacity of these regulatory approaches to generate transformative change. Experts increasingly agree that opposing the use of a quota instrument on one side against employing target and disclosure instruments on the other is not a useful differentiation, even "misleading" (see for example: Mensi-Klarback and Seierstad, 2020; Seierstad et al, 2021; Piscopo and Muntean, 2018; Mensi Klarbach et al. 2021). There are multiple reasons to move away from this false dichotomy. First, the quota instrument is not necessarily the prerogative of the state nor the target instrument of business self-regulation. Self-regulation and state intervention can tap into similar toolboxes to promote equality on boards. Targets and quotas can be found in both self-regulation approaches and state-regulation approaches. True, quotas are more likely in reality to be introduced through state intervention. True, targets are often used in self-regulatory frameworks, but they can also be prescribed in law. A quota requires a minimum proportion of women on company boards. This proportion is set ex-ante and applied to all the companies falling within the scope of the quota instrument. A target also focuses on a proportion to reach but departs from the quota regarding who is in charge of setting this minimum threshold. A target is usually set by the companies themselves as an objective to reach within a specific period. Comply-or-explain mechanisms such as disclosure rules that require companies to explain any discrepancy between the expectation and their actual achievement are found in state intervention and self-regulation.

Second, as the GEPP approach suggests, policy instruments do not operate in isolation. They are often combined with additional instruments (or not) and it is the specific regulatory combination that maximizes or hinders the transformative potential of policy (see also Bothfeld and Rouault, 2019). For example, a quota instrument where implementation is only supported by a reporting obligation may not produce the same effect as a quota that is combined with a financial fine in case of non-compliance (Terjesen et al, 2015; Franceschet and Piscopo, 2013; Humbert et al, 2020 and Bennouri et al, 2020). A target supported by an incentive (positive or negative) may have more teeth than a quota without a sanction in case of non-compliance (Liao et al, 2019; Mensi-Klarback and Seierstad, 2020; Humbert et al, 2020).

This is why the analysis developed in this book takes an analytical deep dive into a lower level beyond the regulatory approach: the level of the policy mix with the possibility of a mix of the four major policy instruments already discussed in Chapter 1—command and control, incentives (negative and positive), capacity, and communication tools. Each instrument mix is analyzed across three continuums measuring pivotal dimensions for assessing implementation success (or failure) and the level of transformative change: regulatory scope and coerciveness examined below. The chapter authors refer to the three continuums to assess the particular policy mix at work in their countries.

The Regulatory Approach Continuum

As shown in Figure 2.1 the regulatory approach continuum goes from the ideal types of self-regulation to state-regulation. The initial regulatory situation was in the hands of the corporate sector, and more often than not at the level of the individual companies. Despite increasing government attention to the issue, the state has rarely fully taken over ownership of the issue. In many cases, if there is state intervention, this intervention has been rather gradual and has left untouched, at least for a period, some areas to self-regulation. These are regulatory situations that are best described as a mixed approach that combines state intervention and corporate action. In addition, it also happens that the corporate sector starts to self-organize under the threat of state action. As result, regulatory situations are often less clear-cut in reality than on paper.

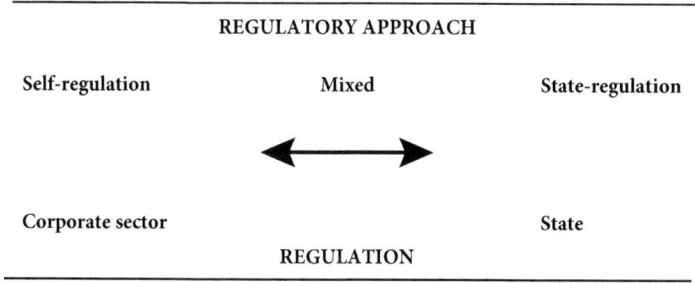

Fig. 2.1 The Regulatory Approach Continuum

The Regulatory Scope Continuum

There is often much negotiation and bargaining about the scope of a given regulation, particularly when resistance to change is high. Indeed, circumscribing the regulatory scope is a way to limit the impact of the regulation. Frequent negotiations are about the legal status, the size of the targeted companies, and the type of boards that should be regulated (see also Meensi-Klarback and Seierstad, 2020). While its successful accomplishment is likely to be easier and faster, a quota mandate that is limited to large companies or companies of a particular legal status only is less likely to boost the overall share of women on boards than a mandate that addresses all the companies regardless of their size and status. A spillover across the sector is possible, but it would be an indirect effect of the regulation only. Figure 2.2 illustrates the regulatory scope continuum with three ideal types. A situation of comprehensive coverage means that the regulation applies to each and every company regardless of the legal status, size, and type of board. A situation of targeted coverage occurs when the regulation is restricted to a finite number of companies, according to their legal status, size, or the type of boards.

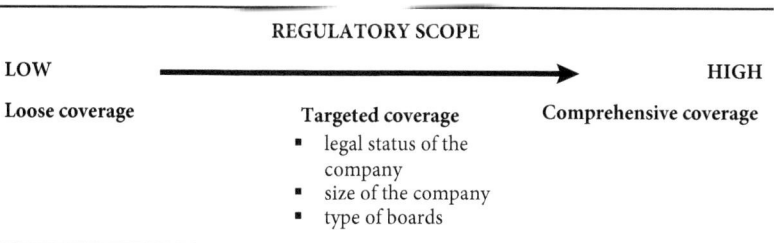

Fig. 2.2 The Regulatory Scope Continuum

The Regulatory Coerciveness Continuum

The third continuum addresses the extent to which the policy mix as a whole is coercive in prescribing compliance to the expected outcome and behavior. We distinguish between two types of policy objectives: the mandate and the recommendation. The mandate is a compulsory requirement a specific behavior. The recommendation is an incitation to adopt for a specific behavior. In other words, what matters is whether the behavior is prescribed or recommended only. As such, a compulsory quota to be achieved or a compulsory target to set are both mandates. On the contrary, a suggested target or quota are both recommendations. A quota instrument is not necessarily more coercive or "harder" in practice than a target if not supported by enforcement-related instruments (Mensi-Klarback and Seierstad, 2020; Mensi-Klarbach et al. 2021). For example, the Norwegian quota policy includes the threat of dissolving companies in case of non-compliance, while the Spanish quota policy has no sanctions. The Norwegian policy is thus more coercive than the Spanish one because it includes a range of sanctions. Moreover, additional behaviors may be prescribed to the main targeted one. The most common ones are the requirement to report or disclose and monitor. When recommendations come with such strings attached, it is often referred to as a comply-or-explain mechanism. The companies are recommended to adopt a specific behavior. If they choose not to do so, they will have to explain why, or, at the very least, they may be required to disclose the gender makeup of their board(s) for example.

The policy output may contain a mix of recommendations and mandates. In this case, there will be variation in terms of coerciveness across the range of instruments within the same policy output. This is why the degree of coerciveness is best conceptualized as a continuum rather than as finite categories. Figure 2.3

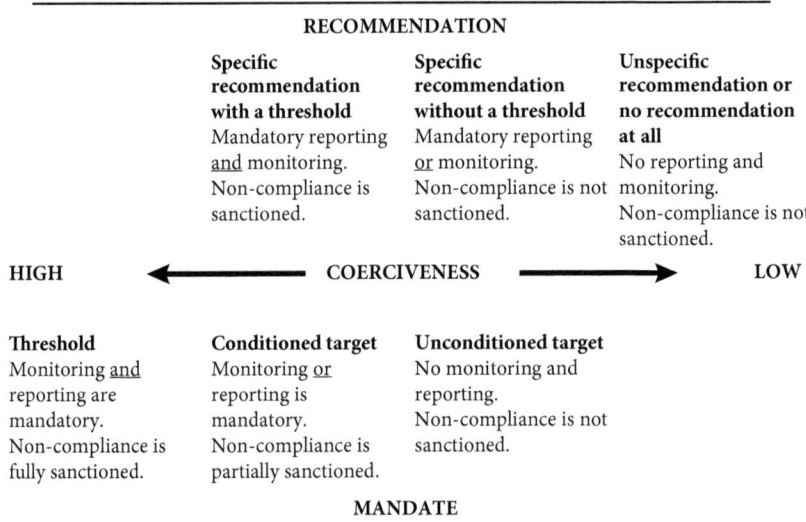

Fig. 2.3   The Regulatory Coerciveness Continuum

displays six examples of coercive situations on the continuum—three for the mandate and three for the recommendation—according to the specificity of the mandate and the recommendation, the requirement for monitoring and reporting, and the existence of sanctions in case of non-compliance.

Assessing Inclusive Empowerment

The analysis of the policy instruments as they read on paper would be rather meaningless without scrutinizing their implementation on the ground. As one of the operating premises of the GEPP approach posits, the implementation process can be a highly contentious process where resistance and opposition can emerge: "Implementation is a battle for power" (Engeli and Mazur, 2018,p. 116). Indeed, for equality advocates to make their voice(s) heard, they need to be included in the implementation process. We contend that assessing the degree of inclusive empowerment requires an intersectional lens that goes beyond the actors who have been included, usually white upper-class men and women, to also scrutinize who are the ones that have been excluded from the implementation process— underrepresented groups of women. Obviously, having a seat at the table does not necessarily mean one voice will be heard. We thus make a distinction between descriptive empowerment that measures whether equality advocates took part in the implementation process and substantive empowerment that captures whether their perspectives and demands have been concretely integrated into the implementation practices. More specifically, in telling the story of if and how the policy instruments were used by policy actors, the analyst is to identify who came forward to speak for women's interests in the post-adoption process. What did they say? For which groups of women were they speaking?—descriptive empowerment—and were their demands actually incorporated in the practice of policy?—the substantive element of empowerment. The hypothesis here is that if there are higher levels of inclusive policy empowerment it should in some ways contribute to policy success. For the highly closed and predominantly white male corporate arena, such intersectional inclusion poses a particular challenge to meaningful policy empowerment that goes beyond bean counting and bringing in "token" white women. Ultimately, policy action must address the deep-seated biases of the business world itself.

Assessing Transformative Change

Assessing the transformative outcome of the policy process is just as, if not more, challenging a task for the corporate sector, as well as for GEPP more generally speaking. In a way, as long as the policy is still being implemented, the final outcome is still in the making, and any assessment is provisory at best. Policy outcomes are also not easy to measure either. Some effects are direct and observable. Other effects are indirect and less observable. A typical direct outcome is whether the problem has been solved. Here, we have to differentiate between the policy goal as defined in the policy itself and the original problem as it exists in reality. A policy may set an unambitious goal. The policy may be successful at achieving its formalized goal but is rather unlikely to solve the problem at its core. A policy goal may also mischaracterize the problem.

To illustrate, as has already been pointed out earlier in the chapter, in the evolution of corporate gender equality where business is king, the predominantly male business leaders have tended to set policy goals in terms of achieving a target number of women on boards in the context of what they identify as a shortage of qualified women. In reality, the problem is that white male business leaders shy away from qualified women who are not white or upper class, making virtually no effort to proactively help women from previously excluded groups. Instead, any demand side initiatives are left to a handful of women business advocates and groups, sometimes connected to international efforts and/or women's policy agencies. While the superficial goal of increasing the number of women on boards might be met, the underlying causes of the problem remain untouched.

Beyond the direct effect, policy can also have indirect or "ripple" effects, which can be positive, neutral, or negative. For example, a policy can achieve the intended effect of increasing women's presence on corporate boards overall but have the unintended consequences of decreasing diversity on the very same boards and/or concentrating board memberships in the hands of a very small pool of privileged women who are members on boards in several different companies—the famous golden-skirt problem. There are two main positive ripple effects operationalized in the GEPP approach for assessing the outcome of policy on gender balance on corporate boards. The first indirect effect is at the level of the gatekeepers and decision-makers, for the most part, business leaders. A policy that successfully pushes forward the promotion of gender equality is likely to have not only reached the direct policy goal but also to have changed the beliefs and behaviors of the gatekeepers and decision-makers. These effects are rarely directly observable. They are often measured through an approximation. In corporate boards policy, an approximation might be to see an increase of women reaching positions of power, like the position of CEO, that are not targeted in the policy. An example of another ripple effect is that companies expand their efforts toward equality to include additional goals related, for example, to diversity or sexuality+ equality that goes beyond heteronormative notions to include a broader range of sexual identities and orientations, or to solve other problems related to gender equality such as the gender pay gap.

The second long-term effect assessed through the GEPP approach is at the societal level operationalized in terms of the extent to which the policy has triggered a progressive change in public opinion and hence contributes to dismantling traditional gender norms and roles more broadly. Short of the use of a policy experiment, a rarity, this second type of long-term effect is difficult to measure, given the effect of a given policy on its own cannot be robustly isolated. Here as well, an approximation can be used as long it is with the utmost caution. An example of such approximation is to study the evolution of media discourse on the issue of women in corporate leadership and the way the media portray women economic leaders and companies that are pioneering leaders or stalling laggards.

Building from the combination of the observed direct and ripple effects, the GEPP framework distinguishes between four general outcomes in terms of the level of **gender transformation**: gender neutral, gender rowback, gender accommodation, and gender transformation. These are to be used as qualitative touchstones to differentiate between different levels of gender transformation (Engeli and Mazur, 2018) rather than static categories.

> **Gender-neutral** outcomes are those that do nothing to change dominant relations in a given sector, usually with no original intent to do so. The refusal of federal regulators in the USA to make any mention of gender-specific considerations in promoting "diversity" in business leadership is a prime example of this first category, particularly given the recent poor performance of US corporations in gender-balanced boards.
>
> **Gender rowback** is even bleaker. Here, while policies may have formally tried to concretely advance gender equality goals and even started to do so, political circumstances and new challenges block any progress. Rowback has clearly occurred in the Central Eastern European countries in all areas of gender equality with the arrival of populist right-wing leaders in many countries, thus, further stalling already weak and symbolic policies targeted at gender equality on boards. Spain also experienced rowback of a quite progressive policy with the arrival of a right-wing majority in power in the mid-2000s. There is some optimism, however, that the pendulum might be swinging back to progress in recent years.
>
> **Gender accommodation**, found to be one of the most common outcomes in GEPP-inspired studies, occurs when dominant gender norms still prevail even in the face of a certain level of authoritative policies. In the pursuit of corporate gender equality, gender accommodation almost seems to be the rule, with corporations willing to enhance numbers, by filling open positions with white upper-class women who do not rock the boat, or sometimes even women business leaders from other countries. The golden-skirt phenomenon is an excellent indicator of accommodation.

Finally, the ultimate prize for gender equality policy is **gender transformation**, the most difficult to achieve of any of the outcomes for obvious reasons. Here, the idea is that the implementation and practice of a given policy actually shift the very deep-seated gender biases and norms on which the targeted gender inequities were seated. Such a shift necessarily involves a changed frame and approach of the gatekeepers in their very activities and interactions. In the corporate world, gender transformation would be achieved if the mostly male business leaders actually understood and embraced the need to promote more gender-equal access to corporate boards for women leaders, for instance through targeted recruitment and training programs, rather than the typical argument that the problem is due to a lack of qualified women and thus essentially the fault of the women themselves.

Given the slow-moving and challenging nature of transformative change, GEPP has allowed for two levels: simple and complex. In **simple gender transformation**, for example, the policy outcome would bring in more upper-class heteronormative white women on corporate boards in positions of power and leadership. **Complex gender transformation** policy outcomes would need to go beyond the "usual suspects" to include women who were not heterosexual, as well as women of color, women from lower socioeconomic groups, and disabled women, to name a few underrepresented groups of women. This is an outcome, as the chapters show in this volume, not to be witnessed in our lifetimes.

The Comparative Strategy: Interrogating the Corporate Sector and the State in Action

Reflecting the larger comparative analytical purview of the GEPP analytical approach, this study adopts a "Most Similar System Design" approach (Przeworski and Teune, 1970) and relies on a selection of democracies from Western, Central and Eastern Europe, North American, and Australasia. This design means that the question of regional patterns in the policy of policy and policy success is addressed in the cross-national analysis. That is, do countries from certain shared historical, political, and cultural settings produce more or less successful policy—put simply, does region matter? This "mid-range" (Merton, 1949) focus also maximizes the reliability and validity of the country and comparative analyses in the book where analytical constructs and concepts can "travel" from one context without overly "stretching" (Sartori, 1970).

The mid-range most similar systems design strategy also provides key conditions for examining policy practices in this particular arena. Whereas on one hand, the development of corporations and their role in national and global economies occurred in post-industrial economies with large service sectors and high levels of technology, on the other, the impulse to promote gender equality on corporate boards in part has come from the expansion of stable democracies to address the rights and status of excluded groups based on principles of justice and equality guaranteed by the rule of law. Although for some countries, the impetus for policy came from extra-national influences as well, including pressure from international and supranational bodies like the EU or the OECD, international NGOs, or even other countries where policies have been put into play, like the path-breaking 2003 quota law in Norway, an important touchstone for policy, and the campaign for corporate gender equality in many other countries.

Case Selection

Our case selection strategy is driven by maximizing the variation on the main factors of interest: the regulatory approach and its implementation process. We have selected cases across the full spectrum of (non) actions toward gender equality on corporate boards as shown in Table 2.1: cases across the self-regulation approach, cases across the state-regulation approach, and cases where there has been no large-scale organized regulation. In addition, for each of the two regulatory approaches, we have selected cases that are on what we have labeled the flagship track and on the alternative track.

Of the countries that have adopted a self-regulation approach, we have selected Australia, the UK, and Sweden. From the state-regulation approach category, we have sampled Norway, France, Spain, Austria, Belgium, and Germany. All

Table 2.1 The Policy Approaches to Corporate Gender Equality in the Fifteen Countries

SELF-REGULATION
Australia
UK
Sweden

STATE REGULATION
Norway
France
Belgium
Spain
Germany

NO SECTOR-WIDE REGULATION
USA
Canada
Poland
Hungary
Croatia
Serbia

these cases have moved from initial self-regulation to state-regulation approaches. Norway, France, and Belgium have seen a major shift toward state-led regulation in the form of legislated quotas with no return to business self-regulation. Once the state took over the regulation of gender equality on corporate boards, the regulatory lead has been kept firmly in the hands of the state. Spain, Austria, and Germany have also seen an increasing intervention of the state over time, but this intervention has mostly been designed to operate in cooperation with self-regulatory efforts led by corporate leadership. Finally, among the countries that have not seen any large-scale regulatory policy efforts, or have only made embryonic attempts, we have selected the USA, Canada, Croatia, Serbia, Hungary, and Poland. All four countries exhibit a piecemeal approach that displays a high level of fragmentation and a lack of cohesion across actions and initiatives toward corporate equality.

The country case selection also provides for a variation on the mix and type of instruments used beyond just the approach. Many scholars and policy practitioners either overtly state or tacitly assume that quotas are the pinnacle for authoritative policy in this area. A 2017 OECD report, for instance, shows that there have been more increases in women's presence in countries with quotas. Other studies have shown that quotas are not the magic bullet for policy success. For example, Smith (2018) points out that gender quotas do not solve the pipeline problem, an absence of qualified women for leadership positions, and that other policies are necessary.

> In many countries the number of women in top executive positions is limited, and it is not clear from the evidence that quotas lead to a larger pool of female top executives, who are the main pipeline for boards of directors. Thus, other supplementary policies may be necessary if politicians want to increase the number of women in senior management.
>
> (p. 1)

A 2015 global study of the issue takes the argument a step further showing that voluntary measures pursued by companies actually go further than quotas and details what measures companies need to take to promote more successful outcomes.

> ... voluntary regimes, unlike quota systems, allow companies and their boards to set their own targets for gender diversity without many repercussions on firm performance and stock prices.... Any quota legislation will dilute the effect of that prerogative. Market forces will force companies to achieve diversity thresholds in their own timeframes with minimal government interference.
>
> (Maseko, 2015, p. 20)

Bothfeld and Roualt (2019) provide a more nuanced argument in their comparative study of corporate board policies in France, Sweden, and Germany;

policy success comes as a product of combining three different types of policy regulation—hierarchical, procedural, and evaluative—with varying levels of coercion and comprehensiveness—reminiscent of GEPP's policy mix.

> progress can be achieved through the design of sound policy packages, that is a smart combination of well-designed rules, accompanying measures and monitoring tools, relying on all three types of regulation.
>
> (p. 1)

The Impact of the Implementation Context

As the GEPP model indicates, implementation does not take place in a vacuum. It is embedded in a context that may also have an impact on the likelihood of policy to lead to a successful outcome (Verloo and Lombardo, 2007; Hughes et al, 2017; Teigen, 2012; Lépinard and Rubio-Marìn, 2018; Terjesen et al, 2015; Mensi-Klarbach and Seierstad, 2020).

The country case selection allows for a secondary level of variation to the approach and policy instruments at play on a number of contextual factors that may also have a mitigating effect on the process and its outcome across the two main regulatory approaches. As a result, this secondary set of contextual factors can be seen, more broadly speaking, to make up the potential ingredients in the pursuit for the "elusive recipe for policy success" in gender equality policy implementation. Table 2.2 maps out the three categories of secondary variations across the fifteen countries in the study.

The first category covers the legal framework of board structures. One-tier systems require companies to have a board of directors that includes the CEO and the other executive members of the senior management, and non-executive directors that are often externally appointed. The executive members are the ones who run the companies, and the non-executive members are the ones in charge of the oversight and the monitoring (Aluchna, 2013a). This is the case in Australia, Belgium (until 2019), Canada, Spain, Sweden, the USA, the UK, and Norway, which requires companies with over 200 employees to also have a corporate assembly. Austria, Germany, and Poland function on a two-tier system where the responsibilities are separated between the two boards. The management board includes the executive members in charge of the executive responsibilities. The supervisory board includes the non-executive members in charge of the oversight and the monitoring and stand above the management board (Aluchna, 2013b). Croatia, Hungary, Serbia, and France allow for multiple structures. The speed of the feminization may likely differ between the types of boards with a higher likelihood for the supervisory boards to progress faster than the executive boards.

Another set of secondary variations is related to the institutional context for state action and the promotion of equality. Our case selection varies across **the**

Table 2.2 Mapping the Secondary Variations across the Fifteen Cases

	Board structure	Corporatism index[d]	EU membership	Legislated political quotas[f]	% Women in parliament[g]	Economic gender gap[h]
PATH 1: SELF-REGULATION						
Australia	One-tier system	−0.22	No	No	30.0	0.70
UK	One-tier system	−1.33	01.01.1973–31.01.2020	No	33.9	0.72
Sweden	One-tier system	1.26	Since 1995	No	47	0.81
USA	One-tier system	−1.65	No	No	23.4	0.75
Canada	One-tier system	−1.55	No	No	29.0	0.74
Croatia	Both systems are available	N/A	Since 2013	Yes	19.2	0.67
Serbia	Both systems are available	N/A	No	Yes	37.7	0.72
Hungary	Both systems are available	−0.93	Since 2004	No		0.67
Poland	Two-tier system	−1.03	Since 2004	Yes (Lower House)	28.7	0.71
PATH 2: STATE-REGULATION						
Norway	One-tier system[a]	1.03	No	No	41.4	0.79
France	Both systems are available	−0.23	Since 1958	Yes	39.5	0.71
Spain	One-tier system	0.59	Since 1986	Yes	44.0	0.70
Belgium	One-tier system[b]	1.21	Since 1958	Yes	40.7	0.71
Germany	Two-tier system[c]	1.01	Since 1958	No	31.2	0.71
Austria	Two-tier system	2.06	Since 1995	No	39.3	0.69

[a]Companies with more than 200 employees should also have a corporate assembly. [b]The 2019 reform of the Code of Governance has introduced the options of a two-tier system. [c]For stock corporations. [d]Source: Jahn 2016. A higher score indicates a higher degree of corporatism. [f]Source: IDEA Gender Quota Database. [g]Source: IPU Parline. Percentages for the Lower/Single House. On January 1, 2020. [h]Source: 2020 WEF Global Gender Gap Report.

level of corporatism, the EU membership status, and the presence of legislated gender quotas for elected office—**legislated political quotas**. The extent to which relations between the state, the trade unions, and the employers are organized and institutionalized may have an impact on the degree of cooperation between the government and the corporate sector toward the promotion of gender equality on boards (see Krook et al, 2009 for political quotas; Mensi-Klarbach and Seierstad, 2020 for corporate quotas) or the capacity of the partners to slow down gender equality policy (Saari et al, 2021). The EU as has been discussed above has dedicated increasing attention to promoting women's access to decision-making. While EU policy has fallen short, so far, of taking an effective lead on corporate quotas, member states have been exposed to the issue since the early 2010s and may have an incentive to show proactive behavior—especially for the members that recently joined the EU (Humbert et al, 2019 and Hughes et al, 2017). In similar fashion, the existence of political quotas is likely to make the concept of quotas more familiar to political and economic actors, providing potential for practices to more easily spillover from the political to economic spheres (Franceschet and Piscopo, 2013; Terjesen et al, 2015, Terjesen and Singh, 2008; Hughes et al, 2017, Lépinard and Rubio-Marin, 2018; Meier, 2013). On the contrary, systems that have encountered strong opposition to political quotas may be less prone to reopening the same controversial debate for corporate boards (Hughes et al, 2017).

The last set of secondary variations addresses the women-friendliness of the system and the overall state of gender equality (Mensi-Klarbach and Seierstad, 2020) captured for case selection purposes through the strength of the **presence of women in parliament**, and the size of the **economic gender gap**. The impact of the presence of women in politics on the gender balance on corporate boards is highly debated (Ibid). Systems that have recently seen steady increases in women's access to political power may be more likely to push the effort toward the apex of economic power (Chizema et al, 2015; Terjesen et al; 2015; but see also Grosvold, 2011). This effect may be more pronounced for systems that have only recently seen such increases (Terjesen and Singh, 2008). Finally, countries with a high level of economic disparities between women and men, such as a weaker integration of women into the labor market and a higher gender pay gap, may be more resistant to corporate equality (Grosvold et al, 2016; Mensi-Klarbach and Seierstad, 2020; Terjesen and Singh, 2008; Terjesen, et al, 2015).

The Issue of Causality

Of course, telling the story of the process and practice of post-adoption is only part of the job. As the GEPP approach indicates, researchers also must focus on coming to the conclusion of whether policy implementation actually mattered in the outcomes of that particular policy over time or whether other factors were

more important in explaining policy impact and outcomes, the "what if?" problem (Engeli and Mazur, 2018, p. 124.; see also Hughes et al, 2017). What if the
outcome—gender policy success—was a result of forces other than the regulatory
approach and its implementation practices? For example, as much research has
shown, it is difficult to implement and evaluate complex policies like gender equality policy in "hard economic times" when public budgets are being cut, particularly
for gender equality policies that may be viewed by some policy actors as "non-
essential" (Annesley et al, 2014). In addition, Hughes et al, (2017) and Piscopo
and Clark Muntean (2018) rightly point out that women's access to parliament
and corporate boards has been naturally increasing over time due to socioeconomic and cultural transformations. Finally, the threat of state intervention may
act as a strong negative incentive for companies to act preemptively (Hughes et al,
2017; Teigen, 2012; Mensi-Klarback and Seierstad, 2020). Therefore, the issue of
whether policy implementation and evaluation were the crucial ingredients for
improvements in gender equality becomes a question for research rather than a
given assumption. Our range of secondary variations at least partially addresses
this first issue over causality through our selection of cases, which provides a laboratory in which certain political, cultural, and economic factors are held constant,
while others are made to vary in order to evaluate the relative importance of our
factors of interest across contextual settings.

A second issue in identifying causality that has received increasing attention across comparative research on gender policy and politics is multi-causality.
Rather than a single causal factor or ingredient being salient, equality gains and
success are often a product of a broader range of determinants acting in combination with each other (Lewellyn and Kuller-Kahle, 2020; Humbert et al, 2020).
For instance, recent comparative research on gender balance in representation has
shown that quotas are not alone a "magic bullet" but are only successful in combination with other factors, in particular, gendered electoral financing (Muriaas et al,
2021). This configurational logic (Ragin, 2014) has helped researchers to concep-
tualize the search for a causal theory of gender policy formation in terms of a recipe
with ingredients, or combination of conditions, where the logic of equa-finality
applies—multiple paths to the same outcome—or no single recipe for success, with
certain ingredients being necessary and sufficient in different settings.

Moving Corporate Equality Forwards in the Corporate World

The remainder of the book now turns to the country analyses of gender equality
policy action in the corporate world using the GEPP framework and measurements laid out in this chapter to conduct individual data-rich country-level
analyses based on primary and secondary source research and, in most cases, elite
interviews. Each chapter hones in on a single case of policy implementation in

corporations and traces it through the pre-adoption and adoption phases through implementation and evaluation, assessing the mix of policy instruments, the practice of post-adoption, the level of policy empowerment, and the transformative impact of the policy in a before and after analysis. While some chapters mention the regulation of board equality in state-owned companies, this book's main focus is on the private sector. With a case selection logic based on a most similar systems design that controls for levels of economic and political development, except for the differences between emerging and consolidated democracies, the range of country cases included also brings under the microscope the effect of cross-national variations in policy approach and contextual factors mapped out in this chapter.

The last two chapters in the book take-up a comparative lens conducting a systematic cross-nation comparison of the politics and outcomes across the fifteen country cases that identify where policies failed and succeeded, what worked and did not, and good practices as well as the complex line-up of factors in terms of variations in policy instruments and contextual factors identified in this chapter. While Chapter 16 assesses the recipe for success in terms of numerical outcomes—increase in women on boards—Chapter 17 dives into the more complex qualitative measurements of policy empowerment and gender transformation. At the end of the comparative story of gender equality policy on corporate boards, in Chapter 17, we return to the larger gender equality policy implementation puzzle, now nourished by the findings of this comparative study—to answer the complex questions of does gender equality policy implementation matter, and if so, how, why, and to what end?—providing further insight into the actual recipe for the effective promotion of equality on the ground. An initial read on these policies suggests that policy success may very well be minimal in all countries regardless of variations in policy and contextual dynamics. The rich empirical analysis conducted on the backdrop of the uniform GEPP framework and comparative good practices of concept traveling, reliability, and validity may very well show something quite different. No matter what the findings reveal, the book ends with, in many ways, what is this study's most important contribution, concrete evidence-based recommendations for moving gender equality forward in the last bastion of male dominance.

References

Aluchna, Maria (2013a) 'One Tier Board', in Samuel O. Idowu, Nicholas Capaldi, Lina-grong Zu, and Ananda Das Guptas (eds) *Encyclopedia of Corporate Social Responsibility*. Berlin, Heidelberg: Springer, https://link.springer.com/referenceworkentry/10.1007%2F978-3-642-28036-8_294 (Accessed December 8, 2021).

Aluchna, Maria (2013b) "Two-Tier Board," in Samuel O. Idowu, Nicholas Capaldi, Linagrong Zu, and Ananda Das Guptas (eds) *Encyclopedia of Corporate Social Responsibility*. Berlin, Heidelberg: Springer, https://link.springer.com/

referenceworkentry/10.1007%2F978-3-642-28036-8_294 (Accessed December 8, 2021).

Aluchna, Maria and Güler Aras (eds) (2018) *Women on Corporate Boards: An International Perspective*, Finance, Governance and Sustainability Series. Routledge: London, New York.

Annesley, Claire, Isabelle Engeli, Francesca Gains, and Sandra L. Resodihardjo (2014) "Gender Equality Policy Advocacy in Hard Times: Comparing the Determinants of Issue Attention to Gender Equality on Executive Policy Agendas," *West European Politics*, 5(37), pp. 886–902.

Armstrong, Jo and Sylvia Walby (2012) *Gender Quotas in Management Boards*. Brussels: European Parliament, Directorate General for Internal Policies, http://www.europarl.europa.eu/RegData/etudes/note/join/2012/462429/IPOL-FEMM_NT(2012)462429_EN.pdf (Accessed December 8, 2021).

Baachi, Carol (1999) *Women, Politics and Policies: The Construction of Policy Problems*. London: Sage.

Bennouri, Morez, Chiara De Amicis, and Sonia Falconieri (2020) "Welcome on Board: A Note on Gender Quotas Regulation in Europe," *Economics Letters*, Volume 190, https://doi.org/10.1016/j.econlet.2020.109055.

Bothfeld, Silke and Sophie Rouault (2019) "Governing Employment Equality by Gender Quotas? Why Authority Does Not Suffice. A Comparative Policy Design Analysis," Discussion Paper. Berlin School of Economics and Law.

Burke, Ronald J. and Mary C. Mattis (eds) (2000) *Women on Corporate Boards of Directors: International Challenge and Opportunities*. Dordrecht, NL: Kluwer.

Chandler, Andrea (2016) "Women on Corporate Boards: A Comparison of Parliamentary Discourse in the United Kingdom and France," (3), pp. 443–468.

Chizema, Amon, Dzidziso. S. Kamuriwo, and Yoshikatsu Shinozawa (2015) "Women on Corporate Boards around the World: Triggers and Barriers," *The Leadership Quarterly*, 26(6), pp. 1051–1065.

Elomäki, Anna (2018) "Gender Quotas for Corporate Boards: Depoliticizing Gender and the Economy," *NORA-Nordic Journal of Feminist and Gender Research*, 26(1), https://doi.org/10.1080/08038740.2017.1388282 (Accessed 1 September 2021).

Engeli, Isabelle and Amy G. Mazur (2018) "Taking Implementation Seriously in Assessing Success: The Politics of Gender Policy in Practice," *European Journal of Gender and Politics* 1(1), pp. 11–29.

European Institute for Gender Equality (EIGE) (2021) *Statistical Brief: Gender Balance in Corporate Boards 2020*. Vilnius: European Institute for Gender Equality, https://eige.europa.eu/sites/default/files/documents/20211100_mh0121080enn_pdf.pdf (Accessed December 8, 2021).

Fagan, Colette, Maria C. González Menéndez, and Silvia Gómez Anson (eds) (2012) *Women on Corporate Boards and in Top Management: European Trends and Policy*. Palgrave Macmillan: New York.

Franceschet, Susan. and Jennifer Piscopo (2013) "Equality, Democracy, and the Broadening and Deepening of Gender Quotas," (3), pp. 310–316.

Grosvold, Johanne (2011) "Where Are All the Women? Institutional Context and the Prevalence of Women on the Corporate Board of Directors," *Business & Society*, 50(3), pp. 531–555.

Grosvold, Johanne, Bruce Rayton, and Stephen Brammer (2016) "Women on Corporate Boards: A Comparative Institutional Analysis," (8), pp. 1157–1196.

Hughes, Melanie, Pamela Paxton, and Mona Lena Krook (2017) "Gender Quotas for Legislatures and Corporate Boards," *Annual Review of Sociology*, 43(1), pp. 331–352.

Humbert, Anne Laure, Elisabeth K. Kelan, and Kate Clayton-Hathway (2019) "A Rights-Based Approach to Board Quotas and How Hard Sanctions Work for Gender Equality," *European Journal of Women's Studies*, 26(4), pp. 447–468.

Kantola, Johanna and Mieke Verloo (2018) "Revisiting Gender Equality at Times of Recession: A Discussion of the Strategies of Gender and Politics Scholarship for Dealing with Equality," *European Journal of Politics and Gender*, 1(1), pp. 205–222.

Klettner, Alice, Thomas Clarke, and Martijn Boersma (2013) "The Governance of Corporate Sustainability: Empirical Insights into the Development, Leadership and Implementation of Responsible Business Strategy," *Journal of Business Ethics*, 122(1), DOI:10.1007/s10551-013-1750-y.

Krook, Mona Lena, Joni Lovenduski, and Squires Judith (2009) "Gender Quotas and Models of Political Citizenship," *British Journal of Political Science*, 39(4) pp. 781–803.

Lépinard, Eléonore and Ruth Rubio-Marín (eds) (2018) *Transforming Gender Citizenship: The Irresistible Rise of Gender Quotas in Europe*. Cambridge: Cambridge University Press.

Lewellyn, Krista B. and Maureen I. Muller-Kahle (2020) "The Corporate Board Glass Ceiling. The Role of Empowerment and Culture in Shaping Board Gender Diversity," *Journal of Business Ethics*, 165, pp. 329–346.

Liao, Rose C., Gilberto R. Loureiro, and Alvaro G. Taboada (2019) "Women on Bank Boards: Evidence from Gender Quotas around the World," *SSRN*, https://ssrn.com/abstract=3346672 (Accessed December 8, 2021).

Maseko, Nelson (2015) "Women Quotas on the Board of Directors: Evidence from the World's Major Markets," 10.13140/RG.2.1.3918.2888

McBride, Dorothy E. and Amy G. Mazur (2010) *The Politics of State Feminism: Innovation in Comparative Research*. Philadelphia, PA: Temple University Press.

Meier, Petra (2013) "Quotas, Quotas Everywhere: From Party Regulations to Gender Quotas for Corporate Management Boards. Another Case of Contagion," *Representation*, 49(4), pp. 453–66.

Mensi-Klarbach, Heike and Cathrine Seierstad (2020) "Gender Quotas on Corporate Boards: Similarities and Differences in Quota Scenarios," *European Management Review*, 17(3), pp. 615–631.

Mensi-Klarbach et al. 2021 https://link.springer.com/article/10.1007/s10551-019-04336-z

Merton, Robert K. [1949] (1968) *Social Theory and Social Structure*. Reprint. New York: Free Press.

Muriaas, Ragnhild, Amy G. Mazur, and Season Hoard (2021) "Payments and Penalties for Democracy: Gendered Electoral Financing in Action Worldwide," *American Political Science Review*. Online First https://www.cambridge.org/core/journals/american-political-science-review/article/payments-and-penalties-for-democracy-gendered-electoral-financing-in-action-worldwide/9A8671265ED91C755324B717B556F7CD.

OECD (2017) *The Pursuit of Gender Equality. An Uphill Battle*. Paris: OECD, http://www.oecd.org/gender/the-pursuit-of-gender-equality-9789264281318-en.htm (Accessed December 8, 2021).

Pande, Rohini and Deanna Ford (2011) "Gender Quotas and Female Leadership," Background Paper for the World Development Report 2012: Gender Equality and Development, https://openknowledge.worldbank.org/handle/10986/9120.

Piscopo, Jennifer M. and Susan Clark Muntean (2018) "Corporate Quotas and Symbolic Politics in Advanced Democracies," *Journal of Women, Politics and Policy*, 39(3), pp. 285–309.

Prügl, Elisabeth (2012) "'If Lehman Brothers had Been Lehman Sisters …': Gender and Myth in the Aftermath of the Financial Crisis," *International Political Sociology*, 6(March), pp. 21–35.

Przeworski, Adam and Henry Teune (1970) *The Logic of Comparative Social Inquiry*. New York: Wiley-Interscience.

Ragin, Charles C. (2014) *The Comparative Method: Moving Beyond Qualitative and Quantitative Strategies*. Oakland, CA: University of California Press.

Saari, Milja Johanna Kantola and Paula Koskinen Sandberg (2021) "Implementing Equal Pay Policy: Clash between Gender Equality and Corporatism," *Social Politics: International Studies in Gender, State & Society*, 28(2), pp. 265–289.

Sartori, Giovanni (1970) "Concept Misformation in Comparative Politics," *American Political Science Review*, 74, pp. 1033–1053.

Seierstad, Cathrine, Ahu Tatli, Maryam Aldossari, and Morten Huse (2021) "Broadening of the Field of Corporate Boards and Legitimate Capitals: An Investigation into the Use of Gender Quotas in Corporate Boards in Norway," *Work, Employment and Society*, 35(4), pp. 753–773.

Smith, Nina (2018) "Gender Quotas on Boards of Directors," *IZA World of Labor*, 7(2), pp. 1–10.

Teigen, Mari (2012) "Gender Quotas on Corporate Boards: On the Diffusion of a Distinct National Policy Reform," in Engelstad, F. and Teigen, M. (ed.) *Firms, Boards and Gender Quotas: Comparative Perspectives (Comparative Social Research, Vol. 29)*. Bingley: Emerald Group Publishing Limited, pp. 115–146.

Terjesen, Siri, Ruth V. Aguilera, and Ruth Lorenz (2015) "Legislating a Woman's Seat on the Board: Institutional Factors Driving Gender Quotas for Boards of Directors," (2), pp. 233–251.

Terjesen, Siri and Ruth Sealy (2016) "Board Gender Quotas: Exploring Ethical Tensions From A Multi-Theoretical Perspective," *Business Ethics Quarterly*, 26(1), pp. 23–65

Terjesen, Siri. and Val Singh (2008) "Female Presence on Corporate Boards: A Multi-Country Study of Environmental Context," (1), pp. 55–63.

Verge, Tania and Emanuela Lombardo (2021) "The Contentious Politics of Policy Failure: The Case of Corporate Board Gender Quotas in Spain," *Public Policy and Administration*, 36(2), pp. 232–251.

Verloo, Mieke (ed.) (2018) *Varieties of Opposition to Gender Equality in Europe*. New York: Routledge.

Verloo, Mieke and Emanuela Lombardo (ed.) (2007) "Contested Gender Equality and Policy Variety in Europe: Introducing a Critical Frame Analysis Approach," in Verloo, M. (ed) *Multiple Meanings of Gender Equality: A Critical Frame Analysis of Gender Policies in Europe*. Budapest, Hungary: Central European University Press, pp. 21–50.

Woodward, A. 2003. "European Gender Mainstreaming: Promises and Pitfalls of Transformative Policy," *Review of Policy Research*, 20(1), pp 65–88.

POLICY PATH 1
SELF-REGULATION

Track 1. Flagship Approach: Self-regulation by Design

3

Accommodating Gender through Self-regulation

A Limited Response for Equity on Boards in Australia

Lucie Newsome and Alison Sheridan

Introduction

Women's poor representation in corporate leadership roles in Australia attracted significant attention in the first decade of the 21st century. The apparent intractability of gender imbalance at the board level and top-level management was made visible through national monitoring annually (Equal Opportunity for Women in the Workplace Agency (EOWWA), 2002, 2008), and the associated media attention decrying the disappointing results when the statistics were released generated lively debate in the popular press accompanied by calls for gender quotas. In this chapter, we track how the corporate sector in Australia lobbied hard to resist the gender quotas being argued for by key lobby groups and high-profile women throughout 2009–2010. Following a government committee inquiry, a self-regulatory approach to increasing women's representation on corporate boards was adopted by the Australian Securities Exchange (ASX) in 2011. The peak body for directors and corporate governance, the Australian Institute of Company Directors (AICD) supported this approach and in 2015 set a target of 30% of board positions to be held by women by 2018 (AICD, 2016).

We focus on the representation of women on the Australian Securities Exchange Top 200 (ASX 200) firms to explore how self-regulation was enacted in 2010/2011, disrupting the previous patterns of board composition. We also draw on the insights of women directors interviewed in 2016 and 2017 about their experiences in accessing director roles after the ASX had required gender reporting by companies (Sheridan et al, 2021). From a mere 8% of ASX 200 directors in 2009, women represent 30% of ASX 200 directors in 2019. We argue that the self-regulatory approach adopted, supported by the actions of key stakeholders, represents gender

Lucie Newsome and Alison Sheridan, *Accommodating Gender through Self-regulation*. In: *Gender Equality and Policy Implementation in the Corporate World*. Edited by Isabelle Engeli and Amy G. Mazur, Oxford University Press. © Oxford University Press (2022). DOI: 10.1093/oso/9780198865216.003.0003

accommodation in so far as its numerical targets have been achieved for the largest companies (AICD, 2019) and attention to board diversity continues to feature in public debates about gender equality with little evidence of the transforming of gender relations through this approach. We note that for smaller companies, even numerical change is lagging, with women's representation on these boards reaching only 15% in 2018. This has attracted key stakeholder attention, and the focus is now on replicating the numerical gains of the larger companies within these smaller companies (AICD and Heidrick and Struggles, 2018) with little attention to the goal of gender transformation.

Gender Equality in the Corporate World

Australia's Liberal Welfare State

As a western industrialized system and market economy, Australia is recognized as a liberal welfare state (Esping-Andersen, 1990; O'Connor et al, 1999), which is guided by notions of market liberalism, a low taxation base, low welfare spending, and individual responsibilities. Australia has a market-oriented gender regime (O'Connor et al, 1999), with residual welfare state benefits to support women's workforce participation. While Esping-Andersen (1990) argued that liberal welfare states would lead to higher levels of female labor force participation, the workforce participation of Australian women with children is low relative to other OECD nations (OECD, 2017). This has been attributed to the cultural strength of the male breadwinner model and the legacy of policies that supported this model (van Egmond et al, 2010).

Authority Instruments to Address Pay Equity

Australia was early in its use of authority instruments (Schneider and Ingram, 1990) to address the gender pay gap created by gender segmentation and the rigidities of the labor market, such as the Affirmative Action (Equal Employment Opportunity for Women) Act 1986. The intent of the original legislation was twofold: to remove sex discrimination from the workplace and to improve employment opportunities for women in private sector organizations with more than 100 employees and higher education institutions (Sheridan, 1995). Gender equality policy developments such as this have been spearheaded by a strong women's policy machinery that has had deep links to women's groups (Sawer, 1996). Despite the use of instruments such as these, the gender pay gap persists at 14.1% (Workplace Gender Equality Agency, 2018). Only 55% of employed women work full-time as compared to 85% of men in Australia. This is despite more females entering higher education in Australia than males since 1989 (ABS, 1994).

Corporate Governance in Australia

There are over 2,200 companies listed on the Australian Securities Exchange (ASX), which has operated as a national exchange since 1987. Corporate governance in ASX companies is shaped by the principles of common law, with laws governing directors' duties coming from three areas—common law, statute law, and a company's constitution. Australia's corporate governance tends to a single-tier board system, with a few exceptions of two-tiered boards found in private health care (Laverty, 2017). The ASX oversees compliance with its operating rules and promotes standards of corporate governance among listed companies (Australian Securities Exchange, 2018).

Female Representation on Corporate Boards

The 2010 Census of Women in Leadership in Australia reported an overall lack of progress for women in executive levels within organizations (Equal Opportunity for Women in the Workplace Agency, 2012). From 2002–2010 women's representation on boards was only 8.4% of the top 200 ASX companies and women made up only 8% of senior executive teams (Table 3.1). Only 3% of the ASX 200 had a female CEO. Insurance, consumer services, banks, diversified financials, and software and services were the industries that had the highest percentage of female board directors. In 2008, women held a significantly higher proportion of board positions on government boards and committees (38%) and the not-for-profit sector (30%) than in commercial companies as a result of government policies to encourage this (Braund and Medd, 2008).

Table 3.1 Percentage Share of Women on Boards in Large Listed Companies in Australia, 2002–2018

| | AUSTRALIA | | | | | |
	2002[a]	2004[a]	2008[a]	2012[a]	2015[b]	2018[b]
ASX 20	—	—	—	18.8	24.2	35.4
ASX 50	—	—	—	15.7	23.7	31.6
ASX 100	—	—	—	11.8	23.8	31.5
ASX 200	8.2	8.6	8.3	12.3	20.6	29.7
ASX 200 CEOs	1.3	3.0	2.0	3.5	5.5	7.0

Source: [a]Equal Opportunity for Women in the Workplace Agency (2002–2012); [b]AICD 2015–2019.

Getting Political and Corporate Attention, 2008–2010

In 2008, following years of women's representation on corporate boards stagnating, the issue reached the political agenda. Critical actors to emerge in this debate included Elizabeth Broderick, the Sex Discrimination Commissioner (2007–2015) with the Australian Human Rights Commission (an independent statutory authority reporting to the federal Parliament), and the lobby group Women on Boards, who were arguing for quotas as progress for women on boards had been "glacial" (Ross-Smith and Bridge, 2008) and intervention was required. This issue did not attract the interest of trade unions or more mainstream women's groups, who were largely absent from the debate. Other influential actors included the ASX, the AICD, and the Workplace Gender Equality Agency (WGEA). Debate occurred through the media rather than a formal consultation process and did not reach the parliamentary level at this time. Under a federal Labor government, political agents debated the efficacy of quotas, mentoring programs, and targets (Watson, 2014), and centered on gender diversity rather than diversity more broadly. Proponents of regulatory intervention challenged the accepted norm that ASX boards be dominated by men and pointed to the Norwegian quota system as an example of how to meet ambitious targets (Sheridan et al, 2014).

Broderick's (2009) arguments for intervention to improve women's representation on boards related to economic growth at a macro level, democratic legitimacy of decision-making/better corporate governance, better company performance, and that the pace of voluntary change was too slow. She did not draw on arguments of transforming gender patterns or a more equal society—in Australia, these arguments have not been pivotal to gender policy development in other areas, such as paid parental leave (Newsome, 2017). In 2010, Broderick and the Australian Human Rights Commission's (AHRC) position was that by 2015 all publicly listed companies should establish a target of a minimum of 40% female board representation. As the AHRC had no statutory rights to require this, all it could do was make recommendations to the Australian government that "[i]f progress is not made, the Australian Government should consider legislating to require publicly listed companies and other large employers to achieve a mandatory gender diversity quota of a minimum of 40% of both genders within a specified timeframe [five years], failing which penalties will be imposed" (Broderick et al, 2010).

The AICD dominated the Australian debate around the gendered composition of corporate boards in Australia when it emerged following Norway's final enforcement of a 40% quota of women on boards in 2008. The AICD promoted the view held by company representatives that quotas would represent "tokenism" (AICD, 2011) rather than the earning of board positions through merit and experience. The AICD was successful in framing the problem around the limited supply of qualified and capable female candidates and that company autonomy should be preserved. This argument was supported by a number of high-profile businesswomen who argued against regulation and for the "merit" approach to continue (UWA Business School, 2010).

The AICD proposed self-regulation by the sector (AICD, 2011). Its position was supported by corporate Australia more broadly, which was strongly opposed to the introduction of quotas (Sheridan et al, 2014). The AICD drew on arguments associated with company autonomy and that corporations should be the drivers of change rather than the state to make its case for self-regulation. The CEO of the AICD argued that "[t]he idea of mandated quotas for female representation on boards is wrong in principle, has difficulties in practice, is tokenistic and is counterproductive to the end goal of increasing board diversity" (AICD, 2011). Further, the AICD's public statements continued to frame the lack of women on corporate boards as a pipeline problem that needed to be addressed through both short- and long-term measures. It argued for companies to be given the freedom to set targets on gender and board composition. The chair of the ASX also opposed the introduction of quotas (Braund, 2010). As the AICD is part of the ASX Governing Council, it was in a privileged position to influence its preferred policy solution.

WGEA, which sits within federal government, promoted industry leadership rather than legislated intervention to improve gendered board composition. Sheridan et al, (2014) argued that this positioning was strategically important for WGEA in maintaining its influence within corporate Australia. It is also consistent with its general approach to measuring gender and leadership in corporations without adopting hard regulation. While the AHRC's position was important for setting ambitious targets for debate, the Human Rights Commission was not substantially represented in the debate that followed. The WGEA, on the other hand, had a more moderate approach and was able to maintain its seat at the table. The AICD was in a powerful position as part of the ASX Governing Council and was able to successfully frame the debate as an issue of supply of female candidates for board positions, which shaped the ensuing policy.

Self-regulation Process

The Minister for Superannuation and Corporate Law, Senator Nick Sherry responded to the growing public debate on the gendered composition of Australian corporate boards by referring the matter to the Corporations and Markets Advisory Committee (CAMAC) for further investigation into possible solutions. In the terms of reference, Sherry pointed to a soft regulatory approach, requesting an investigation into "the options for creating an environment that will encourage companies in Australia to foster a governance culture that embraces diversity in the composition of their boards" (CAMAC, 2009, p. 3). Sherry framed diversity around gender, ethnicity, education, professional backgrounds, and demography but believed that gender diversity was particularly worthy of further investigation.

CAMAC was formed in 1989 and comprises a group of people appointed by the Minister for Superannuation and Corporate Law representative of industries relevant to its remit. At the time of CAMAC's (2009) report *Diversity on Boards of Directors*, the advisory committee comprised seven men and four women, three of whom were lawyers, three academics, three company directors, one chartered accountant, and the deputy chair of the Australian Securities and Investments Commission (CAMAC, 2009). The report presents that there was consensus among the advisory board.

Referring the issue to CAMAC served to empower a new group in the debate on gender diversity on Australian boards but to marginalize others that had been involved earlier. The AHRC and the Sex Discrimination Commissioner were not consulted in the development of the report and nor were women's groups, the AICD, or traditional lobby groups for employment issues, such as employer associations or trade unions. The WGEA and the Federal Office for Women were descriptively represented in this process in that they were identified as being consulted.

In its final report, CAMAC did not clearly present the low representation of women on Australian boards as a major problem. Instead, it represented diversity as a trade-off with an effective board. For example, CAMAC (2009, p. 20) argued that a "balance needs to be struck" between diversity and the ability of the board to be harmonious and make decisions as an "overly diverse board may run the risk of becoming divided and dysfunctional" CAMAC (2009) was forceful in its dismissal of quotas of any kind, either regulatory or self-regulatory. CAMAC (2009) maintained that in the private sector, the accountability of board members to shareholders was paramount, and imposing quotas would undermine effective governance. It argued: "There would be obvious dangers in any initiative to cut across their choice and dictate elements of board composition" (Ibid, p. 9). CAMAC's report delegitimized quotas as a policy response.

CAMAC (2009) attributed the low numbers of women on boards to a limited supply of suitable female candidates. In responding to EOWWA's (2008) census demonstrating the stagnating number of women's board representation, CAMAC (2009, p. 27) argued: "The census does not provide information on the number of women who are seeking, or are otherwise open to, board appointments in Australia." CAMAC (2009) proposed self-regulation but failed to endorse a specific solution to the issue of low female board representation in Australia. The report recommended that "boards and shareholders, in their own interest, give full consideration to issues of diversity in board composition" (Ibid, p. 48). In advocating private sector accountability, the report recommended that the government aim at convincing leaders and shareholders of the value of a more open approach to identifying and selecting directors, a more structured approach to candidate selection, and more information to shareholders on board appointments rather than relying on social and informal networks. This reflected the ASX Corporate

Governance Council Corporate Governance Principles and recommendations to seek to promote better processes for the selection and evaluation of directors of public listed entities. Following the framing of the problem as one related to the supply of suitable candidates, CAMAC (2009) pointed to programs for the skill development for women, such as mentoring programs and websites where women can register their interest for board membership.

The AICD (2009) quickly responded to CAMAC's (2009) report and endorsed the recommendation that boards should "take a more open approach to board selection" and regularly review their composition as part of a formal process of evaluating the effectiveness of the board. The AICD welcomed CAMAC's (2009) rejection of quotas as a policy instrument on the basis that it was likely to undermine company governance and success. The AICD (2009) highlighted CAMAC's conclusion that "it is not a case of diversity at all costs; there needs to be some common purpose and ability to work together" and that the "mix of directors is a matter for consideration by each company in the context of its own business and needs." Drawing on CAMAC's (2009) argument that the issue was caused by the supply of female candidates, John Colvin, Chief Executive Officer of AICD, said, "One of the challenges in introducing new non-executive directors to top listed company boards is the need for candidates to demonstrate that they have required competencies" (AICD, 2009).

By referring the issue to the CAMAC, the Australian Labor Party (ALP) government and Minister Sherry were able to distance themselves from the gender ideology associated with women's representation on corporate boards and place decision-making power in the hands of a conservative, independent entity. Despite the Labor party being left-leaning, it was not willing to significantly intervene in the market to improve women's representation on corporate boards. CAMAC responded to Sherry's instructive terms of reference by proposing self-regulation and delegitimizing quotas as a policy instrument. AICD supported this policy outcome and the framing of the issue around the inadequate supply of suitable female candidates.

Outputs

Consistent with CAMAC's (2009) recommendations, the ASX implemented a private governance mechanism to respond to the issue of low female representation on Australian boards. The chosen policy instrument mix to increase women's representation on corporate boards was one of self-regulation, specifically disclosure, reporting, transparency, and accountability to shareholders. In response to the CAMAC recommendations, the ASX revised the 2007 edition of its principles and released the *Corporate Governance Principles and Recommendations with 2010 Amendments*. From January 1, 2011, Principle 3 of the ASX Corporate Governance

Table 3.2 Policy Measures on Corporate Gender Equality in Australia

---

SELF-REGULATION

ASX Corporate Governance Principles and Recommendations, 2010 Amendments

Principle 3.2: Companies should establish a **policy concerning diversity** and **disclose the policy** or a summary of that policy. The policy should include requirements for the board to establish **measurable objectives** for **achieving gender diversity** for the board to assess annually both the objectives and progress in achieving them.

Principle 3.3: Companies should disclose in **each annual report** the **measurable objectives for achieving gender diversity** set by the board in accordance with the diversity policy and progress toward achieving them.

Recommendation 3.4: Companies should disclose in **each annual report** the **proportion of women employees** in the whole organization, women in senior executive positions, and women on the board.

---

guidelines was amended (ASX Corporate Governance Council, 2010, p. 25) to specifically address gender diversity. The revisions are summarized in Table 3.2.

The ASX has the capacity to delist corporations not complying with the diversity principles. Therefore, the added principles together can be categorized as an "incentive instrument" in Schneider and Ingram's (1990) classification system, as they aimed to nudge the desired behavior with negative incentives of being delisted if companies failed to comply.

The principles, however, do not set specific targets, and there is wide scope for companies to interpret the principles (Klettner et al, 2016). As they state: "Increased gender diversity on boards is associated with better financial performance, and that improved female workforce participation at all levels positively impacts the economy AICD" (2010c, p. 6). The ASX Corporate Governance Council (2010) also framed the decision to include a diversity principle very firmly in the business case for diversity, which focuses on the benefits for the company of embracing the spirit of the changes to the ASX principles.

This self-regulation covers all listed companies but does not extend to not-for-profit entities or unlisted companies and has allowed companies to set their own targets. Recommendation 3.3 of the ASX Corporate Governance Guidelines suggests companies establish and disclose measurable objectives for achieving gender diversity, as well as progress toward achieving those objectives. It is targeted at a high level so that heads of companies need to ensure compliance and are therefore aware of how their company is tracking.

Similarly, the new gender principles were moderately coercive as monitoring and reporting are required with a comply-or-explain mechanism. Non-compliant corporations must outline reasons for non-compliance in their annual report. In this way, a company is required to make publicly available its failure to comply with the guidelines. There is some capacity for the ASX to coerce companies to comply through the threat of being delisted, and positive incentives for compliance exist in terms of gains to be made through stakeholder perceptions of the corporation's social justice commitment and company performance and governance (Sheridan et al, 2014).

In anticipation of the introduction of the gender guidelines, the ASX worked closely with the AICD to make visible the progress of women to corporate boards through a publicly available "real-time" report on the AICD website tracking women's appointments to ASX boards and their cumulative share. This bean-counting approach is a metric that is easy to monitor and report, but there is a well-established critique of such metrics' failure to address underlying gender norms and practices (Alvesson and Due Billing, 2002).

In its tips for assisting companies to adopt the new principles (AICD, 2010c, p. 3), companies were advised to "target professional development programs aimed at helping women to develop skills and experience." The AICD company directors' course was promoted as a means for better preparing women for corporate directorships, with scholarships available to women to complete this course (AICD, 2010b). This reflects the initial framing of the issue by AICD, which was then picked up by CAMAC (2009), that the problem is one of limited supply, rather than demand for women to become members of corporate boards. In this way, the incentive instrument of companies being delisted if they failed to comply was coupled with capacity and learning instruments (Schneider and Ingram, 1990) of providing resources, knowledge, and skills in order to empower the desired change.

The Chairmen's Mentoring Program was another AICD activity to support women to become "board-ready" through matching women with experienced chairs of ASX companies. It attracted 350 applications in 2011 for its 2012 program, resulting in 86 women being matched with 76 chairs of boards (Schmidt and Hooper, 2011). The criteria for this program was that women must be ASX 200 "board ready," including having "experience on the boards of ASX 200 and other listed companies, unlisted public companies, large private companies, government bodies and not-for-profits, as well as senior executive women within ASX-listed companies" (AICD, 2010a). Given these criteria, it raises the question of why these women would even need mentoring. The beneficiaries of this program were women who were already at senior levels in the corporation and likely to have privileged socioeconomic backgrounds. As such, it is unlikely to empower more diverse groups of women, particularly as diversity more broadly conceived was not part of CAMAC's initial terms of reference.

The amendment to the AICD's principles served to allow for company autonomy while forcing a level of action on the issue of women's corporate board representation. The key policy instruments deployed in Australia for increasing women's representation on corporate boards are self-regulation through the ASX's reporting requirements for listed companies. In response to the problem established during the debate regarding the supply of female candidates, the AICD, in collaboration with the ASX, implemented training programs for women to ensure they are "board ready." Thus, soft guidelines have been produced to assist corporations to comply with the principles of gender diversity.

Implementation and Evaluation Practices

From 2010 to 2018 the principles instituted by the ASX and AICD were complemented by a specific target, that female board representation should reach 30% by 2018. To monitor progress toward this goal the reporting mechanism was instituted that also served to encourage compliance from ASX listed firms. The monitoring strategy was crucial to ensuring the efficacy of the self-regulatory approach.

The ASX was the agent responsible for implementing the change to its guiding principles. The ASX delegated reporting to the corporate sphere, which provided a level of transparency to the monitoring of the policy outcome. One of Australia's top accounting firms, KPMG, was commissioned by the ASX's Education and Research Program to analyze the first year's set of disclosures by companies under the new Principle. KPMG conducted a quantitative analysis of a sample of the companies listed on the ASX as of September 30, 2012 (KPMG, 2013). The sample comprised the top 200 companies, 200 of the next largest 300 companies, and 200 of the remaining 1,688 companies. KPMG (2013) found a high level of compliance, with over 90% of listed companies establishing a diversity policy or explaining why not, although a smaller percentage reported setting measurable objectives. The smaller the organization the less likely it was to report (Sheridan et al, 2015).

Elizabeth Broderick, in her position as Sex Discrimination Commissioner, drew attention to the issue of women's low representation on corporate boards but was sidelined through the decision-making and implementation process, predominantly due to her support of the introduction of mandatory quotas. Broderick was effective, however, in convening the Male Champions of Change (MCC) in 2011. Fifteen male CEOs were the initial signatories to the MCC who publicly championed their commitment to increasing female representation in leadership positions in business (Male Champions of Change, 2011). This created normative pressure for other business leaders to advocate for change (Sheridan et al, 2014) and empowered individual companies to become leaders in this space. Australia's first female prime minister, Julia Gillard, supported leadership by individual companies: "We are strenuously urging the private sector to act to get more women onto their boards. I view regulating as the last option—I want to see self-motivated change from Australian companies" (The Australian, 2011). The impact of MCC has been significant, as evidenced by the following quote from one of the women directors of an ASX 50 company:

I think Fortescue [one of the signatories to the MCC] going above 50 per cent has set a whole new benchmark. It's got very good media and stuff out of it. The ASX and AICD as well are all talking about the companies that don't have enough women on their boards.

(ASX 50 Women director)

The 30% Club, the international charter to bring women's board representation to 30%, emerged as a substantively empowered group during the implementation of the ASX principles. From July 2015, the AICD formalized publishing quarterly reports on the progress to achieving the 30% target (AICD, 2015, 30% Club, 2019). As the monitoring evolved, there was greater attention to the segments where most gains were being made, with the details of the gender composition of the top 20, 50, and 100 ASX companies included.

As well, insiders were working to enact gender transformation at the board level. Influential women directors described their (largely invisible to the wider community) role in reinforcing ASX Principle 3, and bringing to life the AICD's 30% target for those companies that have been laggards.

A couple of us do ring the chairmen of these companies and they know why we're calling and we're not going to give up. The AICD has been absolutely fabulous because they have operated as the core of the 30% Club in terms of providing, not only all the administrative support, but a lot of the strategic input to what we're doing.

(ASX 50 female director)

Since the introduction of the gender diversity recommendation in 2011, there has been an increase in the number of women on corporate boards. As part of the process, the AICD urged ASX 200 boards to meet the target of 30% women on the boards by 2018 (AICD, 2018).

The ASX has been pushing hard, the AICD has been pushing hard, the BCA (Business Council of Australia), there's also scrutiny from the Shareholders' Association. There's real pressure and scrutiny now on boards that don't have women. So I think that pressure and momentum will continue until we reach about 30%. I worry then whether it will continue on to 40 and 50.

(ASX 50 Women director)

The lobby group, Women on Boards, played a role in producing guidelines that influenced the way that the ASX Principles for Diversity were implemented. This group, however, was only descriptively empowered in this process as it acted within the regulatory guidelines established by CAMAC and ASX, which acted in close collaboration with the AICD. WGEA was descriptively empowered, as it was constrained in its ability to challenge the federal government in which it sits and acted, to maintain its seat at the corporate table. No gender transformation is evident at a decision-maker/gatekeeper level in the Australian context. With the supply of suitable candidates identified as the reason for the low number of women on boards, the capacity for societal gender transformation has been limited as demand-side factors were not recognized by the decision-makers, key stakeholders, or evaluators.

During the implementation of the ASX revised principles, Elizabeth Broderick and the 30% Club mobilized to promote greater gains for women's representation on corporate boards than would have occurred without their agency. The ASX principles were not specific in their aims and the self-regulatory approach gave key agents, such as Broderick and the 30% Club, room to maneuver to promote their agenda for change and be substantively represented in the implementation process in a way that was not represented in the policy development process. In the implementation process, there has been a mixed collaboration here between public agents (AICD) and private agents (female directors and Broderick) as well as established lobby groups.

Assessing Empowerment and Gender Transformation

The implementation of the ASX diversity principles has had a medium positive effect in terms of gender transformation, and in terms of its stated goals and the cost of implementation, there is evidence of the policy's effectiveness and efficiency. In 2015, the AICD set a target of 30% of women board appointments to ASX 200 boards by 2018. Since 2009, the AICD has published the new board appointments of the ASX listed companies every quarter (AICD, 2018), with additional reporting around progress toward meeting the 30% target from 2015, including reports of those performing well, and making visible the laggards. From 8.3% of directors in ASX 200 companies in 2009, women now make up 29.7% (AICD, 2018), close to the 30% target.

Women agents have had a significant impact on improving the level of female board representation in Australia, despite being sidelined at various points of the policy's development. Elizabeth Broderick was able to mobilize to create normative change through the empowerment of leaders in the MCC program. The 30% Club entered the policy space to influence the setting of specific targets at the implementation phase. The setting of this target was important for creating buy-in from board members who sat on more than one board. Gilding et al, (2018) found the only significant predictor of whether boards will reach the 30% target was if it has a director that sits on another board that has reached the 30% target. They did not find that the presence of a Male Champion of Change on the board per se made a significant difference to reaching the 30% point.

According to directors of ASX 50 companies, the shift that occurred in the recruitment of directors following the introduction of the ASX Principle 3 was dramatic. Sex had become a more visible and salient factor in board appointments (Sheridan et al, 2021). Directors made it clear that no board in the ASX Top 50 would now not have women appearing on their shortlists for new appointments, and that gender composition was now part of the discourse of board appointments for those companies that perceived themselves as leaders. As one interviewee noted, "There has been a material change in the past five years. No company would have said it must have women on its shortlist of board candidates five years ago" (ASX 50 female director).

Ross-Smith and Bridge (2008) argue that Australian corporate governance guidelines with their stated preference for a majority of non-executive directors can help explain the comparative success of women in achieving non-executive director appointments. This is a necessary but not sufficient way to achieve more female board appointments in the absence of women in other major pathways to boards—namely senior executive leadership roles in the corporate sector. While there has been an increase in women on boards in Australia, the number of women in the executive management teams of the ASX 200 has remained low. In 2018, only fourteen of the ASX 200 companies had a female CEO (Korn Ferry Institute, 2018), although this has increased from four in 2008. There are 430 women in the ASX200 executive leadership teams, compared to 1,428 men (CEW, 2018). This is up from 125 women in 2008. Among ASX 500 companies, there was a total of 731 executive directors, and, of these, only 28 were female (3.8%) and 12 were CEOs (2.4%) (Table 3.1). Australia's gender pay gap has stayed at approximately the 15% mark for the last two decades (Workplace Gender Equality Agency, 2020).

There is some evidence of social reproduction with the increased numbers of women on Australian boards. Smith (2018) found that social connections drive board appointments and that social identity is a significant selection criterion for board membership. The golden skirt is also evident, with women more likely to hold more than one board seat. Women comprised 35% of those, with two or more board seats, of ASX 200 companies and 45% of those with three or more seats (Australian Council of Superannuation Investors, 2015). Women's representation in executive and board leadership roles remains low, with women holding just 6% of ASX 100 chair roles (Australian Council of Superannuation Investors, 2016). The challenge of this policy change to traditional gender relations and gender norms is limited by its framing as a supply-side issue.

The ASX's implementation of diversity principles has a medium/positive likelihood of being successful in the future. Klettner et al, (2016) argue that while quotas may achieve significant results directly following their implementation, voluntary targets may create a more significant cultural shift that may improve gendered board composition in the long run. As Braithwaite (2002, p. 47) argues:

"As the regulated phenomena become more complex, principles deliver more consistency than rules." The Australian system of self-regulation is limited, however, in its capacity to capture all corporations, as it only covers listed companies and does not include smaller firms or not-for-profit entities. Of listed corporations, larger firms are more likely to increase the numbers of women on their boards as they are subject to greater public scrutiny and are more likely to provide leadership on issues such as this (Luoma and Goodstein, 1999). Nagarajan (2011) argues that the stakeholders in smaller and medium-sized listed corporations do not have the same influence, so these firms lag behind movements by larger ASX listed corporations to improve the gender compositions of their boards. The discourse on board diversity has most commonly been contained to gender diversity, with other dimensions of diversity such as race, ethnicity, disability, and age largely ignored.

There was a medium/positive gender transformation at the decision-maker/gatekeeper level following the implementation of the ASX guideline change to incorporate gender. For example, the current chair of the AICD, Elizabeth Proust argued that if the 30% goal was not met by the end of 2018, then the ASX 200 would likely have to face mandated quotas (Khadem, 2016). Proust argued: "But quotas will have to be on the table. We will have to have a debate and I would like to broaden it from being about gender to all aspects of diversity." Angus Armour the AICD Chief Executive said that the AICD was considering its next move, which included the possibility of introducing a so-called 40-40-20 target. Under that model, boards would be required to appoint a minimum of 40% men and 40% women, while the remaining 20% could be of either gender (Patten, 2019). Khadem (2017) found evidence that chairs of Australian companies support quotas and Sheridan et al, (2014) argued that there is a growing realization that board appointments were not necessarily linked to merit.

It is unlikely that the ASX revised principles would have improved the levels of female representation on Australian boards without the setting of the 30% target. This allowed for norm diffusion between boards, particularly where a board member was on the board for a company that had achieved this target (Gilding et al, 2018). Self-regulation was an important policy instrument for creating buy-in from corporate Australia and it enabled agents such as Broderick to maneuver to create and support leaders in this space. The gender-transformative effects of this policy are limited by the golden-skirt phenomenon, the framing of the issue as a supply-side problem and the persistence of the glass ceiling and stagnant gender pay gap.

Conclusion

The AICD dominated the debate regarding the gender composition of corporate boards in Australia when it emerged following Norway's enactment of quotas in

2008. The AICD was successful in framing the problem around the limited supply of qualified and capable female candidates and that company autonomy should be preserved. The early advice to companies seeking to increase women's representation included "fixing" the women by providing more training and development. Over time, the institutional pressures on firms to demonstrate they were leaders through their more representative board profiles, through the 30% target set for ASX 200 companies by the AICD, the AICD reports of those performing well, and the MCC have yielded an increase in women's representation on boards.

This case supports the literature on the impact that critical agents can have on gender policy outcomes rather than supporting critical mass theory. Elizabeth Broderick, the Sex Discrimination Commissioner, was a critical agent moving within the space created by self-regulation to influence individual companies to improve their female board representation. The institutionalized power of the office of the Sex Discrimination Commissioner bore fruits in this situation and is consistent with the historic strength of this position in influencing gender equality policy development. Broderick was influential in the early stages of the debate and then sidelined through the policy development phase. Through the implementation process, she was able to exert considerable influence over individual companies to become norm setters through leadership on the issue. The 30% Club was empowered through the implementation phase and was able to fill the policy gap to influence the AICD's setting of a 30% target by 2018.

The policy instruments of self-regulation reflect the philosophy of market liberalism underpinning Australia's welfare state and economy as well as its regulatory tradition. Self-regulation was framed as an appropriate policy in the Australian case as it allowed buy-in from corporate Australia and has been acceptable to both Labor and Coalition governments. The capacity of this policy to create gender transformation is limited due to the initial framing of the issue as one of inadequate supply of qualified women and the golden-skirt problem that has emerged with women holding multiple board memberships. Rather, it is clear the self-regulatory approach in Australia, with its focus on the numerical representation of women on boards, exemplifies gender accommodation.

References

30% CLUB (2019) *Business Leadership: The Catalyst for Accelerating Change*. Sydney: 30% Club, https://30percentclub.org (Accessed March 19, 2019).

ABS (1994) *Participation in Education: Gender Differences in Higher Education*, https://www.abs.gov.au/ausstats/abs@.nsf/7d12b0f6763c78caca257061001cc588/0660ad7a5d3e0e31ca2570ec00786347!OpenDocument (Accessed May 15, 2019).

AICD (2009) *AICD Endorses a More Open Approach to Board Appointments*, http://www.companydirectors.com.au/-/media/resources/media/media-releases-and-speeches/2009/aicd-media-release_board-diversity-report_13-august-2009.ashx (Accessed May 15, 2019).

AICD (2010a) *Directors Take the Lead in Helping Put Women on Boards*, http://
www.companydirectors.com.au/General/Header/Media/Media-Releases/2010/
Directors-take-the-lead-in-helping-put-women-on-boards (Accessed October 14,
2011).

AICD (2010b) *New Scholarships to Increase Diversity on Boards*, http://www.
companydirectors.com.au/General/Header/Media/Media-Releases/2010/New-
scholarships-to-increase-diversity-on-boards (Accessed December 19, 2011).

AICD (2010c) *New Corporate Governance Recommendations on Diversity: Tips for
Getting Started*, http://www.asxgroup.com.au/media/PDFs/new_cg_recommendati
ons_diversity_aicd_tips_started.pdf (Accessed December 19, 2011).

AICD (2011) *Quotas Are Not the Answer*, http://www.companydirectors.com.au/Gene
ral/Header/Media/Media-Releases/2011/Quotas-are-not-the-answer   (Accessed
January 9, 2012).

AICD (2015) *30% by 2018: Gender Diversity Progress Report*. Sydney: Australian
Institute of Company Directors.

AICD (2016) *30% by 2018: Gender Diversity Progress Report*. Sydney: Australian
Institute of Company Directors.

AICD (2018) *30% by 2018: Gender Diversity Progress Report*. Sydney: Australian
Institute of Company Directors.

AICD (2019) *30% by 2018: Gender Diversity Progress Report*. Sydney: Australian
Institute of Company Directors.

AICD and Heidrick and Struggles, (2018) *Beyond 200: A Study of Gender Diversity in
ASX201-500 Companies*. Sydney: Australian Institute of Company Directors.

Alvesson, Mats and Due Billing, Yvonne (2002) "Beyond Body Counting: A Discussion of the Social Construction of Gender at Work," in Iiris Aaltio and Albert Mills
(eds) *Gender Identity and the Culture of Organizations*. London: Routledge, pp. 72–
91.

ASX Corporate Governance Council (2010) *Corporate Governance Principles and
Recommendations* (2nd edn) Sydney: Australian Securities Exchange.

Australian Council of Superannuation Investors (2015) *Board Composition and NED
Pay*. Melbourne: Australian Council of Superannuation Investors.

Australian Council of Superannuation Investors (2016) *Board Composition and NED
Pay*. Melbourne: Australian Council of Superannuation Investors.

Australian Securities Exchange (2018) *Corporate Overview*, http://www.asx.com.au/
about/corporate-overview.htm (Accessed January 4, 2018).

Braithwaite, John (2002) "Rules and Principles: A Theory of Legal Certainty," *Australian Journal of Legal Philosophy*, 27, pp. 47–82.

Braund, Claire (2010) *Where to in 2011?*, http://www.womenonboards.org.au/pubs/
articles/cb1012-summary.htm (Accessed December 19, 2011).

Braund, Claire and Medd, Ruth (2008) *Women on Boards Road Map for Gender
Diversity on Australian Boards*. Gosford: Women on Boards.

Broderick, Elizabeth. (2009) "Make Room at the Table for Women." The Australian
Financial Review, 29 October, https://humanrights.gov.au/about/news/opinions/
make-room-table-women-2009 (Accessed December 23, 2011)

Broderick, Elizabeth, Cassandra Goldie, and Elena Rosenman (2010) *Gender Equality
Blueprint*. Sydney: Australian Human Rights Commission.

CAMAC (2009) *Diversity on Boards of Directors*. Sydney: Corporations and Markets
Advisory Committee.

CEW (2018) *Senior Executive Census 2018*. Sydney: Chief Executive Women.

Equal Opportunity for Women in the Workplace Agency (2002) *Australian Census of Women Board of Directors*. Sydney: EOWWA.

Equal Opportunity for Women in the Workplace Agency (2008) *Australian Census of Women in Leadership*. Sydney: EOWWA.

Equal Opportunity for Women in the Workplace Agency (2012) *Australian Census of Women in Leadership*. Sydney: EOWWA.

Esping-Andersen, Gøsta (1990) *The Three Worlds of Welfare Capitalism*. Cambridge: Polity Press.

Gilding, Michael, Dean Lusher, and Helen Bird (2018) "'Network Contagion' Is Key to Getting Healthier Numbers of Women on Company Boards," *The Conversation*, July 11.

Khadem, Nassim (2016) "Australia Will Not Hit 30% Women on Boards by 2018, Time for Quotas: Elizabeth Proust," *The Sydney Morning Herald*, June 8.

Khadem, Nassim (2017) "Australia's Top Chairmen Came to Support Quotas, When Will We?," *The Sydney Morning Herald*, March 29.

Klettner, Alice, Thomas Clarke, and Martijn Boersma (2016) "Strategic and Regulatory Approaches to Increasing Women in Leadership: Multilevel Targets and Mandatory Quotas as Levers for Cultural Change," *Journal of Business Ethics*, 133, pp. 395–419.

Korn Ferry Institute (2018) *Australian Women CEOs Speak: How Female Leaders Rise and How Organisations Can Help*. Sydney: AICD.

KPMG (2013) *ASX Corporate Governance Council Principles and Recommendations on Diversity*. Sydney: KPMG.

Laverty, Martin (2017) "One Board for Mission, Another Board for Margin: Exploring Two-tiered Boards and Links to Not-for-profit Organizational Performance," PhD thesis, University of New England, Armidale.

Luoma, Patrice and Jerry Goodstein (1999) "Special Research Forum on Stakeholders, Social Responsibility and Performance," *Academy of Management Journal*, 42, pp. 553–563.

Male Champions of Change (2011) *Our Experiences in Elevating the Representation of Women in Leadership—A Letter from Business Leaders*. Canberra: Australian Human Rights and Equal Opportunity Commission.

Nagarajan, Vijaya (2011) "Regulating for Women on Corporate Boards: Polycentric Governance in Australia," *Federal Law Review*, 39, pp. 258–279.

Newsome, Lucie (2017) "The Rise and Fall of Paid Maternity Leave Policy in the Years of the Keating Government," *Australian Journal of Politics and History*, 63(20), pp. 223–237.

O'Connor, Julia. S., Anne Shola Orloff, and Sheila Shaver (1999) *States, Markets, Families: Gender, Liberalism, and Social Policy in Australia, Canada, Great Britain, and the United States*. Cambridge: Cambridge University Press.

OECD (2017) *Connecting People with Jobs: Key Issues for Raising Labour Market Participation in Australia*. Paris: OECD Publishing.

Patten, Sally (2019) "'Fantastic': ASX200 Boards Close on 30pc Women," *Australian Financial Review*, January 29.

Ross-Smith, Anne and Jane Bridge (2008) "'Glacial at Best': Women's Progress on Corporate Boards in Australia," in Susan Vinnicombe, Val Singh, Ronald J. Burke, Diana Bilimoria, and Morton Huse (eds.) *Women on Corporate Boards of Directors*. Cheltenham: Edward Elgar, pp. 67–78.

Sawer, Marian (1996) *Femocrats and Ecorats: Women's Policy Machinery in Australia, Canada and New Zealand, Occasional Paper 6*. Paris: OECD.

Schmidt, Lucinda and Narelle Hooper (2011) "The Network Effect," *AFR Boss*, January 4, 28–32.

Schneider, Anne and Helen Ingram (1990) "Behavioral Assumptions of Policy Tools," *The Journal of Politics*, 52, pp. 510–529.

Sheridan, Alison (1995) "Affirmative Action in Australia–Employment Statistics Can't Tell the Whole Story," *Women in Management Review*, 10, pp. 26–34.

Sheridan, Alison, Linley Lord, and Anne Ross-Smith (2021) "Disrupting board appointments: Australia's governance guidelines and gender capital," *Equality, Diversity and Inclusion: An International Journal*, 40, pp. 615-630.

Sheridan, Alison, Anne Ross-Smith, and Linley Lord (2014) "Institutional Influences on Women's Representation on Corporate Boards: An Australian Case Study," *Equality, Diversity and Inclusion: An International Journal*, 33, pp. 140–159.

Sheridan, Alison, Anne Ross-Smith and Linley Lord (2015) "Women on Boards in Australia: Achieving Real Change or More of the Same?," in Broadbridge Adelina and Sandra, L. Fielden (eds.) *Handbook of Gendered Careers in Management: Getting in, Getting on, Getting out*. Edward Elgar: Cheltenham, UK, pp. 322–340.

Smith, Sherene (2018) "Company Boards Are Stacked with Friends of Friends so How Can We Expect Change?," *The Conversation*, May 4.

The Australian (2011) "PM Against Quotas for Women on Boards," *The Australian*, March 9.

UWA Business School (2010) "To Quota or Not to Quota: Women in Leadership," *UWA News*, http://www.news.uwa.edu.au/201007092652/quota-or-not-quota-women-leadership (Accessed December 19, 2011).

Van Egmond, Marcel, Janine Baxter, Sandra Buchler, and Mark Western (2010) "A Stalled Revolution? Gender Role Attitudes in Australia, 1986–2005," *Journal of Population Research*, 27, pp. 147–168.

Watson, Katie (2014) "Gender Diversity on Corporate Boards," *Journal of the Australasian Law Teachers Association*, 2, pp. 1–8.

Workplace Gender Equality Agency (2018) *The National Gender Pay Gap*, https://www.wgea.gov.au/topics/gender-pay-gap/national-gender-pay-gap (Accessed May 15, 2019).

Workplace Gender Equality Agency (2020) *Australia's Gender Pay Gap Statistics*, https://www.wgea.gov.au/data/fact-sheets/australias-gender-pay-gap-statistics (Accessed August 3, 2020).

4

Self-regulation Comes at a Cost: Closing off Authoritative Policy for Gender Equality on Corporate Boards in the UK

Susan Milner

Introduction

This chapter analyzes the British case of "limited government pressure" on companies to increase gender diversity on corporate boards (Burk and Hartmann, 2017, p. 136) based on government-backed, voluntary target-setting and monitoring led by business (Goyal et al, 2018). The chapter tracks the origins, development, and implementation of the voluntary review process established in 2011. The process is run by two high-level reviews, known by the name of their respective chairs: the first review chaired by Lord Davies ran from 2011 to 2015 and was followed by the Hampton-Alexander Review (chaired by Sir Phillip Hampton and also by Dame Helen Alexander until her death in 2017) from 2016 to 2020. The review process consists of target-setting and annual monitoring of progress through a high-level committee, steering group, and wider network of business leaders, on a purely voluntary basis, and applicable only to the largest companies (principally FTSE 100 and to a lesser extent, although increasingly, FTSE 250). The review is supported by data gathering, through individual company reports sent voluntarily to the committee, and annual monitoring of company reports by a team of academics at Cranfield University.

Under this process, action on vertical segregation follows the dominant policy path in the UK where a problem is identified, but the state prefers a voluntary business-led solution, relying on soft instruments which deploy data collection and publication, capacity-building, and voluntary codes. Moreover, as will be argued below, the outputs and implementation method themselves embed the voluntary approach and have the effect of closing off more thorough-going transformation. While the question of women on corporate boards regularly receives public attention through the review process and its discussion in mainstream media, the agenda is located within business and related (academic and practitioner) elites

Susan Milner, *Self-regulation Comes at a Cost*. In: *Gender Equality and Policy Implementation in the Corporate World*. Edited by Isabelle Engeli and Amy G. Mazur, Oxford University Press.
© Oxford University Press (2022). DOI: 10.1093/oso/9780198865216.003.0004

and has not significantly broken into mainstream political debate. Business elites own the process and set the parameters for evaluation, and alternative proposals for regulation are marginalized and delegitimized.

Through the review process, change has taken place: the initial target set in 2011 of 25% of the Financial Times Stock Exchange (FTSE) 100 board members to be women was met by 2015, and in 2020, it was announced that not just the FTSE 100 but FTSE 350 (100+250) companies had overall reached the target set in 2016 of 33% female board members. The number of all-male boards had fallen from 152 in 2011 to just one (Aston Martin) in September 2020. The timing of change in descriptive representation (larger numbers of women on corporate boards) means that it is likely to have been caused by the setting of targets, but change has been circumscribed, and it has not (yet) had any impact on wider substantive representation.

Feminization remains limited to less challenging actions (greater numbers of women in non-executive board positions) and "pioneer" companies, while the pace of change is slow outside these large firms. The number of women in the top decision-making positions remains tiny, most sectors having no female CEO. Only 6% of CEOs are female, none of them women of color (Kaur, 2020). Only 3% of top positions in FTSE 100 organizations (CEO, finance director, executive board chair) are occupied by people of color, and these are twice as likely to be men as women (Green Park, 2020). This chapter shows, therefore, the strengths and weaknesses of limited pressure through intensive self-regulation (which includes high-profile exhortation, annual monitoring, and reputational pressure). The British case constitutes "gender accommodation," as cultural change has taken place through limited modernization of business elites, but the review process has not fundamentally challenged gendered assumptions.

Gender Equality in the Corporate World: The Long Struggle for Equality in a Liberal Market Economy

The imbalance in representation in economic decision-making, outlined briefly above and discussed further below, is also found in earnings. The gender pay gap for low earners working full-time has narrowed since 1997 when the series began, due at least in part to improvements in minimum wage provision. However, for high earners, it remained stable for much of this period and has risen in recent years, particularly in the private sector (ONS, 2019). The Trades Union Congress's (TUC) analysis of 2015 Office for National Statistics (ONS) data found that within the top 10% of earnings the gender pay gap rose with each percentile, reaching 45.9% for the top 5% of earners and 54.9% for the top 2% (TUC, 2015).

Overall, the unadjusted gender pay gap remains high by European standards, at 19.9% in 2020, compared to 14.8% on average for the European Union's twenty-seven member states (Eurostat, 2020a). As noted above, the gender pay gap is attributable in part to strong vertical segregation. It also reflects the penalties attached to low-pay traps in the labor market for women, which are particularly associated with part-time work (Grimshaw and Rubery, 2007). Not only do a high proportion of women work part-time (39.4%, compared to an EU average of 31.3%) (Eurostat, 2020b), but the gender pay gap for part-time workers is exceptionally high by European standards, especially for maternity returners, as they are concentrated in high feminized low-pay occupations (caring and low-grade administrative work) (Harkness et al, 2019).

The part-time penalty for mothers is likely to remain throughout their professional life and to result in pension inequalities (Olsen et al, 2018). This structural characteristic of the British labor market has led it to be classed as a "modified breadwinner regime" or a "one-and-a-half breadwinner regime," typical of liberal market economies, which rely heavily on female part-time work to raise employment levels, increase labor market flexibility, and avoid public expenditure on childcare (Ciccia and Bleijenbergh, 2014). It is historically embedded in cultural norms about gender and parenting (McCarthy, 2020).

Like other Anglo-American liberal market economies, the UK has a distinctive model of corporate governance that previously has been seen to be able to resist moves within the EU to promote a common approach (Aguilera and Jackson, 2010; Horn, 2012). The predominant policy preference is for "light touch" regulation, voluntary codes of conduct, and self-reporting. In the British case, corporate governance (starting with the Cadbury code in 1992) is based on comply-or-explain expectations that private actors will respond to reputational pressures, which gives companies a large degree of latitude in explaining away divergence from expected behaviors (Seidl et al, 2013). The system lacks an overarching regulatory body (Keay, 2013) and has significant enforcement and monitoring weaknesses (Arcot et al, 2010; Shrives and Brennan, 2017). As discussed further below, the corporate governance code has been revised several times in order to include equality and diversity objectives in the range of principles on which publicly listed companies should report annually, and there is evidence that increasing numbers of annual reports cover such areas, but no action is taken in respect of companies that fail to provide equality and diversity information, and there is evidence of the variable quality of reporting.

Table 4.1 presents the trends in gender equality on corporate boards in the UK in comparison to European-wide figures. In line with the European trend, it shows increased female board membership after 2011, suggesting an impact on the domestic practice of debates sparked by EU-level proposals to introduce quotas, and further increases in 2019. This chapter discusses the pace of change in female board membership in relation to the chosen mode of implementation, whereby monitoring has been intensified in response to perceived slowness of progress, with limited results.

Table 4.1 Percentage Share of Women on Boards in the Largest Listed Companies in the UK, 2004–2020[a]

	EU-28 Board members	UK				
		Board members	President	CEO	Executives	Non-executives
2004	9	13.2	0	—	—	—
2005	9.8	12.7	0	—	—	—
2006	9.7	12.1	0	—	—	—
2007	10.4	11.4	1.8	—	—	—
2008	10.8	12.4	0	—	—	—
2009	11	12.3	0	—	—	—
2010	11.9	13.3	0	—	—	—
2011	13.7	16.3	0	—	—	—
2012	15.8	18.8	0	3.8	6.4	11.1
2013	17.8	21	0	3.8	2.2	12.9
2014	20.2	24.2	2	3.7	2	16.6
2015	22.7	27.8	2	7.7	4	18.1
2016	23.9	27	2	11.5	6	16.4
2017	25.3	27.2	0	7.1	4	17.9
2018	26.7	29.9	4.1	7.7	6.1	18.7
2019	28.8	32.6	4	3.8	4.1	20.7
2020	29.2	34.6	8	7.7	4.1	22.5

Source: EIGE Database. [a] Data for October each year, except for 2020 [April].

Political Attention on Corporate Gender Equality: Establishing the Business Case for Women on Boards

From the beginning of the 1980s, businesses took the lead in identifying the problem of female underrepresentation in economic decision-making. Policy-making on women in the corporate world was initially driven by a coalition of business leaders, including the Confederation of British Industry (CBI), under Conservative governments. The Conservative leader Margaret Thatcher herself was famously scornful of initiatives to improve women's representation, stating in several interviews that quotas undermined principles of merit (see Murray, 2013). However, business leaders persisted, under the influence of North American initiatives led by the international consultants Deloitte and McKinsey.

In 1988, a commission chaired by Lady Howe, who headed Business in the Community's initiative on Women's Economic Development, and including CEOs of seventeen large public and private organizations as well as the CBI's director John Banham, was established by the Hansard Society (an independent institute established to provide information on parliament) in order to examine women's underrepresentation in public life. Regarding economic decision-making, the commission made a series of recommendations: first, that businesses should not only put in place measures to support women at work and advance their career development but that they should also carry out audits and measure their progress; second, that employer bodies such as the CBI should promote good practice by private sector firms; and third, that companies should be required to report on their equal opportunities practice in their annual financial reporting (Hansard Society, 1990).

The 1990 commission recommendations were followed by a series of academic reports measuring the slow pace of change in women's representation in political and economic decision-making. In 1995, Professor Susan McRae's report for the Hansard Society showed that the percentage of women executive directors in 120 of the Times Top 200 companies had increased from 0.5% in 1989 to just 1% in 1996, and the percentage of women in non-executive positions from 3.9% in 1989 to 10.4% in 1995 (McRae, 1995). Business in the Community, a charity that promotes "responsible business" through its network of member companies, responded to the Hansard Society Commission's report by setting up Opportunity 2000, with the support of Conservative Prime Minister John Major. Sixty-one organizations signed up to the initiative, pledging to implement measures to support female employees and to share practice, and this number had almost doubled within twelve months. The Opportunity 2000 teams worked with signatory employers to put in place equality projects. The initiative was born of frustration with the lack of progress attributed to low awareness and commitment among employers (Hammond, 1992). Although Opportunity 2000 raised awareness of women's underrepresentation in economic decision-making, it resulted in mostly minimalist actions, even in the large organizations where the potential for change seemed greatest (see Richards, 2001). It did not challenge the prevailing rejection of forceful initiatives in favor of "enabling" market solutions.

The Labour manifesto in 1997 did not mention underrepresentation of women in economic life. However, public discussion of women's underrepresentation on corporate boards continued during the period of Labour government, under the influence of two sets of concerns, one about corporate governance and its impact on economic performance, the other about the gender pay gap, in the context of rising female labor market participation. A series of business scandals led the government to review the regulation of corporate governance. Sir Derek Higgs, a businessman then working for Price Waterhouse Cooper, was commissioned by the Labour government to review the effectiveness of the corporate governance code. The Higgs report drew attention to the predominance on British boards of "white males nearing retirement age with previous experience of PLC director experience" (Higgs, 2003, p. 42). Its main outcome was the establishment of a working group of business leaders to look at ways of encouraging company managers to deploy active recruitment strategies in order to attract and appoint suitable female candidates from non-commercial backgrounds and the public sector.

According to Lord Davies of Abersoch, a former banker who at that time headed the Department of Trade and Industry (DTI), the Labour government was influenced by business guru Michael Porter, who was invited to visit the UK to advise policy-makers on competitiveness. In Davies' account, Porter described the UK as "a joke" and advised the DTI to focus on three areas: infrastructure, skills training, and equality and diversity in the workplace to harness talents (Davies, 2015). The business case for action to encourage greater diversity on boards was underpinned by research by academics and consultants, which not only set out the business case (Catalyst, 2008; McKinsey, 2007) but also drew attention to the UK's comparative weakness. An academic study of FTSE 100 boards by researchers at Cranfield University's business school argued, based on evidence from North America, that greater diversity on boards would result in better corporate governance and better economic performance (Singh et al, 2001). It showed the UK lagging behind the USA, with only 6.4% of female directors in 2001, and 39% of top UK companies having no women on their board. The Cranfield research highlighted the need for regular monitoring using the same dataset, such as those produced in the USA by multinational consultants like Catalyst, which had been tracking the number of female-held seats on US Fortune 500 companies since 1996 (Singh and Vinnicombe, 2004).

Labour's 2001 manifesto showed concern about the gender pay gap but was vague in its proposals: "We will work with employers and employees to develop effective proposals, building on good practice and the sound business case, in both the private and public sectors." During the Labour years, three reviews into the gender pay gap were conducted, reflecting a lack of consensus about how to tackle it (see Grimshaw and Rubery, 2007). These reviews focused on the concentration of women in low-paid occupations and part-time work, although they also noted in passing the need to diversify business leadership.

The second major review, conducted by former employment lawyer Denise Kingsmill (then deputy chair of the Monopolies and Mergers Commission) who set out to develop "practical proposals and solutions that work with the grain of the market" (Kingsmill, 2002, p. 5), recommended the inclusion of gender equality objectives in annual business reporting. The third review, by the Women and Work Commission (WWC), chaired by former trade union leader Baroness Margaret Prosser, and including a range of business leaders, trade unionists and experts, made no recommendations on the gender diversity of boards but included the observation by its chair that "There are still 22 companies in the FTSE 100 that have all-male boards" (WWC, 2009, p. 5). Harriet Harman MP, as a backbencher, set out to measure the number of women on corporate boards, employing a parliamentary researcher to trawl through the company reports for FTSE 100 companies. In 2000 they found that half the FTSE 1000 boards were men-only (Harman, 2017, p. 222). She was joined in 2001 by Susan Vinnicombe at Cranfield School of Management, whose team took over responsibility for compiling the data. When Harman became Women and Equalities Minister in 2007 (for the second time) the new Government Equalities Office took over responsibility for funding the annual FTSE 100 reports prepared by the Cranfield team and set itself the task of publicizing the findings (Government Equalities Office, 2009, p. 25). In 2009, Harman advocated using government contracts to oblige companies to meet targets for female executive representation, but this did not find its way into the Equality Act 2010.

Despite the mobilization of business actors and networks, and the work of the Equal Opportunities Commission, which worked with businesses to encourage them to carry out gender pay audits (Miller and Neathey, 2004), and despite improved data on the presence of women on boards, the pace of change remained glacial. Repeatedly, studies showed that male CEOs cited a lack of experienced female candidates as a reason for not appointing women to board positions. Noting that even among its members there had been little change since 1990—although their boards had greater gender balance than the national average—Opportunity 2000 (renamed Opportunity Now) recommended that there should be gender balance in all public appointments by 2020 and asked its members to commit to carrying out full gender pay audits and publishing the results, ensuring gender parity in appointments bodies dealing with top positions, and putting in place pipeline measures to support women's career advancement (Business in the Community, 2011). The idea of setting ambitious voluntary targets, which could be publicly monitored in order to increase reputational pressure, became widely floated in business circles.

Under the (Conservative-led) Coalition government, a review process was set up in September 2010, chaired by Lord Davies. Although neither Conservatives nor Liberal Democrats had mentioned women's representation on boards, the Coalition agreement drawn up in 2010 as a program for government stated that "We will look to promote gender equality on the boards of listed companies," without specifying how this would be done.[1] The Davies report set out the situation as one of stark gender inequality at the top, with the boards of FTSE 100 companies composed of 87.5% men and 12.5% women in 2010 (7.8% for FTSE 250). Although this represented an increase from 9.4% in 2004, progress appeared to have plateaued: "At the current rate of change it will take over 70 years to achieve gender-balanced boardrooms in the UK" (Davies, 2011, p.1). The business case for gender diversity in the boardroom was defined under four headings: improving business performance by having a broader set of perspectives in decision-making and reducing risk; accessing the widest possible talent pool; being more responsive

---

[1] The *Guardian*, publishing a comprehensive review of Coalition agreement pledges in September 2010, noted that it had not featured in either party's manifesto promises and observed a wait and see approach making any initiative dependent on wider moves to review financial reporting requirements in 2011: see https://www.theguardian.com/news/datablog/2010/sep/17/coalition-agreement-programme-for-government.

to the market, that is, the gender composition of the client base; and achieving better corporate governance, with better planning and oversight (Ibid, pp. 8–10). The Davies report, based on the conviction that voluntary action achieves change by mobilizing business leaders, became the foundation for policy.

Adopting the Self-regulatory Approach: Justifying the Preference for Voluntary Action over Quotas

Although the Davies report emphasized the need for urgent and far-reaching change, it did not favour mandatory regulation. It recommended oversight of self-regulation through the existing corporate governance code (in other words, with no additional reporting requirements, but monitoring by the Financial Reporting Council and pressure from shareholders and investors),

> to require listed companies to establish a policy concerning boardroom diversity, including measurable objectives for implementing the policy, and disclose annually a summary of the policy and the progress made in achieving the objectives.
>
> (Davies, 2011, p. 4)

In line with the corporate governance code, it recommended attention to nominations committees and consultation with shareholders and other stakeholders. It also suggested requirements on gender composition reporting, although it did not specify the means to do so.

This approach was adopted despite recognition that where statutory regulation had been introduced significant change had taken place, as in Norway, and to a lesser extent in France and Australia (Davies, 2011, p. 14). A decisive reason not to adopt statutory regulation was given as weak support for it in the consultation which the Davies Review had conducted: out of the 2,654 responses received, only 11% had advocated the introduction of quotas. The voluntary approach was also preferred because of the business need for flexibility. The approach recommended in the Davies report was described as "a more focused business-led approach" (Ibid, p. 18) and as a third way between coercion (Norway) and liberal voluntaristic positions, defined as "collaborative approaches, which rely upon cooperative measures across a range of public and private sector stakeholder groups" (Ibid, p. 24).

The voluntary approach, preferred by all three main political parties at the time, was strongly promoted by the main business organizations. The president of the CBI, Helen Alexander, expressed the prevailing view in a newspaper interview in 2011 when she argued that "Quotas would not have tackled the real issue of how we bring about a cultural change. It should be for companies, not government, to set an appropriate target" (Wood, 2011). Proposals in 2011–2012 by the European Commission to introduce legislation on quotas appear to have hardened opposition to them within the British political establishment: the House of Lords Select Committee on the European Union looked at the question in 2012, noting the opposition of the government and also all the business leaders who contributed to their inquiry, and concluding:

> The European Commission has stressed that "sufficient time has already been given to the industry to make credible commitments to change the current situation." We acknowledge that challenges remain, but the idea that time has run out, whether in the EU as a whole or particularly in the United Kingdom, is not convincing. We urge the Commission to refrain from proposing legislation that would seek to introduce a quota mechanism.
>
> (House of Lords, 2012)

Opposing this view were a range of feminist scholars and labor lawyers who pointed to the gains made by countries that introduced mandatory quotas (Villiers, 2011) but whose views were dismissed by the government and the House of Lords. A particularly influential report was written by Rowena Lewis and Katherine Rake for the Fawcett Society, the UK's leading gender equality campaign group named after the suffragist Millicent Fawcett. This report outlined a number of possible voluntary measures including better databases on available recruitment opportunities, inspired by the New Zealand case, and while it fought shy of recommending mandatory quotas outright, it nevertheless asked whether the intractable nature of the problem called for more vigorous measures than those envisaged by the government (Lewis and Rake, 2008). The 2011 *Sex and Power* report produced by the Equalities and Human Rights Commission emphasized the need for swift, vigorous action given the lack of progress to date. Commenting on the report, the Fawcett Society's director Anna Bird said it showed "that we can't afford to wait but need to introduce some form of positive action" (Hill, 2011).

However, given the stated preferences of the Coalition government, and the absence of commitments to regulate in the Coalition agreement, it was not surprising that the business-led voluntary approach put forward by Lord Davies prevailed. Welcoming the Davies report recommendations, (Liberal Democrat) business secretary Vince Cable commented that:

> The report is clear that a business-led approach is the best way to increase the number of women on company boards, and we will therefore engage with business in considering his recommendations. Likewise we encourage regulators, investors and executive search firms to take forward those recommendations that fall to them.
>
> (BIS, 2011)

Once this choice was made, it set up a path dependency whereby quotas had been excluded as an inappropriate mechanism, and further actions followed the initial choice of voluntary action.

The initial threat of mandatory quotas should, however, not be overlooked. Lord Davies also later acknowledged the importance of the shadow of hierarchy as a lever for change among the more reluctant business leaders: "The threat of quotas did cause a bit of stomach acid for one or two chairmen. And that was good. Very useful. I think the threat of quotas should be used a lot more" (Davies, 2015).

Outputs: An Intensive Form of Self-regulation

Table 4.2 summarizes the measures that have been developed since the first 2011 review, all of which take an intensive self-regulatory approach.

Table 4.2 Policy Measures on Gender Equality on Corporate Boards in the UK

SELF-REGULATION

Voluntary targets

Davies Review (2011–2015)	**Hampton-Alexander Review (2016–2020)**
* **Voluntary targets** for FTSE 100 companies: 25% of board members to be women by end 2015.	* **Voluntary targets** for FTSE 100 companies: 33% of board members to be women by end 2020.
* **Annual review** published on Davies Review website, based on a combination of (a) information provided in writing by CEOs to Davies Review and (b) research by Cranfield School of Management, using company annual reports.	* **Annual review** published on Davies Review website, based on a combination of (a) information provided in writing by CEOs to Davies Review and (b) research by Cranfield School of Management, using company annual reports.

Reporting and monitoring

UK Corporate Governance Code 2016	**UK Corporate Governance Code 2018**
* **Listed companies**	* **Listed companies**
* Board recruitment should "**consider diversity, including gender**	* Recruitment processes must be transparent and should "**promote diversity of gender, ethnic and social backgrounds**"; board composition should be reviewed annually (FTSE 100) or every three years (FTSE 250)"
* **Comply-or-explain**	
* **Annual report** should include work of nominations committee	* **Comply-or-explain**
* **Monitoring** by FRC	* **Annual report** should include an account of nominations process and wider policy on diversity and inclusion
	* **Monitoring** by FRC

The output decided in 2011 was intermediate in its coverage, consisting of a voluntary target of 25% of women board directors (with no separate targets for executive and non-executive) among FTSE 100 companies, that is, the very largest publicly listed companies, by 2015. As well as the 25% target for FTSE 100 companies, the Department for Business, Innovation and Skills accepted the Davies report recommendation that these and the 250 next biggest businesses (the FTSE 250) should set their own "challenging" targets, of at least 25%, and the Davies commission would review progress for both sets of companies.

Lord Davies called upon chief executives voluntarily to announce their targets and to publish annual progress reports, not just on the gender composition of boards but of the wider workforce. He wrote to all CEOs of the largest firms asking them to report on their targets for 2013 and 2015 concerning the number of women on their boards. The voluntary approach was supported by the government: in October 2011, the Conservative prime minister himself wrote to all the FTSE 100 companies that had not responded earlier to Lord Davies. In that letter, David Cameron expressly ruled out quotas or other forms of mandatory regulation, "as coercion can undermine the real talent that is out there," but called upon CEOs personally to commit to diversifying their leadership (Cameron, 2011).

There was no legal requirement for companies to take any reporting action or to sign up to any code of conduct, although companies were required to publish information on boards in their annual reports under the British Code of Corporate Conduct according to the comply-or-explain approach, with oversight by the Financial Reporting Council. The corporate governance code was revised in 2010 to include a requirement for listed companies to consider gender diversity on boards. It has been amended since 2010 in order to encourage reporting on workforce diversity (Sealy, 2018; see Table 4.2). The 2016 code stipulated that annual reports should include a section detailing the process for board appointments, and the 2018 code specified that it should demonstrate how this process met requirements for a formal, rigorous, and transparent procedure, subject to annual review (Parker Review, 2020, p. 38).

The incorporation of reporting on gender and diversity targets into the Corporate Governance Code gives self-regulation more teeth in the sense that there is an expectation that all publicly listed companies will comply, professional bodies are responsible for compliance by their members, and public monitoring by the Financial Reporting Council (FRC) takes place. This approach is described by the FRC as market-led voluntary compliance.

> We believe that market participants and their professional advisers, encouraged by the investor community, have the primary responsibility for achieving high standards of governance and reporting. Our approach is based as far as possible on facilitation rather than dictation and on principles rather than rules.
>
> (FRC, 2014, p. 5)

The review process itself, and the informational resources it provided, also formed part of the output. The steering group, which met every six months to review progress, was chaired by Lord Davies, and also included Dominic Casserley (CEO of Willis Group, and formerly of McKinsey), Denise Wilson OBE (chief executive of the Davies Review, and formerly an executive in financial services, then oil and gas), Sir John Parker GBE (chair of Anglo American and Pennon Group), Amanda Mackenzie OBE (seconded from Aviva Group Executive), and Professor Susan Vinnicombe CBE of Cranfield University. Researchers from Cranfield University, with sponsorship by multinational consultancies (initially by KPMG, then by EY), analyzed the data reporting for the review.

The combination of voluntary targets and review by a high-level commission is best described as light voluntary on the coerciveness continuum. The voluntary target has had strong symbolic value as a focal point for business campaigns. The biggest incentive for businesses to comply is reputational since the Davies commission reported annually to parliament, and its reports received widespread coverage particularly in the business press but also in mainstream media. They did not just publish aggregate figures but gave a detailed ranking of individual companies by name, using a "traffic light system" to classify businesses not just by absolute figures but also by progress made. Outside the annual ranking, this incentive effect was most obviously seen in the later reviews, which increased the naming and shaming pressure: individual companies were associated with specific aspects of good practice as defined by the Davies Review. Conversely, those with no or female representation were named as giving cause for concern.

Cranfield University research in 2011 showed that businesses responded quickly to the call from the Davies report to take greater account of equality and diversity in their annual reporting, and already had started to change practices of recruitment to boards, particularly non-executive boards before the review was formally launched. In the eight months following Lord Davies' report, the percentage of female FTSE 100 board members had risen from 13% to 22.5%, and the number of all-male boards had dropped from 21 to 14 (Sealy et al, 2011, p. 6). The first monitoring report showed that considerable progress needed to be made, however, and referred to a range of foot-dragging responses to the Davies initiative from employers, including complacency (we appoint on merit) and wait and see comments, as well as outright opposition to target-setting from a range of companies (Sealy et al, 2011, pp. 26–28).

By 2013, Davies expressed satisfaction with the progress to date. In an interview in the *Financial Times* (October 17, 2013) he said that "we need to keep up the momentum." In his final report in 2015, he referred to a "near revolution" and "profound cultural change," which had taken place in British companies (BIS, 2015, p. 4). The triumphalist 2015 five-year report claimed that the UK was a world leader, having achieved significant change in a short period and now having reached sixth place in international rankings, just behind countries that had introduced compulsory quotas (Ibid, p. 6). A FTSE chairman was quoted as claiming that businesses were effecting change as a way of rejecting the perceived European approach based on statutory regulation: "We're standing alone against the rest of Europe and saying that this is a better way of doing it" (Ibid, p. 11). Business respondents highlighted the motivation of benchmarking and peer pressure in effecting change, while the pressure on executive search (recruitment) agencies was also seen as having been an important lever.

The 2015 report argued explicitly that the motor for change was the business case and not the social justice argument ("business case versus equalities issues": Ibid, p. 8). In particular, the business case was narrowed to a focus on increasing the talent pool. Although the target had been exceeded, with companies doubling their female boardroom representation in four years to 26.1%, the report argued that more could be done, using the same method, to increase it further and extend the process to get more women into executive as well as non-executive directorships. It recommended an increased target of 33% by the end of the following five years to 2020. The Conservative manifesto in 2015 stated that the 2011 target had been reached. However, following the election, Conservative Equalities Minister Nicky Morgan stated that "A major milestone has been achieved but we are only halfway there" (DfE, 2015). Although the proportion of female non-executive directors had doubled, only 9.6% of executive directors in FTSE 100 companies were women and only 5.2% in FTSE 250 companies. In order to take the process forward, work toward a new target of 33% women in boardroom positions, and support work by the Institute of Directors on women in executive management, she stated that a new review would be established to focus on women in executive positions.

A new commission was therefore set up in February 2016, chaired by Sir Phillip Hampton, chair of GlaxoSmithKline, and Dame Helen Alexander (who died in 2017), former director of the CBI and chair of UBM plc, as deputy chair, and sponsored by KPMG. A new target of 33% by 2020 was set, in line with the recommendations of the outgoing Davies panel and steering group. The initial report of the Hampton-Alexander Review that published in November 2016 sounded a cautious note, acknowledging a certain amount of "nervousness" among business organizations (Simon Collins, Melanie Richards, KPMG, quoted in Hampton Alexander Review, 2016, p. 6) and recognizing that the new target would be "stretching for many, and not without challenges ahead" (Phillip Hampton and Helen Alexander in Hampton-Alexander Review, 2016, p. 5). The early output of the Hampton-Alexander Review also discussed possible ways of making the process more extensive (considering wider gender workforce composition and talent pipelines) and intensive (finding ways of working with business organizations to put in place support programs such as mentoring and training). These discussions about the method reflected growing criticism from some quarters of the self-regulation process and the limited progress it had achieved, as discussed further below.

The Davies Review process, including data analysis by the same Cranfield School of Management researchers, was also transferred to a separate initiative on race and ethnicity, chaired by Sir John Parker who sat on the Davies steering group. In his foreword to the group's initial report, Parker stated that the lessons of the Davies group could be applied to promote racial and ethnic diversity.

> Based on my experiences as a member of Lord Davies' review of "Women on Boards," I am confident that by setting out practical issues and coming up with aspirational and realistic objectives and timescales, progressive business leaders will respond and act.
>
> (Parker, 2017, p. 5)

Noting that, in total, executives of color represented only 8% of board members (compared to 14% of the total population), mostly in multinationals headquartered outside the UK, and that 44% of these executives were women (37 out of 85), the Parker Review set the voluntary target of one in ten board members to be black or from an ethnic minority background by 2021. The Parker Review followed an independent inquiry chaired by Baroness McGregor-Smith CBE (former CEO of utilities company Mitie Group, who was made a life peer in 2015 and invited to join the Department for Education as a non-executive board member). Her review was scathing in its assessment of businesses' willingness to tackle race-based disadvantage in the workplace; a quarter of organizations had failed to answer her call for information, and half of those who responded said they were unable to provide data (McGregor-Smith Review, 2017, p. 3). "The time for talking is over. It is time to act," the report argued (McGregor-Smith Review, 2017, p. 7). The report ruled out quotas but insisted on the need for aspirational targets within a five-year timetable and set out a business rationale for intensive networks of employee support led by top management. The voluntary approach taken by the McGregor-Smith and Parker reviews has had a very limited impact. 54% of FTSE 100 corporate boards in 2017 did not have a single person of color (Green Park, 2017). By 2020, when the Parker Review published its first update, this figure had fallen to 37%, but for FTSE 350 companies it stood at 59% (Parker Review, 2020). The report also noted that a relatively high non-response rate meant the true figure could be as high as 70% and made it difficult to measure progress over time. In the 2020 report, faced with the slow and uncertain pace of change, attention shifted from the aspirational target of 10% board membership to another target of zero boards with no member from a BAME background.

Encouraging Business Responsiveness in Practice: Academic Research, Recruitment Specialists, and Investor Mobilization

A key feature of the Davies Review process was the range of actors it sought to mobilize to achieve the voluntary targets, which the Hampton-Alexander Review (2019, p. 42) describes as forming the wider landscape of equality and diversity.

The Davies Review created an exceptionally close relationship between policy-makers (specifically, ministers in the business department), business practitioners and leaders, and academics. The Hampton-Alexander Review worked in partner-ship with a number of large firms that sit on its steering group, notably McKinsey. The Parker Review emulated this model and was sponsored by Ernst & Young.

Academics at Cranfield University not only provided much of the monitor-ing research but participated directly in the review panels. Reflecting on this relationship, the researchers involved noted that the lack of a gender theoretical perspective facilitated contacts in the business world; research had to be "factual" and "issue-driven," not normative (Sealy et al, 2017, p. 67). As their relationships with business leaders became more established, researchers could adopt a more normative tone, highlighting the need for thorough-going organizational change in order to achieve headline targets. However, overt use of social justice frames would not have been possible in the context of the steering group (Ibid, p. 70). The Cranfield reports explicitly endorsed the voluntary approach.

Executive search firms or headhunters, especially the six largest firms, were de-scribed as prominent change agents in Lord Davies' press conference launching the 2011 report, and by academics also involved in the review as that of "acciden-tal activists" and "marginal" agents of change (Sealy et al, 2017). Nineteen leading recruitment firms developed and signed a voluntary code of conduct in July 2011 to support the recommendations of the Davies report, with the aim of producing gender-balanced shortlists for top posts, starting with a target of 30% women on longlists. As part of the Davies Review, diversity consultant Charlotte Sweeney was appointed to evaluate the code in 2013, by which time sixty-eight search firms had signed. She found, among some large companies, a willingness to go further and set voluntary targets of gender-equal longlists and women-only shortlists. However, she also found that such companies were in a minority and that most executive search firms did not display awareness of the code. Accordingly, she recommended more visibility for the code, including in FRC guidelines, and on the website of all executive search firms, as well as the publication by the Davies Review of a database of women with the skills to be appointed to top positions in FTSE 350 firms (Sweeney, 2014). The code was revised in 2014 and updated in 2017 un-der the Hampton-Alexander Review, taking up Sweeney's recommendations, and signed by thirty-nine firms. It was further strengthened in 2018 to include recom-mendations from the Parker Review, and a new clause requiring that firms identify at least two women their client should meet for every chair and non-executive director post.

The role of shareholder and investor mobilization has been less forceful than the 2011 Davies report anticipated, as an annual series of reports by Grant Thornton on compliance with the UK corporate governance code showed. The 2016 report suggested that improved formal compliance with reporting under the governance code has resulted in weaker substantive compliance. It noted that because increasing numbers of female non-executive directors have been appointed, greater numbers of companies report on gender diversity and related issues in their annual statements; however, reporting has become more general and generic: "Companies are therefore reverting to saying less, rather than expanding on what they are doing to nurture and develop talent, even if it may take longer" (Grant Thornton, 2016, p. 36). With the shift toward a broader set of reporting areas, to include other areas of diversity including race and ethnicity, and workforce risk assessment, the tendency toward underreporting and limited compliance has grown (CIPD, 2018). A 2018 survey for the FRC found that while nearly all FTSE 100 companies (and 85%) provide information on at least one area of diversity in their reports (most often gender), only around a third referred to ethnicity as well as gender (Sealy, 2018).

Investor engagement also emerged more slowly than anticipated. In 2019, however, the Investment Association, which represents asset managers, collaborated with the Hampton-Alexander Review by jointly writing to sixty-nine listed companies with no female board representation or only one female board member, asking them to set out how they would increase board diversity. Leading companies such as Legal & General Investment Management announced that they would vote against companies that had not acted to improve gender diversity on their board. This action, which followed similar moves in the USA, resulted in a reduction in the number of "one and done" boards from sixty-six to twenty-eight, as over half of the companies contacted took action to appoint at least one woman to their board (Hampton-Alexander Review, 2019, p. 42).

The Davies/Hampton-Alexander Review process is supported by a dense network of business organizations including the CBI, the Institute of Directors, and Business in the Community. It has also drawn on the activism of organizations and networks of female business leaders, in particular the 30% Club, and the expertise of Women on Boards and other associations set up to provide training, toolkits, and programs for business. The 30% Club, founded by Dame Helena Morrissey (formerly a bond trader and then investment executive at Newton before becoming asset manager at Legal & General), was formed specifically in 2010 to promote business action to increase women's representation at board level. Its vision as outlined on its web page defines the business case based on the impact of executive performance on business outcomes:

> The 30% Club believes that gender balance on boards not only encourages better leadership and governance, but diversity further contributes to better all-round board performance, and ultimately increased corporate performance for both companies and their shareholders.
>
> (30% Club, 2017)

It explicitly rejects the idea of formal quotas and aims to reach its target of 30% women at the executive level through engagement with business networks. The method promoted by the 30% Club is to draw together CEOs willing to commit to a 30% target, initially from a group of directors directly contacted by Morrissey, and to extend the network through high-profile events and awards.

In the male-dominated finance sector, Jayne-Anne Gadhia (former CEO of Virgin Money) has promoted a target of 50:50 representation on corporate boards. In her preface to her government-commissioned 2016 report on women in the finance industry, Gadhia argued in favor of voluntary targets because they require companies to measure and monitor, "and what gets measured gets done" (HM Treasury/Virgin Money, 2016, p. 6). The Davies Review acted as a spur to businesses, she argued, but companies need to identify their own targets and review their own processes in order to achieve them, audit, and report annually, and appoint an executive with responsibility for equality and diversity. Launching the report in March 2016, and supported by the Treasury, she announced a charter signed by her own company, four high street banks, a mutual, and an asset management firm, committing them to put into practice the report's recommendations. The Women in Finance Charter, which now has around 370 signatories, commits organizations to appointing a board-level diversity champion, setting internal targets for diversity and publishing annual monitoring updates on the company website, and to "having an intention to ensure the pay of the senior executive team is linked to delivery against these internal targets on gender diversity." The Charter is credited with a significant increase (9% since 2015) in the proportion of women on the boards of British banks to 37%, higher than in the USA or the European Union average (McCulloch, 2020).

The close collaboration between the Davies and Hampton-Alexander steering groups, executive search firms, investor associations, business associations, and influential business figures, highlights the diffuse nature of the change process. Following an initial phase of institutionalization intended to raise awareness and to jolt business actors into changing their behavior, the role of business support networks and headhunters highlights the de-institutionalization that followed (Doldor et al, 2016). This de-institutionalization, typical of a voluntary self-regulation approach, creates a path-dependent trajectory of change because change is seen as self-generating rather than dependent on an externally verifiable process of monitoring and enforcement. According to this logic, change will occur through endogenous processes, which excludes the need for and therefore the possibility of more formal mandatory processes.

Assessing Empowerment and Gender Transformation: The Limitations of Self-regulated Change

The review process, as outlined above, has placed heavy emphasis on implementation as a practice to shift cultural attitudes over years. Denise Wilson, the CEO of the Hampton-Alexander Review, argues that the question of women on boards has shifted in less than a decade from "water-cooler conversation" to a mainstream issue (Wilson, 2019). More starkly, Lord Davies has stated that his panel initially faced resistance from "a club of men" and widespread skepticism from business leaders, while shareholders showed "a lack of interest" in the subject, and head-hunters argued that there was no supply of female candidates (Davies, 2015). He saw the key to changing attitudes as being the leadership shown by "one or two chairmen who really stepped up and said I'm gonna take this on, and they then went to their friends and said to them, I'm absolutely fixing my company." Stake-holder groups organized by the review panel early on also helped to legitimate this behavior and disseminate it. Helena Morrissey confirmed that business lead-ers were initially polarized between most "saying this is a women's issue, this is not our issue, why are you interfering in our board" and those committed to the goals of the 30% Club. Like Lord Davies, she referred to the hate mail she had received from some quarters but also claimed that the hostile view "has com-pletely changed. Many of those same individuals are now advocates" (Morrissey, 2015).

While sending positive messages to encourage cultural change through the mo-bilization of key actors, the Davies and Hampton-Alexander steering groups were also forced to acknowledge the slow pace of change. Indeed, in later years, the Hampton-Alexander steering group became more critical of employer attitudes, in order to remobilize change agents, as attention shifted from the aspirational targets to issues of non-compliance or weak compliance. As well as congratulating the companies that have reached the 33% target, it began to name "poor perform-ers" where little or no change was observed. In 2018, despite seven years of action by executive search firms and employer associations to demonstrate that the talent pool already existed, the business ministry revealed the following range of reasons given to the Hampton-Alexander steering group by employers for not appointing more women onto corporate boards:

1) incompatible attitudes: "I don't think women fit comfortably into the board environment"; "My other board colleagues wouldn't want to appoint a woman on our board"; "Most women don't want the hassle or pressure of sitting on a board";

2) tokenistic box-ticking: "We have one woman already on the board, so we are done—it is someone else's turn"; and

3) claims of insufficient numbers of suitably-qualified women: "There aren't that many women with the right credentials and depth of experience to sit on the board—the issues covered are extremely complex"; "All the 'good' women have already been snapped up" (Hampton-Alexander Review, 2018, p. 23).

Given the outright sexism of many of these comments, the report was widely covered in the media (see e.g., Pickard and Murphy, 2018) and the government website called the reasons for inaction "outrageous" (BEIS, 2018).

Even while celebrating the achievement of the headline target in 2020 (see Table 4.3), the Hampton-Alexander Review acknowledged that 41% of FTSE 350 companies still failed to reach the target of 33% female board members (Hampton-Alexander Review, 2020). Eighteen of these boards included only one woman member. The most notable increase took place in the appointment of non-executive directors. Thus, whereas the percentage of female non-executive directors rose to 40.8% at the end of the decade of review, the proportion of executive board members had increased only slightly to 13.2%. The Cranfield academics leading the annual monitoring, therefore, argued that although targets had enabled increased non-executive board presence of women, they had not succeeded in driving change through top-level appointments (Cranfield School of Management, 2020).

The voluntary review process, therefore, enabled some degree of attitudinal change through mobilization of key actors with credibility in the business world but also failed to challenge deep-seated resistance. It has not led to gender transformation. The term "chairmen" was not challenged by the Davies Review and continues to be routinely used in all communications, as the above quotation shows (for example, Sir John Parker was described on the review website as "chairman" of Anglo-American). Probably the most visible sign of empowerment is

Table 4.3 Share of Women on Boards in FTSE 100 and FTSE 250 Companies in the UK, 2011–2019

	2011	2013	2015	2017	2019
FTSE 100					
Board members	135	194	286	294	341
(%)	(12.5%)	(17.3%)	(26.1%)	(27.7%)	(32.4%)
Non-executive directors (%)	117	176	260	269	311
	(15.6%)	(21.8%)	(31.1%)	(33.3%)	(38.5%)
Board chairs	2	1	3	6	5
CEOs	5	3	5	6	6
FTSE 250					
Board members	154	267	396	453	582
(%)	(7.8%)	(13.2%)	(19.6%)	(22.8%)	(29.6%)
Non-executive directors (%)	127	235	368	415	538 (35%)
	(9.6%)	(16.6%)	(26.6%)	(27.8%)	
Board chairs	—	—	10	11	20
CEOs	10	—	11	9	8

Source: Hampton-Alexander Review, 2019, p. 48.

the greater presence of women in business networks and public discourse on leadership, as well as increased numbers of female candidates at higher levels of management recruitment. As the 2018 Hampton-Alexander report argued, the issue of women leaders has become inescapable in the corporate world. More widely, underrepresentation of women in boardrooms has been highlighted as a policy concern in public debate such as mainstream newspaper articles and television discussions, alongside the related issues of executive pay and the gender pay gap, although it struggles for attention as austerity accelerates its grip on low-paid occupations where female employment is predominantly located.

However, the empowerment of women in implementation and evaluation is quite low. The voice of campaign groups such as the Fawcett Society (Kaur, 2020) or the TUC calling for stronger regulatory action such as mandatory quotas has been sidelined to a significant extent, although the intervention of the parliamentary all-party Women and Equalities Committee in 2016 gave a wider space for women's groups and equality campaigners to set out the case for alternative action, including quotas (UK Parliament, 2016). In parliamentary debates, the discourse of voluntary self-regulation is dominant. The last tabled debate on women on boards took place in May 2018, when the Minister for Women Victoria Atkins cited the Hampton-Alexander Review as the reason to adhere to voluntary self-regulation while acknowledging that more could be done to encourage business compliance through the provision of more informational and supportive resources (business toolkits). Attention by the bigger political parties has also remained low. In the 2017 and 2019 general election campaigns, the main political parties did not broach the question of women on boards. Only the Women's Equality Party (WEP, 2017) and the Scottish National Party (see O'Hagan and Thompson, in this volume) called for statutory action to place a duty on employers to work toward parity on corporate boards. Substantive representation remains low in the outcome of the policy. The process of target-setting, monitoring, and reporting on gender has been broadened to include race and ethnicity diversity. As noted above, the corporate governance code now asks companies to report on a wider range of workforce data, including diversity at the corporate board level. Women's groups, particularly women's business networks and campaign organizations, and equality campaigners have been empowered through greater visibility of the issue of women in economic decision-making.

Descriptive representation has increased since 2011, but there are signs of stalling, and although the number of women board members has increased, they have generally not been able to break the glass ceiling of company directorships. The pipeline problem remains sizable and business resistance to tackling it is extensive (see Barnes et al, 2019). Female board members are 89.2% white, a "really poor picture," although they are less likely than their male counterparts to have been Oxbridge-educated (11%, compared to 24% overall) (Vinnicombe, 2019). Despite a great increase in the public visibility of the issue of women in economic decision-making. Table 4.2 shows the progress made since 2011, based on the Davies and Hampton-Alexander annual reports. It reveals the steady rise in absolute and relative terms of female board members in FTSE 350 companies. This progression led to claims that the "combination of leadership, transparency and collaboration, is firmly placing the UK as a world leader" on the question of diversity in the business world (Hampton-Alexander Review, 2018, p. 40). However, progression has required significant investment by business leaders close to the government, and it has made only limited inroads into wider business practice. Beneath this success story lies a more challenging situation for women wishing to make their way to the top of business on equal terms with men. After ten years, the progress made by the Davies and then Hampton-Alexander Reviews is fragile and partial at best.

First, although the number of female directorships has risen, the number and proportion of female executive directors have grown more slowly, particularly outside the FTSE 100. The number of female executive board chairs and CEOs has remained stubbornly low. The focus on FTSE 100 companies, where headline change can take place based on the appointment of just a few individual highly-skilled women, means that debates are kept within a very small circle of the business elite.

Second, anecdotal evidence of tokenism and lip-service compliance is plentiful, as the 2018 Hampton-Alexander Review revealed. As well as the reasons given by CEOs for not increasing female board presence, the report cited several prominent female business leaders who suggested that the experience is as difficult as ever. Dame Inga Beale (former CEO of Lloyds of London) said that many female executive directors know that they will be succeeded by men: "Speaking to several of them, the common view is that Chairs think they have done their bit by hiring a woman, now the role can go back to a man. It feels as though we took two steps forward and are now taking one step back" (Hampton-Alexander Review, 2018, p. 7). In June 2019 she argued that companies not increasing female board representation should be obliged to pay some kind of levy that could be used for the purposes of helping women to access promotion (Beale, 2019). The consequence of tokenism and "one and done" appointments of women is not just that descriptive representation remains limited to a small circle (Vinnicombe, 2019) but also that these few women lack resources to enact change and may end up being "pillars of representation" whose workload increases by virtue of their isolation (Céline Thomas, interview, August 2020).

Third, the process does not challenge the organizational cultures and behaviors that perpetuate the exclusion of women's voices. Céline Thomas (Policy Officer, Women's Equality Party) argues that the pipeline approach reinforces internalization by women of the values and behavioral preferences of the existing decision-makers, rather than promoting diversity of behaviors (interview, August 2020). In order to make it to the top, women are coached, mentored, and socialized into the existing way of working. Beyond the debate between voluntarism and quotas, this feminist perspective locates transformative change as a broader agenda, which could start, for example, with pay transparency.

Given this situation, the overall outcome of this policy in terms of the GEPP approach is most appropriately characterized as one of gender accommodation, where a space has been opened up for women's representation, the public profile of women has increased in business as in many other aspects of public life, and a dense network of women's networks has grown up to support change and resist roll-back. The business world has been feminized, and leadership has been recast as a women's domain as well as that of men, but only to a certain extent. Strong pressures for roll-back exist in the form of stereotyped attitudes that are increasingly challenged but remain embedded. Race and ethnicity remain intractable areas where the Parker Review process has generated only a slight increase in the knowledge base and limited action.

Conclusion

The UK has innovated in its intensive form of self-regulation. On the coerciveness spectrum, this policy approach may best be characterized as fitting the description of light intermediate and partial self-regulation, with monitoring mechanisms but no compulsion, rather an expectation to report, and limited to the largest public limited companies. The key output features as outlined above consist of (a) voluntary target; (b) voluntary measures in a voluntary but strongly expected corporate governance code, in particular, expectations about reporting via annual statements, attributions of a nomination committee, and expectations about consultation with shareholders and other stakeholders; and (c) annual monitoring and reporting by a high-level independent steering committee, with attention to reputational pressures, including both best practice distinctions and naming and shaming of companies that do not respond to exhortations to appoint women. Besides the review panel itself, the process relies on a supporting network of high-profile business leaders, particularly women business leaders. The Hampton-Alexander Review did not change this approach, although it has sought to strengthen links with existing networks such as the Institute of Directors and Women on Boards, which work on programs to support individual women, and collaboration with executive search firms, and investors.

The British case shows the strengths and weaknesses of the self-regulation approach and the implementation method chosen to support it, as outlined above. As Table 4.1 shows, the percentage of female executives (for the very largest firms, at least) has been consistently higher than the EU average, for the period since 2003 when comparative data have been available. However, change has so far remained limited to the outer circles of business decision-making, despite the efforts of the high-level review panel to effect change through information, public reputational pressures, and direct appeals to CEOs. As the reviews have shown, change has trickled out beyond the largest firms more slowly. Furthermore, board diversity on race and ethnicity is still not being addressed at all in most companies.

During the period of the Davies Review, an advocacy coalition of equality campaign groups called for an alternative approach based on mandatory quotas and wide-ranging support measures for women at work. While stopping short of recommending quotas, the Women and Equalities Parliamentary Select Committee, along with other parliamentary committees headed by women, such as the business and finance committees, have attempted to keep the debate about methods open and also called for a broader approach that would help to tackle structural inequalities. Viewed from this perspective, the prevailing approach appears narrow, and so far the government has not been able to justify the lack of stronger action in the face of evidence that companies have paid little heed to the targets or sought ways to avoid taking action. The Hampton-Alexander Review (2019, 32) argues that the British voluntary approach "is clearly working." The announcement in 2020 that the 33% target had been met by FTSE 100 companies further strengthens the argument of those opposed to regulatory action but may end up weakening the impetus for change. The need for a "step change" is widely acknowledged, but preferences about how to achieve it exhibit strong path dependency.

The business-led British case shows that non-binding targets can achieve results when allied to compliance norms for corporate governance reporting and significant activism by business actors; however, progress falls short of that achieved in countries where formal quotas are introduced. Moreover, there are indications that the progress achieved may be hollow (reaching only a small number of women without changing practices within organizations) and short-lived (failing to tackle pipeline issues). In this case, reliance on strong business actors and networks achieved only partial change and created a path-dependent narrowing of the agenda for change (avoidance of quotas or strong enforcement mechanisms), which worked with the existing grain of relying on the market and "enabling" rather than enforcing mechanisms. Given the effort invested in embedding the voluntary approach and its fit with dominant policy preferences to date, it is unlikely to be overcome in the short term, despite strong activism by equality campaigners to introduce authority measures. The result is gender accommodation.

References

30% Club (2017) "Who we are," https://30percentclub.org/about/who-we-are (Accessed June 4, 2018).

Aguilera, Ruth V. and Gregory Jackson (2010) "Comparative and International Corporate Governance," *The Academy of Management Annals*, 4(1), pp. 485–556.

Arcot, Sridar, Valentina Bruno, and Antoine Faure-Grimaud (2010) "Corporate Governance in the UK: Is the Comply or Explain Approach Working?" *International Review of Law and Economics*, 30(1), pp. 193–201.

Barnes, Claire, Rachel Lewis, Joanna Yarker, and Lilith Arevshatian (2019) "Women Directors on FTSE Company Boards: An Exploration of the Factors Influencing their Appointment," *Cogent Psychology*, 6(1), pp. 1–24.

Beale, Inga (2019) Interview, BBC Radio 4, Woman's Hour, June 25.

Burk, Martha and Heidi Hartmann (2017) "Gender Parity on Corporate Boards: A Path to Women's Equality?" in Shannon N. Davis, Sarah Winslow, and David J. Maume (eds) *Gender in the Twenty-first Century. The Stalled Revolution and the Road to Equality*. Oakland, CA: University of California Press, pp. 127–146.

Business in the Community (2011) *Opportunity Now. Twentieth Anniversary Review. Celebrating Two Decades of Advancing Women in the Workplace*. London: Business in the Community.

Cameron, David (2011) Letter to Chief Executives, October 12, https://webarchive. nationalarchives.gov.uk/20121205130129/http://www.number10.gov.uk/news/pm-welcomes-progress-on-women-on-boards/ (Accessed August 24, 2020).

Catalyst (2008) *Women on Boards. Census of the Women Board Directors of the Fortune 500*. New York: Catalyst.

Chartered Institute for Personnel and Development (CIPD) (2018) *Hidden Figures. How Workforce Data is Missing from Corporate Reports*. London: CIPD.

Ciccia, Rossella and Inge Bleijenbergh (2014) "After the Male Breadwinner Model? Childcare Services and the Division of Labor in European Countries," *Social Politics*, 21(1), pp. 50–79.

Cranfield School of Management (2020) "Targets Bring More Women on Boards, but They Still Don't Reach the Top," Press release, September 24, https://www.cranfield. ac.uk/som/press/targets-bring-more-women-on-boards-but-they-still-dont-reach-the-top (Accessed September 25, 2020).

Davies, Mervyn (2011) *Women on Boards*. London: BIS.

Davies, Mervyn (2015) "Women on boards: closing the gap," Speech at Oxford Brookes Centre for Diversity Research and Practice, November 12.

Department for Business, Energy and Industrial Strategy (BEIS) (2018) "Revealed: The Worst Explanations for not Appointing Women to FTSE 100 boards," News story, May 31, 2018, https://www.gov.uk/government/news/revealed-the-worst-explanations-for-not-appointing-women-to-ftse-company-boards (Accessed June 4, 2018).

Department for Business, Innovation and Skills (BIS) (2011) Women on Boards, February 24, https://www.gov.uk/government/news/women-on-boards (Accessed September 25, 2020).

Department for Business, Innovation and Skills (BIS) (2015) *Women on Boards—A Five Year Summary*. London: BIS.

Department for Education (DfE) (2015) "Nicky Morgan: Lord Davies Review on Women on Boards," Speech, October 29, https://www.gov.uk/government/speeches/ nicky-morgan-lord-davies-review-on-women-on-boards (Accessed June 4, 2018).

Doldor, Elena, Ruth Sealy, and Susan Vinnicombe (2016) "Accidental Activists: Head-hunters as Marginal Diversity Actors in Institutional Change towards More Women on Boards," *Human Resource Management Journal*, 26(3), pp. 285–303.

Equality and Human Rights Commission (EHRC) (2014) *An Inquiry into Fairness, Transparency and Diversity in FTSE 350 Companies*. London: EHRC.

European Institute for Gender Equality (EIGE) (2020) Gender Statistics Database: Business, https://eige.europa.eu/gender-statistics/dgs/browse/wmidm/wmidm_bus/wmidm_bus_bus (Accessed October 12, 2020).

Eurostat (2020a) Gender Pay Gap in Unadjusted Form, https://ec.europa.eu/eurostat/databrowser/view/sdg_05_20/default/table?lang=en (Accessed September 25, 2020).

Eurostat (2020b) Part-time Employment as Percentage of the Total Employment, by Sex and Age (%), https://ec.europa.eu/eurostat/web/products-eurostat-news/-/DDN-20180608-1 (Accessed September 25, 2020).

Financial Reporting Council (FRC) (2014) *The UK Corporate Governance Code. September 2014*. London: FRC.

Government Equalities Office (GEO) (2009) *Business Plan 2009–2010*. London: Her Majesty's Government.

Goyal, Rita, Nada Korac Kakabadse, Felipe Morais, and Andrew P. Kakabadse (2018) "Gender Diversity on Boards in Norway and the UK. A Different Approach to Governance or a Case of Path Dependency?" in Maria Aluchna and Güler Aras (eds) *Women on Corporate Boards. An International Perspective*. London, New York: Routledge (e-book), https://www.routledge.com/Women-on-Corporate-Boards-An-International-Perspective/Aluchna-Aras/p/book/9780367591366 (Accessed July 5, 2019).

Grant Thornton (2016) *The Future of Governance: One Small Step. Corporate Governance Review 2016*. London: Grant Thornton LLP.

Green Park (2017) *The Green Park Leadership 10,000. 2016–2017*. London: Green Park.

Green Park (2020) *Green Park Business Leaders 2020. Britain's Top Firms Failing Black Leaders*. London: Green Park.

Grimshaw, Damian and Jill Rubery (2007) *Undervaluing Women's Work*. Manchester: Equal Opportunities Commission.

Hammond, Val (1992) "Opportunity 2000: A Culture Change Approach to Equal Opportunity," *Women in Management Review*, 7(7), pp. 3–10.

Hampton-Alexander Review (2016) *Improving Gender Balance in FTSE Leadership*. London: FTSE Women Leaders/KPMG.

Hampton-Alexander Review (2018) *Improving Gender Balance in FTSE Leadership*. London: FTSE Women Leaders/KPMG.

Hampton-Alexander Review (2019) *Improving Gender Balance in FTSE Leadership*. London: FTSE Women Leaders/KPMG.

Hampton-Alexander Review (2020) Press release, September, https://ftsewomenleaders.com/wp-content/uploads/2020/09/UNDER-STRICT-EMBARGO-HA-Review-BEIS-PR_Sept-2020.pd (Accessed September 25, 2020).

Hansard Society (1990) *Women at the Top*. Report of the Hansard Society Commission. London: Hansard Society.

Harkness, Susan, Magda Borkowska, and Alina Pelik (2019) *Employment Pathways and Occupational Change after Childbirth*. London: Government Equalities Office.

Harman, Harriet (2017) *A Woman's Work*. London: Allen Lane.

Higgs, Derek (2003) *Review of the Role and Effectiveness of Non-executive Directors*. London: Department of Trade and Industry.

Hill, Amelia (2011) "More than 5,400 Women 'missing' from 26,000 Top Posts in Britain, Report Finds," *The Guardian*, August 17.

HM Treasury/Virgin Money (2016) *Empowering Productivity: Harnessing the Talents of Women in the Finance Industry*. London: HM Treasury.

Horn, Laura (2012) "Corporate Governance in Crisis? The Politics of EU Corporate Governance Regulation," *European Law Journal*, 4(1), pp. 83–107.

House of Lords (2012) *Women on Boards*. Fifth report of session 2012–2013, House of Lords Select Committee on European Union, https://publications.parliament.uk/pa/ld201213/ldselect/ldeucom/58/5802.htm (Accessed September 25, 2020).

Kaur, Sanmeet (2020) *The 2020 Sex and Power Index*. London: Fawcett Society.

Keay, Andrew (2013) "Comply or Explain in Corporate Governance Codes: In Need of Greater Regulatory Oversight?" *Legal Studies*, 34(2), pp. 279–304.

Kingsmill, Denise (2002) *Report into Women's Employment and Pay*. London: Department for Education and Employment.

Lewis, Rowena and Katherine Rake (2008) *Breaking the Mould for Women Leaders: Could Boardroom Quotas Hold the Key?* London: Fawcett Society.

McCarthy, Helen (2020) *Double Lives: A History of Working Motherhood*. London: Bloomsbury.

McCulloch, Adam (2020) "UK Banks Increase Number of Female Board Members," *Personnel Today*, August 18.

McKinsey (2007) *Women Matter. Gender Diversity, a Corporate Performance Driver*. Paris: McKinsey.

McGregor-Smith Review (2017) Race in the Workplace, https://www.gov.uk/government/publications/race-in-the-workplace-the-mcgregor-smith-review (Accessed July 5, 2019).

McRae, Susan (1995) *Women at the Top. Progress after Five Years*. London: Hansard Society.

Miller, Linda and Fiona Neathey (2004) *Advancing Women in the Workplace*. Manchester: Equal Opportunities Commission.

Morrissey, Helena (2015) "Women on Boards: Closing the Gap," Speech at Oxford Brookes Centre for Diversity Research and Practice, November 12.

Murray, Jenni (2013) "What Did Margaret Thatcher Do for Women?" *Guardian*, April 9, https://www.theguardian.com/politics/2013/apr/09/margaret-thatcher-women (Accessed August 18, 2020).

Office of National Statistics (ONS) (2019) "Gender Pay Gap in the UK: 2019," https://www.ons.gov.uk/employmentandlabourmarket/peopleinwork/earningsandworkinghours/bulletins/genderpaygapintheuk/2019 (Accessed August 18, 2020).

Olsen, Wendy, Vanessa Gash, Sook Kim, and Min Zhang (2018) *The Gender Pay Gap in the UK: Evidence from the UKHLS*. London: Government Equalities Office.

Parker Review (2020) *Ethnic Diversity Enriching Business Leadership: An Update from the Parker Review*. London: Parker Review/Ernst & Young.

Pickard, Jim and Hannah Murphy (2018) "UK Companies Using 'Pitiful' Excuses to Keep Women Out of the Boardroom," *Financial Times*, May 31, https://www.ft.com/content/6432085c-649d-11e8-90c2-9563a0613e56 (Accessed June 4, 2018).

Richards, Wendy (2001) "Evaluating Equal Opportunities Initiatives: The Case for a 'Transformative' agenda," in Mike Noon and Emmanuel Ogbonna (eds) *Equality, Diversity and Disadvantage in Employment*. Basingstoke: Palgrave, pp. 15–31.

Sealy, Ruth (2018) *Board Diversity Reporting*. London: Financial Reporting Council.

Sealy, Ruth, Elena Doldor, Val Singh, and Susan Vinnicombe (2011) *Women on Boards. 6 Month Monitoring Report*. London: Government Equalities Office.

Sealy, Ruth, Elena Doldor, Susan Vinnicombe, Sirin Terjesen, Deirdre Anderson, and Doyn Atewologun (2017) "Expanding the Logic of Dialogic Trading Zones: The Case of Women on Boards Research," *British Journal of Management*, 28(1), pp. 48–63.

Seidl, David, Paul Sanderson, and John Roberts (2013) "Applying the 'Comply-or-Explain' Principle: Discursive Legitimacy Tactics with Regard to Codes of Corporate Governance," *Journal of Management and Governance*, 17(3), pp. 791–826.

Shrives, Philip J. and Niamh M. Brennan (2017) "Explanations for Corporate Governance Non-Compliance: A Rhetorical Analysis," *Critical Perspectives on Accounting*, 42(9), pp. 31–56.

Singh, Val and Susan Vinnicombe (2004) "Why So Few Women in Top UK Boardrooms? Evidence and Theoretical Explanations," *Corporate Governance*, 12(4), pp. 479–488.

Singh, Val, Susan Vinnicombe, and Phyl Johnson (2001) "Women Directors on Top UK Boards," *Corporate Governance: An International Review*, 9(1), pp. 206–216.

Sweeney, Charlotte (2014) *Women on Boards: Voluntary Code for Executive Search Firms*. https://www.gov.uk/government/publications/women-on-boards-voluntary-code-for-executive-search-firms (Accessed June 4, 2018).

Trades Union Congress (TUC) (2015) "Gender Pay Gap for Britain's Top Earners Hits 55%, Says TUC," Press release, November 9, https://www.tuc.org.uk/news/gender-pay-gap-uk's-top-earners-hits-55-says-tuc (Accessed June 4, 2018).

UK Parliament (2016) "Why Are so Few Women Running British Businesses?" February 2, https://www.parliament.uk/business/committees/committees-a-z/commons-select/women-and-equalities-committee/news-parliament-2015/women-in-executive-management-evidence-15-16/ (Accessed June 4, 2018).

Villiers, Charlotte (2011) "Achieving Gender Balance in the Boardroom: Is It Time for Legislative Action in the UK?" *Legal Studies*, 30(4), pp. 533–547.

Vinnicombe, Susan (2019) "Women in the Workplace: Beyond the Numbers," Speech to Westminster Business Forum policy conference, December 19.

Wilson, Denise (2019) "Hampton-Alexander Review: Next Steps for Improving Representation," Speech to Westminster Business Forum Policy Conference, December 19.

Women and Work Commission (WWC) (2006) *Shaping a Fairer Future*. London: WWC.

Women and Work Commission (WWC) (2009) *Shaping a Fairer Future. A Review of the Recommendations of the Women and Work Commission Three Years On*. London: WWC.

Women's Equality Party (WEP) (2017) "Conservative Plans Won't Work for Women," May 18, http://www.womensequality.org.uk/conservative_manifesto (Accessed June 4, 2018).

Wood, Zoe (2011) "Lord Davies Tells Big Firms to Double Number of Women Directors," *The Guardian*, February 24.

5

Avoiding Quotas at all Costs

How Self-regulation Undermines Gender Transformation in Sweden

Lenita Freidenvall

Introduction

In a report by the European Institute for Gender Equality (EIGE), it is noted that the biggest boost to gender equality in Europe over the past ten years has been in the domain of power, especially on corporate boards (EIGE, 2017). Although women are still largely left out of decision-making, it is stressed that this result reflects recent political pressure to increase gender balance on the boards of the largest publicly listed companies. It is also emphasized that the progress, particularly since 2010, can largely be attributed to "major legislative initiatives taken both at the national and EU levels and the extensive public debates in this area" (EIGE, 2017, p. 63). A similar conclusion is made by OECD, noting that countries that have adopted corporate gender quotas have seen a more immediate increase in the number of women board members, while those that have embarked upon a "softer" approach, using disclosure rules or targets, have seen a more gradual increase over time (OECD, 2017, p. 14).

Based on these observations, Sweden represents an interesting puzzle; the percentage of women on corporate boards has more than doubled since 2005 (from 16% in 2005 to 34% in 2020) despite not having any legislative corporate gender quotas, and putting Sweden at the same level as its Nordic counterparts (see the chapter on Norway in this volume; see also Heidenrich, 2012). In fact, as Table 5.1 indicates, in 2020 with 38.6% women on the boards of the largest listed companies, Sweden ranked second (after France) among all the European Union countries, and was even outperforming countries with legislative corporate gender quotas—33.7% average.

Although attempts to adopt corporate gender quotas have been made, self-regulation in the form of a voluntary corporate governance code, similar to the

Lenita Freidenvall, *Avoiding Quotas at all Costs*. In: *Gender Equality and Policy Implementation in the Corporate World.*
Edited by Isabelle Engeli and Amy G. Mazur, Oxford University Press. © Oxford University Press (2022).
DOI: 10.1093/oso/9780198865216.003.0005

Table 5.1 Percentage Share of Women on Boards in the Largest Listed Companies in Sweden, 2004–2020

	EU-28 Board members	SWEDEN				
		Board members	President	CEO	Executives	Non-executives
2004	9	21.3	0.0	—	—	—
2005	9.8	24.0	0.0	—	—	—
2006	9.7	24.4	0.0	—	—	—
2007	10.4	23.8	0.0	—	—	—
2008	10.8	26.9	0.0	—	—	—
2009	11	26.8	0.0	—	—	—
2010	11.9	26.4	0.0	—	—	—
2011	13.7	24.7	0.0	—	—	—
2012	15.8	25.5	0.0	3.8	19.2	27.1
2013	17.8	26.5	3.8	3.8	21.5	27.8
2014	20.2	27.6	7.4	3.7	22.4	28.5
2015	22.7	32.6	7.7	7.7	23.7	33.8
2016	23.9	36.9	7.7	11.5	23.9	38.5
2017	25.3	36.3	7.1	7.1	24.8	38.7
2018	26.7	36.1	11.5	7.7	24.8	38.2
2019	28.8	37.5	19.2	3.8	23.7	39.3
2020	29.2	38.6	15.4	7.7	24.7	40.3

Source: EIGE database. Data for October each year, except for 2020 [April].

ones adopted in Australia and the UK (see the chapters on each country in this book), has been the preferred strategy. This Code, adopted in 2005, contains a gender equality stipulation that "equal gender distribution on the board is to be an aim." A few years earlier, in 1999, a policy on gender balance (with a sub-goal of a minimum of 40% of women by 2003) on the boards of state-owned (and partially state-owned) companies was introduced by the government. This rule was initiated by the Gender Equality Minister in order to set a good example and to encourage private companies to take initiatives on their own.

This chapter analyzes the adoption, implementation, evaluation, and outcome of the gender equality stipulation in the 2005 Code. It argues that this self regulatory solution has been introduced by the corporate sector itself in order to avoid the adoption of legislative corporate gender quotas. The adoption of this Code has resulted in a gradual, but slow, increase in women on corporate boards, although without leading to gender-balanced boards or substantial transformation in gendered norms of representation in the economic sector. The adoption of the policy on gender balance on the boards of state-owned companies, in contrast, seems to have been more successful.

Gender Equality in the Corporate World

A key characteristic of gender equality in Sweden is its close connection to the social democratic welfare state ideology, often referred to as the Swedish model (Bergqvist et al, 1999; Hernes, 1987; Sainsbury, 1996). The notion generally refers to the economic and social policy model that developed in Sweden after WWII, a model that combines free market economy with a comprehensive welfare state, which provides universal health care and tertiary education for its citizens, and collective bargaining at the national level. It is based on the support of a universalist welfare state that promotes individual autonomy and social mobility, a corporatist system involving a tripartite arrangement of social partners (employer organizations, trade unions, and the state) negotiating wages and labor market policies and a commitment to private ownership, free markets, and trade. Key to the model is also collaboration between government and industry, a relation that has been labeled "Harpsund democracy," based on the idea that private owners enjoy considerable autonomy, given that they take responsibility for their employees and society in general (Agnblad et al, 2001, p. 251). As in many other countries, the system of governance has gradually been revised in line with neoliberal principles, including privatization, deregulation, and new public management.

The Swedish model is also based on the principle that women and men are independent and self-supporting individuals. This means that a "dual-income earner-and-care giver model" has been established, replacing a "male breadwinner model" (Sainsbury, 1996). Following this logic, a series of key reforms were introduced in the 1970s, such as individual taxation (1971), gender-neutral parental leave (1974), and publicly subsidized daycare for children. Generous parental leave schemes, including reserving days for each parent (30 days for each parent out of a total of 480 days in 1995, 60 days for each parent in 2002, and 90 days for each parent in 2016) as well as wide-ranging childcare facilities, have contributed to reconciling work and family by promoting women's participation in paid work and men's participation in the unpaid work at home and the care of children. The Swedish Gender Equality Act, which came into force in 1979, prohibited discrimination in the labor market on the basis of sex and provided for affirmative action to promote gender equality. For instance, since 1991, employers with ten employees or more must have a gender equality plan detailing how the employers are promoting an equal distribution of women and men in different types of work. In 2009, the Gender Equality Act was amalgamated into the Anti-Discrimination Act, and the Gender Equality Ombudsman established in 1980 to oversee the law was merged with other ombudsmen into the Anti-Discrimination Ombudsman (Borchorst et al, 2011). As of 2020, all employers are to promote gender balance in different types of work, among different categories of employees, and among management positions by means of education and training, skills development, and other appropriate measures. Employers who employ twenty-five workers or more are to document in writing the active measures taken during the year.

Equal representation of women and men in decision-making bodies is an old phenomenon in Sweden. In the 1970s, political parties adopted voluntary measures, ranging from general goals and recommendations to party quotas in order to increase women's representation in elected bodies (Freidenvall, 2018; Freidenvall, 2021). In the 1980s, the government introduced formal rules for the representation of women and men on the boards of state agencies and national commissions of inquiry (Freidenvall, 2018). Since 1988, all state agencies, as well as national commissions of inquiry, must abide by the formal rule for gendered representation on their boards (30% of the underrepresented sex by 1992, 40% by 1995, and 50% by 1998 (Government bill, prop. 1987/88:105, bet. 1987/88:AU17, rskr. 1987/88:36)). As mentioned in the introduction, since 1999 the boards of wholly or partially state-owned companies must be gender balanced (with a sub-goal that the proportion of women is to reach 40% by 2003) (Government communication, 1999). These rules for the public sector were initiated by Gender Equality Ministers, who used the gender equality of public firms as leverage in relation to the private sector. Hence, several rules for the gendered composition of decision-making bodies have been adopted, albeit not via any legislative measures.

With regard to the company structure of Sweden, there are two types of limited companies (a limited company (*aktiebolag*) is a legal entity owned by its shareholder or shareholders): 1) private limited companies (usually owned by one or two people); and 2) public limited companies (the shares of a public limited company can be sold to the public). As of 2020, more than 300 public limited companies, ranging from small-cap to mid-cap to large-cap, are registered on Nasdaq OMX Stockholm. Two of these companies are owned by the state. The board of these companies manages the company on behalf of the company shareholders. The board members are elected by the shareholders at the annual general meeting or a general meeting. The board is responsible for the management of the company's affairs, summoning to attend general meetings, paying taxes, and filing the annual report with the Swedish Companies Registration Office (*Bolagsverket*). Importantly, board members can be held personally liable for decisions that have been made when serving on the board.

Gaining Political and Corporate Attention through a Focus on State-owned Companies, 1987–2003

The representation of women in management positions, particularly on the boards of companies, was long considered an internal matter for the business sector (Freidenvall and Hallonsten, 2013). It was not until the 1990s when the lack of gender balance in the political sphere had been a topical issue for some time that male dominance in the economic sphere also began to attract attention (Freidenvall, 2018). The pursuit of increased representation of women on company boards was promoted primarily by two sets of actors: ministers for gender equality and the corporate sector itself. As the story of gender balance on company boards in Sweden reveals, the two groups of actors have followed the same pattern since the issue was first placed on the political agenda. Ministers for gender equality took the lead, establishing national commissions of inquiry to analyze how gender balance on company boards could be achieved, and corporate sector representatives responded by introducing self-regulatory measures in order to avoid regulation.

In the final report of the first national commission of inquiry, appointed by the Minister for Gender Equality Anita Gradin in the Social Democratic Government, it was noted that women were underrepresented in decision-making positions in all major spheres of power: in politics, in the business sector and the public administration (SOU, 1987:19). In 1988, based on the proposals made by the national commission of inquiry, the government decided to increase the proportion of the underrepresented sex on the boards of state agencies to at least 30% by 1992, 40% by 1994, and 50% by 1998 (Ds, 2006:11). By focusing on the public administration and persistent gaps in its own backyard, the government could both avoid regulating the political and economic spheres via legislative gender quotas and respect the principle of non-interference of the state in the inner life of the business sector.

The topic of women's underrepresentation in the business sector did not disappear. In 1993, it was placed on the political agenda in its own right. Bengt Westerberg (Liberal Party), Deputy Prime Minister and Minister for Gender Equality in the right/center coalition government (1991–1994), appointed a national commission of inquiry to study how a more equal distribution of women and men in management positions in the business sector could be achieved. In the final report of the inquiry, *Men's Perceptions about Women and Leadership* (SOU, 1994:3), it was noted that 51% of all companies (state-owned and privately owned) in the survey had no women on their boards and that this figure was even higher for privately owned companies, of which the lion's share (72%) had all-male boards. In more than half of all companies (56%), top management consisted entirely of men; in almost all (99%), men dominated in top management (more than 60% men), while the average proportion of women was consistently lower among privately owned companies (66% of these had entirely male top management). Male dominance in the business sector was explained as the result of men's lack of knowledge of the importance of gender in working life and their privilege in society as well as the result of the Swedish corporate tradition, which was based on collaboration between large capital owners and the labor movement, both normally led by men.

Almost ten years later, in 2002, Margareta Winberg (Social Democratic Party), Deputy Prime Minister and Minister for Gender Equality in the Social Democratic Government (1994–2006) appointed a new national commission of inquiry to follow up the 1994 study. In the final report of this inquiry, *Male Dominance in Transition* (SOU, 2003:16), it was concluded that male dominance in management positions in the business sector, including on boards, persisted. At that time, 87% of all companies studied (state-owned and privately owned) and 93% of the privately owned companies had boards dominated by men, in other words, more than 60% of board members were men. However, the proportion of boards comprised only of men had decreased to 42% of all companies (and 50% of the privately owned companies). Although there was increased awareness of women's underrepresentation in leading positions in the business sector as compared to the 1993 study, gender gaps remained. It was noted that increased knowledge is important but does not necessarily lead to action for change; the will to change is also needed. The dominance of men even among young executives signaled that the problem would continue.

Despite the growing political attention to women's underrepresentation on company boards, few initiatives to improve the situation were taken, and the proportion of women increased slowly. In 1993, the private company boards were comprised of 1.4% women members, and ten years later, in 2002, the proportion of women board members had only increased to 5.8% (Nilsson, 2009; Niskanen, 2009).

Given the difficulty in intervening in the business sector and the inner life of corporations, the Social Democratic government, and Minister for Gender Equality Margareta Winberg, decided on a two-step approach: to first focus on its own companies—the state-owned companies—and then on the publicly listed companies. In 1999, as a first step, a policy was introduced mandating the achievement of gender balance on the boards of state-owned companies (Government communication, 1999). The policy stipulated that the proportion of women on state-owned company boards had to reach 40% by 2003 and that the results be reported on an annual basis to Parliament in the budget bill. The regulation was successful. In 2003, state-owned company boards were comprised of 43% women, and since then the rule has been complied with, the results have been reported in the budget bill and the objective has been reached.

As a second step, and in the same year (1999), Minister for Gender Equality Margareta Winberg proposed that legislative gender quotas be adopted for all companies listed on the Stockholm Stock Exchange (out of about 300 publicly listed companies, two were state-owned). A minimum of 25% of the underrepresented sex was to be included on the boards of these companies. The promotion of gender equality on the boards of listed companies was based on the argument that power and influence in all sectors of governance are to be shared by women and men. With more women on company boards, dialogue, collaboration, and networking in companies also would be improved. Thus, arguments targeting the democratic legitimacy of decision-making as well as better company performance and utilization of the talent pool were used. Minister Winberg gave listed companies five years to improve the share of women board members; if the share did not increase substantially, legislative corporate gender quotas were to be adopted. In 2002, the demand was repeated; if the share of women board members did not increase to 25% by 2004, legislative corporate gender quotas would be adopted (Fredell, 2005). Ironically, these threats were the starting point for the introduction of a corporate governance code as a way of avoiding legislative corporate gender quotas.

Major actors in society were opposed to legislative corporate gender quotas. Parliamentarians from the center/right claimed that quotas conflicted with the Swedish Companies Act, which stipulated that listed companies had the right to appoint their own board members. Increased representation of women on boards was not to be achieved by compromising the autonomy of companies. Rather, it was to be achieved through other measures, such as general discussions on gender equality in the business sector and leadership courses for women executives. The influential Confederation of Employers' Organizations (*Svenskt näringsliv*) emphasized the principle of self-regulation in the composition of company boards and claimed that the number of women on boards would increase by itself when the number of women in management positions (mid and top level) in the business sector increased (Bohman, Bygren, and Edling, 2012). The social partners were generally in favor of continued self-regulation, stressing the role of the corporate organizations as the driving force for change, in line with the Swedish model of corporate governance. Many women managers were also against gender quotas. A survey of 500 women leaders in 2000 had shown that 93% of the respondents were against the introduction of legislated corporate gender quotas (Fredell, 2005). Businesswomen claimed that they wanted to earn a board position on the basis of merit and experience, not on the basis of their gender.

Self-regulation in the Corporate Code Wins Out Over Quotas, 2003–2005

As a reaction to the government's repeated threats to adopt legislative corporate gender quotas, processes began within the business sector to avoid such regulations. A plausible solution to this critical problem was the introduction of voluntary and self-regulatory measures for the representation of women on company boards. The process to develop these self-regulatory measures was linked to a larger process of improving corporate governance in Sweden. Although some regulations and guidelines existed, particularly the Swedish Companies Act, there was no comprehensive code of corporate governance in Sweden. In 1993, the Swedish Shareholders' Association had decided on an ownership policy for the first time. Since then, larger Swedish institutional owners had drawn up their own guidelines on how the ownership role should be exercised. In 2003, the Swedish Academy of Directors had issued Guidelines for Good Board Practice, the first comprehensive description of good practice for boards of directors of Swedish companies. Hence, the business community shared the opinion that there was a need for a more comprehensive compilation of good practice in corporate governance in Sweden. The aim was not only to codify what was considered good practice for corporate governance in Swedish companies but also to advance practice in certain areas. The topic of women's representation on company boards fitted well into this larger effort.

The process of adopting the Code took place in two stages. In the first stage, between October 2003 and April 2004, a working group composed of nine members (three members appointed by the Commission on Business Confidence (*Förtroendekommissionen*) and six members appointed by bodies and organizations in the business sector) were tasked with presenting a proposal for a corporate governance code. This proposal was then circulated for comment. In the second stage, between October and December 2004, a national commission was appointed by the government, composed mainly of the same members as in the working group. The chairperson was Erik Åsbrink, later Minister of Finance in the Social Democratic Government, and the other members consisted of well know industrialists. The task of the commission was to propose a corporate governance code that could take effect in 2005. In its final report, the commission presented a set of guidelines for good corporate governance—*the Swedish code of corporate governance* (the Code). The Code included a passage on the representation of women members on company boards, stipulating that "equal gender distribution on the board is to be an aim" (The Swedish Code of Corporate Governance, 2005, p. 25).

The Social Democratic Government (1998–2006) was not completely satisfied with this voluntary solution. It stressed that the share of female board members did not increase at the pace needed to reach the established target (Freidenvall, 2018). Therefore, in 2005, Jens Orback, Gender Equality Minister in the Social Democratic Government, commissioned legal scholar Catarina af Sandeberg to investigate how a possible corporate gender quota law could be designed. In her report, *The Gender Composition on Corporate Boards* (Ds, 2006:11), legislative corporate gender quotas were framed as a matter of equal rights and democracy, being inherently connected to one of the sub-goals of the national gender equality policy in Sweden—"equal access by women and men to positions of power and influence." According to the proposal presented, members of the boards of public listed companies (companies listed on the Stockholm Stock Exchange) should be comprised of at least 40% of each sex. It was proposed that the new regulation enter into force on January 1, 2008, for public listed companies and on January 1, 2010, for unlisted companies. Non-compliance was to be sanctioned financially by a fine of SEK 150,000 (EUR 15,000) to be paid to the Swedish Companies Registration Office (*Bolagsverket*). The idea of adopting legislative corporate gender quotas came to an abrupt halt in 2006. The general election in September 2006 resulted in a change of government, and the Social Democratic Government had to turn over leadership to a right/center coalition government (2006–2014) comprised of the Moderate Party, the Center Party, the Liberal Party, and the Christian Democratic Party.

The new right-center government was not in favor of regulating the gender composition of boards through any legislative means. Quite the contrary, it claimed that the composition of boards was a matter for the company owners. The right of the company owners must be respected, and a hands-off policy was to be taken by the state. The Minister for Gender Equality Nyamko Sabuni (Liberal Party) insisted that candidate selection should be guided by meritocratic principles, not gender (Freidenvall and Hallonsten, 2013; Freidenvall, 2018).

While the right-center government was opposed to legislative corporate gender quotas, it was not opposed to voluntary measures to achieve gender balance on company boards. In fact, the 2005 Code, adopted by the business sector itself, represented a good solution to the continued problem of women's underrepresentation on boards. The government also emphasized the Swedish model as the backbone of the Swedish economy and stressed the important role played by the social partners.

The Instruments of Self-regulation

As Table 5.2 illustrates, Swedish policy takes a self-regulatory approach with regards to private sector business and a state regulatory approach for state-owned companies. The corporate governance code (the Code), which was adopted by the business sector itself in 2005, applied to all large companies listed on the Stockholm Stock Exchange. The Code was based on the Swedish Companies Act (*Aktiebolagslagen*) (1975:1385) and the tradition of self-regulation. The general aim of the Code was to help improve corporate governance in Swedish companies through self-regulation. Even though the Code was directed primarily at stock market companies, sound corporate governance in these companies was expected to serve as an example and a model for other types of companies, including small and middle-sized companies (SMEs).

According to the Code, "equal gender distribution on the board is to be an aim" (The Swedish Code of Corporate Governance, 2005, p. 25). As all rules in the Code, equal gender distribution on the board was based on the principle of comply-or-explain. Under this principle a company may depart from individual rules; however, in that event, it must provide an explanation stating the reasons for the departure. Thus, applying the Code meant neither that every rule must always be observed nor that departing from a rule constituted a breach of the Code. Quite the contrary, deviating from a rule could in some instances signify good corporate governance, particularly if the rule was not perceived as suitable for the company. Hence, the emphasis was on the reason for the deviation being the most essential element.

Table 5.2 Policy Measures for Gender Equality on Corporate Boards in Sweden

SELF-REGULATION

Swedish Corporate Governance Code 2005	Swedish Corporate Governance Code 2016
* Listed companies * "Equal gender distribution on the board is to be an aim" * Comply-or-explain No deadline No minimum annual increase	* Listed companies * "The company is to strive for gender balance on the board" * Comply-or-explain No deadline No minimum annual increase

STATE-REGULATION

Government Policy on gender balance on the boards of state-owned companies 1999
* State-owned companies (listed and unlisted companies)
* The goal is gender balance on the boards of state-owned companies
* The proportion of women on state-owned company boards is to reach 40 percent by 2003
* The result is presented in the annual Budget Bill presented to the Parliament
Government Strategy on Gender Equality in the Labor Market 2009–2010
* National government program for women leaders during 2009–2010

Importantly, the Code included rules for the gender composition of boards. The Code stipulated that a board should have "a size and composition that enables it to embrace the various qualifications and experience needed" and to "meet the independence criteria required to manage the company's affairs effectively and independently" (Corporate Governance Code, 2005, p. 25). The renewal of the board should be paced with "due consideration for the development of the company operations as well as for the 'need for continuity' in the work of the board" (Ibid). Specifically, with the company's operations, phase of development, and other conditions taken into consideration, the board was to have an "appropriate composition, exhibiting diversity and breadth in the directors' qualifications, experience and background" (Ibid). There were no sanctions for non-compliance, except for the possible negative publicity a violation of the Code could generate.

Since 2005, the Swedish Corporate Governance Board (*Kollegiet för svensk bo lagsstyrning*) has managed and administered the Code. The Code has been revised on a couple of occasions, most recently in 2020. The policy of gender-balanced boards has been kept intact, but it was reformulated in 2016 into "the company is to strive for gender balance on the board" (Corporate Governance Code, 2016). The Code includes some instruments for implementation and evaluation. For instance, the Code stipulates that the board of directors is to inform shareholders and the capital market annually as to corporate governance functions in the company and how the company applies the Code. This information is to be published in a corporate governance report and on the company's website. The requirement to produce a corporate governance report is stipulated in Chapter 6, Sections 6–9 of the Annual Accounts Act (1995:554). In the corporate governance report, the company must state which Code rules it has not complied with, explain the reasons for each case of non-compliance and describe the alternative solutions it has adopted. The report must also include information on the composition of the company's nomination committee, the division of work among board members, and how the work of the board was conducted during the most recent financial year, including the number of board meetings held and the attendance of each of the board members at board meetings. The corporate governance section of the website is to include information regarding the members of the board, the chief executive, and the statutory auditor.

To complement the work of the business sector, the government itself initiated a series of measures to stimulate increased numbers of women on company boards. For instance, a National Strategy for Gender Equality in the Labor Market 2009–2010 was adopted in 2009, including more than seventy activities. Within the framework of this strategy, Almi (a company owned by the Swedish state, which provides loans to businesses and engages in venture capital activities) was commissioned to undertake and coordinate a national government program for women leaders during 2009–2010 (National Strategy for Gender Equality in the Labor Market 2009–2010). The program aimed at identifying competent women to be recruited to company boards, disseminating good examples, and initiating a debate about the importance of having "more women" on boards based on an "economic growth perspective" (Ibid, p. 48). As a result of the program, at least 200 women were invited to an exclusive mentorship program and received a scholarship grant of SEK 10,000 for optional board education.

In terms of regulatory approach, Sweden takes a self-regulation approach on the part of corporate stakeholders themselves. Since the policy entails comprehensive coverage of boards, in other words, all listed companies on the stock market regardless of size or legal status, Sweden can be placed at the middle to high end of the regulatory scope continuum. The selection of this approach can be explained primarily by norms and practices of gender balance in elected bodies and on the boards of state agencies and state-owned companies, and in national commissions of inquiry. Sweden can also be placed at the low end (as light coercion or light voluntary) of the coerciveness continuum. Self-regulation is binding; monitoring and reporting are required; and, there are formal comply-or-explain mechanisms, but non-compliance is not sanctioned. This placement on the coerciveness continuum can be explained by the fact that gender equality is established as a norm in Swedish society, but the preferred solutions to achieve gender balance have never included legislated gender quotas. The placement can also be explained by the tradition of non-interference by the state in the private sector.

Symbolic Implementation and Evaluation in Practice, 2005–2020

The implementation of the Code was quite a simple task, due to its design. Gender balance on corporate boards is the ultimate goal, but the Code does not regulate when this objective is to be achieved or according to what measures. In fact, if companies "strive" to increase the share of women board members, they can continue upon a "business as usual track." What is more, sanctions for non-compliance do not exist, except for the "bad reputation" or "ill will" that companies would risk and the negative publicity it could result in. A brief analysis of compliance to the Code in 2019 among a selection of companies shows that companies do publish reports on their websites, as part of their ordinary annual reporting systems, in which the proportion of women board members is mentioned. A table of the gender composition of the board is often included, although without any comments. The government, in turn, reports the results in the annual budget bill, often noting that there is little, though continuous, progress and sometimes also referring to gender quotas as a possible solution if the upward trend does not continue.

The implementation of the Code was affected to a great degree by at least three mechanisms. First, the government promoted the strategy of leading by example. Referring to the gender composition of state-owned company boards, on which the sub-goal of a minimum of 40% women had been reached in 2003 due to the implementation of government targets, it was recommended that the business sector do its part—in other words, implement company targets. It was argued that if gender balance could be achieved on the boards of state-owned companies (and on the boards of state agencies and in national commissions of inquiry), it could also be achieved on the boards of listed companies. As part of the Swedish model and Harpsund democracy, the state as well as the business sector must lead by example.

Second, threats of legislative corporate gender quotas continued to be utilized. For instance, by referring to the introduction of gender quotas in Norway and also to the 2012 EU Commission proposal for a 40% quota for the underrepresented sex in non-executive board member positions by 2020, the Minister of Finance Anders Borg (Moderate Party) in the right-center government (2006–2014) warned the Swedish business sector that legislative corporate gender quotas would be introduced, either by the government or through an EU directive, unless more equal representation of women and men on company boards was achieved. Threats of legislative corporate gender quotas were close to being realized when there was a change of government, and Prime Minister Stefan Löfven (Social Democratic Party) for the Social Democratic Party and Green Party minority government (2014–2018), announced in 2014 that corporate gender quotas were to be adopted if the representation of women on company boards did not reach 40% by the end of 2016. A legislative proposal was even prepared within the government offices, which was based on the 2006 proposal (Ds, 2016:32). This shows that the party in government matters in Sweden as pertains to promoting corporate gender quotas.

Third, name-and-shame strategies were used by private non-profit organizations to induce companies to improve the number of women board members. The Allbright Foundation, for instance, published reports on an annual basis in which companies with an equal gender distribution were placed on a "green list," companies that had made progress but not yet reached equal gender representation were placed on a "yellow list," and companies with no women board members were placed on a "red list." Following the name-and-shame strategy, companies on the green lists were praised and celebrated for their work ("evidently worth investing in for career-driven women"), while companies on the red lists should be boycotted (Allbright Foundation, 2017, p. 6). Consumer politics were highlighted as a way forward, and male-dominated companies were to be "ditched" (Ibid, p. 2). It was argued that if the rhetoric about gender equality was followed by action, gender equality would be achieved. Therefore, "inequality seems to be the best friend of hypocrisy" (Allbright Foundation, 2017, p. 2). According to an interview with a staff member at Allbright, the method of "black listing" companies can drive change, influencing decision-makers in the business sector to work consciously and purposefully to increase the proportion of women in senior positions (Interview 1). However, an interview with a board member of a listed company in the IT sector stated that gender balance on business management teams and company boards has never become a subject for discussion (Interview 2).

In order to evaluate progress in terms of women's representation in leadership positions in the corporate sector, including the gender composition of private company boards, the right/center government, and Minister for Gender Equality, Nyamko Sabuni (Liberal Party), commissioned a national inquiry in 2011, the Delegation on Gender Equality in Working Life. In one of the many research reports from the inquiry, it was noted that there was increased awareness on the matter of gender balance in leadership positions in the corporate sector, but processes of change were slow (SOU, 2014:80). According to the study, which was conducted by the well-known scholar Professor Anna Wahl and her team, the gender gap in leadership positions had decreased over the past ten years, 2004–2014, but male dominance persisted. For instance, company boards were comprised of 23% women and 77% men in 2014, compared to 17% women and 83% men in 2004, and 33% of private company boards were comprised only of men, compared to 42% in 2004. Hence, despite the massive public attention over the past ten years, a third of the private company boards were comprised solely of men. Nonetheless, the reduced gender gap was explained as the result of both structural changes in the labor market and attitudinal changes (SOU, 2014:80). Increased privatization of public sector tasks, including women-dominated professions such as health care, childcare, and education, had contributed to higher levels of women in leadership positions and on boards within these fields. Increased knowledge among business leaders on gender equality as well as on gendered power structures, organized efforts for gender equality within companies, and the framing of gender equality as a matter of profit and economic growth had also affected gender distribution in a positive way (SOU, 2014:80).

Assessing Outcomes: Medium Policy Empowerment and Gender Accommodation

Medium Policy Empowerment

In terms of direct participation, few women were involved in the adoption and implementation of the Code. Since this was the result of the corporate sector itself, it mainly involved male business leaders not wanting legislative gender quotas on company boards to be introduced. Ministers for Gender Equality in the right-center government 2006–2014 noted progress and were passively engaged in the implementation process as part of the leading by example strategy. Amanda Lundeteg, the outspoken CEO of the Allbright Foundation, was actively involved, exposing top performers and laggards by utilizing the name-and-shame strategy. As the front figure for the Allbright Foundation, she noted that "Anders" or "Johan" were the most common names among CEOs, arguing that candidate selection was permeated by mechanisms of homosociality, in other words, men selectors selecting other men with similar backgrounds. In harsh words, she proposed that "sooner or later discriminatory fossils must die too" (Allbright Foundation, 2017, p. 2). Additional measures were introduced by Gender Equality Ministers, such as national commissions of inquiry, and male ministers threatened to adopt legislative gender quotas if the business sector did not show results.

However, when it comes to the placement of the topic of male dominance in the business sector on the political and corporate agenda, Gender Equality Ministers—both women and men—were instrumental. They framed the issue as a problem in need of an urgent solution. Margareta Winberg, in particular, was a key actor, both descriptively and substantively, by threatening the business community with the adoption of legislative corporate gender quotas if no results were seen, and by introducing rules for gender balance in state-owned companies. Female scholars were indirectly represented both descriptively and substantively by presenting analyses of the (lack of) progress made and proposals for change. Women in the business sector were generally absent from the process, as were the women's organizations. In general, women's representation on company boards was not a top priority for the women's organizations, based on the argument that a focus on a few privileged women should not be prioritized at the expense of a focus on real problems, such as men's violence against women (Freidenvall, 2018). Hence, the descriptive and substantive empowerment of women in the policy adoption and implementation process can be described as medium (low for Code; high for agenda setting, production, and dissemination of knowledge and adoption of rules for state-owned companies).

Direct Impacts: Increase in Women's Presence but with Little Change in Power

To what extent was the problem of the skewed gender composition of company boards solved in accordance with the goals of the Code as defined in its original statement?

As shown in Figure 5.1, the proportion of women on the boards of private companies increased slowly, but gradually, from 1% in 1993 to 34% in 2020. While this is a noteworthy result that may be classified as a medium to high positive impact, it differs markedly from the gendered composition of state-owned companies, where the proportion of women increased from 31% in 1991 to 48% in 2020. In contrast to the minimum representation (40%) of women and men on the boards of state-owned companies that was achieved immediately upon the adoption of the 1999 rule, male dominance on the boards of private companies persists.

The difference between the two types of companies is ever more profound if one considers the gender composition of chairpersons and CEOs. In 2020, the proportion of female chairpersons on private company boards was 9%, as compared to 91% men. Among corporate CEOs, 10% were women, as compared to 90% men. The corresponding figures for the state-owned boards are 51% female

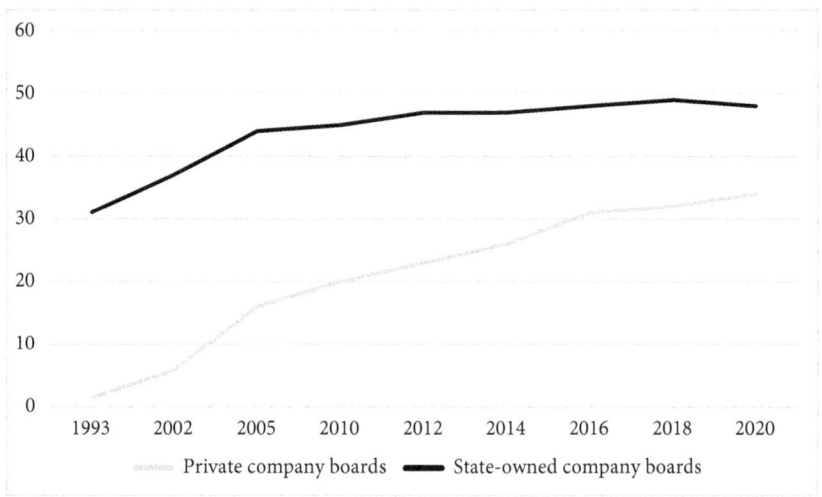

Fig. 5.1 Percentage Share of Women on Private (Listed) and State-owned Company Boards in Sweden, 1993–2020

chairpersons and 42% female CEOs. In addition, there is a significant difference between the public and private sectors when it comes to leadership positions in general. Unsurprisingly, the gender distribution in leadership positions is more gender equal in the public sector, particularly within the state, than in the private sector. In 2019, the state sector was comprised of 50% women and 50% men in leadership positions, while the private sector was comprised of 33% women and 67% men (SCB, 2020). However, leadership positions within the public sector at the municipal level and county level are women-dominated (more than 70% of leaders at these levels are women).

Although developments within state-owned companies are more positive than for private companies, threats of legislation seem to be an effective tool. As a response to these threats, the proportion of women on the boards of listed companies tripled (from 6% to 18%) from 2002 to 2006 (Nilsson, 2009; Bohman, Bygren, and Edling, 2012) and from 18% to 26% from 2006 to 2014. In 2016, after the renewed threat by Prime Minister Löfven (Social Democratic Party), the share of women increased to 32%. However, since the 40% threshold was not reached, the government was about to submit its legislative proposal for corporate gender quotas. However, it was stopped short when the Parliament and its Standing Committee on Civil Affairs, while dealing with a series of private member motions on legislative corporate gender quotas, called in January 2017 for gender balance on corporate boards to be achieved in other ways than through legislative measures (Committee Report 2016/17:6). With this parliamentary decision, legislative corporate gender quotas became a dead issue, given the situation with a minority government. The many twists and turns around legislative corporate gender quotas show that party politics matters.

Indirect Impact: Gender Norms of the Gatekeepers

To what extent did the framing on the part of gatekeepers of gender roles change? According to the 2014 inquiry, which is based on a series of interviews with business leaders (women, men, young people, and gender equality profession als), increased awareness and criticisms of gaps in gender-equal representation within the business sector can be noted. The views on the problem of unequal dis tribution of women and men in leadership positions of the interviewed groups are summarized in Table 5.3.

According to the gender equality professionals (recruited by companies to work on gender equality), the business community regards women business leaders as deficient, lacking the necessary resources to advance to leadership positions. In particular, it is claimed that women business leaders are affected by the so-called life puzzle, having problems in juggling their work-life balance. What is new, according to the gender equality professionals, is that the business sector

Table 5.3 Perspectives on the Problem of Unequal Distribution of Women and Men in Leadership Positions, 2013

The corporate sector[a]	Gender equality professionals	Men business leaders	Women business leaders	Young business leaders
Women's lack of resources (competence, will, and time due to child rearing)	Unequal distribution of power	Structures exist	Structures exist	There is no problem any longer
The brand of the company will be damaged	Men are afraid of or unwilling to yield power	Men select men	Men select men	Homogeneous groups are unprofessional due to a lack of different perspectives
—	Women are not aware of or lack strategies to promote equal representation	The timetable for careers in business life does not fit women	Lack of support for women	—
—	Women are faced with resistance and do not endure	Women are unnecessarily shy	Working life conditions	—
—	—	—	Women's choices in life differ from men's choices	—

Source: SOU 2014:80, p. 127. [a] According to gender equality professionals.

itself perceives male dominance in leadership positions to be outdated, backward-looking, and unfashionable. However, in the views of gender equality professionals themselves, power is unequally distributed between the sexes, and men, in general, are afraid of yielding power to women. Women business leaders do not lack resources, but they lack an awareness of the structures that impede them, and when faced with resistance, they lack the motivation to continue.

Men business leaders claim that there are indeed structures that prevent women from competing on equal terms with men. They also argue that there is a strong tendency in the business sector to select people that look like themselves. However, while they perceive women as equally competent as men, they argue that women many times do not promote themselves, at least not to the same extent as many men. Women business leaders articulate criticism of impeding structures and male dominance in the sector. In line with theories of homosociality (e.g.,

Holgersson, 2003), they believe that men select men that resemble themselves in terms of background, residence, education, and so forth. Women business leaders also claim that they are forced to adapt to challenging working life conditions in order to succeed and that they experience problems of reconciling work and family life. However, some of them state that they have been favored by being the lone woman and that male dominance in leadership positions is the result of individual choice.

Young business leaders deviate to quite an extent from more senior ones. In their view, unequal representation of women and men in leadership positions is not a problem. Recruitment to top management positions has nothing to do with gender; it is a matter of individual competence and choice. Some of them also claim that gender imbalance in leadership positions is part of history that will disappear in due course. Gender equality efforts are also perceived as something unnecessary, even unfair. To the extent that unequal representation is framed as a problem, it is claimed that homogenous groups lack important perspectives and that diversity, particularly in terms of age and ethnicity, will contribute to achieving dynamic corporate boards.

Based on this finding, it is difficult to claim that substantial gender transformation has taken place. Previous research corroborates this finding, demonstrating that young men in the business sector expect a career, while young women hope to receive one (e.g., Linghag, 2009). Studies have also shown that many young women business leaders are described as being "diligent/good girls" (In Swedish, *duktig flicka*)—they are diligent, well prepared, and work hard. In the business sector, however, this trait is not interpreted as competence but as an expression of insecurity (e.g., Regnö, 2013). It implies that a competent business leader does not have to "overwork" as a leader; he can be unprepared and a bit sloppy without risking his reputation. Thus, to be diligent is not seen as an advantage for women but almost as something to be ashamed of (Ibid).

Positive changes have, though, taken place. For instance, more women business leaders are increasingly critical of the unequal representation of women and men on company boards and in leadership positions (SOU, 2014:80). They argue that there is no longer any need to educate women or to show candidate selection committees that there are competent women; if the business sector wanted more women on company boards or in top management positions, they would just recruit them. Thus, the problem, according to them, is demand, not supply. To redress the situation, men need to change. Moreover, as another example of change, men business leaders more actively promote gender equality today as compared to the 1990s (SOU, 2014:80). Men in top management positions not only (passively) support gender equality but also actively promote gender equality efforts. The need to recruit more women board members and to achieve more mixed management groups are no longer deviant opinions but rather part of a company's image and

marketing strategy for recruiting and retaining competent personnel and for sell-
ing its products or services. Also, the framing of men as part of the problem, but
also as a part of the solution, has been increasingly highlighted. The picture of the
business leader himself as an actor in favor of gender equality efforts is more man-
ifest in 2014 than twenty years ago (SOU 2014:80, p. 134). On the basis of all of
these studies that highlight both structural and individual factors, it may be concluded that gender transformation at the gate-keeper level has been achieved at a
medium/positive level.

Gender Transformation at the Societal Level

To what extent have social attitudes about gender roles and equality in this particular area changed? Equal representation of women and men in decision-making
positions, including in the business sector, is increasingly seen in Swedish society
as something right, fair, and natural. Although the descriptive goal of gender-
balanced company boards has not been achieved and many gaps and challenges
remain, not least of all sexual harassment as shown by the #MeToo movement,
the idea of gender balance has been more or less established as an axiom at the
normative level. It has even been argued that the large #MeToo wave in Sweden
occurred "not despite, but because of" gender equality—in other words, because
of certain norms on equality that have been established in Swedish society. Research has shown that citizens' endorsement of quotas is low in countries with
high levels of formal gender equality, and support is higher in countries in which
interventionist policies are widely accepted (Möhring and Teney, 2019). The discourse in Sweden seems to fit into that analysis. Today, the critical discussion on
the gender composition of company boards does not revolve around IF but HOW
this is to be achieved, particularly since there is still resistance to legislative measures, including gender quotas—or intervention in the autonomy of corporations
and their entrepreneurial freedom. Gender transformation at the societal level can,
therefore, be classified as medium to high positive.

Taken together, the level of gender transformation in Sweden may be classified
as accommodation; it has taken place, at least to some extent. This having been
said, direct changes in the composition of corporate boards and women's actual
power in the corporate world as well as indirect changes in gendered norms are
complex; they have been slow, and the pattern of gender accommodation presents
many challenges to the achievement of meaningful equality. In general, views on
gender relations among decision-makers (gatekeeper level) have shifted in a slow
but positive way over time. The lack of awareness among young business leaders of gender equality gaps, however, signals that gender-equal boards will not be
achieved automatically as time goes by. The problem will most likely linger on.

Conclusion

This chapter has studied the adoption and implementation of a corporate governance code in Sweden. It shows that this self-regulatory solution was introduced by the corporate sector itself in order to avoid legislation on corporate gender quotas. The implementation of the Code has resulted in a gradual, but slow, increase in women on corporate boards, while not leading to gender-balanced boards. Gendered norms of equal representation of women and men in leadership positions in the economic sector have changed as well, though challenges remain, particularly when it comes to the number of women chairpersons and CEOs. What is more, the lack of awareness of gender equality gaps among young business leaders indicates that automatic and linear progress is not a given. In addition, the chapter clearly shows that party politics matter. Right and center parties supported the adoption and implementation of the Code in 2005 but rejected legislative corporate gender quotas. The most serious attempt on the part of the Social Democratic Party to adopt legislative corporate gender quotas failed due to a change of government in 2006 in favor of the right/center parties. Once in office in 2014, the pro-quota Social Democratic/Green Party government could not proceed with a legislative proposal on gender quotas due to it being a minority government.

In general, the implementation of the Code has promoted women's descriptive representation in the business sector and empowered women. Although increased awareness of the problem of women's underrepresentation on company boards has been achieved, even among business leaders, substantial gender transformation has not been achieved. This discursive change can to some extent be regarded as a result of the Code and practice in the implementation. However, these developments are complex, particularly when considering the motive behind the adoption of the Code—to avoid legislative corporate gender quotas. There is indeed a need for more studies on gender-equal representation on company boards, especially studies that focus on resistance among young business leaders to gender equality and gender-balanced decision-making.

References

Agnblad, Jonas, Erik Berglöf, Peter Högfeldt, and Helena Svancar (2001) "Ownership and Control in Sweden: Strong Owners, Weak Minorities, and Social Control." in Fabricio Barca and Marco Becht (eds) *The Control of Corporate Europe*. Oxford: Oxford University Press, 228–259.

Allbright (2017) *VD-kvinnor väljer jämställdhet. Allbrightrapporten 2017*. Stockholm: Allbright.

Bergqvist, Christina, Anette Borchorst, Ann-Dorte Christensen, Viveca Ramstedt-Silén, Nina C. Rauum, and Auður Styrkársdóttir (1999) *Equal Democracies? Gender and Politics in the Nordic Countries*. Oslo: Scandinavian University Press.

Bohman, Love, Magnus Bygren, and Christofer Edling (2012) "Surge under Threat: The Rapid Increase of Women on Swedish Boards of Directors," in Colette Fagan, Marie González Menèndez, and Silvia Gómez Ansón (eds) *Women on Corporate Boards and in Top Management: European Trends and Policy.* Houndmills, Basingstoke: Palgrave Macmillan, 91–108.

Borchorst, Anette, Lenita Freidenvall, Johanna Kantola, Liza Reisel, and Mari Teigen (2011) "Institutionalizing Intersectionality in the Nordic Countries: Anti-Discrimination and Equality in Denmark, Finland, Norway, and Sweden," in Andrea Krizsan, Hege Skjeie, and Judith Squires (eds) *Institutionalizing Intersectionality: The Changing Nature of European Equality Regimes.* Houndmills, Basingstoke: Palgrave Macmillan, pp 59–88.

Committee Report 2016/17:CU6. Associationsrätt. Swedish Parliament.

Ds 2006:11. *Könsfördelningen i bolagsstyrelser.* Stockholm: Justitiedepartementet.

Ds 2016:35. *Jämn könsfördelning i bolagsstyrelser.* Stockholm: Justitiedepartementet.

EIGE (2017) *Gender Equality Index 2017. Measuring Gender Equality in the European Union 2005–2015.* Vilnius: EIGE.

Fredell, Åsa (2005) "Lagstadgad könskvotering i bolagsstyrelser? En analys av den svenska mediadebatten," *Working Paper Series, No 2.* The Research program on gender quotas. Stockholm: Stockholm University.

Freidenvall, Lenita (2015) "Gender Quotas Spill-over in Sweden. From Politics to Business?" *EUI Working Paper LAW* 2015/28. Florence: European University Institute, Department of Law.

Freidenvall, Lenita (2018) "Gender Equality without Gender Quotas in Sweden," in Éléonore Lépinard and Ruth Rubio Marín (eds) *Transforming Gender Equality: The Irresistible Rise of Gender Quotas in Europe.* Cambridge: Cambridge University Press, 366–399.

Freidenvall, Lenita (2021) *Equal Representation without Legislation: Gender, Institutions and Power in Sweden.* New York: Rowman & Littlefield.

Freidenvall, Lenita and Hanna Hallonsten (2013) "Why Not Corporate Gender Quotas in Sweden?" *Representation,* 49 (4), 467–485.

Government Bill (1987) Prop. 1987/88:105. *Om jämställdhetspolitiken inför 1990-talet.*

Government Communication (1999) Skr. 1999/2000:24 *Jämställdhetspolitiken inför 2000-talet.*

Heidenrich, Vibeke (2012) "Why Gender Quotas on Company Boards in Norway— and not in Sweden?" in Fredrik Engelstad and Mari Teigen (eds) *Firms, Boards, and Gender Quotas in Comparative Perspectives* (Comparative Social Research) 29, 147–183.

Hernes, Helga (1987) *Welfare State and Woman Power. Essays in State Feminism.* Oslo: Norwegian University Press.

Holgersson, Charlotte (2003) *Rekrytering av företagsledare: en studie i homosocialitet.* Stockholm: EFI vid Handelshögskolan i Stockholm.

Kollegiet för svensk bolagsstyrning (2016) *The Swedish Code of Corporate Governance 2005.*

Linghag, Sophie (2009) *Från medarbetare till chef: kö och makt i chefsförsörjning och karriär.* Stockholm. Kungliga Tekniska Högskolan.

Möhring, Katja and Teney, Celine (2019) "Equality prescribed? Contextual determinants of citizens' support for gender boardroom quotas across Europe," *Comparative European Politics,* November 4, 2019, https://link.springer.com/article/10.1057/s41295-019-00199-w#citeas (Accessed December 16, 2021).

Nilsson, Tomas (2009) "Kön och makt i svenskt näringsliv," in Kirsti Niskanen and Anita Nyberg (eds) *Kön och Makt i Norden del 1 Landsrapporter*. Oslo: Nordic Council of Ministers, 289–320.

Niskanen, Kirsti (ed) (2009) *Gender and Power in the Nordic Countries. With Focus on Politics and Business*. NIKK Publications 2011:1. Oslo: the Nordic Gender Institute.

OECD (2017) *The Pursuit of Gender Equality. An Uphill Battle*, http://www.oecd.org/gender/the-pursuit-of-gender-equality-9789264281318-en.htm (Accessed December 16, 2021).

Regnö, Klara (2013) *Det osynliggjorda ledarskapet. Kvinnliga chefer i majoritet*. Stockholm: Kungliga Tekniska högskolan.

Sainsbury, Diane (1996) *Gender, Equality and Welfare States*. Cambridge: Cambridge University Press.

SCB (2013) *Kvinnor och män i näringslivet 2013*. Örebro: Statistics Sweden.

SCB (2020) *På tal om kvinnor och män*. Örebro: Statistics Sweden.

SOU (1987:19) *Varannan damernas*. Stockholm: Fritzes.

SOU (1994:39) *Mäns föreställningar om kvinnor och chefskap*. Stockholm: Fritzes.

SOU (2003:16) *Mansdominans i förändring*. Stockholm: Fritzes.

SOU (2004:130) *Svensk kod för bolagsstyrning*. Stockholm: Justitiedepartementet.

SOU (2014:80) *Ökad medvetenhet men långsam förändring – om kvinnor och män på ledande position i svenskt näringsliv*. Stockholm: Fritzes.

Track 2. Piecemeal Approach: Self-Regulation by Default

6

Set to Fail?

Scattered Regulation Leaves the Glass Ceiling "Unbroken" in the USA

Season Hoard

Introduction

As recent as 2017, an OECD report on gender equality shows glass ceilings are "still unbroken" in the USA for women in politics, on corporate boards, and senior management (OECD, 2017, p. 177). The USA continues to underperform in women's representation on corporate boards compared to many postindustrial democracies, well below the OECD average. Rather than directly regulate corporate board composition, US policy takes a piecemeal approach that includes symbolic federal regulation focused on "diversity" reporting, but it allows corporations to adopt their own definitions of diversity, limited administrative oversight, sub-national level regulation that targets gender inequities on corporate boards in a handful of states, and scattered efforts by individual businesses to enhance women's presence at the top, which are mostly from investor pressure rather than any of the highly limited government initiated policies. This multi-level patchwork of policies has unfolded since 2008 in the highly decentralized context of the US federal system, with most business regulation occurring at the state level, and federal law providing only minimum standards. It relies on numerous factors including geographic location, state of incorporation, employment sector, and investor activism. When federal government policies addressed corporate board diversity beginning in 2008 through disclosure policies, the regulations were limited and vague, allowing for self-assessment of progress, and either not defining diversity or allowing corporations to add their own broader interpretations. This has led to corporations co-opting definitions of diversity to serve their purposes. Thus, the transformative potential of these policies is limited as they were never designed to be truly transformative. Policy outcomes in the USA have, therefore, been at best incremental with limited progress in women's presence on corporate boards, with gender-biased norms still dominating the corporate world.

Season Hoard, *Set to Fail?* In: *Gender Equality and Policy Implementation in the Corporate World.* Edited by Isabelle Engeli and Amy G. Mazur, Oxford University Press. © Oxford University Press (2022).
DOI: 10.1093/oso/9780198865216.003.0006

This chapter maps out this fragmented terrain by first presenting in more detail the highly decentralized context for limited business regulation and the promotion of corporate gender equality in the USA. The next section covers agenda-setting, adoption, and administrative outputs for the two pieces of federal regulation on reporting: an obscure and poorly followed rule put into place by the Securities Exchange Commission in 2009 and an equally unknown regulation in Section 342 of the Dodd-Frank Wall Street Reform and Consumer Protection Act in 2010 for government agencies only regulating the financial business sector. The last two sections of the chapter cover the practice of implementation and evaluation and then the policy outcomes for all parts of the policy patchwork.

Gender Equality in the Corporate World

Progress in gender equality in the corporate world has been comparatively slow in the USA due to limited corporate regulation, especially of private businesses, and decentralization of corporate policy, which has led to powerful corporations with much autonomy. The USA's one-tier corporate board structure emphasizes independence and shareholder primacy (Ho, 2010, p. 59). As of 2015, there were approximately 4.6 million corporations in the USA, including 2.9 million S corporations, one million C corporations, and 0.7 million partnerships (Keightley and Hughes, 2018, p. 3). Most corporations are private and thus not subject to many of the government regulations required of public corporations (companies that have shares publicly traded on a stock exchange). As of 2017, there were approximately 3,600 companies on the US stock exchange (Editorial Board, 2018). Corporate regulation in the USA is highly decentralized with most of the regulation occurring at the state- and territory-level with federal law providing only minimum standards. While incorporation is possible in any state, more than two-thirds of Fortune 500 firms are incorporated in Delaware due to its corporate-friendly laws (Deleware Division of Corporations, 2018). Moreover, given that businesses can incorporate in the state of their choice, and a company may be headquartered in one state but subject to the regulations of another, the implementation process is fragmented and confusing. As a result, the push for more women on corporate boards has mostly come from investor pressure and individual business initiatives rather than government regulation. More generally, the autonomy of private business is sacrosanct in the USA, and business regulation has been highly controversial and circumscribed, particularly with regards to gender equality (Mazur, 2002). The primacy of private businesses and big corporations has been indeed a major limitation to policies that seek to promote gender equality in the workplace (Parry and McBride, 2016). For example, the USA remains the only OECD country that has no nationally mandated maternity leave policy, and only five states and the

District of Columbia have instituted paid family leave (Brainerd, 2017). Instead, businesses may offer paid paternal-leave policies as a "perk" to aid in business recruitment and retention which produces disparity in maternity leave.

Despite women constituting over 45% of the workforce since the 1990s, women's share of corporate board seats, called the Board of Directors in the USA, has remained low. Private companies do not have to report their board composition; thus, board diversity data that is reported tends to be from public companies, such as those on the S&P 500 (a stock market index of the 500 largest publicly traded US companies), and the largest private companies that are included on lists, such as the Fortune 100 (100 largest US private and public companies by revenue) and the Fortune 500 (500 largest US private and public companies by revenue). In 1999, only 11.1% of corporate board seats on the Fortune 500 were held by women (Arfken et al, 2004, p. 181). By 2010, women comprised only 15.7% of total board seats. As shown in Table 6.1, the rate of growth for CEOs of Fortune 500 has been even slower, with only one CEO in 1996, and twelve in 2011 (2.4%) (Lipman, 2011). Progress increased beginning in the early 2000s with the percentage of women on corporate boards for Fortune 500 companies reaching 19.7% by 2015 (2020 Women on Boards, 2016, p. 4) and 22.5% of total board seats by 2018 (Deloitte and Alliance for Board Diversity, 2019, p. 17).

Progress also depends on the type of companies being examined. Young companies have fewer women on their board. The top 25 IPOs (Initial Public Offering) had only 9.2% of their board seats filled by women in 2017 (2020 Women on Boards, 2018, p. 3). In contrast, the Fortune 100 had 25.7% women on their boards in 2018, while the Fortune 1000 had 22% (2020 Women on Boards, 2018, p. 4). Table 6.1 shows that progress has also been slow for the S&P 500, but in 2020, women held 28% of board seats, and in 2021 this increased to 30%, an all-time high, and all S&P companies had at least one woman on their board. In fact, in 2020, 46% of new directors for the S&P 500 were women (an increase from 40% in 2018) and 43% of new directors were women in 2021 (Spencer Stuart, 2019, p. 1; Spencer Stuart, 2021, p. 4). Women constituted only 26.5% of chief executives and only 6.4% of CEO positions at S&P 500 companies in 2019 (Catalyst, 2019b). The slow pace of women's progress on corporate boards is multi-causal in the USA, however, the low rate of corporate board renewal—S&P companies average less than one new director on the board of directors per year (Spencer Stuart, 2018, p. 2)—is certainly an important impediment. While trends for the Fortune 500 and S&P 500 show a gradual but steady increase over time, it is important to note that a study of the 200 largest venture-backed private companies found 60% of these companies had no women on their board in 2019 (Teare, 2019) and 49% had no woman on their board in 2020 (Shepherd and Teare, 2021). As most corporations are private, this shows that progress in women's total share of board seats in the USA is much slower than reported metrics suggest.

Table 6.1 Percentage Share of Women on Boards in Fortune 500 and S&P 500 in the USA, 2000–2020

	USA				
	Fortune 500		S&P 500		
	Board members	CEOs	Board members	CEOs	Executives/ Senior managers
2000	11.7	0.4	—	—	—
2001	12.4	0.8	—	—	—
2002	12.4	1.2	—	—	—
2003	13.6	1.4	—	—	—
2004	13.6	1.6	16.0	2.2	—
2005	14.7	1.8	—	2.2	—
2006	14.6	2.0	—	3.4	—
2007	14.8	2.4	—	3.4	—
2008	15.2	2.4	—	3.4	—
2009	15.2	3.0	16.0	3.8	—
2010	15.7	3.0	—	3.8	—
2011	16.1	2.4	16.4	4.4	—
2012	16.6	3.6	17.1	5.0	—
2013	16.9	4.0	18.0	5.4	—
2014	—	4.8	19.0	6.4	—
2015	—	4.8	19.2	6.6	25.1
2016	20.2	4.2	19.9	6.4	25.1
2017	22.2	6.4	21.2	7.0	26.5
2018	22.5	4.8	24.0	6.2	26.5
2019	22.5	6.6	26.0	6.4	26.5
2020	26.5	7.4	28.0	6.4	26.5
2021			30%	6%	–

Sources: Pew Research Center (2018); Ebrahimji (2020); Catalyst (2015); Catalyst (2016); Catalyst (2017); Catalyst (2018); Catalyst (2019b); Catalyst (2020); Ghosh (2019); Spencer Stuart (2019), Spencer Stuart (2020, p. 3), Spencer Stuart (2021, p. 4).

Agenda-setting, Adoption, and Policy Outputs in Highly Symbolic Federal Regulation

Getting Political and Corporate Attention up to 2008: Business is Free to Self-regulate until Governments Respond to Crisis

Prior to the 2000 regulations, it was primarily individual businesses themselves who took any initiative on promoting women on boards. After the adoption of the Civil Rights Act of 1964, corporations began to focus more on overall diversity, although corporations have co-opted the diversity discourse to appear supportive of racial and gender equality while largely avoiding substantive change (Embrick,

2011, p. 544). In the late 1990s and early 2000s, individual companies started appointing more women to their boards due to investor pressure, media attention, and employee recruitment and retention. For instance, the board of General Motors (GM), a publicly traded company (since 2010) on both the S&P 500 and the Fortune 100, had over 50% women in 2019. However, in 2000, only 6.4% of their corporate officers were women (Williams, 2000). In less than 20 years, GM went from a laggard in women's representation on their boards, to a leader, implementing several policies in the 1990s and 2000s to increase the number of women and minority executive officers, including mentoring and networking programs, diversity training, and sexual harassment training. A major reason for these initiatives was due to losing promising employees, many women, who sought opportunities elsewhere after failing to move up in the organization (Williams, 2000).

Corporate scandals were instrumental in placing corporate governance and diversity issues on the federal agenda in the early 2000s. The Enron Scandal resulted in the Sarbanes-Oxley Act of 2002 (SOX) which increased investor protections and transparency, created more independent corporate boards, impacted the type of directors sought (those with financial expertise), and led to a reduction in the number of CEOs serving on multiple boards (Spencer Stuart, 2012). While not focused on diversity, research suggests that SOX has increased board diversity (Upadhyay and Triana, 2020), especially in the wake of higher board turnover after SOX was initially adopted, which created more opportunities for women (Dalton and Dalton, 2010, p. 264). Arguments in support of Sarbanes-Oxley were framed as an issue of transparency, and many subsequent attempts to intervene in corporate governance at the federal level, including the Securities and Exchange Commission (SEC) diversity disclosure discussed in this chapter, have been framed similarly. Corporate board diversity again gained federal government attention due to the 2008 global economic crisis. The financial crisis was partially blamed on excessive risk-taking of global financial institutions enabled by an unregulated shadow banking system with little oversight or transparency. Barack Obama's platform included several planks to address the housing and banking crisis to increase regulation and transparency, and his election in 2008 and a democratic majority in both Houses of Congress paved the way for new policies that still allowed extensive self-regulation on the part of corporations in the composition of their boards. These policies, as adopted and implemented, have had little impact on corporate board composition due to their vagueness and the unwillingness of federal actors to truly hold companies accountable for diversity. Instead, relying on investor pressure to achieve these goals.

While the causes of the eventual global crisis were indeed numerous, some were partially attributing the financial crisis to the lack of women on corporate boards, with some questioning whether the "Lehman Sisters" would have reduced the impact (Morris, 2009). By 2009, much media attention was on the women tasked with leading the financial recovery both within the USA and internationally. With this unprecedented attention to the issue of women on boards, the stage was set for two corporate diversity initiatives that were focused on diversity: SEC Item 407(c)(2)(vi) of Regulation SK and Section 342 of the Dodd-Frank Wall Street Reform and Consumer Protection Act of 2010. However, this attention did not transpose into a process that was open to groups speaking for women and gender equality in business with both regulations having little if any direct focus on addressing the underrepresentation of women on corporate boards.

The Decision-making Process: Women's Movement Organizations Ignored and Excluded

SEC Item 407(c)(2)(vi): Reporting Diversity Considerations With No Mention of Gender

Mary L. Shapiro, the Chair of the SEC, argued that the financial crisis was partially caused by a regulatory system that had failed investors, and more transparency was needed (Labaton, 2009). She embarked on an ambitious regulatory agenda that included several changes to reporting requirements to enhance transparency (US Securities and Exchange Commission, 2012). While Shapiro took the lead in developing and promoting many of the new reporting requirements, SEC Commissioner Luis Aguilar led the development of the rule requiring companies to report on how diversity is considered when selecting new board members. His argument for diversity-focused on better corporate governance and economic growth and referenced several studies showing that diversity was good for firm financial performance, and helped investors make better economic decisions (Aguilar, 2010). However, the focus remained on diversity with no specific attention to women's representation on board per se.

On July 10, 2009, the SEC proposed a series of amendments to its disclosure rules for publicly traded companies to increase transparency and promote "informed voting and investment decisions" (US Securities and Exchange Commission, 2009, p. 5). These disclosure rules included substantial revisions to the reporting process, including specifying diversity considerations when identifying director nominees. The SEC sought comment on whether they should require companies to provide diversity considerations of nominating committees when selecting board positions. Supporters of the disclosure argued that the rule would improve economic performance. Two groups that promoted gender equality in business, Catalyst and the Social Investment Forum noted the impact of diversity on corporate financial performance and recruitment and retention (US Securities and Exchange Commission, 2009, p. 38). For Catalyst, women's representation on corporate boards was important for the increased economic performance of corporations and that the current pace of change was too slow. The Forum for Executive Women also argued that diversity, especially gender diversity, was important for economic performance, and it enhanced corporate governance and decision-making.

Much of the response to the proposed diversity disclosure rules was positive, at least in terms of whether a diversity disclosure rule should exist. Only five comments opposed the adoption of a disclosure rule, these arguments ranged from concerns that the disclosure rules would not be helpful in that race and ethnicity should not be considered when selecting board members. While accepting that diversity disclosure was useful for investors, corporations preferred a more self-regulatory approach to maintain corporate independence in determining the composition of their boards, arguing that definitions of diversity, and how much information to provide should be left to individual corporations to determine. To put it bluntly, corporations mainly focused on making disclosures as least onerous for businesses as possible. For example, the Teachers Insurance and Annuity Association of America-College Retirement Equities Fund (TIAA-CREF) argued that diversity "should not be defined in the same way for all companies. Each company should consider factors based on its own business model and specific needs" (Choi, 2009, p. 1). NACCO Industries argued that diversity should not be disclosed on an individual basis as "such individual disclosure of qualifications, attributes and skills fails to recognize that a well-constructed board is a diverse collection of individuals bringing a variety of complementary skills and experiences to the boardroom" (Taylor, 2009, p. 1). Ultimately, the final disclosure rule was adopted by the SEC with little amendment. The proposals of the business sector which focused on allowing much leeway for corporations in diversity disclosure won over women's groups and organizations representing people of color. Based on feedback, the SEC adopted Item 407(c) of Regulation S-K (Item 407(c)(2)(vi)) but did not define diversity, allowing companies to determine their own definitions and conceptualizations. Thus, the final policy has limited power to achieve transformative change as it allows corporations to reframe diversity to avoid true change and highlights the unwillingness of the SEC to create a stronger policy with effective enforcement mechanisms. These rules went into effect on February 28, 2010.

Section 342 in 2010 Act: Consumer: Financial Regulatory Agencies Receive Administrative Authority to Oversee Gender Diversity

The Obama Administration also sought to reform the financial sector by proposing a series of reforms in July of 2009 that eventually became the Dodd-Frank Act. Members of the Congressional Black Caucus and the Congressional Hispanic Caucus worked on Section 342 to draft a rule requiring federal regulatory agencies to assess the diversity of women and minorities within their institutions and the companies they regulate (Backman, 2016). Representative Maxine Waters took the lead in making the case that part of the problem in the financial industry was a lack of women and minorities (Roby, 2015) and that Section 342 would correct the underrepresentation of women and people of color on Wall Street (Roose, 2010).

Arguments made in support of the new rule focused on the democratic legitimacy of financial institutions, and the pace of change within these institutions was too slow.

There was little debate or focus on this portion of the overall act while it was being crafted. Unlike for the SEC Item, no women's groups were consulted. The bill was adopted with very little revision from the initial proposal. In fact, Representative Waters was the only member to discuss Section 342, or diversity of women and minorities in the financial sector, during floor debates. The final bill, described more fully below, focused on representation in the financial sector and financial regulatory agencies, requiring regulatory agencies, federal reserve banks, and the Consumer Financial Protection Bureau to establish an Office of Minority and Women Inclusion (OMWI).

Policy Outputs: A Patchwork of Highly Symbolic Federal Regulations, State-level Regulation, and Limited Business Self-regulation

Following the adoption and implementation of these two highly symbolic federal regulations, a handful of states presented in Table 6.2, several corporations, and one regional investors' association directly took up the call for gender equality on corporate boards. A call that had been virtually ignored in both federal regulations. Here just the policy outputs at the federal level are discussed. The next two sections turn to the post-adoption practice and outcomes of this highly piecemeal and incremental approach.

Both regulations are very low in terms of overall policy coercion given that neither specifically makes mention of gender equality on corporate boards and the SEC Item does not require that gender even be mentioned in the required reports. Moreover, there are no stipulations of what should be included in the diversity reports, which are only required of publicly listed companies. Similarly, Section 324 of the 2010 Act has very low coercion and limited coverage to actually regulate the presence of women on corporate boards given that it only requires financial regulatory agencies to establish an OMWI, which is responsible for developing standards for 1) equal employment opportunity and diversity of agency workforce, 2) diversity and inclusion, particularly for minority and women-owned businesses in agency programs and contracts, and 3) assessing diversity policies of entities regulated by the agency. Each OMWI is required to submit annual reports to Congress on their activities and actions with a number of elements, including steps to seek diversity in terms of recruitment at universities that serve women and minority populations, recruitment at urban community job fairs, employment advertisements in magazines that serve minority populations, and women among others (Federal Reserve Bank of San Francisco, 2010, p. 2). Thus, the law only

Table 6.2 Policy Measures for Gender Equality on Corporate Boards in the USA

SELF-REGULATION

Individual corporations (examples)[a]
* 10 companies with 50% women or more (Amazon, American Water Works, Best Buy, Capri Holdings, CBS, General Motors, Omnicom Group, Progressive, Ulta Beauty, and Viacom).
* GM over 50% women purposive appointment and mentoring programs.
* Amazon: 30% of women on board in 2018.
* 24 Midwest companies adopt the "Rooney Rule."

STATE REGULATION

FEDERAL REGULATION	STATE REGULATION
SEC Item 407(c)(2)(vi) 2010 and 2019 * Publicly traded companies. * Companies to report diversity considerations for nominations of directors. No specific mention of gender. Begins in 2010. * 2019 Reform in SEC regulation makes the first mention of taking into account "demographic" characteristics in reporting. **Section 342 of Dodd-Frank Act 2010** * Financial regulatory agencies, financial sector. * Goal is to increase diversity in financial sector, create Offices of Minority and Women Inclusion (OMWIs) in financial regulatory agencies. * Annual reporting, standards required, no mechanism to ensure compliance.	**California: Women On Boards 2018** * Public companies with principal executive offices in California. *One woman on all boards by 2019; two women on boards with five members by 2021; three women on boards with six members by 2021. * Minimum of 40% women. * $100,000 for first violation; $300,000 for following violations. **Washington: Washington Business Corporation Act (WBCA)** *Public companies incorporated in Washington with some exceptions *Gender diverse board by January 1, 2022 (at least 25% of directors) *Reporting on an annual basis *No monetary consequences, must deliver an analysis and discussion of board diversity to shareholders if fail to meet. *Shareholders can sue company for remedy if fail to meet **Colorado 2017** * Resolution on increasing women on corporate boards. **Maryland 2019** * Businesses headquartered in state must disclose number of directors and female directors in annual reports (ten-year sunset provision). **Illinois 2019** * Board diversity disclosure for publicly held companies with principal executive office in state; minimum-level requirements for female directors. **New York 2020** * Conduct study on board diversity; to do study requires all companies doing business in New York must report number of directors and total female directors.

Sources: Oliver and Norris (2022); Chang and Milkman (2020, pp. 3–4); Federal Reserve Bank of San Francisco (2010, p. 2); Hatcher and Latham (2020); McCarthy (2019); Molla (2018); US Securities and Exchange Commission (2009, p. 39)

covers the administration of the financial sector, does not specifically mention gender equality and boards, and has no real oversight process for the newly created agencies. While the two regulations do not preclude treatment of gender equality on boards, without any formal authority to promote and police the goal, the new regulations have been since the get-go empty containers.

Implementation and Evaluation in Practice at Different Levels: Limited Descriptive and Substantive Empowerment of Women

With these severe limitations, it is no surprise that the post-adoption practices have not produced effective policy responses to gender inequities on boards. The regulatory gap at the federal level has left states and businesses to go it alone and self-regulate and set the stage for certain states to follow the lead of empty policy outputs by considering and adopting similar disclosure laws at the state level. The implementation of the federal regulations and the state and business level policy responses shows the same disappointing pattern in practice with the participation of some actors who promote gender equality and some minor developments in better addressing gender inequality on boards in the implementation and evaluation.

Practice in Federal Regulation

SEC Item 407(c)(2)(vi)

As the item focuses on reporting requirements to receive trading securities from the SEC, implementation and evaluation have been handled by the SEC. The SEC has the sole ability to formally sanction non-compliance with the new reporting rules. Once comments on the initial proposed rule were concluded in the adoption stage, descriptive and substantive empowerment has been limited; women's movement actors and organizations (as well as other organizations) have not directly participated in the implementation or evaluation of the new reporting requirements. However, government actors outside of the SEC, including the House of Representatives and New York State, have evaluated diversity statements provided by companies.

Implementation was swift and initial evaluation was conducted by the SEC to ensure that companies were compliant with the new rule, requiring further written comment or additional data from only a few companies who were found not in compliance by the SEC. Commissioner Aguilar has suggested that implementation failed to meet the goals of adoption, stating that if some companies did well in addressing the rules, providing information "in the spirit of the SEC rule," many did not provide much detail in their diversity disclosures (Aguilar, 2010). In addition, an independent study conducted by Dhir (2015) found that less than 10% of the Fortune 100 firms sampled received a request from the SEC for further comment in the first year of implementation, and no further requests for clarification or comment were made in 2011 to 2015 (Dhir, 2015, p. 206).

Some government evaluation outside of the SEC has led to clarification in the disclosure rule. In 2018, the US House of Representatives Subcommittee on Capital Markets, Securities, and Investment of the Committee on Financial Services conducted an oversight hearing on the SEC's Division of Corporation Finance. At this hearing, William Hinman, the Director of the Division of Corporation Finance of the SEC, was asked to address concerns that the SEC diversity rule does not provide robust disclosures for effective evaluation by investors. Specifically, Mr. Hinman was asked whether diversity disclosures have been adequate and whether the Division of Corporation Finance would eventually provide a public recommendation to the SEC on whether it should adopt proposals to improve the rule. Mr. Hinman noted the criticism the policy has received and that they would put the public recommendation to the SEC on the agenda (Hinman, 2018). This suggests that diversity disclosure provided enough information on women on corporate boards for investors to evaluate companies, but disclosure of other diversity considerations is lacking. However, independent analysis of disclosures found that only half of the proxy statements of the Fortune 100 firms referenced gender in their consideration of diversity, and race and ethnicity were referenced in similar amounts (Dhir, 2015, p. 191). The most referenced category in diversity considerations of corporations was the diversity of experience. This highlights the issue with allowing corporations to define diversity; they co-opt diversity to serve their own purpose while avoiding transformative change. As the goal of women's groups was to increase the number of women on corporate boards, the fact that most corporations listed experience as their primary consideration limits the ability of the diversity disclosure to substantively empower women over time.

In 2019, due to pressure from investor groups, some states, and the House of Representatives oversight hearing, some progress was made when the SEC provided clarification on the diversity disclosure rules through Compliance and Disclosure Interpretations (c&DIs). This opened the door for a focus on promoting women as candidates for open positions on boards through "how the company considers self-identified diversity attributes of nominees as well as any other qualifications in its diversity policy takes into account, such as diverse work experiences, military service, or socio-economic or demographic characteristics" (US Securities and Exchange Commission, 2020). It is unclear how this update will impact diversity disclosures in the future, and it does not actually mention gender; thus, this is a very minor and incremental shift in highly limited policy.

Section 342 of the Dodd-Frank Act

In contrast to the decision-making process where Section 342 received little attention, the implementation of the Dodd-Frank Act had more descriptive empowerment of women and women's organizations, but substantive empowerment was lacking. Section 342 was to be implemented by the federal bureaucracies who were tasked with setting up an OMWI and developing their own standards for assessing diversity. While the regulatory agencies are required to submit yearly reports, there are no sanctions in Section 342 to ensure compliance. There are also limited mechanisms for evaluation. Congress monitors whether the annual reports are being submitted and published by OMWI directors, but evaluation of the diversity standards within the financial industry is left to the federal regulatory agencies who have not evaluated these policies. As with the SEC Item, the evaluation of OMWIs has been mostly conducted by outside actors and relatively few at that, which severely limits the ability of this policy to meet its goals.

Some aspects of the bill have been implemented quickly. For instance, OMWIs were set up, directors were selected by each regulatory agency, and initially, directors were submitting regular reports for all agencies (Backman, 2016). However, in later years, implementation of reporting requirements has stalled. Reports from the OMWI Director for the Department of Treasury were delayed in 2015 and 2016, and the Treasury Department indicated that their OMWI would not be able to fulfill the reporting requirements under 342 in 2018 due to hiring freezes and insufficient staffing (Thorson, 2018, p. 3).

Developing standards to assess diversity policies of regulated entities has also proven more elusive. Two years after Dodd-Frank Act was passed, the OMWIs had not yet developed diversity standards for senior management (Vissa, 2013). While women's movement organizations participated in the process of developing these standards, the final content of the standards remained largely unchanged, not incorporating many of these concerns. The OMWIs of six regulatory agencies, the Consumer Financial Protection Bureau (CFPB), Office of the Comptroller of the Currency (OCC), Board of Governors of the Federal Reserve System, Federal Deposit Insurance and Corporation (FDIC), National Credit Union Administration (NCUA), and the SEC, worked together to establish joint standards that were submitted for public comment in October of 2013. The proposed rules for assessing diversity policies and practices of regulated entities were less far-reaching than advocates of Article 342 had hoped. The initial proposal did not define diversity, the standards allowed for self-assessment of diversity policies and practices, and voluntary disclosure to regulating agencies on the self-assessment (Federal Register, 2015, p. 33,017). The agencies also provided a set of proposed assessment factors but allowed for regulated entities to develop standards and assessments that fit their unique environment (Federal Register, 2015, p. 33,022).

It is during the comment period for these rules when women's movement organizations were most represented. Several individuals and entities commented on the proposed rules (more than 200 letters were received), including the National Women's Law Center, the Center for Diversity in Finance and Industry, members of the House of Representatives Committee on Financial Services, the National LGBT Bar Association, among others. Those groups and individuals supportive of Article 342 spoke out against the proposed rules for lack of transparency and accountability, specifically stating that self-assessment is inadequate and standardized evaluation systems need to be established. The House of Representatives Committee on Financial Services, many of whom were the architects of Article 342, stated, "[W]e believe it is necessary to achieve both the spirit and the plain letter of Section 342, that the final standards include: 1) mandatory diversity assessments and disclosures… 2) information on both workforce and supplier diversity practices and policies … and 3) that the diversity data be made available to the public" (Waters et al, 2014, p. 1). The failure to define diversity was noted by advocacy groups and business organizations alike, and some businesses spoke out against the rule due to implementation costs and the possibility it would encourage quotas (Federal Register, 2015, p. 33,019).

The final rules were altered very little from the proposal. They kept self-assessment of diversity policies and practices to be conducted at least yearly, allowed entities to determine their own assessment standards, retained voluntary disclosure to regulating entities, and allowed regulating agencies to determine what information to publish while protecting the confidentiality of the entity (Federal Register, 2015, pp. 33,023–33,024). An important change from the proposed rule to the final policy statement was the adoption of a definition of diversity that included minorities (Black Americans, Native Americans, Hispanic Americans, and Asian Americans) and women (Federal Register, 2015, p. 33,023). However, the final policy statement allows the regulated entities to adopt broader definitions of diversity. Representative Maxine Waters stated the final rules were too ambiguous, failed to establish uniform criteria to assess diversity policy and practices, and ignored the intent of Section 342 by making diversity assessments voluntary (NAWRB, 2015). Luis Aguilar also criticized the joint standards, noting that the final rules failed to meet the goals of 342 (Aguilar, 2015).

While reports are being produced by most of the OMWIs annually, little evaluation of the law's impact on diversity in financial services has been conducted. The Greenlining Institute, an organization focused on racial and economic justice, examined racial and ethnic diversity in the financial sector by requesting diversity data from OMWI directors in 2012. They found considerable variation in racial and ethnic diversity in financial regulatory agencies (Vissa & Sundar, 2012, p. 14). While these federal policies have received relatively little formal evaluation, it is important to note that much informal evaluation of women on corporate boards has occurred, including by state-level government actors, interest groups such as Catalyst, and investor groups. Many of these evaluations began in earnest prior to both federal laws as public and media attention to this policy area increased in the late 1990s and early 2000s.

Business and State-level Practice

Beginning in the late 2010s, social movement and media attention propelled more state-level and investor action in this area. Given the limits of the federal regulation, several states took the lead. California's state legislature, for example, passed a corporate board law requiring one woman on corporate boards of publicly held companies based in California in 2018. Since the passage of the California law, Connecticut, Hawaii, Massachusetts, Michigan, New Jersey, Pennsylvania, Oregon, and Washington State introduced similar laws, while Maryland, Illinois, and New York introduced laws amending filing requirements to make publicly held companies report diversity characteristics of board members and/or provide information on how diversity characteristics are used to nominate executive offers similar to the SEC Item (Hatcher and Latham, 2020). Washington State became the second state in the USA to mandate specific board diversity requirements in 2020 with the Washington Business Corporation Act (WBCA). This legislation required a gender diverse board defined as 25 percent women by January 1st, 2022 (Jaeger, 2020). Most states that have passed some form of legislation in this area but have not mandated corporations appoint women to their boards. A few states, such as Colorado and Pennsylvania, have passed legislation "encouraging" companies to appoint women to their boards while most, including Maryland, Illinois, and New York, have focused on requiring diversity disclosure (Jaeger, 2020). Thus, many states have considered a similar approach to the federal policies by focusing on diversity disclosure rather than forcing businesses to nominate women to their boards, but California and Washington are the exception. However, state regulation of corporate composition to this extent are rare and the constitutionality of California's law is being challenged in the courts. One challenge, *Meland v. Padilla* (now *Meland v. Weber)*, was initially dismissed in 2020 for lack of standing but this decision was reversed in 2021 by the United States Court of Appeals for the Ninth Circuit (Posney, 2021), while another, *Crest v. Padilla*, began a bench trial in the Las Angeles County Superior court in December of 2021 with an expected decision in 2022 (Milstead, 2022). It will likely be several years before the constitutionality of California's law is decided.

Despite this, California's and Washington's laws may already be having an impact on the number of women on corporate boards. In 2021, Washington, California and Utah had the highest growth rates of women on the boards of companies on the Russell 3000 Index (the 3,000 largest companies in the US). Notably, only Minnesota had more than 25% of women on the boards of these companies in 2020, but by 2021 the top three states for percentage of women directors were Washington, California, and Michigan (50/50 Women on Boards, 2021). However, how much of this and similar trends in the S&P 500, in which 2020 was the first year every S&P 500 company had at least one woman board member, is questionable. Betsy Bogart, Business Programs Division Chief for the California Secretary of State (who enforces the law), testified in the Los Angeles Superior Court that the law is not enforced so it is "essentially voluntary" (Melley, 2021). Despite the legislated penalties, Bogart's testimony revealed that fewer than half of the corporations complied with the law, there is no penalty for corporations who lied about compliance, and no follow up for corporations who do not report as required by law (Melley, 2021). As few states have attempted to regulate board composition to this extent and California's law is largely symbolic due to lack of enforcement, progress in women on corporate boards is more attributable to decisions by individual businesses as they are mostly free to determine their board's composition with limited interference from either state or federal actors.

This self-regulation is illustrated with the case of GM, not only a leader in their industry in gender equality but also among the S&P 500 and Fortune 500 companies. In fact, GM was only one of ten companies in 2019 whose board was 50% or more women, an impressive feat given that the automobile industry is male dominated. GM was implementing initiatives to increase women executives in the 1990s and 2000s, yet for every diversity disclosure since 2010, GM has stated that it does not have a formal diversity policy and the content of these disclosures has changed very little. In its 2020 Proxy Filing, GM states, "Your Board recognizes the value of overall diversity and considers members' and candidates' opinions, perspectives, personal and professional experiences, and backgrounds, including gender, race, ethnicity, and country of origin" (General Motors Company, 2020, p. 11). Over half of GM's board is women, yet they report having no formal diversity policy, which suggests gains for women and minorities are due to other factors. In fact, six other companies in Delaware have at least 20% of their directorships filled by women and minorities in 2019. This highlights that the largely self-regulatory approach used in the USA does not prevent increasing women's presence on corporate boards, especially in a state known for limited regulation of corporations, but corporations maintain the ability to determine their own corporate board composition with limited government interference.

Amazon was one of the companies with at least 50% of women on their board in 2019, but in 2018, the company was criticized for having an all-white board and only three women on their ten-member executive board. After investor pressure and media scrutiny, Amazon adopted the "Rooney Rule" requiring at least one woman or minority candidate to be interviewed for an open-board seat, a principle first followed by the National Football League (Molla, 2018). This illustrates the potential effectiveness of external pressure to force companies to increase women and people of color on their boards; however, Amazon's board composition was similar to their competitors, which also highlights the disadvantages of this largely self-regulatory approach.

These self-regulatory efforts are not only limited to individual businesses either. An investor-led effort in the Midwest undertaken by the Midwest Investors Diversity Initiative (MIDI), an institutional investor coalition created in 2016 to diversify corporate boards focused specifically on promoting diversity on boards, convinced twenty-four companies to adopt the Rooney Rule. The NASDAQ, the major stock exchange for most publicly listed companies, adopted a board diversity rule which was approved by the SEC in 2021. The rule requires all companies listed on the exchange to disclose diversity statistics of their board directors, and "have at least two diverse board members or explain their failure to meet the requirement" (Aberg and Lin, 2021).

Assessing Outcomes of the Policy Patchwork: Limited Progress and the Absence of Transformative Potential

Overall, neither federal policy has had an impact on gender equality and corporate board composition. Changes in corporate board composition for the largest companies were already changing well before the implementation of either policy, and neither policy has impacted these trends. Changes at the state level in response to social movements, except for California, seem likely to also be gender neutral as they similarly require diversity policy disclosure rather than mandate what those policies should contain, although the impact of these potential changes can only truly be known over time. Despite largely gender-neutral outcomes at both the federal and state level, the largely self-regulatory approach has also achieved some gender accommodation. As decision-makers at the corporate level have increasingly appointed women to their boards, we do see incremental and piecemeal change that accommodates traditional gender roles rather than attempts to transform them. Nonetheless, investor pressure to add women to corporate boards seems to be increasing and has already led to successes. While these successes are likely to continue to produce only incremental and sporadic change across industries, with more companies reaching at least 50% women on their corporate boards, we may see transformative potential in the future.

Direct Impact: More Women on Boards?

In terms of increasing women's presence on corporate boards, trends do not suggest that either federal policy has had much of an impact. The SEC Item has the potential to be more far-reaching in increasing the number of women on corporate boards considering it applies to all publicly traded companies, and implementation of the rule happened rather quickly. As Section 342 only applies to the finance industry and implementation of diversity standards was delayed for two years, its ability to impact corporate board composition is much more limited. While women's presence on the corporate boards of Fortune 100 and Fortune 500 companies is increasing and the rate of change appears to increase after the adoption and implementation of these policies, women's presence on corporate boards is less than 30% for the Fortune 100 and the Fortune 500, and the S&P 500 just reached 30% in 2021. Overall, progress is still slow. The increases that have been seen over time cannot be attributed to these specific policies, especially considering the policies themselves have neither no real enforcement mechanisms to ensure compliance nor are vague to ensure businesses can self-regulate.

Approximately ten years after the adoption and implementation of both federal policies, women's representation on the S&P is just over a quarter of seats (26%), which is an all-time high (Catalyst, 2019b); this is slightly double what it was in 2000 when women constituted only 12% of seats (Guttner, 2001). In 2019, for the first time, no S&P 500 boards contained all men, and nearly half of all new appointments were women. By 2019, ten companies in the S&P 500 have at least 50% of women on their boards and a total of thirty-eight have at least 40% of women on their boards (McGregor, 2019). Twelve Fortune 500 companies had boards with 50% or more women and over two dozen had at least 40% women (Hinchliffe, 2019).

When considering the finance industry, which was targeted by Section 342, women have made even fewer gains. Women in financial services constitute 48% of first/mid-level managers, and only 29% of executive/senior-level management from 2007 to 2015 (Catalyst, 2019a). No woman has ever led a Wall Street Bank, and women's representation in the C-Suite of the financial sector was only 19% in 2017. Women of color represented only 1% of C-Suite representation in 2017 (McKinsey and Company, 2018). Thus, the impact of Section 342 so far has been limited and, with diversity in the finance sector barely changing from 2007 to 2017, it is difficult to argue that 342 has made any transformative change. There is little evidence it has had an impact on gender equality or diversity within the very industry it targets.

Trends in the Fortune 100, Fortune 500, and the S&P 500 illustrate that women's presence on corporate boards was slowly increasing beginning in the early 2000s prior to the federal and state law changes discussed above. Moreover, gains made by the S&P 500 in 2020 and 2021 have been attributed by some to the 2018 California law requiring public companies headquartered in the state to appoint at least one woman to their board by 2019 and for private financial firms and investors requiring businesses to add women and minorities to their boards (Gupta, 2020; 50/50 Women on Boards, 2021). However, as stated previously, Bogart's testimony that the law has not been enforced places some doubt on these assertions. An interview with a Catalyst representative in February 2020 suggests these changes are not due to federal policy, rather they are primarily driven by external pressure from large investor groups and regional diversity initiatives as in the case of the MIDI discussed above.

While the increase in women's presence on corporate boards, especially record-breaking trends in the S&P 500 may seem promising, research suggests that S&P 1500 and 500 companies practice "tokenism" where businesses only symbolically address gender inequality on their boards by appointing a minimum threshold of women, referred to as "twokenism" by Chang et al, 2016 (p. 8). In fact, US companies are "disproportionately likely to include exactly two women on their boards," which allows these companies to avoid claims of tokenism (by including more than one woman) while simultaneously avoiding true commitment to board diversity (Chang and Milkman, 2020, pp. 3–4). Thus, only just slightly over a quarter of the S&P 500 have shown any commitment to move beyond tokenism or "twokenism" by having at least 30% of women on their boards. This, in combination with often empty regulations at the federal and state levels, leads to an incremental and piecemeal change in women on corporate boards.

Impact on Decision-makers and Gatekeepers: Limited Potential for Gender Transformation

When considering potential impacts at the decision-maker and gatekeeper level, there is little evidence that either federal policy has transformed views on gender relations or will lead to gender transformation in future state or corporate actions. Looking at changes from the date each policy was passed to 2020, neither policy has had any impact on decision-maker/gatekeeper attitudes. If we consider the SEC Item, the implementation of the SEC diversity disclosure rule remains largely unchanged despite the transition to a new administration. For Section 342, the law failed to provide any enforcement mechanisms to ensure compliance of the regulatory agencies. This, combined with other issues including lack of resources, limit its ability to transform attitudes at the decision-maker and gatekeeper level. As several regulatory agencies elected to enact policies counter to the intentions of the section's sponsors, this law has had no impact on decision-maker attitudes overall and limited ability to transform them in the future. Instead, they can adopt diversity policies that allow them to avoid a true commitment to gender equality and diversity on their corporate boards.

However, outside of federal laws, evidence suggests that attitudes among decision-makers, especially at the state level may be changing as indicated by the state-level policies discussed above. Unfortunately, the policies considered are predominately diversity disclosures like the SEC rule, which will impact gender transformation potential. If diversity is not defined or corporations are allowed to consider other factors in their definitions, these policies will be as weak as their federal counterparts. Nonetheless, this suggests that attitudes of state-level decision-makers and gatekeepers are changing, as these actors have failed to act in this area in the past. Evidence also shows that individual companies are including more women on their boards, and both private and public investor groups have taken an active role in pressuring companies to add more women to their boards. This pressure has been successful in forcing companies to act, but this does not indicate that gender transformation is occurring at the corporate level. Rather, companies are electing to add more women in response to external pressure and many are appointing just a minimum threshold of women to avoid true change that reflects gender accommodation. Nevertheless, this could be an indication of decision-maker/gatekeeper attitudes changing, albeit slowly and in a patchwork fashion.

Impact on Society: Social Movements Impacting Attitudes and Action on Women on Corporate Boards

With the low level of impact on gender relations and attitudes in the entities they were designed to regulate, the lack of impact on societal attitudes is unsurprising. Support for women in leadership remains high, as surveys consistently show most US respondents believe women and men would make equally good political leaders (Kohut, Wike, and Horowitz, 2007, pp. 48–49; Parker, Horowitz, and Rohal 2015). Women and men are also believed to be equally good leaders in business, but analysis reveals that whether men and women are rated as equally capable by most respondents depends on the industry being analyzed, illustrating that gender stereotypes still impact views on women's leadership in several industries (Parker et al, 2015). As with corporate board increases discussed above, high support for women in leadership existed prior to both laws, and evidence suggests that there has been very little change in these attitudes. Further, gender stereotypes of women in leadership have changed little since these laws were implemented, suggesting no gender transformation.

However, outside of the federal policies, social movement and media attention may indicate changing attitudes regarding women on corporate boards and the government's role in ensuring companies diversify. For instance, the #MeToo and Time's Up movements have focused the public's attention on sexual harassment in the workplace and equal pay. As these movements began getting more public attention, particularly #MeToo, several states introduced legislation dealing with sexual harassment, equal pay, and corporate board composition. As stated, most of these potential reforms take the form of diversity disclosure like the federal policies suggesting limited potential for gender transformation over time. Additionally, as early as 2018 a pushback to these movements was already identified by several media sources. Nonetheless, this may signal changing attitudes that will have more transformative potential over time. The full impact of #MeToo and Time's Up on gender relations and attitudes both publicly and in the corporate sector, as well as ongoing impacts, will need more time to be fully assessed.

Conclusion: The Limits of the Policy Patchwork without Teeth

The piecemeal approach of US policy, which allows much self-regulation on the part of businesses to determine whether to appoint more women to their boards, currently has limited impacts on gender equality and gender transformation over time. The analysis illustrates that the presence of women on corporate boards was increasing prior to the federal regulation implemented in 2010, and these successes were due to larger societal trends and businesses pursuing diversity on their boards as a business necessity rather than a commitment to true gender equality. While the federal government had the opportunity to create policies that were less symbolic through defining diversity, requiring reporting of diversity statistics, an external assessment of these policies in the case of Section 342, both policies failed to adopt a stronger regulatory approach. Thus, the decision to include more women on corporate boards is almost entirely left to individual corporations, which leads to only incremental change in women's presence on corporate boards overall, and increases are not uniform across all industries.

While policy outcomes at the federal level seem to be almost gender neutral in terms of the GEPP outcomes measures, states are becoming increasingly more active in this policy area. These prospective state-level changes have been in response to social movements including #MeToo and Time's Up. While these movements have had the most impact on sexual harassment policies, several states have considered corporate board legislation in response, with California and now Washington State leading the way. Unfortunately, it seems, the California Secretary of State had limited resources to ensure compliance with the law (Melley, 2021) and California's law is already being challenged in the courts. It is unclear whether it will survive the court challenges. Additionally, many states are considering diversity disclosures similar to federal policy and thus relying on investors to pressure companies to diversify their boards. This makes the impact of #MeToo and similar movements unclear, at least in terms of corporate board composition. However, these movements could be early indications of an attitude shift in the proper role of government in ensuring gender diversity on corporate boards. At present, these policies will likely have little impact on the incremental and disjointed increases that have been ongoing for the past three decades, but if these movements remain active, we may see more extensive policies in this area at the state level.

Despite the limitations of US incrementalism, women's presence on corporate boards is increasing and made substantial gains from 2018 to 2020. These changes reflect ongoing trends in US corporate board composition in the last decade that are driven by individual businesses due to external investor pressure, media attention, social movements, and employee recruitment and retention. Thus, self-regulation on the part of businesses to determine their own diversity policies can and has increased the presence of women on corporate boards in the USA. As more investor groups pressure companies to adopt the Rooney Rule, the presence of women on corporate boards is likely to increase. However, evidence suggests that except for a few companies that have pursued gender equal boards, most businesses currently appoint a bare minimum of women to their boards to avoid criticism. This currently produces gender accommodation at the business level, where the self-regulatory approach has led to increases in women on corporate boards but without transformation of gender relations and attitudes.

The ultimate questions are whether trends of state action, social pressure, and investor pressure will continue and what will be the impact of these trends on representation of both women and people of color on corporate boards. If disclosure rules do not improve, holding companies accountable for the composition of their boards will be difficult, especially in terms of race and ethnicity where these rules are especially inadequate. This suggests that improving disclosure rules at the state level could aid investors in pressuring companies to diversify, especially if more expansive policies in California and Washington State are overturned by courts. However, if this is the dominant method of increasing women's presence on corporate boards then this piecemeal process will continue to have a limited impact on the glass ceiling and the potential for gender transformation for the foreseeable future.

References

2020 Women on Boards (2016) *2020 Women on Boards Gender Diversity Index: 2011–2016 Progress of Women Corporate Directors by Company Size, State, and Sector*. Jamaica Plain: MSCI ESG Research.

2020 Women on Boards (2018) *2020 Women on Boards Gender Diversity Index: 2018 Progress of Women Corporate Directors by Company Size, State and Industry Sector*. Los Angeles: MSCI ESG Research.

50/50 Women on Boards (2021) *Gender Diversity Index: 2021 Progress of Women Corporate Directors by Company, Size, State and Industry Sector*. 50/50 Women on Boards. Los Angeles: MSCI ESG Research.

Aberg, Sarah E. and Matthew T Lin (2021) "SEC Approves Nasdaq Diversity Rule." *National Law Review* XI (232). https://www.natlawreview.com/article/sec-approves-nasdaq-diversity-rule.

Aguilar, Louis. A. (2010) "Diversity in the Boardroom Is Important and, Unfortunately, Still Rare," *Harvard Law School Forum on Corporate Governance*, September 23.

Aguilar, Louis. A. (2015) *Dissenting Statement of the Final Interagency Policy Statement: Failing to Advance Diversity and Inclusion*, https://www.sec.gov/news/statement/dissent-interagency-policy-statement-diversity.html (Accessed January 1, 2019).

Arfken, Deborah. E., Stephanie. L. Bellar, and Marilyn. M. Helms (2004) "The Ultimate Glass Ceiling Revisited: The Presence of Women on Corporate B\boards," *Journal of Business Ethics*, Volume 50, 177–186.

Backman, Melvin (2016) "Inside the Piece of Dodd-Frank that's Trying—and Will Likely Fail—to Diversify Wall Street," *Quartz*, March 14.

Beecham, Wendy (2000) *Letter to the Securities and Exchange Commission: Proxy Disclosure and Solicitation Enhancements*. s.l.: s.n.

Brainerd, Jackson (2017) "Paid Family Leave in the States," *National Conference of State Legislatures Legis Brief*, August.

California Senate Office of Research (1999) *Women and Equality: A California Review of Women's Equity Issues in Civil Rights, Education and the Workplace*. Sacramento, CA: California Senate Office of Research.

Catalyst (2015) *Pyramid: Women in S&P 500 Companies*. [Online]. (Accessed June 15, 2019). https://www.catalyst.org/research/2016-catalyst-census-women-and-men-board-directors/.

Catalyst (2016) *Pyramid: Women in S&P 500 Companies*. February 2016. [Online]. (Accessed June 15, 2019)

Catalyst (2017) *Pyramid: Women CEOs of the S&P 500*. August 22. [Online]. (Accessed June 15, 2019) https://www.catalyst.org/research/2016-catalyst-census-women-and-men-board-directors/.

Catalyst (2018) *Pyramid: Women in S&P 500 Companies*. [Online]. (Accessed June 15, 2019).

Catalyst (2019a) *Quick Take: Women in Financial Services*, https://www.catalyst.org/research/women-in-financial-services/ (Accessed June 15, 2019).

Catalyst (2019b) *Pyramid: Women in S&P 500 Companies*. February 25 [Online]. (Accessed June 15, 2019) https://www.catalyst.org/research/women-in-sp-500-companies/.

Catalyst (2020) *Pyramid: Women in S&P 500 Companies*. January 2020. [Online]. (Accessed August 1, 2020). https://www.moneysmart.ae/en/Pages/5_reasons_why_women_make_great_leaders.aspx

Catalyst (2021) *Pyramid: Women in the United States Workforce*. September 19 [Online]. (Accessed January 25, 2022). https://www.catalyst.org/research/women-in-the-united-states-workforce/.

Chang, Edward., Katherine. L. Milkman, Dolly Chugh, and Modupe Akinola (2016) *"Twokenism" on Corporate Boards: Threshold Effects and Gender Diversity*. s.l.: Working Paper.

Chang, Edward. H. and Katherine. L. Milkman (2020) "Improving Decisions that Affect Gender Equality in the Workplace," *Organizational Dynamics*, 49(1), 1–7.

Cheffins, Brian. R. (2015) Delaware and the Transformation of Corporate Governance. *Delaware Journal of Corporate Law*, Volume 8, 1–77.

Choi, Hye-Won (2009) *Comment Letter to the Securities Exchange Commission*. s.l.: s.n.

Dalton, Dan R. and Catherine M. Dalton. 2010. "Women and Corporate Boards of Directors: The Promise of Increased, and Substantive, Participation in the Post Sarbanes-Oxley E"a." *Business Horizons* 53 (3): 257–268.

Delaware Division of Corporations (2018) *Annual Report Statistics*, https://corp.delaware.gov/stats/ (Accessed January 15, 2019).

Deloitte and Alliance for Board Diversity (2019) *Missing Pieces Report: The 2018 Board Diversity Census of Women and Minorities on Fortune 500 Boards*. s.l.: Deloitte.

Dhir, Aaron (2015) *Challenging Boardroom Homogeneity: Corporate Law, Governance, and Diversity.* New York: Cambridge University Press.

Ebrahimji, Alisha (2020) "Female Fortune 500 CEOs Reach an All-time High, but It's Still a Small Percentage," *CNN Business*, May 20.

Editorial Board (2018) "Wheaveave All the Public Companies Gone?" *Bloomberg Opinion*, April 9.

Embrick, David (2011) "The Diversity Ideology in the Business World: A New Oppression for a New Age," *Critical Sociology*, 37(5), 541–556.

Federal Register (2015) *Final Interagency Policy Statement Establishing Joint Standards for Assessing the Diversity Policies and Practices of Entities Regulated by the Agencies.* Washington, DC: Federal Register.

Federal Reserve Bank of San Francisco (2010) *The Dodd-Frank Wall Street Reform and Consumer Protection Act of 2010.* San Francisco: s.n.

General Motors Company (2020) *Proxy Statement Pursuant to Section 14(a) of the Securities.* Washington, DC: United States Securities and Exchange Commission.

Ghosh, Iman (2019) "All the S&P 500 CEOs in One Timeline (2000–2019)," *Markets*, September 17.

Government Publishing Office (2010) *Conference Report on H.R. 4173, Dodd-Frank Wall Street Reform and Consumer Protection Act.* Washington: s.n.

Gupta, Alisha Haridasani (2020) "Why 2019 Was a Breakthrough Year for Women in the Boardroom," *The New York Times*, March 3.

Guttner, Thomas (2001) "Wanted: More Diverse Directors," *Business Week*, April 30, p. 134.

Hatcher, Michael and Weldon Latham (2020) "States Are Leading the Charge to Corporate Boards: Diversify!" *Harvard Law School Forum on Corporate Governance*, May 12.

Hinchliffe, Emma (2019) "GM's Board Will Have More Women Than Men. It's Not the Only One," *Fortune*, May 20.

Hinman, William (2018) *Oversight of the SEC's Division of Corporation Finance.* Washington DC: US House of Representatives.

Ho, Virginia Harper (2010)" "Enlightened Shareholder Value: Corporate Governance beyond the Shareholder-Stakeholder Divide," *The Journal of Corporation Law*, 36(1), 59–112.

Jaeger, Jaclyn (2020) "Emerging state board laws encourage proactive approa"h." *Compliance Week*, November 3.https://www.complianceweek.com/boards-and-shareholders/emerging-state-board-diversity-laws-encourage-proactive-approach/29681.article.

Keightley, Mark. P. and Joseph. S. Hughes (2018) *Pass-throughs, Corporations, and Small Businesses: A Look at Firm Size.* Washington, DC: Congressional Research Service.

Kilborn, Peter. T. (1995) "For Many in Work Force, the 'Glass Ceiling' Still Exists," *The New York Times*, March 16.

Kohut, Andrew, Richard Wike, and Menasce Juliana Horowitz. (2007) *World Publics Welcome Global Tr—e–But Not Immigration.* Washington, DC: Pew Research Center.

Labaton, Stephen (2009) "S.E.C. Nominee Offered Plan for Tighter Regulation," *The New York Times*, January 15.

Lang, Ilene. H. (2009) *Letter to the US Securities Exchange Commission: Request for Comment—File No. S7-13-09.* s.l.: s.n.

Lipman, Becca (2011) "Here Are the 12 Female CEOs of Fortune 500 Companies," *Business Insider*, July 9.

Mazur, Amy G. (2002) *Theorizing Feminist Policy*. Oxford: Oxford University Press.

McCarthy, Patricia (2019) "Companies Adopt Rooney Rule, Add Women and Minorities to Boards as Midwest Investors Diversity Gains Momentum," *GlobeNewswire*, August 13.

McGregor, Jenna (2019) "After Years of 'Glacial' Change, Women Now Hold More Than 1 in 4 Corporate Board Seats," *The Washington Post*, July 17.

McKinsey and Company (2018) *Closing the Gap: Leadership Perspectives on Promoting Women in Financial Services*. s.l.: McKinsey & Company.

Melley, Brian (2021) "California official say Women on Boards law is toothle"s." *U.S. News & World Report*, December 2. https://www.usnews.com/news/politics/articles/2021-12-02/california-official-says-women-on-boards-law-is-toothless#:~:text=The%20law%20required%20publicly%20held,members%20must%20have%20three%20women.

Milstead, Virginia (2022). "Rulings in 2022 Could Bring Clarity on California and Nasdaq Board Diversity Mandates," *JDSUPRA*. https://www.jdsupra.com/legalnews/rulings-in-2022-could-bring-clarity-on-5383656/.

Molla, Rani (2018) "Amazon's 10-Person Board Has Only Three Women. That's on par With the Company's Peers," *Vox*, 16 May.

Morris, Nigel (2009) "Harriet Harman: 'If Only It Had Been Lehman Sisters,'" *The Independent*, 4 August.

NAWRB (2015) *OMWI Update from Congresswoman Maxine Waters*, https://www.nawrb.com/omwi-update-from-congresswoman-maxine-waters/ (Accessed January 19, 2019).

OECD (2017) *The pursuit of Gender Equality: An Uphill Battle*. Paris: OECD Publishing.

Oliver, Lori A and Norris, Jessica M (2020) "Corporate Governance Emerging Best Prac." *National Law Review* XI (232). https://www.natlawreview.com/article/sec-approves-nasdaq-diversity-rule.

Parker, Kim, Juliana Menasce Horowitz, and Molly Rohal (2015) *Women and Leadership: Public Says Women Are Equally Qualified, But Barriers Persist*. s.l.: PEW Research Center.

Parry, Janine and Dorothy McBride (2016) *Women's Rights in the US: Policy Debates and Gender Roles*. New York and London: Routledge.

Pew Research Center (2018) "The Data on Women Leaders," *Pew Research Center Social & Demographic Trends*, September 13.

Posney, Cydney (2021) "Hearing on Board Diversity Statute," *Harvard Law School Forum on Corporate Governance*, November 16. https://corpgov.law.harvard.edu/2021/11/16/hearing-on-board-gender-diversity-statute/.

Roby, Karen Wells (2015) "Diversity and Inclusion: The Financial Services Sector and Dodd-Frank," *American Bar Association*, September 1.

Roose, Kevin (2010) "Seeking Guidance on Dodd-Frank's Diversity Clause," *The New York Times*, 11 November.

Shepherd, Ann, and Gené Teare (2021) "2020 Study of Gender Diversity on Private Company Boar"s," *Crunchbase News*, March 1. https://news.crunchbase.com/news/2020-diversity-study-on-private-company-boards/.

Spencer Stuart (2012) "10 Years Later: Sarbanes-Oxley Act Continues to Shape Board Governance," *PR Newswire*, 30 July.

Spencer Stuart (2017) *2017 Spencer Stuart US Board Index*. Chicago, IL: Spencer Stuart.

Spencer Stuart (2018) *2018 United States Spencer Stuart Index*. Chicago, IL: Spencer Stuart.

Spencer Stuart (2019) *2019 US Spencer Stuart Board Index*. Chicago, IL: Spencer Stuart.

Spencer Stuart (2020) *2020 U.S. Spencer Stuart Index*. Chicago, IL: SpencerStuart.

Spencer Stuart (2021) *2021 U.S. Spencer Stuart Index*. Chicago, IL: SpencerStuart.

Taylor, Susan Shulze (2009) *Letter to the Securities and Exchange Commission*. s.l.: s.n.

Teare, Gené (2019) "2019 Study of Gender Diversity in Private Company Boardroo"s," *Crunchbase News*, December 11. https://news.crunchbase.com/news/2019-study-of-gender-diversity-in-private-company-boardrooms/.

The Washington Times (2010) "Editorial: Quotas by Proxy in Dodd-Frank Bill," *The Washington Times*, July 14.

Thorson, Eric. M. (2018) *Department of the Treasury letter to the Committee on Financial Services*. s.l.: s.n.

US Securities and Exchange Commission (2009) *Proxy Disclosure Enhancements: 17 CFR Parts 229, 240, 249, 274*. s.l.: Securities and Exchange Commission.

US Securities and Exchange Commission (2012) *SEC Biography: Chairman Mary L. Schapiro*, https://www.sec.gov/about/commissioner/schapiro.htm (Accessed January 12, 2019).

US Securities and Exchange Commission (2020) *Regulation S-K Questions and Answers of General Applicability*, https://www.sec.gov/divisions/corpfin/guidance/regs-kinterp.htm#116-11 (Accessed August 28, 2020).

Upadhyay, Arun and Maria del Carmen Triana (2020) "Drivers of Diversity on Boards: The Impact of the Sarbanes-Oxley A"t." *Human Resource Management* 8–9. doi:0.1002/hrm.22035.

Vissa, Preeti (2013) "Why 20 Government Offices You've Never Heard of Are Key to Financial Recovery," *The Huffington Post*, May 8.

Vissa, Preeti and Divya Sundar (2012) *Government That Looks Like America? Racial Diversity in Financial Regulator Institutions*. Berkely, CA: The Greenlighting Institute.

Waters, Maxine, Joyce Beatty, Gregory Meeks, Al Green, Keith Ellison, Terri Sewell, Gwen Moore, and William Lacy Clay. 2014. Final Interagency Policy Statement Establishing Joint Standards for Assessing Diversity Policies and Practices of Entities Regulated by the Agencies: Comments. Washington, DC: The Board of Governors of the Federal Reserve System, April 11. https://www.federalreserve.gov/SECRS/2014/May/20140509/OP-1465/OP-1465_041514_126311_475617696392_1.pdf.

Williams, Mary WallacZe (2000) "Where G.E. Falls Short: Diversity at the Top," *The New York Times*, September 3.

7

Implementing Corporate Equality through Québec Inc.

The Promise and Pitfalls of a Feminist Outlier in Canada

Joan Grace

Introduction

Women in Canada are underrepresented within the halls of executive decision-making and at the upper echelons of corporate governance. While some progress has been achieved as corporate Canada has become more aware of gender disparities within business, much more needs to be accomplished to ensure women take their place in the executive halls of power and influence. Arguments advanced by various associations in Canada advocating for women's appointment to corporate boards include improving the company's public image, increasing profitability by extending the company's marketing reach, and facilitating good board governance by the inclusion of alternative perspectives and opinions (Burgess and Tharenou, 2002, pp. 40–41; see also Status of Women Canada, 2014). It has also been argued that women's so-called power-sharing style of management reduces CEO dominance on boards (Burgess and Tharenou, 2002).

Québec, one of ten provinces and three territories in Canada, is an interesting outlier to the pattern of implementing a purely self-regulatory approach consisting of businesses taking a voluntary comply-or-explain approach to monitor and encourage board diversity in private enterprises. Québec has taken a more authoritative and concrete approach that differentiates between self-regulation for privately-held companies and legislation that established a gender quota on state-owned companies—the 2006 Act Respecting Governance of State-Owned Enterprises. This chapter brings in policy on state-owned corporations because this has been the only effort to regulate gender equality on corporate boards through a gender quota law in Canada, albeit for state-owned companies. As the chapter argues, Québec is a feminist outlier offering a potentially more authoritative policy and

Joan Grace, *Implementing Corporate Equality through Québec Inc.* In: *Gender Equality and Policy Implementation in the Corporate World.* Edited by Isabelle Engeli and Amy G. Mazur, Oxford University Press.
© Oxford University Press (2022). DOI: 10.1093/oso/9780198865216.003.0007

implementation through a supportive feminist political culture and a more collective approach to industrial relations referred to as Québec Inc. This policy response and setting are in contrast to the more symbolic voluntary approach to corporate equality that has produced quite disappointing results in the rest of Canada.

The chapter begins by situating Québec's distinctive approach to corporate gender equality in the broader Canadian context. Next, the analysis traces how the more symbolic voluntary efforts to promote gender equality on corporate boards throughout Canada produced disappointing results. The placement of corporate gender equality on the political agenda and the adoption of the 2006 Act in Québec is then discussed. The following sections take a closer look at the instruments and outputs created by the 2006 law, the practice of implementation of evaluation, and the outcome of the Québec policy in terms of policy empowerment and gender transformation. It is argued that the Canadian experience is one of gender accommodation rather than transformation, given the purposeful focus on public companies only in Québec, due to a political and corporate preference for self-regulation approaches of comply-or-explain in the private sector.

Québec and the Canadian Landscape

Regulation of most corporations in Canada falls under provincial jurisdiction. Types of corporations include government-owned entities (referred to as Crown corporations across Canada but as state-owned enterprises in Québec), publicly traded corporations (listed on the Toronto Stock Exchange), and entities that are family (privately) owned. In 2019, there were 277 publicly traded companies on the FP 500, 267 of which are traded on the Toronto Stock Exchange (TSX). The FP 500 (short for the Financial Post 500) are Canada's premier, highest-earning corporations accounting for $2.33 trillion reported revenue (Holloway, 2019, p. 2). Of the 277 noted above, 162 are private companies, 44 are Crown corporations and 17 are cooperatives (Ibid).

At the time of writing, there were thirty-three corporations "owned" at the federal level that include some of Canada's largest corporate enterprises such as Canada Post. There are also many Crown corporations at the provincial level, although they differ in size and number. In 2016 in the province of Québec, there were forty-six state-owned enterprises collectively representing sixty-three billion dollars in revenues, employing 65,000 people (Allaire and Dauphin, 2017, p. 4). A more recent report by Finances Québec puts that number at sixty enterprises (Finances Quebec, 2017), although not all have a business or corporate function. A more precise number of state-owned companies in Canada is better determined and based on a definition that at least 50% of its revenue is from "market activity" (Crisan and McKenzie, 2013, p. 3). Looking at data from 2013, according to this definition, there were twenty-five state-owned corporations in

Québec (Ibid, p. 13). Two of Canada's largest government-owned enterprises are Québec companies: Hydro-Quebec and Caisse de dépôt et placement du Quebec. In 1962, hydroelectricity was nationalized in Québec and is operated by Hydro-Quebec. The Caisse, established in 1965, manages several provincial and para-public pension plans in Québec.

What accounts for why Québec, more often than in any other jurisdiction in Canada, implemented quota legislation to increase the number of women on boards of public corporations? The political culture of Québec is significant in explaining a political commitment to discussing and strategizing ways, such as state interventions and public ownership, to promote an egalitarian Québécois society. Provincial leaders have for almost two decades undertaken substantive consultations with women's groups, and many other civil society communities, gauging how best to develop and implement equality initiatives. And since the time of the provincial consultations in 2005, which led to the enactment of the Act, the province underwent a follow-up consultation in 2016, publishing findings, recommendations, and objectives in *Together for Equality: Government Strategy for Gender Equality Toward 2021* (Secrétariat à la condition féminine, 2017).

Québec's distinctiveness is also evident when one looks at the dynamics of its industrial relations systems. As Lévesque et al noted in 1997, the industrial/economic development model which unfolded in Québec is quite different from other provinces and territories in Canada (p. 485). Referred to as Québec Inc., three key state-market pillars have characterized industrial development in Québec: the creation of a significant number of publicly owned companies, development of cooperative societies, and social economy companies, along with the presence of a diverse array of small firms and large corporations solely owned by French-Canadians (Ibid). It is argued that a social democratic model developed in Québec framed by the Québec nationalist agenda in the province, distinguishing this region from the rest of Canada's (ROC) production systems, which are rooted in Anglo-Saxon market liberalism (Haddow and Klassen, 2006).

As such, there is much more integration of the state and market in Québec than in other jurisdictions across Canada. Indeed, the Québec model, Haddow (2015) argues, involves much more consultation and collaboration compared to pluralist tendencies in other provinces and territories. Noting that "distinct political coalitions underlie different welfare state regimes," as Haddow and Klassen have argued, "Quebec's policy setting diverges from the Canadian norm" (2006, p. 123; see also Bouchard, 2013). A social economy model is evident due to Québec's emphasis on public spending, social partnership policy commitments (Bouchard, 2013), and equality-producing programs (Haddow and Klassen, 2006). The province runs a public auto insurance system and owns and administers the Quebec Pension Plan—the only mandatory pension scheme among Canadian provinces. And like some Nordic countries, the province has available parental leave and a universal childcare system, both of which have contributed to increasing women's paid employment (Petersson et al, 2017, pp. 25 and 30). Since 2000, and up to 2014, investment intentions in public sector capital spending, as a share of GDP, nearly doubled, along with slowed private-sector business investment—the lowest business investment in Canada as a share of GDP prior to a slight rebound in 2012 (Cross 2014, pp. 6–7).

Corporate boards across Canada are organized under a one-tier governance structure. This provides an opportunity for a focused investigation on the employment and participation of women within the upper executive echelons of the corporate elite, the highest single entity tasked with management and monitoring of the corporation. Upon investigation, what is clear is that corporate Canada is male dominated. In 2009, women accounted for only 0.3% of senior managers (Statistics Canada, 2011; see also Wohlbold and Chenier, 2011), and from 1987 to 2009, the proportion of women in middle management rose by only 4% (Statistics Canada, 2011). Even when fast-forwarding to 2018, 90% of chief executive level office holders (or C-level) were men, with women accounting for just over a third (35.1%) of all managers and 32.6% senior managers (Catalyst, 2016). As for Canada's largest publicly traded companies, women accounted for just 10% of high-ranking C-level executives (Ibid).

And across all sectors, women were paid less than men in Canada with wage disparities more significant for women who are employed in non-unionized precarious job situations. In comparison to Québec, at the time the 2006 gender parity law was debated and passed in the province (just prior to 2010), the wage gap was a few points higher in Canada, nonetheless narrowing in both jurisdictions between 2000 and 2015 (Conference Board of Canada, 2016). By 2015, the gap was 16.4% in Québec compared to 18% in the ROC.

Over the years, the wage gap has narrowed in part due to increased rates of women's completion of university degrees, changes in women's and men's employment across occupations, and a decrease in men's employment in unionized workplaces (Statistics Canada, 2019). During the 1960s, 1.7% of women (of the total workforce measured as hours worked) had university degrees compared to 4.8% for men (Petersson et al, July 2017, p. 7). Between 2010 and 2016, 25% of women obtained university degrees compared to about 22% of men (Ibid), although this completion rate has not translated into well-paid, executive employment for women. Yet even with increased educational attainment, in 2018 women aged 25–54 on average earned 13.3% less per hour than men (Pelletier et al, 2019, p. 4).

Progress has been slow in the appointment of women to corporate boards in Canada. In 1998, women only accounted for 7.5% of persons on all corporate boards in Canada (Catalyst, 1998, p.4). In later years and across provinces in Canada, for all types of companies (listed, private, and government owned) the advancement and appointment of women to corporate boards continued to indicate disparate and disappointing results (as executive and nonexecutive participants). Executive board appointees are senior executives who are employees of the company. Nonexecutive board directors are external to the company yet are appointed because of their expertise, professional networks, or corporate/industry specializations. From 2002 and 2012, for example, all ten provinces improved, although gains were marginal in British Columbia, Alberta, Manitoba, and New-foundland; only two provinces (Nova Scotia and Saskatchewan) were at or near 25% by 2012 (Catalyst, 2014). As an aggregate across the nation, women accounted for 19.4% of board of directors in 2016, with female representation the highest on the boards in the financial, management, and service industries (Statistics, 2019, pp. 1 and 4). If one removes government-owned entities from these numbers of women on FP 500 companies, women comprised only 10% of board membership (Conference Board of Canada, 2013, p. 2; see also Conseil, 2014). It matters, then, as to the type of corporate entity that is examined.

The representation of women on Financial Post 500 company boards had only risen to 15.9% in 2013, a mere 1.5% increase from 2011 with approximately 40% of these same Financial Post 500 (FP 500) companies having no female board representation (Catalyst, 2014). Financial Post 500 companies are the largest cor-porations, in terms of revenue, listed on the Toronto Stock Exchange (TSX). More recent data indicates marginal improvement. According to Catalyst reports, 24.5% of women were present on FP 500 company boards in 2018; a slight increase from 22.6% in 2017 (2020) compared to more significant increases since 2011 with a 14.4% share of women on boards and in 2013 at 15.9% (2011 and 2016).

In comparison to other countries, according to 2013 data collected by the OECD, women's presence on company boards traded on the stock exchange in Canada was 20.8%, well below that of Norway (35.5%), Finland (29.9%), and France (29.7%)—all countries with government quota laws (Catalyst, 2016, p. 16). Just over one year later, the number of women grew just slightly. For example, the OECD reported in 2015 that women accounted for 12% of board members among the world's largest corporations, with women representing 13.4% of directors in developed markets (2016, p. 19). Based on 2015 or latest data, the OECD further noted that in comparison to other countries, Canada stood at just 21%, continu-ing to lag behind many other countries such as Iceland (44%), Norway (36%), and France (33%). It is worth noting, however, that Canada—at 21%—was just ahead of the OECD average of 20% (Ibid, p. 21).

Symbolic Policy at the Canadian Level: A Voluntary Comply-or-Explain Approach Leads to Disappointing Outcomes

Due to this discouraging record, over the last several years there has been an increasing number of high-profile organizations, corporations, and professional associations either researching or promoting board diversity, arguing that more women on boards can facilitate better organizational governance and corporate

Table 7.1 Policy Timeline on Promoting Gender Equality on Corporate Boards in Canada

2006	Government of Québec releases its gender equality strategy Act "Respecting Governance of State-Owned Enterprises" directing twenty-three public corporations to achieve gender parity on boards by 2011
2010	Canadian Board Diversity Council publicly advocates promoting diversity and appointing women to Boards of Directors Individual Businesses begin discussing the "comply-or-explain" model
2011	Institute of Corporate Director announces support for advancing women on boards
2012	Minister's mandate directing the creation of a federal Advisory Council to promote women on boards
2014	Status of Women Canada publishes the final report of the federal Advisory Council to promote women on boards making eleven recommendations, one of which is setting a volunteer target of 30% increase of women on boards within five years Canadian Securities Administrators members, except Alberta, British Columbia, and Prince Edward Island, amend National Instrument 58-101 (Disclosure of Corporate Governance Practices) to include disclosure information on the number of women on boards for all non-venture TSX listed companies
2016	Alberta agrees to the disclosure amendment of National Instrument 58–101 The Liberal party passes formal policy resolution at its biannual convention committing to gender parity on boards Introduction to the House of Commons Bill C-25
2018	On May 1, Bill C-25 receives Royal Assent

performance. Increasing attention has been directed to understanding why there has been a persistent lack of gender diversity in management positions and women's presence within the upper echelons of corporate decision-making (Burke and Mattis, 2000; Burgess and Tharenou, 2002). Table 7.1 illustrates the main policy efforts that have been taken across Canada since 2005 to address the gender gap on corporate boards, including the 2006 Act examined in more detail in the next section.

An early advocate for increasing the representation of women on boards was the Institute for Governance of Private and Public Organizations, urging companies to "pick up speed" on the appointment of women (2009, p. 10). It was the Canadian Board Diversity Council, however, that led the primary charge through a broad-based strategy with industry. The Canadian Board Diversity Council, an organization created in 2009 by forty-three "founding members" included at the time a few large corporations (Canadian Tire, Enbridge, Ford of Canada, Shoppers Drug Mart, Suncor Energy, and TELUS), Canada's largest banks (CIBC, BMO Financial Group, Desjardins, RBC, Scotiabank, and TD Bank Financial Group), and a wide variety of professional and industry groups/associations (the Canadian Society of Corporate Secretaries, Canadian Women in Communications, the Institute of Corporate Directors and the Women's Executive Network)—all committed to the Council's "vision … to increase Financial Post 500 and public sector board representation of women, visible minorities, Aboriginal Peoples including First Nations, Inuit, and Métis, persons with disabilities, and members of the LGBT community" with a "goal of increasing women on FP 500 board from 14 per cent in 2009 to 20 per cent by 2013" (Canadian Board Diversity Council, 2010, p. 2).

In their first annual report on diversity improvements, the Canadian Board Diversity Council stated that "boards comprised of directors who bring a wide range of perspectives, skills and experience to corporate governance will be effective contributors to the performance of their organizations (Canadian Board Diversity Council, 2010, p. 2). Since 2010, the Conference Board of Canada has built networks of supporters that have included a research partnership with the Status of Women Canada (the lead federal women's policy agency). The Canadian Board Diversity Council and the Women's Executive Network are two groups now at the forefront, drawing attention to the underrepresentation of women in executive offices and on corporate boards. In 2011, the Institute of Corporate Directors joined this chorus of actors reiterating similar commitments relaying that board diversity "enables boards to deliberate with great perspective and insight, which results in better decision making … [helping to] avoid 'group think'" (Institute of Corporate Directors, 2011, p. 3).

These organizations do not promote, as an intended goal, the transformation of gender norms in corporations related to the appointment of more women to executive and board positions. A notable exception among civil society groups is Women Get on Board Inc., a member-based network of female board members and corporate supporters and funders. Founded and led by Deborah Rosati, Women Get on Board not only promotes the goal of more women on boards, the language used to advocate such are gendered in conjunction with being framed by feminist objectives (although not self-identified as feminist). For example, Ms. Rosati's blog (which she has written since 2015), speaks to the importance of building women's confidence and empowerment of women as board members (Women Get on Board, 2019).

Women's empowerment, however, did not and has yet to become central to industry suggestions on how to increase the number of women on boards. Self-regulation approaches are preferred and take the form of symbolic gestures toward gender equality. Across most provinces, the comply-or-explain voluntary approach prevails. In December 2014, for example, the Canadian Securities Administrators, the national umbrella organization for securities regulators across Canada, announced that all but three provinces (Alberta, British Columbia, and Prince Edward Island) had voluntarily agreed to amend National Instrument 58–101 (Disclosure of Corporate Governance Practices) to include an annual report on the number of women on boards and in an executive position for all non-venture TSX companies, and what efforts the company was taking to promote diversity on their boards (Conference Board of Canada, 2020). Alberta agreed to the disclosure amendment in 2016.

At the federal level, we have seen too an emphasis on self-regulation until recently. For example, the Conservative party government was arguably aware of discussions about increasing women's participation on boards among industry leaders and what was happening at the securities regulatory level. They established an Advisory Council for women on boards in 2012. The Advisory Council, which was administratively attached to the Status of Women Canada, reported in June 2014 offering eleven recommendations (2014, pp. 16–18). Among those recommendations was the suggestion to adopt the comply-and-explain instrument, develop a communications strategy to mobilize key stakeholders, and, interestingly, "aspire" to 30% of women appointed to publicly traded companies by 2019 as a "reasonable national goal" (Status of Women Canada, 2014, pp. 1–2). Members of the Advisory Council included corporate and industry leaders from private-sector corporations (from both English Canada and Québec), financial institutions, business advocacy groups, such as the Canadian Federation of Independent Business, and, as ex officio members, the Executive Director of Catalyst Canada and a representative from the Women's Executive Network (2014, pp. 21–22). The "women on boards" policy idea was picked up by the Liberal party government, newly elected in October 2015, the next year passing a priority resolution at their biennial convention in 2016 committing to gender parity on boards (Liberal Party of Canada, 2016; Interview, Poulin).

The Liberal government eventually introduced Bill C-25 in September 2016 to amend the Canada Business Corporations Act (CBCA), the Canada Not-for-profit Corporations Act, and the Canada Cooperatives Act. The bill received Royal Assent on May 1, 2018, instituting diversity disclosure requirements for federally incorporated public companies. While regulations are yet to be confirmed, there are indications that Crown corporations will be obligated to disclose to shareholders the corporation's policies "related to diversity on the boards of directors and within senior management" of persons appointed from designated groups as defined under the federal Employment Equity Act (Innovation, Science, and Economic Development Canada, 2018). Similar to models at the provincial level, companies can explain and frankly easily justify non-compliance based on economic or bottom-line arguments about what was in the best interests of the corporation.

In sum, the idea of appointing women to corporate boards to improve governance was taking shape notably around 2009 to 2010 emanating directly from many of Canada's leading private-sector corporations via industry associations like the Canadian Board Diversity Council, the Institute of Corporate Directors, and the Women's Executive Network. Yet the self-regulation approach, along with aspirations to meet a 30% target were more a symbolic gesture toward gender equality rather than any authoritative measures to actually move toward the ambitious goal.

Agenda Setting and Decision-making in Québec: Earlier Feminist Attention Leads to More Concrete Policy

In Québec, debates about women's equality had begun much earlier than in other provinces or at the federal level when Jean Charest's Liberal party formed a majority government in April 2003, narrowly winning re-election a few years later and forming a minority government in 2007. Formal consultations were launched in 2005 informed by the government's social inclusion and nationalism goals, setting Québec apart from other jurisdictions and suggesting early on that the province would pursue a more concrete and state regulatory approach to its own public enterprises in sharp contrast with the ROC.

Charest's government won with the lowest popular vote in twenty-six years. The party's main competitor at the time was the Parti Québécois, the provincial sovereigntist party, which had placed itself as the guardian of Québec's distinct economic and social identity, which included promoting and protecting women's equality and the province's egalitarian priorities. The Liberal party had to establish itself as that new protector, arguably keen to do so because of their weakened electoral victory yet also because of proponents in the party. Decision-making and official Liberal party policy about gender parity and women's equality, for example, was consistently advanced by key women in the provincial cabinet (Interview, Poulin). A notable presence during the Charest governments was Monique Jérôme-Forget, a high-profile advocate of women's equal rights in Québec. She was elected to the Quebec National Assembly in 1998 and served as Minister of Government Administration from 2003 to 2008 and Minister of Finance from 2007 to 2008 during Charest governments.

Discussions about board governance and women's participation in decision-making were clearly framed by feminist tenets and arguments advanced in particular by female politicians, various women's groups, and women's policy agencies (the Secrétariat à la condition féminine and the Conseil du statut de la femme). For example, in 2005, the Québec Liberal government, then under the leadership of Jean Charest, approved a consultation process to develop a provincial gender equality strategy. Consultations were instigated by the Conseil du statut de la femme based on their document titled *Vers un nouveau contrat social pour l'égalité entre les femmes et les hommes* (Toward a new social contract between women and men) (Secrétariat à la condition féminine, 2017, p. viii), which mentioned the promotion of women on corporate boards and in decision-making in business. As governing instruments, the various action plans devised by the Liberal party were significant policy frameworks with the goal being to "promote egalitarian models and behavior" across and among civil society (Secrétariat à la condition féminine, 2011, 9).

Emanating from the consultations was the release, in 2006, of the government's gender equality policy called *Pour que l'égalité de droit devienne une égalité de fait* (When formal equality becomes real equality). The policy statement forwarded action plans to implement a range of laws, policies, and strategies to promote women's equality and "to promote equality by taking actions consistent with past efforts, but broader in scope" like enhancing women's participation in decision-making (Secrétariat à la condition féminine, 2017, viii; see also Conseil du statut de la femme, 2006). These goals guided future policy decisions of Québec governments as well as their strategic planning to implement various women's equality measures.

Still, within the private sector, the self-regulation approach of comply-or-explain dominated. Like other provinces, in 2014 all listed companies in Québec were directed to provide annual reporting on their "written policies and goals regarding the representation of women, indicating the number and proportion of women on their board of directors and holding senior management positions" (Québec, 2017, p. 101). And this is also noted in the province's gender and women's equality strategy published in 2017 promoting the goal of "encouraging" companies to achieve parity in decision-making and to monitor the presence of women on boards and the companies (Secrétariat à la condition féminine, 2017, p. 115).

Outputs in Québec: A Mixed Approach Tilted toward State-regulation and Policy Instruments

Consultations with advocates and pressure within the cabinet led the Québec Liberal government to announce in April 2006 that legislation would be introduced to ensure gender parity on publicly owned corporations. Not long after, the government introduced Bill 53, which was unanimously passed by the provincial National Assembly on December 14, 2006. The Act Respecting the Governance of State-Owned Enterprises stipulated that identified boards of provincially owned enterprises include "an equal number of women and men" appointed to their boards by December 2011 (Québec, 2017). Québec has since amended the Act expanding board diversity goals. Along with gender parity, Section 43 directs that at least one member of the board must be thirty-five years or younger, and that board members must reflect the cultural identity of Québecers arguably in keeping with the province's social inclusion efforts.

Self-regulation, however, is also evident given all private-sector corporations employ the voluntary approach of comply-or-explain in reporting of efforts to increase the number of women appointed to their boards. Comprehensiveness, therefore, is rather low given self-regulation in the private sector, a strict focus on state-owned enterprises, and the fact that the Act legislates parity for twenty-three of the sixty state-owned enterprises (Finances Quebec, June 2017). It is unknown why the specific enterprises were selected by the government to be regulated under the parity provision of the Act (all listed in Schedule 1 of the Act). While the Caisse de dépôt et placement du Quebec and Hydro-Quebec are not listed on Schedule 1, it is included in the Act as a notation in Section 43, the parity provision. Other high-profile state-owned enterprises subjected to the parity provision include the provincial auto insurance company, a lotteries regulator, and the corporation responsible for the purchase and distribution of alcohol.

The Act itself does not stipulate budget allocations, nor was there mention of an accompanying budget implementation bill. However, "financial frameworks" were articulated in a key policy document published by the Secrétariat à la condition féminine in 2011 noting that the 2007–2010 government action plan on gender equality included a $24 million financial commitment later extended in the 2010–2011 action plan with an additional $10 million (2011, p. 4). While these budget allocations are not just about equality measures to promote women's participation on boards, the funds nonetheless are part of the government policy priorities and gender action plans out of which the objectives of increasing women's empowerment and decision-making are part.

There are a few reporting requirements in the Act focusing on governance and ethics, financial auditing, and human resources. These are internal reporting procedures, however, which may or may not be included in annual reports made available for public review. Moreover, the Act does not legislate sanctions for failing to meet equity targets, nor are there any stipulated penalties codified in the Act if enterprises do not meet parity. Section 41 of the Act, however, does stipulate that the Minister responsible for state-owned enterprises must report to the government once every ten years, with the report tabled to the National Assembly.

Within the Act, capacity and learning instruments are evident. Section 19, for example, directs the members of the board to establish a committee system comprising of a governance and ethics committee, an audit committee, and a human resources committee. The board can comprise other committees to facilitate its operation. All of these committees are composed of board members. In the Act, there are lists of specific duties of each of three committees including, but not limited to, directing each board to ensure criteria are formulated for evaluating and assessing the performance of board members, creating training programs for board members, establishing a code of ethics for the conduct of the enterprise's operations, financial reporting, risk management, board selection, and board succession planning.

Implementation, Reporting, and Policy Empowerment

Extensive consultations took place within the public service, involving the women's policy agencies and a wide range of civil society actors. From a descriptive representation perspective, moderate empowerment is assessed, due to the wide array of key actors involved in policy development and implementation. The publication and implementation of gender action plans arguably facilitated women's policy empowerment.

Substantively the implementation story differs. Even with the Conseil's reporting as noted above, we have no insight about the implementation of the Act in terms of how the state-owned enterprises reacted to the gender parity clause or how they changed their internal appointment processes to meet the parity expectations codified in the Act. As well, there is no indication of a program evaluation. The absence of program evaluation was noted in Canada's 2016 report to UNESCO on the achievement of UNESCO's global priority on gender equality (Québec is a formal member of UNESCO as is the Canadian government). The report noted that while the Secrétariat à la condition féminine was responsible for coordinating a follow-up on the implementation of the *2011–2015 Government Action Plan on Gender Equality*, the action plan had not been evaluated (UNESCO, 2016).

Other than information made available in corporate annual reports, the only public reporting specific to the appointment of women on boards has been written and published by the province's women's policy agency (the Conseil), which reported on progress on the implementation of gender parity on corporate boards in two reports—one published in 2010, *La gouvernance des entreprises au Quebec: où sont les femmes?* (Company governance in Québec: Where are the women?), the other in 2014, *Les femmes dans les conseils d'administration des entreprises Québécoises* (Women on boards of directors in Québec companies). Both reports provide data, highlighting areas of progress and inertia in the representation of women in state-owned companies in Québec.

Thus, inclusive policy empowerment is only evident from certain vantage points given the participation of women's groups through the many formal consultation processes that led to the development of the government's various action plans on gender equality. The Act is weak in terms of evaluation and implementation in that there are no sanctions for non-compliance, and a bulk of reporting on the Act is firmly situated within the private domain of each enterprise.

Gender Transformation: Québec Leading the Way?

Québec has adopted a differentiated approach that combines state regulation for public enterprises with self-regulation for the private sector, following the voluntary self-regulatory approach of the ROC. At this point, it is uncertain whether the Québec law has led to significant gender transformation or not, even though the passage of the parity law, which made Québec distinct among Canadian provinces and territories as the only jurisdiction in Canada to have legislated quotas, albeit only for state-owned companies. The province, too, appears to be an outlier regarding the time and energy spent on researching, engaging civil society for the development of provincial equality strategies, and the government promotion of women's equality in decision-making. In 2006, 158 men and 60 women were present on the boards of state-owned enterprises in Québec; in September 2008, the number of men decreased to 151, while the number of women increased to 108 (Bagnall, 2008). Put another way, prior to the passage of the Act, women's representation in public enterprises in Québec accounted for 28% of board members (Bagnall, 2008). In 2008, just two years after implementation, women held 42% of board seats—an increase of fourteen percentage points (Ibid, 2008). And increases have continued. By 2014—two years after the parity law stipulated that gender balance had to be achieved by 2011—the Conseil reported that women's presence on boards in Québec increased from 28% to 52.4% (Conseil, 2014, p. 4). This is a laudable achievement and indication of success in terms of meeting the gender parity goal of the Act.

The premier and cabinet acted on and implemented an equality measure of consequence for public enterprises. There clearly was a numerical increase in the number of women on boards in Québec and increased organized advocacy by an array of women's groups and professional women's business groups. For example, the Business Professional Women, Montréal branch, actively advocated the federal government and Liberal cabinet ministers (Personal Interview, BPW) to pass Bill C-25, giving testimony to the Senate of Canada on December 12, 2017.

However, gatekeepers had little interest in directing concrete action in increasing women's representation on private-sector boards. Given the absence of spillover effects from the legislation, there is a clear absence of action in the private sector, and there are no indications from the gender action plans that the provincial government intends to even broach parity on listed corporations—the level of gender transformation is best characterized by gender accommodation. Attitudes among the corporate elite in Québec have not substantively shifted from preferring a comply-or-explain model. As well, there is no legislated sanction codified in the 2006 parity law to address non-compliance with the Act. Moreover, it is unknown if the Act has undergone a formal legislative review, and while the Act stipulates that the Minister of Finance, the office responsible for the administration of the Act, must report to the government after ten years in operation, tabling the report to the National Assembly, these are not readily available for public scrutiny.

Descriptive representation has been promoted through professional advocacy, which increased over the years since the adoption of the gender parity law, as has the attention about why it is important for governance and business results of companies to diversify boards. While descriptive representation is evident, substantive representation is less so given that some boards, notably those of Hydro-Québec and the Caisse, are typically chaired by a man, and quite surprisingly, the position is called "Chairman." The public auto insurance corporation, however, has been chaired by a woman with the office referred to in gender-neutral terms as "Chair."

And what of private-sector corporations across Canada? Concerns were expressed by the Canadian Board Diversity Council that while there had been an increase of women on boards, women continued to be underrepresented in key economic sectors such as oil, gas, mining, and manufacturing (2016). And more currently, the recommendation of the federal Advisory Council advocating a national goal of achieving 30% of women on boards for publicly traded companies, for a majority of Canada's corporations by 2019, was not achieved. The Conference Board of Canada recently reported that representation of women on boards under comply-or-explain is on average only 18%, although it is worth noting that on some of Canada's largest companies, the top sixty on the TSX, met the 30% objective (2020). A quantifiable change and one that, with continued corporate advocacy and civil society persuasion, may provide a foundation for more corporations to consider promoting women on boards.

Conclusion

To be sure, there was some success in implementation—the number of women on state-owned boards increased to meet the parity provision in the Act. As a policy instrument, the parity provision in the Act was a viable option in Québec. Not only did the provincial government implement a policy goal of great interest to women's groups and the general Québec public, but it also responded to vigorous policy advocacy from high-profile corporations and industry. The Charest government was able to take on a leadership role on board parity given its authority over governance structures of state-owned enterprises. Thus, the provincial Liberal party policy in asserting itself as protector of Québécois national identity was a key factor in the development and implementation of gender parity on public enterprises in Québec, particularly with a strong presence of women cabinet members and active femocrats who worked with industry advocacy groups like the Canadian Board Diversity Council and the Women's Executive Network. Certainly, more women in the upper echelons of the corporate world in Québec were empowered because of their appointment to boards of directors, although more research must be undertaken to reveal actual differences their presence has made in terms of shifting gender discourses and integrating diversity practices into corporate practices (Brière, Rinfret, and Lee-Gosselin, 2018).

At the same time, as is the case in the rest of corporate Canada, there remains today little to no appetite for gender parity on private-sector corporate boards, nor is there much motivation for government intervention to compel parity (Interview, Poulin). Indeed, the Institute of Corporate Boards stated that they and their association members do not support mandatory, legislated quota laws. Québec's action on gender parity can act as a potential tool to "nudge" key actors (the government and the private sector) to enhance diversity and equality policy goals (Engeli and Mazur, 2018, p. 115). For private-sector corporations and government-owned companies across the country, diversity disclosure policies and comply-and-explain approaches fix a spotlight on where women are and are not, in corporate governance and overall, in corporate Canada's commitment to diversity (Osler, 2018, p. 20). There is momentum building as more corporations willingly abide by the comply-and-explain mechanism. Liberal market values, however, are deeply engrained among corporate communities in Canada, which will prevent any concerted discussion about quota laws. The corporate world in Canada appears receptive to getting the most out of self-regulation, which may be a substantive way forward as decision-makers in government and industry experience the benefits of diverse voices on boards of directors.

Interviews

Christine Poulin, President Business Professional Women, Montreal, May 21, 2018.

References

Allaire, Yvan and François June Dauphin (2017) *Nos sociétés d'état: Sont-elles bien gouvernées?* Montreal: Institut sur la gouvernance. (In French only)

Bagnall, Janet (2008) "Success with Crown Corporations Shows Affirmative Action Works," *Montreal Gazette*, November 21, http://www.pressreader.com/canada/montreal-gazette/20081121/281835754546527 (Accessed December 17, 2021).

Bernardo, Melissa (2019) "How Canada Stacks up on Women's Representation on Corporate Boards," Canadian Broadcasting Company (CBC), May 14, https://www.cbc.ca/news/business/women-corporate-boards-globally-1.5131113 (Accessed December 17, 2021).

Bouchard, Marie J. (ed.) (2013) *Innovation and the Social Economy. The Quebec Experience*. Toronto: University of Toronto Press.

Brière, Sophie, Natalie Rinfret, and Hélène Lee-Gosselin (2018) "Impact of the Presence of Women on Public Sector and Private Corporations in Quebec: What May Be Learned from the Multiple Discourses of Board Members?," *International Journal of Corporate Governance*, 9(1), pp. 1–22.

Burgess, Zena and Phyllis Tharenou (2002) "Women Board Directors: Characteristics of the Few," *Journal of Business Ethics*, 37, pp. 39–49.

Burke, Ronald and Mary C. Mattis (eds.) 2000, *Women on Corporate Boards of Directors: International Challenges and Opportunities*. Dordrecht the Netherlands: Kluwer Academic Press.

Business Professional Women (2017) *Brief to the Senate of Canada on Bill C-25*. Montreal Chapter December 12. Retrieved at: https://bpwmontreal.com/.

Canadian Board Diversity Council (2010) *2010 Annual Report Card*. Toronto: Canadian Board Diversity Council.

Canadian Board Diversity Council (2016) *2016 Annual Report Card*. Toronto: Canadian Board Diversity Council.

Catalyst (1998) *Women Board Directors of Canada.* https://www.catalyst.org/wp-content/uploads/2019/02/1998_catalyst_census_women_board_directors_of_Canada.pdf (Accessed on November 3, 2019).

Catalyst (2006) *2005 Catalyst Census of Women Board Directors of the FP500.* https://www.catalyst.org/wp-content/uploads/2019/02/2005_Census_FP500_Women_Board_Directors.pdf (Accessed November 3, 2019).

Catalyst (2014) *2013 Catalyst Census of Women Board Directors of the FP500.* https://www.catalyst.org/research/2013-catalyst-census-fortune-500-women-board-directors/ (Accessed November 3, 2019).

Catalyst (2016) *Gender Diversity on Boards in Canada: Recommendations for Accelerating Progress.* https://www.catalyst.org/research/gender-diversity-on-boards-in-Canada-recommendations-for-acceslerating-progress/ (Accessed November 3, 2019).

Catalyst (2020) *Women on Corporate Boards: Quick Take,* https://www.catalyst.org/research/women-on-corporate-boards/ (Accessed December 17, 2021).

CBC (2008) "Women and the Economy Play Big Role in Charest's New Cabinet," https://www.cbc.ca/news/Canada/montreal/women-and-economy-play-big-role-in-charets-s-cabinet-1.724715 (Accessed November 3, 2019).

Conference Board of Canada (2013) *The Business Case for Women on Boards.* Ottawa: Conference Board of Canada.

Conference Board of Canada (2016) *Gender Wage Gap.* https://www.conferenceboard.ca/hcp/provincial/society/gender-gap.aspx (Accessed January 24, 2022).

Conference Board of Canada (2018) *Annual Report Card 2018.* Ottawa: Conference Board of Canada.

Conference Board of Canada (2020) *All on Board,* October 10, 2020, https://www.conferenceboard.ca/research/all-on-board (Accessed December 17, 2021).

Conseil du statut de la femme (2014) *Les femmes dans les conseils d'administraiton des entreprises Québécoises.* Québec: Conseil du statut de la femme.

Conseil du statut de la femme Décember (2006) *Pour que l'egalite de droit devienne une egalité de fait.* Québec City: Conseil du statut de la femme.

Conseil du statut de la femme Décembre (2010) *La gouvernance des entreprises au Québec: ou sont les femmes?* Québec: Bibliothèque et Archives Nationales du Québec.

Conseil du statut de la femme (2014), *Les femmes dans les conseils d'administraiton des entreprises Québécoises,* Québec: Conseil du statut de la femme. (Accessed November 3, 2020).

Crisan, Daria and McKenzie, Kenneth J. (2013) *Government-Owned Enterprises in Canada.* Calgary: University of Calgary, School of Public Policy.

Cross, Philip (2014) *The Public Purse versus Private Wallets: Comparing Provincial Approaches to Investing in Economic Growth.* Vancouver: C.D. Howe Institute.

Engeli, Isabelle and Amy Mazur (2018) "Taking Implementation Seriously in Assessing Success: The Politics of Gender Equality Policy," *European Journal of Politics and Gender,* 1(1–2), 111–129.

Finances Quebec (2017) *List of State-Owned Enterprises.* June. www.finances.gouv.ca/documents/ministere/en/MINEN_ListeENG-2017_SocietesEtat.pdf (Accessed November 3, 2019).

Follett, Arielle (2015) "Feds Propose 'Comply and Explain' Policy for Gender Diversity," *Huffpost.* April 25, 2015. https://www.kelownadailycourier.ca/news/national-news/article-87e07f96--ac06-5129-856f-0a33f5f1-d87a.html (Accessed December 17, 2021).

Haddow, Rodney (2015) *Comparing Quebec and Ontario: Political Economy and Public Policy at the Turn of the Millennium*. Toronto: University of Toronto Press.

Haddow, Rodney and Klassen, Thomas (2006) *Partisanship, Globalization, and Canadian Labour Market Policy: Four Provinces in Comparative Perspective*. Toronto: University of Toronto Press.

Holloway, Andy "Here Are a Few Quick Stats Culled from the FP500," *Financial Post*, September 5, 2019, https://business.financialpost.com/feature/fp500-the-premier-ranking (Accessed December 17, 2021).

Hydro-Quebec (2018) *Quebec Hydropower: Key to the Energy Transition*. Press Release. Montréal: Hydro-Quebec. May 18.

Innovation, Science and Economic Development Canada (2016) *Co-operatives in Canada*, Web Services, Innovation, Science and Economic Development Canada, http://www.ic.gc.ca/eic/site/693.nsf/eng/h_00116.html (Accessed December 17, 2021).

Innovation, Science and Economic Development Canada (2018) *Explanatory Note on Proposed Regulatory Amendments*, www.ic.gc.ca/eic/siTe/cd-dgc.nsf/eng/cs07274.html (Accessed December 17, 2021).

Institute of Corporate Directors (2011) *Diversity in the Boardroom: Findings and Recommendations of the Institute of Corporate Directors*. https://www.icd.ca/ICD/media/documents/2011_BoardDiversity_EN.pdf (Accessed December 17, 2021).

Lévesque, Benoît, Marie-Claire Malo, and Ralph Rouzier (1997) "The 'Caisse de dépôt et placement du Quebec' and the 'Mouvement des Caisses Populaires et d'économie des Jardins': Two Financial Institutions, the Same Convergence towards the General Interest?" *Annals of Public and Cooperative Economics*, 68(3), pp. 485–501.

Liberal Party of Canada (2016) *Adopted Priority Resolutions*. Biennial Convention Winnipeg 2016, https://liberal.ca/legacy-uploads/ (Accessed October 12, 2020).

Moyser, Melissa (2017) *Women and Work*. Statistics Canada, Catalogue no. 89-503X.

Organization for Economic Cooperation and Development (March 8, 2016) *Background Report: Conference on Improving Women's Access to Leadership*. Paris, France.

Osler (2018*) Diversity Disclosure Practices: Women in Leadership Roles at TSX-listed Companies*, https://osler.com (Accessed November 6, 2019).

Pelletier, Rachelle, Martha Patterson, and Melissa Moyser (2019) *The Gender Wage Gap in Canada: 1998 to 2018*. Ottawa: Statistics Canada. Component of Statistics Canada catalogue no. 75-004-M-2019004.

Petersson, Bengt, Rodrigo Mariscal, and Kotaro Ishi (2017) *Women Are the Key for Future Growth: Evidence from Canada*. Washington, DC: IMF Working Paper, WP/17/166.

Québec (2017), *Act Respecting the Governance of State-Owned Enterprises*. Updated to April 1, 2017.

Secrétariat à la condition féminine (2011) *Turning Equality in Law into Equality in Fact*. Québec: Secrétariat à la condition féminine.

Secrétariat à la condition féminine (2017) *Together for Equality: Government Strategy for Gender Equality Toward 2021*. Québec: Secrétariat à la condition féminine.

Statistics Canada (2011) *Women in Canada: A Gender-based Statistical Report*. Statistics Canada, Catalogue no. 89-503–X.

Statistics Canada (2016) "The Surge of Women in the Workforce," *The Daily*, statscan.gc.ca/pub/11-630-x/11-630-x2015009-eng.htm (Accessed December 17, 2021).

Statistics Canada (2017) "Study: Women in Canada: Women and Paid Work," *The Daily*, Wednesday, March 8, 2017. Component of Statistics Canada catalogue no. 11-001–X.

Statistics Canada (2019) "Study: Representation of Women on Boards of Directors, 2016," *The Daily*, Tuesday, May 7, 2019. Component of Statistics Canada catalogue no. 11-001–X.

Status of Women Canada (2014) *Good for Business: A Plan to Promote the Participation of More Women on Canadian Boards*. Report by the Government of Canada's Advisory Council for Promoting Women on Boards. Gatineau: Status of Women Canada. Catalogue No. SW21-162/2014E-PDF.

Status of Women Canada (2015) *Progress Highlights: Increasing Representation of Women on Canadian Boards*. Gatineau: Status of Women Canada. Catalogue No. SW21-164/2015E-PDF.

The Institute for Governance of Private and Public Organizations (2009) *The Status of Women Corporate Directors in Canada: Pushing for Change*. Montreal: Institute for Governance of Private and Public Organizations.

UNESCO (2016) *Canada's Report*, https://en.unesco.org/creativity/governance/periodic-reports/2016/Canada (Accessed August 23, 2020).

Women Get on Board (2019) *About: Women Get on Board*, https://womengetonboard.ca (Accessed December 17, 2021).

Wohlbold, Elise and Louise Chenier (2011) *Women in Senior Management: Where Are They?* Ottawa: Conference Board of Canada.

8

Diffusing Equality without Domestic Gender Champions? Incremental Change and Window-dressing in Croatia and Serbia

Andrea Spehar

Introduction

This chapter analyzes the policy approach in Croatia and Serbia in addressing the (under)representation of women on corporate boards in the context of the role of domestic and international forces at play in agenda setting, policy adoption and implementation. Since the mid-1990s, both countries have made substantial progress in adopting new legislation and policies aimed at ensuring greater gender equality in different spheres of social life owing to the mobilization of women at the domestic level and international pressure (Petricevic, 2012; Spehar, 2012; 2018). As part of the EU membership process and international obligations, Croatian and Serbian governments have set up national machinery for the advancement of gender equality, creating special departments, directorates, agencies, and committees at national and local levels to deal with this matter (Bego, 2015; Spehar, 2018).

The progress in gender equality policymaking is not evident in the area of corporate equality. Even though women in Croatia and Serbia are underrepresented on company boards, the issue has not yet received significant political attention. In 2020, the average representation of women on company boards in Croatia was 26.7% and 15.3% in Serbia. Croatia and Serbia still belong to the group of countries without mandatory gender quotas for management and supervisory boards of companies. They have instead adopted a limited mixed approach, which combines legislative state-driven policy and self-imposed initiatives driven by peak employer associations. In both countries, the state-driven policy approach, influenced by the requirements from the UN Convention on Elimination of Discrimination against Women (the CEDAW) and the EU, allow for positive action measures. Moreover, the Act on Gender Equality in Croatia and the Law on Equality between Sexes in Serbia impose a duty on state-owned companies to respect the prohibition of sex

Andrea Spehar, *Diffusing Equality without Domestic Gender Champions?* In: *Gender Equality and Policy Implementation in the Corporate World.* Edited by Isabelle Engeli and Amy G. Mazur, Oxford University Press.
© Oxford University Press (2022). DOI: 10.1093/oso/9780198865216.003.0008

discrimination and imply that the specific measures are to be introduced when one gender is "substantially underrepresented."[1]

The introduction of corporate quotas is emphasized in policy documents such as the Serbian National Strategy for Gender Equality for the years 2016–2020, which stipulates the introduction of quotas for state-owned company boards.[2] Similarly, the National Policy on Gender Equality, which was adopted by the Croatian Parliament in 2011, aims to create gender balance in supervisory and management board members in the public and private sectors by ensuring that the share of the underrepresented gender, pursuant to the Act on Gender Equality, does not fall below 40%.[3] So far, however, legislators in Croatia and Serbia have not adopted any provisions or measures with a view to explicitly promote corporate equality that targets positive action of any kind, including quota rules.

In the absence of binding state regulations, national business organizations and, in the Croatian case, the Gender Equality Ombuds Office, have taken initiatives for promoting gender diversity in boardrooms. These initiatives, in most cases supported and financed by international organizations and donors, include research and consciousness-raising about the underrepresentation problem and measures that encourage the empowerment of businesswomen. As this chapter argues, the different efforts to put the issue on the public agenda have been very fragmented and limited in scope, consisting of for the most part just one-off interventions with no strategic follow-up. In both Croatia and Serbia, aside from national gender equality machinery, international organizations, and a few local women business actors, there has been a lack of any visible gender champions and advocates lobbying for authoritative provisions or preferential measures of any kind, including quota rules, to be put into place with a view to promoting the number of women on company boards.

While in both countries, the engagement and advocacy work carried out by women's NGOs and movements generally laid the groundwork for the spread and implementation of different gender equality policies, this was not the case for gender equality policy in the corporate world. In the context of the complexity of the post-communist transition, other feminist issues such as abortion rights, domestic violence, economic insecurity, and political representation were considered more pressing to mobilize around than corporate equality. Indeed, over the past two decades, both countries had been confronted with a complex heritage of an ambiguous commitment to gender equality during the communist period, then complicated by a transition in the 1990s in which there were

---

[1] Act on Gender Equality, Official Gazette no. 82/08 and Law on Gender Equality, Official Gazette no. 104/2009.
[2] National Strategy for Gender Equality 2016–2020 with the Plan of Action for the Implementation for 2016–2018, "Official Gazette of the Republic of Serbia," No. 4/2016.
[3] The National Policy for Gender Equality 2011–2015 (Official Gazette, No. 114/06).

prominent calls for "re-traditionalization" (Funk and Mueller, 1993; Gal and Klig-man, 2000). There were, for example, arguments that women should be liberated from their "forced (sic)" participation in the labor market under communism and retreat to domesticity. At the same time, the dual breadwinner model was under-mined by economic insecurity where higher unemployment brought an increase in women's dependence on men's incomes, and by a reduction of welfare state intervention, as a consequence of hard budget constraints and market austerity reforms (Hassenstab and Ramet, 2015).

The research conducted for this comparative study consists of content analysis of policy documents and open-ended interviews with key policy in the agenda-setting and policy adoption and implementation processes actors (see list at the end of the chapter). After a brief contextualization of gender equality in the Croa-tian and Serbian labor market and corporate world, the issue of how women's presence in corporate boards was placed on the political agenda is analyzed. Next, the policy instruments that were adopted and their enactment and monitoring in practice are examined, followed by an assessment of women's empowerment and the limited extent of gender transformation.

Persistent Gender Inequality in the Corporate World

Croatia and Serbia are examples of European post-socialist countries with a long tradition of state socialist measures to promote women's engagement in economic life. The socialist regime in the former Yugoslavia was characterized by a de jure gender equality in labor relations, which translated into equal access to educational opportunities and high levels of employment among men and women. However, women were underrepresented in leadership positions in the economic world (Hassenstab and Ramet, 2015).

The transition to a market economy was marked by sectoral restructuring, pri-vatization of state-owned enterprises, price adjustments, growth of the informal sector, and a rapid increase in unemployment. Today, the Croatian and Serbian labor markets stand among the weakest in the EU, with high unemployment and low employment rates (IMF, 2015). Companies in Croatia and Serbia are orga-nized under a one-tier or two-tier system, the latter being more common among the largest listed companies. For example, all ten of the largest listed companies in Croatia are organized under the two-tier system.[4] While a code of corporate gov-ernance exists in both countries, it makes no mention of gender equality issues, including representation at the board level.

---

[4] A dual board or two-tier system is a corporate structure system that consists of two separate boards of directors, the "management board" and the "supervisory board"; each of these serves a particu-lar purpose. Under a one-tier system, the company is governed by a unified board performing both management and supervisory functions.

Slow Progress and Stagnation in Women's Corporate Representation

Due to the absence of any official monitoring of women's corporate leadership positions, there is no official data in either country on women's presence on boards. Best estimates are made through periodic research conducted by different institutions and organizations, like the European Institute for Gender Equality (EIGE). The legacies of the communist period in combination with economic and political changes, set off by the political transition, made it difficult for women to break through the glass ceiling into the corporate world, where their status matches the predominant indicators on the position of women and men in the Croatian and Serbian labor markets more broadly speaking. Traditional gender roles dictate the division of jobs at the executive level, just as they produce horizontal gender segregation in the labor market. Women reach leadership positions at a later point in life and leave them earlier, which corresponds with their earlier exit from the labor market. Between 2008 and 2020, similar to the development within the EU, we can witness a slight increase in the proportion of women on the boards of the largest listed companies: four percentage points in Serbia and thirteen percentage points in Croatia (see Tables 8.1 and 8.2). The improving gender balance at the board level includes also some progress at the very top. In Serbia, the proportion of women among board chairs (presidents) has more than doubled from 2.8% in 2012 to 14.3% to 30% in 2020. Improvement is slower, however, among top executives. Just 9.5% of the largest listed companies in Croatia have a woman CEO

Table 8.1 Percentage Share of Women on Boards in the Largest Listed Companies in Croatia, 2008–2020

	EU-28	CROATIA				
	Board members	Board members	President	CEO	Executives	Non-executives
2008	*10.8*	11.5	4.5	—	—	—
2009	*11*	15	4.5	—	—	—
2010	*11.9*	15.6	4.5	—	—	—
2011	*13.7*	19	4.2	—	—	—
2012	*15.8*	16.3	4.3	4.3	16.7	15.6
2013	*17.8*	13.3	4	4	17	13.7
2014	*20.2*	15.3	8	4.3	17.8	15.3
2015	*22.7*	20.3	8	4	16.9	20.3
2016	*23.9*	22.2	8.7	4.3	19.5	22.2
2017	*25.3*	22.6	8	8	22.1	22.6
2018	*26.7*	19.3	4.5	4.5	16.7	19.3
2019	*28.8*	24.3	0	6.3	14.3	27
2020	*29.2*	26.7	4.5	9.5	10	27.1

Source: EIGE Database. Data for October each year, except for 2020 [April]

Table 8.2 Percentage Share of Women on Boards in the Largest Listed Companies in Serbia, 2008–2020

	EU-28	SERBIA				
	Board members	Board members	President	CEO	Executives	Non-executives
2008	10.8	13.5	—	—	—	—
2009	11	14.3	7.7	—	—	—
2010	11.9	12.4	21.4	—	—	—
2011	13.7	17.3	21.4	—	—	—
2012	15.8	16.5	14.3	16.7	18.3	19.1
2013	17.8	19.4	13.3	20	25	18.1
2014	20.2	15.3	23.1	0	23.9	15.2
2015	22.7	15.3	23.1	7.7	29.9	15.2
2016	23.9	19.8	23.1	15.4	27	20
2017	25.3	20.3	27.3	0	22.4	20.6
2018	26.7	21.2	27.3	0	19	20
2019	28.8	17.9	27.3	0	21.9	15.5
2020	29.2	17.5	30	0	20.7	15.1

Source: EIGE Database. Data for October each year, except for 2020 [April]

(Chief Executive Officer). Serbia is also struggling when it comes to the number of female CEOs, with no women holding the position in leading companies in the country in 2020.

Comprehensive research conducted in 2014 and 2015 by the Croatian Ombuds for Gender Equality within an EU-financed project provides additional valuable sources of information in this area (Ombuds for Gender Equality 2016a).[5] A survey was conducted electronically of the top 500 Croatian companies with 168 companies responding (33.6%). According to the survey results, women make up on average 19% of these boards (Vranješ Radovanović et al, 2016), which corroborates the EIGE figures in Tables 8.1 and 8.2. According to the CROBEX Index, which measures the share of women in management and board positions in the most important companies on the Zagreb Stock Exchange, the share of women on boards of the leading companies in Croatia in recent years was 20.9% in 2016, 17.3% in 2017, 19.7% in 2018, and 14.5% in 2019. Among Croatian companies in the composition of *CROBEX*, the number of "zero companies," or companies that do not have a single woman on their boards in 2019, was 55%.[6]

In Serbia, a study was conducted in 2016 by the faculty of economics and public administration of the composition of Beleks, Belgrade Stock Exchange in the

---

[5] https://staklenilabirint.prs.hr/info/o-projektu/, accessed 15.03.20.
[6] https://lider.media/aktualno/crobex-u-upravama-vodecih-hrvatskih-tvrtki-sve-manje-zena-39422, accessed 19.03.20.

period 2005–2014 (Misckovic 2016). The data show no major changes from EIGE data. The average share of women on boards was 21.5%, with the lowest share of 19.53% in 2008 and the highest share of 24.85% in 2012 (Ibid, p. 41). In January 2013, the International Finance Corporation (IFC) launched a research project entitled women on corporate boards in Bosnia and Herzegovina, FYR Macedonia, and Serbia (Djulic and Kuzman, 2013). The purpose of the study was to gather information on the representation of women on corporate boards and to learn about the determinants of female board representation in these countries. The study found that on average women need a higher level of education and more work experience to become board members relative to their male colleagues. Considering the development over the past ten years, it could be concluded that Croatia and Serbia are far from breaking the glass ceiling holding women back in the corporate world, an indication of the very low level of political interest in corporate equality among a wide range of different actors in Croatia and Serbia. The analysis now takes a deeper dive into this apathy and disinterest.

Limited Interest in Advocating for Corporate Equality

In the second half of the 1990s, western governments and international organizations such as the UN and EU have made Balkan countries a laboratory to test the idea that getting women involved politically facilitates war-to-democracy transitions (Irvine, 2013). The democratic transitions in the Balkans defined intervention and assistance efforts with an increased focus on women's empowerment and gender policy development (Spehar, 2018). Thus, the transition to democracy created an opportunity for women in Croatia and Serbia to start establishing new groups and mobilizing other actors with similar policy preferences to pressure the political establishment to take action on a range of issues relevant to gender equality. Research on women's movement activism in Croatia and Serbia shows that the movements played an important role in the formation of gender policy during the transition period. Women's movements were influential in raising a number of issues related to domestic violence, political representation, and antidiscrimination to the public agenda as well as in the actual formation of gender policies (Spehar, 2012; 2018). In contrast, they were not actively involved in the policy process related to the issue of gender equality on corporate boards. On one hand, it is surprising that the most prominent advocates of gender equality since the 1990s, Croatian and Serbian women's rights NGOs, did not mobilize around corporate gender inequality. On the other, considering the great need of tackling the challenges and threats to women's rights in other important gender policy related areas, it is less surprising.

While the political (under)representation of women was, in the past two decades, publicly debated and covered by the media in both countries, the issue of the representation of women on corporate boards in private and public companies did not even reach the public agenda through the media, much less become an object of political debate. The question of achieving gender equality in the corporate world appeared on the political agenda to some extent from 2010 onward, when women representing Croatian and Serbian national employer associations organized several public workshops with the aim of supporting the career development of businesswomen and discussing different measures that would increase the representation of women in the corporate world. Inspired by international practices in the area of corporate equality, women from the Serbian Chamber of Commerce initiated in 2010 a project "Employers and Gender Equality" with financial support from UNIFEM and the Norwegian embassy. The main objective of the project was to conduct research on women in management positions and on company boards. The three-year project also included seminars, workshops, and round tables on the issue in order to educate and *raise consciousness* of employers, for the most part, men, on gender equality related issues in the Serbian corporate world.

In the case of Croatia, the Gender Equality Ombuds together with the Croatian Employers' Association (HUP) staged several campaigns in the 2000s to sensitize the public to the question. According to the Croatian Ombuds, the 2012 Commission Proposal for a Directive of the European Parliament and of the Council on improving the gender balance among non-executive directors of companies listed on stock exchanges and related measures triggered these campaigns (Interview 1). From October 2013 until April 2016, the Ombuds for Gender Equality carried out the project "Dismantling the Glass Labyrinth: Equal Opportunity Access to Economic Decision-making in Croatia," financed from EC funds as part of the Progress program. The total project value was 250,000 euros (Ombuds for Gneder equality 2016b). The aim of the project was to raise awareness and promote the need for a balanced representation of women and men in management positions in companies. Four studies were conducted as part of the project, including on the representation of women and men in management positions, the way men and women employers perceive the benefits of gender balance in business decision-making, and the way businesswomen perceive possible obstacles to management positions.

The results of the project were presented in several public workshops in different Croatian cities and through public media. The international actors also influenced the Croatian Employer Association (HUP) to engage on the issue. In 2018, HUP launched together with the Canadian Embassy the initiative to set up the globally recognized "30% Club" in Croatia, in a bid to encourage greater representation of women on companies' management and supervisory boards.[7] The then Croatian Minister for Economy and Entrepreneurship, Martina Dalic, stated that the

---

[7] The 30% Club is a global campaign led by chairs and CEOs taking action to increase gender diversity at board and senior management levels. see https://30percentclub.org/.

Croatian government supported this initiative and advocated stronger representation of women in top managerial positions through its activities to achieve a
ratio of at least 30% on the management boards of companies (Jutarnji list, 2018).
However, since making that statement, no governmental effort has been made to
adopt any measures with the aim of improving the gender balance in the corporative world. Furthermore, in terms of any feminist advocacy alliances in the state
or society, they seem to be still lacking any strong support on the domestic level.

Concrete Decision-making or Window-dressing Supported by the European Union?

To date, the national legislators in Croatia and Serbia have been rather reluctant
to adopt positive action measures in the form of quotas in the area of corporate
board equality. In principle, national laws simply provide permission to take positive action and leave the actual decision to employers. Table 8.3 presents the mixed
approach of a variety of soft and symbolic measures adopted in both countries.

The only explicit mention of a quota was put in national gender equality strategies. The Serbian National Strategy for Gender Equality for the years 2016–2020[8]
stipulates the introduction of quotas for state-owned company boards. According
to the policy document,

> The Ministry responsible for monitoring the implementation of the Law on Gen-
> der Equality should amend instruments to stipulate a legally mandated quota of
> at least 30% of women in the boards of directors—managing and supervisory
> boards of public enterprises.
>
> (p. 94)

In the National Economic Reform Program for 2016–2018, the Serbian Government also commits to increasing the participation of women directors and
members of managing boards to 20% in 2018 targeting to reach 30% in 2020.[9]
Similarly, the National Policy on Gender Equality that was adopted by the Croatian
Parliament in 2011 says that,

> In appointing members of supervisory and management boards of companies
> in the public and private sector, account will be taken of the need to establish a
> balanced representation of both genders, so that the under-represented gender,
> pursuant to the Act on Gender Equality, does not fall below 40%.
>
> (p. 58)

---

[8] National Strategy for Gender Equality 2016–2020 with the Plan of Action for the Implementation
for 2016-2018, "Official Gazette of the Republic of Serbia," No. 4/2016.
[9] National Economic Reform Programme for 2016–2018, http://www.mfin.gov.rs/UserFiles/File/
dokumenti/2016/Economic%20Reform%20Program%202016%202018.p.

Table 8.3 Policy Measures for Gender Equality on Corporate Boards in Croatia and Serbia

SELF-REGULATION	
CROATIA	**SERBIA**
* In 2016, the Croatian Gender Equality Ombuds and the Croatian Employers' Association (HUP) created the *Database of Business Women in Croatia* * In 2018, the Croatian Employers' Association (HUP) launched, together with the Canadian Embassy, the initiative to set up a "30% Club" in Croatia * In 2020, the Croatian Employers' Association (HUP) launched a mentoring program for businesswomen who have the ambition to advance in their professional careers and take senior and leading positions in companies	* In 2010, the Serbian Chamber of Commerce initiated a project "Employers and Gender Equality" with financial support from UNIFEM and the Norwegian embassy. The project aimed to raise the consciousness of the employers on gender (in)equality in the Serbian corporate world * In 2014, the IFC "Corporate Governance Program," together with the Serbian Chamber of Commerce, launched several events in Serbia specifically targeting existing or aspiring female leaders and board members

STATE-REGULATION	
CROATIA	**SERBIA**
Act on Gender Equality 2008 * State-owned companies should introduce specific measures when one gender is "substantially underrepresented," less than 40% * State-owned companies should produce periodical equality action plans every four years Lack of effective implementation mechanisms Poor implementation of the Law **National Policy on Gender Equality 2011–2015** * Aims for a gender balance in private and state-owned company boards by ensuring that the share of the underrepresented gender does not fall below 40% Not implemented	**Law on Equality between Sexes 2009** * State-owned companies should apply * Affirmative measures if the representation of the less represented sex is under 30% Lack of effective implementation mechanisms Poor implementation of the Law **National Strategy for Gender Equality for the years 2016–2020** * Stipulates the introduction of a mandatory quota of at least 30% for state-owned company boards Not implemented

The above-mentioned provisions were not adopted due to the active lobbying by different national actors. They were rather an outcome of the Council of Europe Committee of Minister Recommendation REC (2003) to Member States on balanced participation of women and men in political and public decision-making, and the two countries obligations derived from the process of accession to the

European Union. In neither country has there been, thus far, any efforts to actually implement or enforce the stipulations related to gender equality on company boards in the national gender equality strategies.

The adoption of the 2008 Act on Gender Equality in Croatia and the adoption of the 2009 Law on Equality between Sexes in Serbia marked a first step toward integrating the international standards and EU Directives on gender equality and non-discrimination in the national legal framework. Actors from several relevant ministries, the representatives of women's civil society organizations, and legal experts participated in drafting the laws. The Croatian Act on Gender Equality includes a special chapter on positive action measures (Chapter III—Articles 9–12). Article 12(1) in the Act stipulates the obligation to promote equal participation of men and women across the legislative, judiciary, the executive, and public sectors. Article 12(3) stipulates that a noticeable imbalance exists when members of one sex constitute less than 40% of members participating in "bodies involved in political decision-making and decision-making of public interest." The Law imposes very few obligations on private-sector employers beyond the duty to respect the sex discrimination ban (Selanec and Senden, 2013, pp. 5455). It is not explicitly mentioned that the promotion of the representatives of the less represented sex in advisory and managerial bodies applies to state-owned companies. It is, however, explicitly mentioned that these companies must produce periodical equality action plans according to Article 11. These plans have to be submitted every four years. An action plan must include an analysis of the existing situation within the state institution or a company. It must also include the reasons for introducing or not introducing specific positive action measures, the goals to be achieved, the manner in which they are to be achieved, and the method of supervision.

In Serbia, the 2009 Law on Equality between Sexes requires public authorities to develop active equal opportunity policies in all spheres of public life and across all phases of planning, formulating, and implementing decisions that affect the position of women and men. The Law prescribes a series of obligations for public and private employers in respect of equal opportunities and the introduction of special measures to increase employment and opportunities for employment of the less represented sex. It also aims to increase the participation of the less represented sex in professional training and provision of equal opportunities for advancement (Article 11), keeping of records and documentation about the gender structure of employees (Article 12) as well as with respect to planning of measures to mitigate or eliminate unequal representation of sexes and any reporting on those measures (Article 13). The Law also prescribes equal access to jobs and positions. If the representation of the less represented sex in the management and supervision bodies is less than 30%, the public institutions, including state-owned companies, are obliged to apply affirmative measures in accordance with the Law on Civil Servants and the Law on State Administration (Article 14). Private companies that have more than fifty employees are also obliged by the law to adopt and implement a plan of measures for the elimination or mitigation of unequal representation of women and men every year.

The idea of introducing corporate gender quotas with effective sanction mechanisms, although not discussed extensively, has been controversial in both countries and it was not the subject of organized advocacy in the process of drafting the gender equality related legislation. No political party has ever advocated corporate gender quotas. When publicly discussed in the media or at the seminars, corporate gender quotas are usually advocated by individual femocrats and the female representatives of the business organizations. Arguments in favor of corporate gender quotas and effective implementation mechanisms advocated by these actors are framed in terms of social justice claims for equal representation, of the diversity of perspective and contributions possible from different lived experiences, and business case arguments of improved performance through a wider skill set and professional experience.

In both countries, several studies have assessed the perception of gender equality in the corporate world (Djulic and Kuzman, 2013; Miskovic 2016; Vranješ Radovanović and Šurina Hanzl, 2016). Vranješ Radovanović and Šurina Hanzl's study on Croatia shows that the majority of women on company boards and in managerial positions (57%) believe that women are exposed to discriminatory barriers in business surroundings but still opposes binding legal instruments enacting a certain gender quota on company boards. A relatively high percentage of women (45%) consider that gender-balanced company boards are not a decisive factor for company success.

Another study conducted in Serbia shows that a large majority of interviewees (89% of women and 82% of men) believe that board diversity is important and that it adds value to board work; most women believe that the double-burden syndrome is the single biggest obstacle and the main reason why women still cannot "have it all"; 75% of women and 59% of men in the region agree that current legislation and policies do not support women in their career aspirations (FEFA, 2016). However, a large majority of interviewed men (76%), as well as a majority of interviewed women (62.5%), were against quotas (Ibid).

To conclude, Croatia and Serbia show striking similarities regarding the promotion of women's leadership in the economy. The issue has, so far, not become more salient in recent years and has not led to the implementation of binding quotas for boards of public or private companies. The agenda-setting and the decision-making were clearly more influenced by international requirements and recommendations. The commitment to corporate quotas through policy documents such as national gender equality strategies was not implemented. The current legislation imposes very few obligations on private and state companies beyond the duty to respect the sex discrimination ban and should be described as proactive rather than mandatory duties. In principle, national laws simply provide permission to take positive action and leave the actual decision to companies which, in Croatian and Serbian context, has been shown to be a rather weak policy mechanism. Moreover, although international pressure from the EU and other international actors has been an important driver in this policy area, there has been little feminist mobilization around the issue either on the part of individual actors, women's groups, or even women's policy agencies at the national level.

The Limits of Voluntary Measures: Fixing "Women" not the Systems

In the light of the weak state legislative mechanisms and the absence of the mobilization of women, some voluntary measures are utilized to increase the representation of women in the boardroom. Mostly it is about voluntary initiatives that include training, mentoring, and sponsorship of programs, which assist in the development of so-called female talent. These voluntary efforts also include setting up databases of women interested in and qualified to sit on boards in order to make it easier for companies to find board-ready women. Even in the case of voluntary measures, international efforts seem quite important. Different initiatives, in both countries, were in most cases supported and financed by international organizations and donors. In spring 2014, the IFC through its Corporate Governance Program,[10] together with the Serbian Chamber of Commerce launched several events in Serbia specifically targeting existing or aspiring female leaders and board members. The training aimed at improving their corporate governance skills and focused on educating participants in areas where there is a presumed need for better knowledge and skills among women executives, i.e. corporate finance and the role of board members in monitoring company risk. According to the vice-president of the Serbian Chamber of Commerce,

> The Serbian Chamber of Commerce is keen to contribute to the development of skills of women on boards through targeted and dedicated trainings. Formally, we have fulfilled the conditions for achieving equality, but it does not work in practice. Therefore, Serbian Employers' Association actively supports and will support all initiatives aimed at achieving true equality of women and men in the business world, but also in the wider community.
>
> (Interview 2)

In 2016, the Croatian Gender Equality Ombuds and the Croatian Employer Association (HUP) initiated the creation of the Database of Business Women in

---

[10] IFC's ESG Program helps to promote sustainable investment into seven selected priority countries in Eastern Europe and Central Asia, through a programmatic approach targeting ESG in both the financial and real sector: https://www.ifc.org/wps/wcm/connect/topics_ext_content/ifc_external_corporate_site/ifc+cg/regional_advisory_programs/europe+and+central+asia.

Croatia, launched in spring 2016, and is hosted on the HUP´s website.[11] The Croatian database of Business Women was largely inspired by similar databases across the world and was part of a wider EU-funded Progress program that aimed at removing the glass labyrinth. The main purpose of the database was to encourage companies to hire more women in management positions because they are still significantly underrepresented in comparison to men. The Croatian Ombuds for Gender Equality explained the need for launching the Base of Business Women in the following way.

> Although as the Base will prove we have enough trained, qualified and competent women who can be executive directors, members or presidents of management boards of companies, it is still more common to find men on such positions. Progress is present, but it is still too slow and needs to be stepped up.
>
> (Interview 1)

During 2016 and 2017, the Croatian Ombuds Office organized several workshops on leadership for members of the Base. The Base of Business Women includes over 100 members on average and is renewed every six months. This is one of the rare voluntary measures that has, after the international financing ended, been institutionalized and further developed by domestic actors. After the completion of the EU project in 2017, HUP took over the management of the Base. In 2020, the HUP has also launched a mentoring program for businesswomen who have the ambition to advance in their professional careers and take senior and leading positions in companies.[12] The mentoring cycles will last six months, and the mentors are successful women and men from various fields, in the positions of presidents or members of the management boards of leading companies or have leading roles in HUP's associations. To what extent these voluntary measures will be effective in the long run is difficult to predict. As Tables 8.1 and 8.2 showed, the figures for recent years witness a slight increase in the proportion of women on the boards of the largest listed companies in Croatia.

The Absence of Authoritative Implementation Mechanisms

So far, the key positive action measure prescribed by the gender equality legislation and the policy documents such as national gender equality strategies, have not yet been implemented by the Croatian and Serbian governments and the corporate world. A formal evaluation made by the Croatian Ombuds for Gender Equality

---

[11] www.hup.hr and http://staklenilabirint.prs.hr/
[12] https://www.ictbusiness.info/leadership/hup-pokrece-program-mentorstva-za-poslovne-zene-hrvatske, accessed 15.03.20

clearly states that positive action measures in the Croatian Act on Gender Equality from 2008, are rarely implemented in practice (Ombuds for Gender Equality, 2017). Several factors hamper effective implementation. While the equality action plans for state-owned companies in Croatia have the potential to be an effective measure, what is clearly lacking is an institutional mechanism capable of managing and monitoring their implementation. The action plans must be approved by the Government's Office for Gender Equality; however, this office is lacking the institutional capacity for such a demanding task since it is understaffed with only four employees and has insufficient financial resources (Interview 1). Moreover, the gender equality officers working as part of the state institutions and companies, who are directly responsible for monitoring the equality plans, lack expertise and independence and no additional pay is provided for their effort (Ombuds for Gender Equality, 2017).

Another significant implementation challenge is related to the lack of interest and political will to tackle the underrepresentation of women in the corporate world. For example, the action plans drafted by public companies in Croatia show a rather simplistic approach toward increasing employment-related opportunities of the less represented sex. The most significant part of the equality plans is the generation of gender-sensitive statistics. However, the goals and measures set by these plans are very vague and general. Many plans admit that women are in an unfavorable position. However, the action plans do not identify concrete discriminatory barriers. Similarly, they do not suggest specific measures that should be introduced to increase the representation of women (Interview 1). The Serbian Law on Equality between Sexes from 2009 has similar deficiencies that prevent effective implementation (Interview 3).[13] Serbian women's NGOs also assess that the law lacks efficient implementation mechanisms, clear mandates, and sufficiently specific provisions that would govern the gender equality mechanisms at all levels, and effective penalties for non-compliance with the statutory provisions (Ignjatovic, 2016).

The absence of authoritative implementation mechanisms seems to be one of the most obvious weaknesses of positive action practice in Croatia and Serbia. Consequently, a considerable number of positive action measures remain ineffective in the corporate world. This ineffectiveness suggests that positive action tends to be a result of ad hoc decisions rather than some coherent equality policy. In other words, although strong on paper, positive action is very low on the political agenda of Croatian and Serbian governments. Moreover, without any strong gender champions at the national level in state or society to hold the government's feet to the fire, this policy dynamic will more than likely continue.

---

[13] See for example, Regular Annual Report of the Commissioner for the Protection of Equality for 2017, available at: http://ravnopravnost-5bcf.kxcdn.com/wp-content/uploads/2018/03/RGI-2017_PZR_FINAL_14.3.2018-1.pdf, accessed 10.05.19, accessed 05.06.20.

The Absence of Gender Transformation and Policy Empowerment

The lack of systematic and longitudinal data makes the assessment of the transformative potential of the various initiatives toward promoting corporate equality in Croatia and Serbia complex. For example, one survey that was conducted in Croatia in 2014 showed that the majority of women in managerial positions were not in favor of mandatory quotas. However, no surveys were conducted in consecutive years and thus it is not possible to determine if any change took place. The data shows slow progress in the last two decades related to the average share of women on corporate boards. What has changed since 2010 is the increasing engagement on the topic of gender underrepresentation due to the different initiatives that were organized by business associations and, in the Croatian case, by the Gender Equality Ombuds. The issue gained more attention in the media since 2000. However, this media attention is mostly about covering the specific events and the interviews with the event organizers rather than a groundswell of public interest in corporate gender equality.

There are virtually no signs that the frames used by the Croatian and Serbian political elites have changed at all regarding women on corporate boards. Their willingness to put the issue on the public agenda and implement concrete measures is low if not completely inexistent. The vast majority of concrete initiatives toward the promotion of corporate equality have been launched, financed, and driven by international donors, most prominently UNIFEM and the EU. So far, corporate equality has not been prioritized in their party programs or lobbying for measures such as corporate quotas. Moreover, the issue of gender equality in the corporate world is still not even on the list of policy priorities for women's movements and groups or the women's policy machinery in either country; thus, any inclusive policy empowerment where actors come forward to represent and speak for women in the implementation process has been non-existent. Indeed, the policy outcomes in both countries are a textbook case of "gender-neutral" in terms of GEPP measures. In this outcome, the policy has failed in transforming gender relations or has even not attempted to do so. It is unlikely that much money or resources were invested in the implementation. There are numerous policies that did not result in any tangible effect on the promotion of gender and sexual equality or that were not even implemented at all. As a result, these policies are likely, at best, to be gender-neutral in their generated outcome.

Conclusion

This study reveals that calls for gender equality in the corporate world in Croatia and Serbia coming from outside of the countries failed to mobilize any champions in state or society on behalf of women themselves; as a consequence, there has been an absence of any concrete implementation efforts regarding promoting women on boards in either public or private companies. All in all, corporate gender equality policymaking in the two countries appeared to have failed to move beyond the very first step in the process—the agenda-setting (very important in itself, though), consciousness-raising about the women's absence on corporate boards, and pursuing concrete and authoritative measures to promote gender equality in the corporate boardroom.

To be sure, there was some superficial difference in certain corporate leadership positions in Croatia compared to Serbia according to the EIGE data. But given that no official statistics are being collected by either government, there is no way of verifying whether this is an anomaly of the EIGE data. That there is a lack of consistent progress across all corporate leadership positions as shown in Table 8.2 in Serbia further highlights the possibility of inaccuracy in the EIGE statistics. For example, the EIGE figures do show that while the proportion of women on the boards of the largest listed companies in Croatia increased, there is considerably lower representation among top executives and board chairs. Thus, until there are more systematic studies of women in corporate-level leadership in all firms, it is impossible to say what these more aggregate increases actually mean. But what is clear is that there has been little effort to pursue any systematic implementation or enforcement of formal state regulations and only a handful of women's groups and individual actors in the business sector have asked for more authoritative policy; thus, any policy outcomes remain gender neutral.

The lack of progress can be explained by a variety of factors. First, according to previous research findings by comparative women's movement and gender policy research, the mobilization of women's movement—agency alliances are important for the attainment of certain goals in the area of gender equality (Mazur, 2002; Htun and Weldon, 2018). This process did not happen in Croatia or Serbia; corporate board reform failed to prompt broad and effective cooperation among the different women's NGOs, femocrats, and individual actors making up the women's movements in both countries.

Second, the international involvement in this policy area has not proven to be particularly effective. In Croatia and Serbia, international assistance and the international diffusion of norms have contributed to putting the issue of corporate gender equality on the public agenda. Political elites can no longer be bluntly dismissive about the importance of corporative gender equality. At the same time, however, donor support and international involvement have been shown to have their drawbacks as well. One of them is the tendency toward international policy ownership and financial dependency. While having demonstrated their value in helping to spread new ideas to relevant stakeholders such as business sector and governmental institutions, the external assistance has also contributed to a fragmented, inconsistent, technocratic, and short-term corporate reform agenda. Moreover, the EU enlargement process was a unique opportunity for both countries to advance the promotion of gender equality, but the results were mostly superficial. Despite EU-influenced efforts to introduce positive measures in order to promote equal participation of men and women in all institutions and organizations, there has been no real improvement in corporative gender equality in Croatia and Serbia in the last decade. Part of the problem is that the EU-related adaptational pressures do not automatically translate into domestic structural and policy change. Pre-existing institutions, actors, and policy environments mediate these pressures and affect the ultimate outcome. The lack of litigation from women's movements, a lack of support by governments, weak gender equality governmental bodies, and shortcomings in the judiciary has led much of the transposed EU legislation remaining dead letters without any tangible effect on the representation of women on corporate boards.

Third, the slow progress can be attributed to poor implementation. The key positive action measure prescribed by the gender equality legislation and the policy documents such as national gender equality strategies have not yet been implemented by the Croatian and Serbian governments and the corporate world. Several factors such as lack of political will and limited financial and human resources hamper effective implementation. In both countries, the absence of serious implementation is also symptomatic of deeply ingrained gender stereotypes, which cannot be uprooted through legislation alone. In an ideal scenario, the agenda-setting and implementation of each political activity or action is the result of a sincere wish of decision-makers and political power holders. But in both countries is a shortage of decision-makers and advocates who instinctively, based on their personal beliefs and values, support corporate gender equality.

The public neglect of gender issues during the transition period in Croatia and Serbia, as well as in many other Central and Eastern European (CEE) countries, may be considered as one of the elements that has represented an aspect of continuity with the previous communist systems. Even then, gender equality was important in rhetorical terms, with many aspects of gender equality in practice neglected or made subordinate to other policy areas considered to be of more imminent political importance. Thus, the implementation gaps in corporate gender equality reforms as well as in other gender policy areas must be considered in the light of their common past based on contradictory attitudes toward gender equality made up of a combination of "socialist emancipation" provisions and a rather patriarchal structure of society with strong inbuilt gender role stereotypes.

While much progress has been made in adopting and implementing gender equality in general in both countries, policy on corporate gender equality has lagged significantly behind. In the coming years, a bigger emphasis should be placed on strengthening institutional mechanisms for the effective implementation of adopted policies. Further institutional changes with regards to the rule of law and political culture must take place in Croatia and Serbia so that gender champions may come forward to overcome the poor implementation and disappointing outcomes of corporate gender equality policies.

Interviews

Interview 1. Gender Equality Ombuds in Croatia
Interview 2. Vice-President of the Serbian Chamber of Commerce
Interview 3. Serbian Commissioner for the protection of Equality
Interview 4. President of the Croatian Employers' Association

References

Babovic, Marija (2016) *Gender Equality Index 2016: Measuring Gender Equality in Serbia 2014*. Belgrade: Social Inclusion and Poverty Reduction Unit, Government of Republic of Serbia.

Bego, Ingrid (2015) *Gender Equality Policy in the European Union: A Fast Track to Parity*. London: Palgrave Macmillan.

Djulic, Katarina and Tanja Kuzman (2013) *Women on Corporate Boards in Bosnia and Hercegovina, FYR Macedonia and Serbia*. IFC: the World Bank Group.

Funk, Nanette and Magda Mueller (eds) (1993) *Gender Politics and Post-Communism: Reflections from Eastern Europe and the Former Soviet Union*. New York: Routledge.

Gal, Susan, and Gail Kligman (eds) (2000) *Reproducing Gender: Politics, Publics, and Everyday Life after Socialism*. Princeton: Princeton University Press.

Hassenstab, Christine and Sabrina P. Ramet (2015) *Gender (In)equality and Gender Politics in Southeastern Europe: A Question of Justice (Gender and Politics)*. New York: Palgrave Macmillan.

Htun, Mala and Weldon, Laurel S. (2018) *The Logics of Gender Justice: State Action on Women's Rights around the World*. New York: Cambridge University Press.

Ignjatovic, Tanja (2016) "Draft Law on Gender Equality: Will (Just Any) Amendment to the Law Lead to the Improvement of the Situation?" PrEUgovor—Practical Policy Proposal 08/12, Belgrade: Autonomous Women's Center.

IMF (2015) *The Western Balkans: 15 Years of Economic Transition*. Washington, D.C.: International Monetary Fund.

Irvine, Jill (2013) "Electoral Breakthroughs in Croatia and Serbia: Women's Organizing and International Assistance," *Communist and Post-Communist Studies*, 46 (2), pp. 243–254.

Jutarnji list (2018) *Žene su ključ poslovnog uspjeha, ali samo su rijetke tvrtke prepoznale njihove potencijale*, https://novac.jutarnji.hr/karijere/zene-su-kljuc poslovnog uspjeha-ali-samo-su-rijetke-tvrtke-prepoznale-njihove-potencijale/7317771/ (Accessed March 16, 2020).

Mazur, Amy G. 2002. *Theorizing Feminist Policy*. New York: Oxford University Press.

Miskovic, Tamara 2016. *Žene na upravljačkim položajima u preduzećima u Srbiji.* Beograd: FEFA – Fakultet za ekonomiju, finansije i administraciju, Univerzitet Singidunum, Beograd.

Ombuds for Gender Equality (2015) *Annual Report 2014*. http://www.prs.hr/index.php/izvjesca/2014, accessed 15.03.20 (Accessed December 20, 2021).

Ombuds for Gender Equality (2016a) *Annual Report 2015*. http://www.prs.hr/index.php/izvjesca/2015, accessed 15.03.20 (Accessed December 20, 2021).

Ombuds for Gender Equality (2016b) "Impact of Gender Division of Family Responsibilities and Housework on Professional Life of Employed Women," Zagreb: Ombuds for gender equality

Ombuds for Gender Equality (2017) *Provedba aktivne politike zapošljavanja u 2016. godini. Analiza Pravobraniteljice za ravnopravnost spolova.* http://www.prs.hr/attachments/article/2188/Smjernice%20APZ%20_2016_za%20WEB%20ozujak%202017.pdf. (Accessed April 4, 2020).

Petricevic, Ivana (2012) *Women's Rights in the Western Balkans in the Context of EU Integration: Institutional Mechanisms for Gender Mainstreaming.* Brussels: European Parliament.

Selanec, Goran and Linda Senden (2013) *Positive Action Measures to Ensure Full Equality in Practice between Men and Women, Including on Company Boards.* Publication of the European Network of Legal Experts in the Field of Gender Equality, http://ec.europa.eu/justice/gender-equality/files/gender_balance_decision_making/report_gender-balance_2012_en.pdf> (Accessed January 1, 2020).

Spehar, Andrea (2012) "This Far, but no Further? Benefits and Limitations of EU Gender Equality Policy Making in the Western Balkans," *East European Politics & Societies,* 26 (2), pp. 362–279.

Spehar, Andrea (2018) "The Pursuit of Political Will: Decision Makers' Incentives and Gender Policy Implementation in the Western Balkans," *International Feminist Journal of Politics,* 20(2), 236–250 https://doi.org/10.1080/14616742.2017.1391709 (Accessed December 20, 2021).

Vranješ Radovanović, Ines, Gabrijela Šurina Hanzl, and Selanec, Goran (2016) *Istraživanje o zastupljenosti žena i muškaraca na upravljačkim pozicijama u poslovnim subjektima u Republici Hrvatskoj/Top 500.* http://staklenilabirint.prs.hr/wpcontent/uploads/2014/08/PRSRH_Izvjesce_muskarci-zene500_web.pdf. (Accessed August 10, 2019).

Vranješ Radovanović, Ines and Gabrijela Šurina Hanzl (2016) *Istraživanje percepcije poslovnih žena o eventualnim barijerama na putu prema upravljačkim pozicijama.* http://staklenilabirint.prs.hr/wpcontent/uploads/2014/08/istrazivanje_percepcije_poslovnih_zena.pdf (Accessed August 10, 2019).

World Bank (2015) *Why Should We Care About Care? The Role of Childcare and Eldercare in Serbia,* Working paper. Washington, D.C.: World Bank.

World Bank (2016) *Women's Access to Economic Opportunities in Serbia.* Social Inclusion and Poverty Reduction Unit, Government of Serbia & World Bank.

9

Designed for Failure? Advocating Equality against Adversity in Hungary and Poland

Beáta Nagy, Ewa Lisowska, and Ewa Rumińska-Zimny

Introduction

Similar to other Central East European countries, gender equality in the corporate world presents a conundrum in Poland and Hungary. In socialist times, women in both countries occupied management positions at higher levels than in Western Europe, were an important part of the full-time labor market, and attained the same level of education as men. With the transition to democracy and a market economy, accession to the European Union, and the rise to power of populist right-wing governments, women's overall economic status has declined, and the presence of women on corporate boards and in top managerial positions has remained at quite low levels (ILO, 2015; Fodor, 2004). In 2021, women hold 9.4% of the positions on corporate boards in Hungary and 24.7% in Poland, well below the European Union average of 30,6% (EIGE, 2021).

Moreover, in both countries, symbolic policies without teeth have been adopted, despite policy pressure for gender equality measures through the EU membership process, to address these imbalances in the democratic era. In 2010, the Warsaw Stock Exchange stipulated that listed companies provide reports on the presence of women on their executive boards, and in 2014, the Hungarian Business Leaders Forum set a target of 20% women on corporate boards and in management positions. Alongside these self-regulatory soft policy measures put forward by businesses, women's organizations, like the Women's Congress in Poland and the Hungarian Women's Lobby, have become active players in drawing public attention to gender inequity in the corporate world and in articulating demands for more authoritative policies, like quotas for women on corporate boards. While media attention toward women's leadership has increased significantly in both countries, Polish advocacy groups have been more successful in organizing training for women business leaders than their Hungarian counterparts. Overall,

Beáta Nagy, Ewa Lisowska, and Ewa Rumińska-Zimny, *Designed for Failure?* In: *Gender Equality and Policy Implementation in the Corporate World*. Edited by Isabelle Engeli and Amy G. Mazur, Oxford University Press.

Poland has also had more success than Hungary in actually increasing the presence of women on boards, a 13% difference between 2010 and 2021 compared to the decrease from 13.6% in 2010 to 9.4% in 2021 of women on boards in Hungary (EIGE, 2021).

Thus, both countries are characterized by a lack of governmental commitment to promoting gender equality at the corporate level. The limited attempts have hit a backlash that was released after the transition to democracy, which was embedded in the persistence of conservative values about gender roles where women are seen as family caregivers and men as family breadwinners. Women's movements and other progressive voices have challenged this backlash, but their relative weakness has prevented policy success. Progressive forces have proven to be slightly more successful in Poland, with the corporate-led introduction of soft regulation, than in Hungary where piecemeal initiatives coming from businesses have not led to any long-lasting promotion of women in corporate leadership positions. This chapter seeks to explain the conundrum of backlash and reversal in the post-democratic transition period as well as how and why policy in Hungary has been more stymied by the conservative backlash than in Poland. It sheds light on the conditions under which initiatives to promote women's progress in the corporate world are raised, highlights the limited impact of corporate-led initiatives on transforming gender relations, and shows how mere lip service to equality is likely to result in only trivial increases in women's participation on corporate boards.

To better understand the backlash to gender equality in which corporate equality unfolds, the first section of the chapter assesses the post-transition context first for gender equality in general and then for gender equality in the corporate world in both countries. Next, the analysis tells the story of the development of a highly symbolic soft policy that was poorly implemented and evaluated in both countries, with some limited results in Poland. In the conclusion, the lessons learned from the two countries about the pursuit of corporate equality in Central Eastern Europe are reviewed, as well as why Polish policy has been slightly more authoritative and concrete than Hungarian policy.

Mapping the Backlash in the Post-transition Era

The Context for Gender Equality Policy

After 1989, governments in Hungary and Poland eliminated the key pillars of gender equality policies of the past—women's full-time employment and job security along with universal access to social infrastructure—while failing to put into place new equality policies adjusted to the market conditions. As a result, women's positions in the labor market deteriorated more than men's especially during the first years of the transition process (Rumińska-Zimny, 2009, pp. 25–40). During this period, the signs of the conservative backlash against women's emancipation became noticeable. New voices questioned the appropriateness of women's employment, particularly for mothers, and idealized the segregated world of stay-at-home mothers and wage-earning fathers in both countries (Blaskó, 2005; Lisowska, 2008). The two legacies of emancipation and familialism evoked mixed feelings about women's employment generally and women in managerial positions in particular (Dupcsik and Tóth, 2014; Nagy and Vicsek, 2014).

The accession process to the European Union gave a boost to progressive changes in gender equality legislation in both countries, albeit there was limited effort to implement the new laws after Poland and Hungary became European Union members in 2004. This landscape has changed slightly since 2010, with the publication of research findings on the benefits of gender diversity in top management (EC, 2010; Lisowska, 2010; McKinsey, 2013). Although feminist groups were behind efforts to introduce gender quotas in politics—unsuccessful quota initiatives in 2007 in Hungary and successful initiatives in 2011 in Poland—the growing interest in corporate gender equality was initiated primarily by business actors in both countries (Fodor et al., 2019; Adamska et al., 2009; Lisowska 2021).

Despite initial steps, the lack of political will to promote gender equality has remained dominant in both Poland and Hungary. In Hungary, FIDESZ's electoral victory in 2010 has firmly anchored institutional opposition to "gender ideology" in academia, like the 2019 ban on master programs in gender studies at universities, and more generally to the European Union's gender equality initiatives. Poland has been on track to follow the Hungarian path since the victory of the Law and Justice party in 2015. The Polish government claims that gender equality interferes with the Polish national Christian values and culture, whereas in Hungary, family values are used as a political argument against gender equality, which is seen to erode traditional families without an exact explanation of what it means. A recent development is the questioning of the already ratified Istanbul Convention on preventing and combating violence against women and domestic violence by influential right-wing politicians in Poland and the total rejection of ratification by the Hungarian Parliament. At the time of the final writing of this chapter, convergence between the two countries is even more pronounced, particularly with the Polish ban on abortion. Indeed, by the end of October 2020, the two countries were leading a coalition to oppose EU-led gender equality initiatives more generally.[1]

During the first two decades of democracy and a shift to the market economy, gender equality was not raised in national politics in either Poland or Hungary,

---

[1] *Guardian*, October 28, 2020, https://www.theguardian.com/world/2020/oct/28/hungary-and-poland-to-counter-critics-with-rule-of-law-institute (Accessed October 29, 2020).

except during a short period between 2000–2004 before the European Union accession. Both countries negotiated their membership and had to align their gender equality legislation with the more progressive *acquis communautaire*. After 2004, the main actors advancing gender equality were women's organizations and, after 2010, to some extent, also the private sector, particularly including foreign corporations (Fodor et al., 2019).

The role of the government and political parties in promoting gender equality has remained very limited in the case of Hungary, and since 2015, steadily less so in Poland. In both countries, populist governments transformed the issue of gender equality into the promotion of the family and conservative values. This resulted in the wave of familialism in Hungary and Poland, as well as in other countries in the region, leading to separate gender roles and expectations for women and men, treating men as the main breadwinners, and women as the main caretakers. Familialism and traditional family values were also signs of the declining trust in political, economic, and social institutions (Dupcsik and Tóth, 2014).

The backlash to gender equality in both countries has been framed by conservative family policy and ideology, and lack of supportive labor market solutions such as flexibility and/or part-time employment, as well as insufficient child and elder care arrangements (Saxonberg and Sirovátka, 2006). In Hungary, the prominence of familialism was backed by the retention of a number of parental leave schemes offering a three-year-long paid period for parents—in practice, for mothers. Instead of full-time employment, the ideal of full-time motherhood was promoted. Shortly after the system change, one of the most extreme governmental pronatalist policy initiatives encouraged mothers who had at least three children to stay at home on a paid childcare allowance until the youngest child turned eight.

In Poland, a similar approach prevailed, although until 2015 the financial support to families was less generous than in Hungary. In 2015, the conservative government introduced direct transfers of money to families and children (500+ program) instead of developing nursery schools and kindergartens. Today the care of over 90% of children between 0–3 years of age is provided through informal arrangements, usually mothers and grandmothers (Rumińska-Zimny and Przyborowska, 2016). In Hungary, the availability of public childcare has been relatively good for children between three and six years, however, it has been more problematic to get a place in nursery schools.

Corporate Inequality in the Post-socialist Context

Despite relatively high levels of education for women in both countries (GUS, 2021; HCSO, 2017), there has been little support for gender equality in top managerial or board positions. Women start at a lower level of remuneration, earn less than their male counterparts holding the same position, and are promoted more slowly (Nagy and Sebők, 2019). In Hungary and Poland, the low percentage of women holding executive and non-executive positions as well as the low percentage of women among ministers are due to cultural conditions and stereotyping of the roles of women and men in society (Nagy and Vicsek, 2014).

The representation of women on corporate boards is low in both countries and the progress has been very slow over decades. This relates especially to executive positions and CEOs, whereas women have slightly more opportunities to take a seat on supervisory boards, particularly in Poland. Despite some progress, the number of women on corporate boards is increasing at a very slow pace. This supports the argument that dedicated measures, such as the introduction of binding quotas, are needed in addition to soft measures to achieve significant changes.

In Hungary, a mixed board system has been established by government regulation; thus, the law allows for a supervisory board in addition to an executive board. However, it is only required if companies employ more than 200 full-time employees, and "...the works council did not relinquish employee participation in the supervisory board" (Nagy et al., 2017, p. 211). In Poland, there is a two-tier

Table 9.1 Percentage Share of Women on Boards in the Largest Listed Companies in Hungary, 2004–2021

	EU-28 Board members	HUNGARY				
		Board members	President	CEO	Executives	Non-executives
2004	9.0	8.9	2.1	—	—	—
2005	9.8	9.6	4.7	—	—	—
2006	9.7	11.5	4.8	—	—	—
2007	10.5	10.8	0.0	—	—	—
2008	10.8	16.3	0.0	—	—	—
2009	11.0	13.3	0.0	—	—	—
2010	11.9	13.6	7.7	—	—	—
2011	13.7	5.3	0.0	—	—	—
2012	15.8	7.4	0.0	0.0	2.5	5.1
2013	17.8	11.3	0.0	0.0	7.3	10.7
2014	20.2	11.8	0.0	7.1	10.6	10.5
2015	22.7	17.8	7.1	21.4	11.9	15.1
2016	23.9	12.3	26.7	18.8	11.1	13.3
2017	25.3	14.5	23.5	23.5	13.3	15.6
2018	26.7	14.9	20.0	13.3	13.3	16.7
2019	28.8	12.9	20.0	6.7	20.9	14.9
2020	29.5	9.9	7.1	7.1	18.2	13.0
2021	30.6	9.4	6.3	0.0	17.9	11.8

Note: The data refers to 16 largest listed companies in Hungary.
Source: EIGE Gender Statistics Database. Data for October each year [Accessed October 15 2021]

Table 9.2 Percentage Share of Women on Boards in the Largest Listed Companies in Poland, 2004–2021

	EU-28 Board members	POLAND				
		Board members	President	CEO	Executives	Non-executives
2004	9.0	9.1	10.2	—	—	—
2005	9.8	10.7	8.0	—	—	—
2006	9.7	9.4	12.0	—	—	—
2007	10.4	11.9	10.5	—	—	—
2008	10.8	10.4	10.5	—	—	—
2009	11	9.5	5.3	—	—	—
2010	11.9	11.6	5.3	—	—	—
2011	13.7	11.8	10.5	—	—	—
2012	15.8	11.8	5.3	5.3	5.0	11.8
2013	17.8	12.3	15.8	0.0	4.6	12.4
2014	20.2	14.6	26.3	0.0	4.4	14.9
2015	22.7	19.4	25.0	0.0	10.5	19.9
2016	23.9	18.8	30.0	0.0	11.2	19.3
2017	25.3	20.1	30.0	0.0	13.5	21.0
2018	26.7	21.0	35.0	10.0	13.0	21.9
2019	28.8	23.5	31.6	0.0	13.6	24.5
2020	29.5	22.8	36.8	10.5	15.4	22.8
2021	30.6	24.7	31.6	10.5	15.6	24.7

Note: The data refers to twenty largest listed companies in Poland.
Source: EIGE Gender Statistics Database. Data for October each year [Accessed October 15 2021]

board system: the management and supervisory boards are separate from each other, especially in the case of publicly listed companies (Lisowska, 2010).

The percentage of women in management and on supervisory boards of all companies listed on the Warsaw Stock Exchange in Poland slightly increased from 15% in 2012 to 16% in 2018 (Fundacja, 2016; Deloitte, 2019). The situation seems to be much improving for the largest companies listed on the Warsaw Stock Exchange (Table 9.2). The representation of women on these supervisory boards increased from 12% in 2012 to 21% in 2018 and 25% in 2021. The share of women CEOs was at the level of 5% in 2012 and 11% in 2021. The situation is even worse in Hungary. As Table 9.1 shows, women's presence in corporate senior leadership (board members) has decreased since 2010 when it stalled at 14% and dropped to 9% in 2021 among the listed Hungarian companies. There is a small difference between women's rate in non-executive board positions (12%) and senior executive board positions (18%), signaling that women are doomed to perform less powerful tasks on boards (EIGE, 2021).

It is worth underlining that the role of the state as a major employer and social service provider remained significant in both Hungary and Poland. The proportion of national assets in companies has thus remained rather high over-all (Nagy et al., 2017). At the same time, these state-owned companies have not excelled in having more gender balance on their boards. For example, in Poland, only 20% of the members of supervisory boards of state-owned companies are women (Ministry of State Assets, 2020).

When Demands for Corporate Equality Meet Conservative Opposition in Hungary

The Populist Veto to Corporate Equality

Hungarian decision-makers and stakeholders have not tackled the issue of women's balanced representation in management seriously in the post-socialist period. The issue of women's underrepresentation on corporate boards has reached neither the national political nor broader corporate agendas and only gained minimal media attention. Although Hungarian public employers and state-owned companies are required to develop an equal opportunity plan as per the 2005 Act on Equal Opportunity and Equal Treatment, these plans remain largely symbolic without much concrete action (Kollonay, 2012, p. 106). Moreover, the legal framework for gender equality is rather diluted across all types of inequalities. The situation was not always as grim. At the beginning of 2010, the left-wing government had adopted a more ambitious Strategy for Equality between Women and Men. The strategy was never implemented by the populist government of Orbán, which gained power in May 2010 and has stayed in office since. Moreover, keeping distance from the previous government on this issue was a crucial message of his government.

In October 2020, the current government published the Action Plan "Empowering women in family and society" for 2021-2030 (https://kormany.hu/dokumentumtar/a-nok-szerepenek-erositese-a-csaladban-es-a-tarsadalomban-2 0212030). Most actions and initiatives are framed by traditional ideology focusing on women as mothers. There is one section on promoting women as leaders in the corporate sector, but without setting specific targets. The listed tools for having more women in management remain on the level of soft and vague initiatives, e.g., offering career guidance in secondary education; by showing the example of women leaders; starting mentoring programs; launching awards; and promoting family-friendly workplaces and higher education institutions with family-friendly solutions.

The 2012 recommendation of the European Commission to adopt corporate board quotas (EC, 2012) was not any more successful in providing traction for corporate equality in Hungary. The recommendation was promptly rejected by the Hungarian government, along with nine other member states—the United

Kingdom, Bulgaria, Czech Republic, Denmark, the Netherlands, Lithuania, Malta, Sweden, and Slovenia, which vetoed any stipulations coming from the European Commission (Index.hu, 2012). Deputy Secretary of State Halász gave two reasons for the rejection in Parliament at the time.

1) The government does not support the quota system and prefers different regulatory mechanisms, like campaigns, awareness-raising actions, and voluntary company initiatives.
2) Compared to the introduction of the quota system it is more important to improve the conditions and proportion of working mothers.

(Parliament, Plenary session 241 2012.11.26. Intervention, p. 184)

Five years later the same position was upheld by the government. In an interview in 2017, the deputy secretary of state announced that while government officials began consultations with some CEOs, there was no support for corporate quotas among major stakeholders; and hence the proposal was swiftly removed from the political agenda (Nagy et al., 2017).

The Impact of Women's Organizations: A Velvet Strategy of Informal Initiatives

While Hungarian civil society and particularly women organizations are less powerful than their sister organizations in Poland and across Europe, other than a handful of large multinational companies, few other actors are advocating for corporate gender equality. One of the first and most influential businesswomen's organizations is the Hungarian Women Business Leaders Network (also called Women's Forum), which is a part of the Hungarian Business Leaders Forum (HBLF) founded in 1992. The Women's Forum was launched in the Hungarian Parliament building in 2005, a symbolic step that shows the group's strong social network. The main activities of the network concentrate on getting political and business attention to women's underrepresentation in management and on boards, networking and sponsoring women managers, and mentoring talented businesswomen of younger generations. The rationale behind the group's approach has been a focus on economic efficiency; it is good for business to have more women on boards as they can better utilize female talents, and diversity pays off. The president of the organization expressed this position in a recent interview: "We always say that it is not an equal opportunity issue, it is a business case" (Czakó, 2019).

In 2014–2016, in the framework of an international project, Women Shareholders Demand Gender Equality, a small group of lawyers bought shares of publicly listed companies, then they spoke from the position of shareholders to the company board directors requesting more women board members. These lawyers raised the issue of representation-related questions at the general assemblies of listed companies, which was a highly unconventional intervention into the masculine climate of listed companies. Although this happened only once, it was an effective tool for raising public awarenessand women's empowerment (www.ewsdge.eu/).

The Hungarian Women's Lobby (HWL) (http://noierdek.hu/2/) has also raised its voice and kept the issue of women's increased board representation on its agenda. Being a member of the European Women's Lobby, the Hungarian organization takes an explicitly feminist approach. Following the example of Polish colleagues, it organized the Congress of Women in 2013, where several women managers contributed to the heated discussions on gender equality. Due to the lack of financial resources, this event has not been repeated in Hungary. HWL published both a volume on women's situations in the corporate world and a collection of policy recommendations (Juhász, 2014; 2016). These policy recommendations covered a wide range of possible actions from raising public awareness to the introduction of quota regulation on corporate boards (Nagy, 2016), thus, a menu of different methods to promote gender-balanced leadership.

Influential businesswomen, partly overlapping with the members of the HBLF Women's Forum, launched a network called *Egyenlítő* (Equalizer) with the explicit goal of having more women in management and on boards. The main activities were strongly connected to networking and building women's solidarity in business, and it concentrated on issues such as the confidence gap, forceful communication, and implicit bias. As this organization attracts many influential women managers, they have had a significant media impact as well. On International Women's Day 2019, some members of the foundation collected good practices applied by the most active companies in gender-specific actions in Hungary and published, *Are We There Yet? Programs for Achieving Gender Balance at Companies in Hungary* (www.egyenlitoalapitvany.org/wp-content/uploads/2019/03/noi_angol_march_web.pdf). Professional Women's Association, targeting mid-career women, and Business Women's Network, focusing on early-career women, have also been giving space to networking and mentoring activities mainly in the capital city. All these projects aim to facilitate women's positions in management and not board membership, given that their argument is that women first have to be part of the talent pool before they can be selected for board positions.

Corporate Initiatives

National binding quota regulation is missing from Hungarian public policy, and the government has not proposed the introduction of soft measures either.

Table 9.3 Policy Measures for Gender Equality on Corporate Boards in Hungary

SELF-REGULATION	
HBLF 202020 Club (2014)	**Individual multinational corporations[a]**
* Member organizations of the HBLF * Recommendation to have a minimum of 20% women in companies' management and boards by 2020 * Strategy consisting of four pillars: CEO forums, media awareness, mentoring, and networking * Organized in cooperation with the Diversity Charter	* Women's networks * Mentoring * Training for female talents * Diversity training * Unconscious bias training * Internal company quota * Comply-or-explain targets for women managers

[a] Such as General Electric, Bosch, Deutsche Bank, and Hungarian Telecom

Therefore, it is up to businesses to take proactive measures possibly initiated by multinational companies or NGOs. Table 9.3 summarizes the measures discussed in this section.

The corporate gender equality discussion is mainly dominated by some large multinational companies with soft targets, which shows a strong link between business feminism and capitalist interests (Fodor et al., 2019). Similar actions of public companies have not become known until now. Private companies are more interested in introducing self-regulation, like comply-or-explain, than public companies, which seems to be connected to the neoliberal steps involving more women in the workforce. Behind this self-regulation, the most widely used tool is the establishment of women's networks initiated by General Electric in Hungary in the early 2000s. In addition, mandatory quota systems are also present at some public limited companies, mainly among listed companies with German-based headquarters, like Bosch and Deutsche Bank (German DAX-companies). Magyar Telekom, for example, elaborated a plan "whereby they intend to increase the number of women in board positions and key managerial positions to 30% by 2015" (Kollonay, 2012, p. 107).

Because of the discouragingly low presence of women on corporate boards in Hungary, a notable initiative was launched by the HBLF in February 2014. Based on its previous work through the creation of the Women's Forum and the gender sensibilization of member companies, the organization launched the HBLF 202020 Club (https://hblf.hu/activities/programs/hblf_202020_club), which is a unique example of self-regulation. According to the vision of the club, the target was to reach at least 20% women representation in Hungarian management and boards by 2020. The main initiator and founder of the Women's Forum, Borbála Czakó, recounted in an interview what they did. "Since the situation is very bad in Hungary, we did not think of a 30% club to claim, and rather started with the

20% target. Now this will not be met in Hungary. It is obvious that we still set a high target."

The club was launched by twenty influential businesswomen, mostly CEOs and board members, then it was supported by twenty men CEOs as well. The model of this initiative was the Anglo-Saxon "comply-or-explain" system, pointed out by Czakó who worked as a partner at the global company Ernst and Young in London, where she was responsible also for global diversity and inclusion projects. As the mission statement emphasized, the founders expected progress from CEOs and stakeholders (https://hblf.hu/content/_common/attachments/mission_vision.pdf). The club urged companies to take action and share their best practices to facilitate women's progress. The founders were committed to reaching a better gender balance in organizations. They also requested a change in corporate culture and an increase in gender diversity at all levels of organizations.

To enhance the motivation of company leaders in this matter, the HBLF launched research on gender and management among the TOP 200 Hungarian companies in 2014. The results were presented to an exclusive audience consisting of men and women (deputy) CEOs of the largest companies in Hungary and members of the HBLF 202020 Club. Czakó summarized the aim precisely: "It was important that we contacted those executives who had the power to put women on the boards, so this was one goal. The other goal was to draw attention (to the topic) of all other executives in the long run."

Based on the success of the first steps, the HBLF 202020 Club has followed a strategic plan for the coming years consisting of four pillars, namely regular CEO Forums (4–5 times per year with male and female CEOs to keep the topic on the agenda), constant media awareness of gender issues (strategic partnership with *Forbes Magazine* and other professional media), mentoring at different career stages to fill the talent pool (young professionals, mid-career women, and high fliers), and finally, regular networking with role models. It has been very often organized in cooperation with the Diversity Charter.

Even if some male CEOs officially resist the idea of promoting women on boards in their own companies, they support and sign the mission of the HBLF 202020 Club, and they are involved in the CEO Forum. Although the HBLF 202020 Club launching event earned significant media attention, bottom-up initiatives alone cannot reach a sustainable change in gender equality. They very often depend on personal interests and networks, therefore they remain sporadic. Czakó also pointed out that there has been continuous and deliberate work on reaching the target as well. She perceived these informal solutions in many cases to be even more effective compared to the formal regulation concerning their aptitude for facilitating the change of social environment: "I think we must change Hungary culturally, and it is hard legwork." She shared her negative experience that many people did not treat gender inequality as a real problem, and women managers are hardly accepted outside HR and marketing fields.

Soft Policy Goes Further in Poland, but with Limited Results

The Return to Family Values

Gender equality remained blatantly absent from the agendas and purview of all post-1989 governments in Poland. This can be explained, at least in the first years of the transition process, by the magnitude of challenges related to the development of a market economy and the perception that gender equality had been already achieved and was well protected by the legislation, especially after the adjustments made in 2004. However, from a longer-term perspective over thirty years, it is clear that a major factor behind the lack of attention to gender issues was traditional views on women's roles deeply rooted in Polish society.

There were of course differences in the approaches of different governing majorities to the role of the Gender Equality Office. Centrist and leftist governments maintained the position of the Gender Equality Minister and were more open to a dialogue with women's organizations, ready to look into new areas such as equality in business and monitoring progress, including the implementation of European Union directives such as the directive on the gender pay gap. For example, in 2014 the Minister of Gender Equality commissioned a review of the gender pay gap in the Polish public sector, which was prepared by the Supreme Chamber of Control (NIK, 2014). In the same year, The Ministry of Labor and Social Affairs implemented the project *Equality in Business*, which reviewed the situation of women at the decision-making level in business and provided arguments for why equality pays off. It was accompanied by a practical guide for companies on how to achieve gender equality in individual firms and increase the share of women in top positions (Ministry of Labor and Social Affairs, 2014).

After 2015, with the election victory of the populist Law and Justice Party, the limited interest in gender equality policy turned into a veritable backlash fueled by a return to family values. This was reflected in the downgrading of the Gender Equality Office within the government, adding other dimensions of inequalities to its portfolio, such as matters regarding the disabled, and closing the dialogue with women's organizations, especially those working on violence against women and human rights. Attempts to restrict women's reproductive rights met strong social resistance with massive street "black protests" in 2016, which delayed by four years the introduction of a ban on abortion in 2020.

In contrast to the Hungarian reaction, the 2012 recommendation of the European Commission to introduce gender board quotas launched a campaign and debate around women on corporate boards in Poland. At that time, Poland was governed by a liberal conservative government that gave more consideration to European Union-led initiatives than the government in Hungary. The public debate was long lasting and often emotional with a number of pro-quota arguments advanced by women's organizations. It took place in the media and at various conferences and events organized by the Gender Equality Minister, women's

NGOs, such as the Congress of Women's Association, employer organizations, and academia.

The public debate did not help, however, to pass the European Union proposal through the Polish Parliament. The proposal was rejected a year later based on its non-compliance with the subsidiary principle (resolution of the Parliament of January 4, 2013). In the letter informing the President of the European Commission about the position of Poland, the government stated that there was no need for introducing quotas, as national legislation guarantees equal standards in the corporate world and is "more effective than the proposed EU legislation" (Commissioner for Human Rights, 2019, p. 8). The rejection of the European Union proposal by the Polish Parliament closed the case on the government side even if the debate on quotas continued in 2014–2015 driven by women's organizations that supported quotas along with recommendations on introducing measures to facilitate work-life balance, in particular through investments in caring infrastructure (children and elderly alike) and sharing family responsibilities (also paternal leaves) between women and men (Fuszara et al., 2017).

In the context of the Polish debate, the pro-quota position of the national Commissioner for Human Rights, the constitutional authority for legal control and protection independent from other state authorities, should be noted. After the rejection of the European Union proposal by the Polish Parliament, the Commissioner requested information on two separate occasions from the government to evaluate progress in women's top positions in State Treasury companies and the economy at large. Recently, the Commissioner for Human Rights called the current populist Law and Justice government to take action in ensuring equal opportunities for women and men at top positions in business. The Commissioner's of letter May 31, 2019, requested the prime minister to evaluate the effectiveness of systemic measures aimed at gender equality at top positions referring to the European Union legislative actions after 2012 and good practices of other countries such as Norway, Spain, and France (Commissioner for Human Rights, 2019). The Commissioner also made it clear that quotas are an effective tool to achieve progress and that they should be introduced first of all in State Treasury companies, which should serve as a model for private sector companies. There was neither any reaction from the government to this letter nor any discussion of it in Parliament or the media.

Soft Regulations to Circumvent the Conservative Backlash

Unlike Hungary, Polish policy toward gender corporate equality followed a mixed approach as shown in Table 9.4.

From 2010 to 2017, some regulations were introduced to promote women for board positions. In 2010 and 2011, the Warsaw Stock Exchange introduced soft

Table 9.4 Policy Measures on Gender Equality on Corporate Boards in Poland

SELF-REGULATION	
Resolution of the Warsaw Stock Exchange 2010	**Resolution of the Warsaw Stock Exchange 2011**
* Listed companies * Recommendation for promoting women on company boards	* Listed companies * Recommendation to include in the annual report data the number of women and men holding executive and non-executive board positions * Recommendation to publish the report on the company website

STATE-REGULATION	
Act of the State Treasury 2015	**Act of the Ministry of Development on implementation of the Directive 2014/95/EU 2017**
* Companies with a state share of at least 25% * 35% of women on corporate boards * five-year period (by 2020) * Recommendation to appoint women on corporate boards No minimum annual increase No monitoring No sanction	* Large companies of 250 or more employees * Annual reporting on gender diversity * Obligation to explain no progress No deadline No minimum annual increase No monitoring No sanction

recommendations for listed companies to publish information on their websites about the number of women and men holding executive and non-executive board positions (Resolution, 2010; Resolution, 2011). The surveys carried out in 2009 and 2010 revealed that among listed companies more than half declared that they had taken actions targeted at gender equality. However, only a third of the surveyed companies acknowledged having clearly defined public relations goals. Whereas, very few had introduced special policies related to recruitment and promotion including mentoring and training for women aimed at increasing their share in managerial positions (Adamska et al, 2009; Lisowska, 2010).

In 2015, the State Treasury introduced a soft executive ordinance for companies that had a minimum of 25% of state shares to have gender balance on corporate boards with a target of 35% women by 2020 (Ministerstwo, 2015). Moreover, Poland had to comply with the stipulations from Directive 2014/95/EU on the disclosure of non-financial information and diversity information starting in 2017. The objective was to enforce reporting obligations in large firms (250 or more employees) on presenting data by gender, including managerial positions as well (Ministerstwo, 2017).

These soft regulations had a very limited impact on advancing women in board positions. Regulations at the Warsaw Stock Exchange created some pressure on business leadership only during the first few years. In 2016, the Warsaw Stock Exchange published the last report on women on boards in listed companies, which was a part of publicly available documents presented to stakeholders. Little has been done to monitor the implementation of the executive order of the State Treasury as well as the Directive 2014/95/EU. While the target of 35% women on corporate boards of state-owned companies has not been achieved thus far, there has been a twofold increase in women on private corporation boards, more as a result of the active insider advocacy, examined in the next section, than any of these soft policy measures.

The Impact of Women's Organizations: Expertise and Insider Advocacy

Given the historical absence of government support for gender equality policy, Polish women's organizations were the key actors in lobbying for gender equality and proposing new solutions. They worked toward more gender awareness in politics, business, and social life, initiated public debates as well as created networks to promote role models and publish reports monitoring progress. A number of these organizations sought to support women entrepreneurs by promoting women's careers in the corporate sector. One of the first organizations supporting women in business was the International Forum of Women established in 1993 at SGH Warsaw School of Economics as a research program on women entrepreneurs (www.mfk.org.pl/). Now, many others are active. The Foundation of Women Leaders promotes women on corporate boards by providing mentoring and organizing meetings with women in leadership positions. The foundation, Success Written with Lipstick, organizes an annual competition for Women of the Year in various categories (corporate and self-owned company, and includes an award for male CEOs who help women to move up the career ladder (https://sukcespisanyszminka.pl/).

The most active and influential women's organization is the Women's Congress established in 2009 (www.kongreskobiet.pl). It is now the largest women's NGO in Poland, which has twenty-nine local representatives across the country and organizes annual congresses gathering around 4,500 women nationally to discuss and recommend actions. The association actively promotes women's participation in decision-making and prepared a citizen's project on obligatory quotas for women on the lists of political parties, adopted by the Polish Parliament in 2011. A 35% quota for women candidates in elections is now in force and, as a result, the share of women in Parliament has increased from 21% in 2007 to 29% in 2019. The Women's Congress also actively supported the EU directive on quotas on corporate boards and organized a number of public debates on gender issues. In March 2020, it prepared the first Polish proposal for an equal pay law based on the European Union's recommendations on wage transparency. The project has been already well-received by opposition parties in the Parliament and by the media, and has resulted in the government proposal to amend the Labor Code to formally define mobbing in wage inequality.

Overall, the impact of women's organizations in Poland on advancing positive changes has been significant despite the unfavorable political climate. They initiated research on inequalities and provided arguments why women's economic potential matters for the development of the private sector. Prior to 2015, they also managed to successfully lobby policymakers on issues such as quotas in politics and have put pressure on the conservative Law and Justice government. At the same time, these organizations have strengthened women's self-confidence through mentoring and training, promoting role models, and building networks.

Conclusion: Comparative Lessons for Promoting Corporate Equality in Times of Conservative Backlash

In Hungary and Poland, there have been only limited efforts to improve women's positions on corporate boards and the absence of relevant regulations at the national level. Before 2015, Poland introduced soft regulations recommending companies the fair representation in management, while in Hungary there are only self-regulations at the company level typically guided or set by the international headquarters. The lack of national mandatory regulations in both countries has consequences in terms of lower representation of women on company boards and slower pace or stagnation of progress as compared to countries that have such regulations. Poland, however, had more success than Hungary in introducing gender equality in the corporate world, as has been pointed out, with the share of women on corporate boards in Poland doubling, while in Hungary it decreased in 2021 to compare with the previous years.

There are several reasons why there was this difference in performance between the two quite similar countries. First, with the arrival of the populist right-wing majority in Parliament coming five years later, the populist backlash against gender equality had less time to take hold in Poland. Women's mobilization was also more pronounced around issues of gender equality in the corporate world in Poland than in Hungary, particularly on the national scene. Given the lack of political will, particularly with the advent of the right-wing populist government, bottom-up self-regulatory processes initiated by women's organizations became very important in both countries. Policy recommendations prepared by the Hungarian Women's Lobby have offered a wide range of actions for all stakeholders considering changes. The European women lawyer actions can also serve as good practice on raising awareness on the benefits of regulations and mandatory quotas. Polish women are even more effective in establishing a common platform for action by bringing together thousands of women at annual congresses to empower women in public life and let their voices be heard. The key question today is who will join these organizations to push for long-term efforts aimed at building systemic mechanisms, including quotas, to close the gender gap in the corporate sector, particularly in the context of the hardening conservative backlash in the government. Corporate actors seem to be potential partners of women's movements in bringing the change despite being driven by the business case approach and corporate profit. New media campaigns focused on women in the corporate sector, such as *Forbes Women* launched in 2019 in Poland, could be also a powerful ally.

However, there are also commonalities between the two countries. The aversion to mandatory regulation is rooted in historical antecedents, mainly in the backlash to the socialist emancipation project, and recently in the strong anti-gender attitude of conservative governments blocking policies and measures promoting gender equality. In this setting, traditional gender roles are reinforced implicitly; moreover, the missing political will and a non-supportive environment reduce women's aspirations to compete for demanding jobs to break social norms. Today, none of the political parties that have entered the Parliament in Hungary and Poland have included corporate equality in their programs, not to mention proposals for concrete measures such as corporate quotas. However, in Poland, some references have been made to gender equality as a core value within human rights in the programs of the centrist and leftist parties. Similar attitudes can be observed in Hungary, where some politicians and political parties had intended to introduce gender quotas for elected office in 2007, which was finally rejected by Parliament.

Women in Hungary and Poland are aware that the process of progressive changes in the corporate sector has just begun, and there are many challenges ahead. As founder of the HBLF 202020 Club in Hungary, Borbála Czakó, said, "We cannot change the whole society overnight." Companies may modify their regulations not because of changing attitudes toward promoting women to top positions but to comply with the formal requirements from internationally based headquarters. At the same time, the importance of informal negotiations should not be underestimated.

The debate on quotas in Poland and soft policy measures certainly had a positive effect on raising awareness on the gender gap in top positions in business and on its economic costs. The diversity context is now more often used in public statements and debates to underline the benefits of having more women on corporate boards. There is, however, little or no consensus on introducing quotas and establishing mechanisms to promote women to top positions. Polish CEOs and managers, both male and often female, point out that soft solutions are a better option (changing corporate culture, voluntary target, flextime, and flexplace). In official statements, gender equality is considered "very important for us," as in the prime minister's speech in March 2019 in the Polish Parliament. The current government claims, however, like the previous, more liberal government in 2012, that women's position in the business sector is on target and national legislation already guarantees equal opportunities for women and men.

Despite having many experienced women in middle management, women remain seriously underrepresented in leadership positions in both countries, which goes against the business case for women on boards. There are, therefore, some additional explanations for the limited progress in both countries. The first is the male-dominated power structure in the corporate sector, both as stakeholders and decision-makers, who are not interested in taking action. The second is an increasingly hostile political climate regarding gender issues (often referred to as gender ideology) and toward the implementation of international commitments and treaties. These together slow down the much-needed progress.

In terms of the mechanisms for progress, Poland offers a more optimistic picture, even if it confirms that gender transformation is a long process, and it cannot be taken for granted. Progress is not linear and advancements in gender equality legislation do not guarantee success. Progress depends on the political will of decision-makers at the government, local, and party levels as well as at the level of the firm. As the Polish case demonstrates, progress could be also driven by bottom-up actions of women's movements and good practices of companies. In Hungary, despite some civil society voices promoting more women on boards, the bottom-up approach is less effective due to the general weakness of civil society.

Interviews

Borbála Czakó, President of the Hungarian Business Leaders Forum, July 16, 2019 (Individual interview by Beáta Nagy).

References

Adamska, Lidia, Beata Jarosz, and Ewa Lisowska (2009) "Kobiety w spółkach rynku kapitałowego," [Women in Capital Market Companies] in *Kobiety dla Polski – Polska dla kobiet. 20 lat transformacji 1989–2009* [Women for Poland—Poland for Women. 20 Years of Transformation 1989–2009]. Warszawa: Feminoteka Foundation, pp. 87–114.

Blaskó, Zsuzsa (2005) 'Dolgozzanak-e a nők? A magyar lakosság nemi szerepekkel kapcsolatos véleményének változásai 1988, 1994, 2002,' [Should Women Work? The Changing Attitudes of the Hungarian Population on Gender Roles 1988, 1994, 2002], *Demográfia*, 48 (2–3) pp. 159–186.

Commissioner for Human Rights (2019) *Za mało kobiet we władzach spółek giełdowych i skarbu państwa. Postulaty RPO do premiera* [Small Number of Women on Boards of Listed and State-owned Companies. Demands from the Commissioner for Human Rights to the Prime Minister]. https://www.rpo.gov.pl/pl/content/rpo-do-premiera-za-malo-kobiet-we-wladzach-spolek-gieldowych-i-skarbu-panstwa (Accessed August 13, 2020).

Deloitte (2019) *Women in the Boardroom. A Global Perspective*, 6th edition, https://www2.deloitte.com/global/en/pages/risk/articles/women-in-the-boardroom-global-perspective.html (Accessed August 13, 2020).

Dupcsik, Csaba and Olga Tóth (2014) "Family Systems and Family Values in Twenty-first-century Hungary," in Zsombor Rajkai (ed.) *Family and Social Change in Socialist and Post-Socialist Societies*. Leiden: Brill, pp. 210–249.

EC (2010) *More Women in Senior Positions. Key to Economic Stability and Economic Growth*. Luxembourg: European Commission.

EC (2012) *Proposal for a Directive of the European Parliament and of the Council on Improving the Gender Balance among Non-executive Directors of Companies Listed on Stock Exchange and Related Measures*. Brussels: European Commission Brussels.

EC (2019) *Report on Equality between Women and Men in the EU*, https://ec.europa.eu/info/sites/info/files/aid_development_cooperation_fundamental_rights/annual_report_ge_2019_en.pdf (Accessed August 13, 2020).

EIGE (2021) *Gender Statistics Database: Largest Listed Companies*, https://eige.europa.eu/gender-statistics/dgs/indicator/wmidm_bus_bus__wmid_comp_compbm (Accessed October 15, 2021).

Fodor, Éva (2004) "The State Socialist Emancipation Project: Gender Inequality in Workplace Authority in Hungary and Austria," *Signs: Journal of Women in Culture and Society*, 29 (3), pp. 783–813. https://www.jstor.org/stable/10.1086/381103

Fodor, Éva, Christy Glass, and Beáta Nagy (2019) "Transnational Business Feminism: Exporting Feminism in the Global Economy," (8), pp. 1117–1137. https://doi.org/10.1111/gwao.12302

Fundacja (2016) *Kobiety we władzach spółek giełdowych w Polsce w 2016. Czas na zmiany* [Women on the Boards of the Listed Companies in Poland in 2016. It's Time for Change]. Warszawa: Fundacja Liderek Biznesu [Foundation Women Leaders].

Fuszara, Małgorzata, Ewa Rumińska-Zimny, and Magdalena Środa (2017) *Czas na kobiety* [Time for women], Congress of Women Report, https://www.kongreskobiet.pl/pl-PL/text/inicjatywy/czas_na_kobiety/materialy_do_pobrania (Accessed August 13, 2020).

GUS (2021) *Aktywność ekonomiczna ludności Polski* [Labor Force Survey in Poland]. Warszawa: Statistics Poland.

HCSO (2017) *Nők és férfiak Magyarországon 2016* [Women and Men in Hungary 2016]. Budapest: KSH.

ILO (2015) *Women in Business and Management: Gaining Momentum*. Geneva: International Labour Office.

Index.hu (2012) Nem akar Magyarország több nőt [Hungary Does Not Want to Have More Women], *index.hu*, September 5, 2012, https://index.hu/gazdasag/magyar/2012/09/05/magyarorszagon_bukhat_el_az_unios_noi_kvota/ (Accessed December 20, 2021).

Juhász, Borbála (ed.) (2014) *A nőtlen évek ára: a nők helyzetének közpolitikai elemzése, 1989–2013* [The Price of Years without Women. Policy Analysis of Women's Situation 1989–2013]. Budapest: Magyar Női Érdekérvényesítő Szövetség.

Borbála Juhász (ed.) (2016) *A Magyar Női Érdekérvényesítő Szövetség közpolitikai ajánlásai* [Policy Recommendations of the Hungarian Women's Lobby]. Budapest: Magyar Női Érdekérvényesítő Szövetség.

Kollonay, Lehoczky, Csilla (2012) "Hungary," in G. Selanec and L. Senden (eds) *Positive Action Measures to Ensure Full Equality in Practice between*

Men and Women, Including on Company Boards. Luxembourg: European Commission, European Network of Legal Experts in the Field of Gender Equality, pp. 105–109, http://ec.europa.eu/justice/gender-equality/files/gender_balance_decision_making/report_gender-balance_2012_en.pdf DOI 10.2838/850 (Accessed 8 August 8, 2017).

Křížková, Alena, Beáta Nagy, and Aleksandra Kanjuo Mrčela (2010) "The Gender Implications of Labour Market Policy during the Economic Transformation and EU Accession: A Comparison of the Czech Republic, Hungary, and Slovenia," in Christina Klenner and Simone Leiber (eds.) *Welfare States and Gender Inequality in Central and Eastern Europe. Continuity and Post-socialist Transformation in the EU Member States.* Brussels: ETUI, pp. 329–361.

Lisowska, Ewa (2008) *Równouprawnienie kobiet i mężczyzn w społeczeństwie* [Equality between Women and Men in Society]. Warszawa: SGH Warsaw School of Economics.

Lisowska, Ewa (2010) "Women in Stock Market Companies versus Company Profitability," *Women and Business*, 1–4, pp. 32–41.

Lisowska, Ewa (2021) "Empowering Women in Organizations – Good Practices", *Women and Business*, 1–4, pp. 56–64.

McKinsey (2013) *Gender Diversity in Top Management: Moving Corporate Culture, Moving Boundaries.* Warsaw: McKinsey & Company.

Ministerstwo (2015) *Dobre praktyki w zakresie zapewnienia zrównoważonego udziału kobiet i mężczyzn w organach spółek z udziałem Skarbu Państwa* [Good Practices in Ensuring Balanced Participation of Women and Men in the Bodies of Companies with the State Treasury Share]. Warszawa: Ministry of Finance.

Ministerstwo (2017) *Raportowanie niefinansowe. Poradnik dla raportujących* [Non-financial Reporting. Guide for Reporting]. Warszawa: Ministry of Development.

Ministry of Labor and Social Affairs (2014) *Więcej kobiet w zarządzaniu – to się opłaca. Przewodnik dla firm* [More Women in Management—it benefits. Guide for Companies]. Warszawa: Ministry of Labor and Social Affairs.

Ministry of State Assets (2020) https://www.gov.pl/web/nadzor-kprm/rady-nadzorcze-i-pelnomocnicy (Accessed 13 August 13, 2020).

Nagy, Beáta (2016) "A Magyar Női Érdekérvényesítő Szövetség ajánlásai a nemek közti egyenlőség szempontjainak figyelembe vételére a gazdasági vezetők tekintetében," in Borbála Juhász (ed.) *A Magyar Női Érdekérvényesítő Szövetség közpolitikai ajánlásai* [Policy Recommendations of the Hungarian Women's Lobby]. Budapest: Magyar Női Érdekérvényesítő Szövetség, pp. 17–23.

Nagy, Beáta, Henriett Primecz, and Péter Munkácsi (2017) "The Downturn of Gender Diversity on Boards in Hungary," in Cathrine Seierstad, Patricia Gabaldon, and Heike Mensi-Klarbach (eds.) *Gender Diversity in the Boardroom.* Palgrave Macmillan, pp. 205–233.

Nagy, Beáta and Anna Sebők (2019) "Female and Male Managers," *The Hungarian Labour Market 2018.* Budapest: Institute of Economics, Centre for Economic and Regional Studies, Hungarian Academy of Sciences, pp. 66–69, https://www.mtakti.hu/wp-content/uploads/2019/07/23.pdf (Accessed August 8, 2017).

Nagy, Beáta and Lilla Vicsek (2014) "Exploring Gender Culture at a Telecommunications Company," *Gender in Management: An International Journal*, 29 (6), pp. 318–333.

NIK Report (2014) https://www.nik.gov.pl/aktualnosci/nik-o-wynagrodzeniu-kobiet-i-mezczyzn.html (Accessed 13 August 13, 2020).

Resolution (2010) "Uchwała nr 17/1249/2010 Rady Nadzorczej Giełdy Papierów Wartościowych w Warszawie S.A. z 19 maja 2010 r. w sprawie uchwalenia Dobrych praktyk spółek notowanych na GPW," [Warsaw Stock Exchange: Resolution No 17/1249/2010 of 19 May 2010 on good practices of listed companies]. https://www.gpw.pl/pub/GPW/files/PDF/dobre_praktyki/uch_rg_17_1249.pdf (Accessed August 13, 2020).

Resolution (2011) "Uchwała nr 20/1287/2011 Rady Nadzorczej Giełdy Papierów Wartościowych w Warszawie S.A. z 19 października 2011 r. w sprawie uchwalenia Dobrych praktyk spółek notowanych na GPW" [Warsaw Stock Exchange: Resolution No 20/1287/2011 of 19 October 2011 on good practices of listed companies]. https://www.gpw.pl/pub/GPW/files/PDF/dobre_praktyki/uch_rg_15_1282_2011.pdf (Accessed August 13, 2020).

Rumińska-Zimny Ewa (2009) "Women's Employability in Eastern Europe and CIS," in Rumińska-Zimny, Ewa (eds) *Gender Gap and Economic Policy*. United Nations Economic Commission for Europe, Geneva, pp. 25–40.

Rumińska-Zimny Ewa and Katarzyna Przyborowska (2016) "Polityka społeczna rządu PIS: możliwe skutki i wyzwania" [Social Policy of Law and Justice Party Government: Possible Effects and Challenges], in *Prawa kobiet, prawa obywatelskie pod rządami PIS* [Women's Rights and Civil Rights under the Law and Justice Party Government]. Warszawa: Congress of Women.

Saxonberg, Steven and Tomás Sirovátka (2006) "Failing Family Policy in Post-Communist Central Europe," *Journal of Comparative Policy Analysis*, 8 (2), pp. 185–202.

POLICY PATH 2
STATE REGULATION

Track 1. Flagship Approach: Legislative Regulation by Quota

10

From Shockwave to Ripple?

The Nuanced Impact of Corporate Quotas in Norway

Mari Teigen

Introduction

Male dominance in top business positions in Norway, as in other countries, is difficult to change and serves as a point of departure for the adoption of gender quotas for corporate boards in Companies Legislation in 2003.[1] This development was considered by many at the time to send "shockwaves into Norwegian business-life" and to be "extremely important in focusing on who should have decision-making power in the business community."[2] Although key actors in the business community found the proposal to introduce a 40% gender quota for corporate boards unacceptable, the regulation was adopted by the Norwegian parliament and stood as the very first legislative quota for corporate boards in the world. This chapter examines the introduction, implementation, and results of the highly contested yet pioneering piece of legislation. The central question to be examined is how and why such a highly controversial regulation proved to be quite seamless to implement and what was its outcome in terms of changing gender-biased norms and realities in the corporate world. The chapter argues that although the new controversial quota laws were predicted to introduce important transformations in corporate practices and gender equality, they actually delivered limited change in

---

[1] Stipulations on gender quotas for corporate boards were introduced in the Norwegian Limited Liability Companies Act, as well as in other parts of company legislation, which also covers state-owned, inter-municipal, and municipal companies. In the Norwegian system of corporate governance, all businesses are regulated by "company laws"—the Private Limited Liability Companies Act (Companies Act), the Public Limited Liability Companies Act (Public Companies Act), and the Partnership Act. The following laws and regulations also apply to listed companies: The Securities Trading Act (Securities Act) (Andersen et al, 2018).

[2] See below for the full quote from an interview conducted for the chapter with Turid Solvang who is CEO and founder of Future Boards, a global independent network of corporate governance experts. She is also co-founder and former CEO of the Norwegian Institute of Directors, former chair of European Confederation of Directors Association, and co-founder and vice chair of European Women on Boards 2013–2017. She was a key player in the implementation of gender quotas for corporate boards.

Mari Teigen, *From Shockwave to Ripple?* In: *Gender Equality and Policy Implementation in the Corporate World.*
Edited by Isabelle Engeli and Amy G. Mazur, Oxford University Press. © Oxford University Press (2022).
DOI: 10.1093/oso/9780198865216.003.0010

the deep-seated gender norms in the business world with "few ripple effects" in the first ten years of the implementation of the law; more recently signs of meaningful transformation have been developing.[3]

While gender quotas for corporate boards cover public limited companies and various types of publicly owned companies, this chapter primarily focuses on quotas for the corporate boards of public limited companies, given that the main public controversy over gender quotas on boards concerned this type of company[4]. The following section provides an overview of gender equality in the corporate world. Next, the analysis traces how gender quotas for corporate boards were placed on the political agenda in Norway as well as how the issue was debated. An analysis of the decision-making process that led to the adoption of gender quotas for corporate boards follows. In the last two sections, the outputs, practice, and outcome of the quotas are assessed and discussed with a focus on the first ten years of implementation and then more recent promising developments.

Continued Male Dominance in the Corporate Sector

Norway is often hailed as one of the world's most gender-equal societies. Feminist scholarship on gender regimes states that Norway and other Nordic countries are more equal than others (Walby, 2009). The Nordic countries have been claimed to embody a state form that makes it possible to transform them into "truly woman-friendly societies" (Hernes, 1987). The institutional framework for Nordic welfare state policies is generally seen as beneficial regarding the inclusion of women in paid work. The specific orientation of family policies further promotes such inclusion, at least in part (Ellingsæter, 2014; Ellingsæter and Leira, 2006; Leira, 2012). Norway, as well as the other Nordic countries, is characterized by high female labor participation and close to gender balance in most elected political offices (Teigen and Skjeie, 2017). However, the business sector creates a sharp contrast to the general picture of gender equality advancements, with its persistent male dominance, especially in the highest-ranking positions.

Taken together, the Norwegian business sector consists of about 600,000 registered companies, most with few or no employees. There are a total of about 10,000 companies with fifty employees or more, just under 1,000 of these companies have more than 250 employees. Most of these are limited companies—not listed on the Norwegian stock exchange, around 200 are public limited companies and traded on the stock exchange. The highest governing body of a Norwegian company is

---

[3] Solvang continued the "shock wave" metaphor in her interview by stating that the outcome of the 2003 law had few ripple effects (See full quote from the interview below).
[4] Public limited companies are a form of registration required for limited companies to be listed on the Oslo Stock Exchange (Oslo Børs ASA), which was founded in 1819 and offers the only regulated markets for security trading in Norway.

its general meeting. A Norwegian company's management comprises its boards of directors, its chief executive (CEO), and, when relevant, its corporate assembly. The board has both managerial and supervisory functions. The CEO is responsible for the day-to-day governing of the company and to follow up the decisions of the board. Whereas Norwegian companies are best characterized by a one-tier system with a single board of directors, some companies have additional organizational entities like a corporate assembly for companies with over 200 employees, for example.[5] Figure 10.1 shows the share of women board members and CEOs in all limited and public limited companies from 2004 to 2020. While there has been significant growth of women on the boards of public limited companies, increase for limited companies has been more modest. For women CEOs, progress has been slower, however, slightly more in the limited companies compared to the public limited companies.

The CORE Norwegian Gender Balance Scorecard was established in 2016 to track individuals holding leadership positions in the 200 largest companies through their position, responsibility and by sex in order to provide a more in-depth measurement of gender balance in top positions in Norway's business sector.[6] As presented in Figure 10.3, a CORE survey from 2020 shows that women

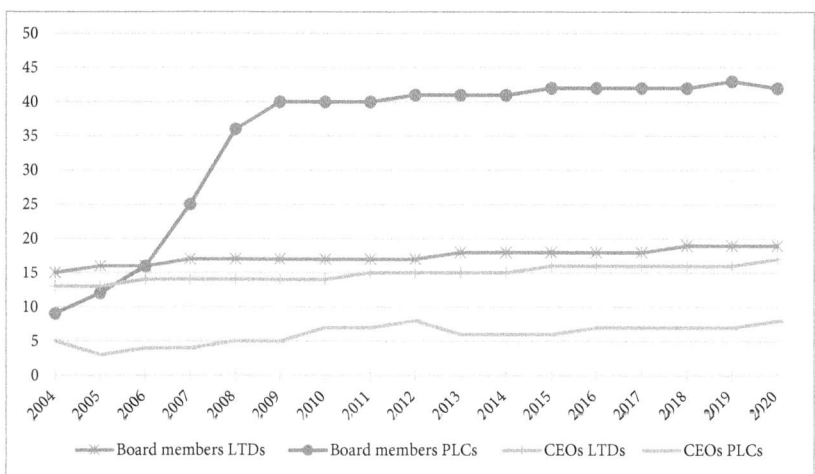

Fig. 10.1 Percentage Share of Women Board Members and CEOs in all Limited Companies (LTDs) and Public Limited Companies (PLCs) in Norway, 2004–2020
Source: Statistics Norway, https://www.ssb.no/styre.

---

[5] This is according to the Norwegian Corporate Governance Code: https://nues.no/english/ (Accessed October 22, 2020).
[6] The data in Figures 10.2–10.3 are from the Gender Balance Core Scorecard Survey. https://www.samfunnsforskning.no/core/english/publications/core-norwegian-gender-balance-scorecard/core-norwegian-gender-balance-scorecard-200---2020.pdf (Accessed October 22, 2020).

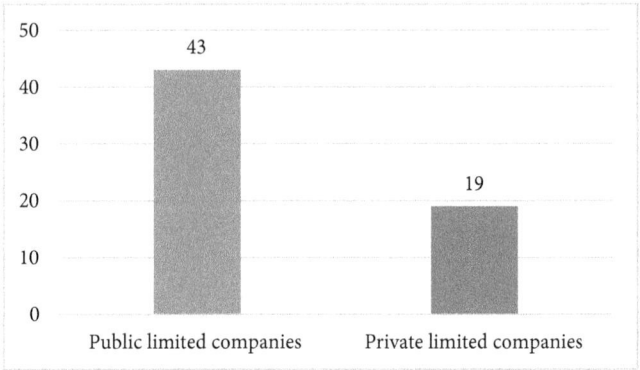

Fig. 10.2 Percentage Share of Women on Boards in Public Limited and Limited Companies in Norway in 2020
Source: CORE Gender Balance Scorecard Survey (2020).

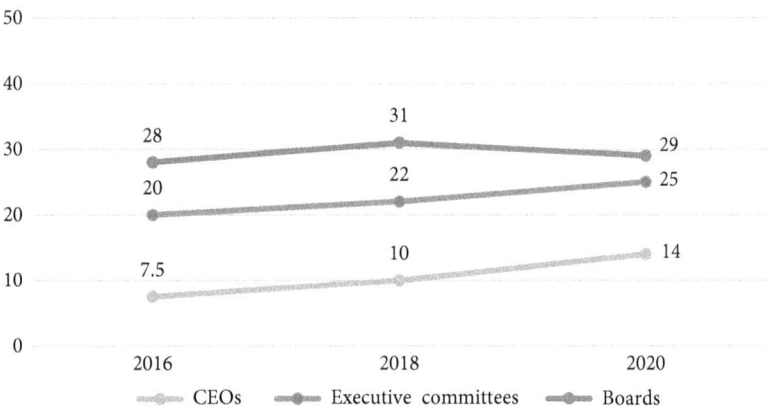

Fig. 10.3 Percentage Share of Women CEOs on Executive Committees and Board Members in the 200 Largest Companies in Norway, 2016–2020
Source: CORE Gender Balance Scorecard Survey (2020).

make up 14% of CEOs, 25% of members of executive committees, and 29% of board members. Figure 10.2 indicates that the 200 largest companies differ little between limited and public limited companies in executive positions, while there is a significant difference in non-executive/board positions: 19% women on limited company boards and 43% women on public limited company boards. The main reason for the difference is that public limited companies are covered by the regulation of gender quotas for corporate boards, while limited companies are not.

Although women are poorly represented in top management positions in the 200 largest companies, a modestly positive development appears from 2016 to

2020. The share of women in CEO positions has almost doubled; it rose from 7.5% to 14%. As seen in Figure 10.3, the share of women in executive committees also increased from 20% to 25%, while the share of women in boards appears to be stable: 28% in 2016 and 29% in 2020.

Putting Gender Quotas on the Agenda: Supporters and Detractors, but "All" Want Gender Balance to Progress

The persistence of men's dominance in top positions in the corporate world became a central issue for public debate in Norway starting in the middle of the 1990s, providing an important backdrop for a discussion that increasingly emphasized gender quotas as the preferred method to evoke real change. This was a new debate, at first furthered by different individual feminist actors from politics, media, and the gender equality apparatus, while the women's organizations did not play an active role (Teigen, 2015). The debate intensified when the Gender Equality Ombud and the Director of the Centre for Gender Equality took on a driving role (Sørensen, 2011). The Gender Equality Ombud suggested to the Ministry of Children and Family, Minister Valgerd Svarstad Haugland from the Christian Democratic Party, that the regulation in the Gender Equality Act of gender quotas for public committees, etc. could be expanded to also cover company boards. When this was included in a major revision of the Gender Equality Act, sent to the public consultation process (Barne—og familiedepartementet, 1999–2000), the debate exploded.

Public debates on gender quota policies are typically characterized by polarized stances (Hughes et al, 2017), and it was no different in the case of gender quotas for corporate boards in Norway. The actor positions in the public consultation were either in support or opposition of gender quotas for corporate boards; there was little middle ground. Those in favor included employee organizations, women's organizations, universities and colleges, and political parties from the left to the center of the political spectrum. Although some women's organizations participating in the public consultation expressed that they were in favor of gender quotas for corporate boards, this issue was not at the heart of their interest, and they did not take an active role in the media debate, as shown in Cvijanovic's (2009) study. Opposing actors in the public consultation comprised employer organizations, industry organizations, and the two main right-wing parties: the Conservative Party and the Progress Party, reflecting what international studies show, that actors in favor of gender quotas often support left-leaning political parties (Hughes et al, 2017).

However, the governments involved with this particular policy process do not fit with the typical positioning of the quota issue along the left-right dimension. The government that first proposed that gender balance on corporate boards could be regulated through the Gender Equality Act was a coalition government that included the Christian Democratic Party, the Liberal Party, and the Centre Party. Then, a short-lived Labor Party government was involved in the process until the final regulation in company legislation was proposed to the parliament by a coalition government with the Christian Democratic Party, the Conservative Party, and the Liberal Party. The arguments put forth in favor of gender quotas for corporate boards emphasized in particular the need to redress the gender composition of company boards specifically. The goal of gender balance would provide men and women with equal access to power and influence, it was argued. Furthermore, it was maintained that there were, in fact, enough qualified women for these roles, mainly with reference to the advancements of women with higher education in fields like law and economics. It was also argued that having more women on company boards would be good for business. The logic behind this was that male-dominated businesses would be inferior to businesses with boards comprising equal numbers of men and women because they would be missing the talents, experiences, and perspectives of women. To provide an example of the tone during the debate, during the first consultation, Ingunn Yssen, Director of the Centre for Gender Equality, emphasized the difficulties for the Norwegian economy not to introduce hard measures:

> The fact that women are not elected to the boards is a problem, for the competent women, but first and foremost for the companies that opt out of half of the country's resources, expertise and impulse. It will be a national problem in the sense that Norway will eventually have a business community that is unable to meet its customers' needs, exposure to competition or demands for restructuring at a time when there is a need for just this.[7]

Nonetheless, central actors in the business community immediately deemed the proposed gender quotas for corporate boards in the Gender Equality Act to be too radical and unrealistic. The main opposing argument was that the government was not in the right to decide the gender composition of private company boards, and that gender quotas for corporate boards would violate owner autonomy, disallowing them to choose individuals that represent their company's best interests. The Confederation of Norwegian Enterprises, the largest employer association, stated the following as its main argument: "The board members are the owners' representatives. The owners have made investments with associated risks, and must be free

---

[7] Public consultation response letter from The Center for Gender Equality in 1999: "*At kvinner ikke velges inn i styrene er et problem, for de flinke kvinnene, men først og fremst for bedriftene som velger bort halvparten av landets ressurser, kompetanse og impulser. Et nasjonalt problem blir det i den forstand at Norge etter hvert vil få et næringsliv som ikke er i stand til å møte sine kunders behov, konkurranseutsetting eller krav om omstilling i en tid med behov for nettopp dette.*"

to choose who is best suited to look after their interests."[8] Similar arguments were expressed by several actors in the business community. The Norwegian Savings Bank Association, for example, maintained that "in the boards of limited companies, the introduction of gender quotas will be problematic because it deprives the owners of the right to elect board members on a sovereign basis to manage owners' assets."[9]

Another strong opposing argument emphasized the importance of selecting the best-qualified board representatives, which was the owner's right. The Confederation of Norwegian Enterprises stated the following:

> Which competence is "correct" will vary from company to company, and depend on different characteristics of the company.... However, the fact that women are not always found to have the right competence does not mean that women are not generally as competent as men.[10]

Finance Norway, the main employer association for finance companies, was less cautious; it stated that "it will be a real problem to get enough qualified women who are interested."[11]

In addition, the Confederation of Norwegian Enterprises responded on the high level of gender segregation in the Norwegian labor market, "The traditional gender segregation in the labor market and thus also the educational choices, therefore also plays a decisive importance for the representation of women in such positions."[12] In other words, the organization stated that the structural conditions of gender segregation were the underlying reason why there were too few women with relevant experience and competence in the business sector as an argument against the introduction of gender quotas for corporate boards. Although the Confederation of Norwegian Enterprises was in strong opposition to this policy, it created a distinction between their principal stance against gender quotas and their responsiveness to the issue of male dominance in the business sector. It stated that it was "natural to elect board representatives you know and who others know. This

---

[8] Public consultation response letter from The Confederation of Norwegian Enterprises in 1999: "*Styremedlemmene er eiernes representanter. Eierne har foretatt investeringer med tilhørende risiko, og må selv fritt kunne velge hvem som er best skikket til å ivareta deres interesser.*"
[9] Public consultation response letter from The Norwegian Savings Bank Association in 1999: "*I styrene i private aksjeselskap vil innføringen av kjønnskvotering være problematisk fordi det fratar eierne retten til på suveren basis å velge styremedlemmer som skal forvalte eiernes eiendeler.*"
[10] Public consultation response letter from The Confederation of Norwegian Enterprises in 1999: "*Hvilken kompetanse som er 'riktig' vil variere fra foretak til foretak, og være avhengig av ulike karakteristika ved foretaket....Det at man ikke alltid finner kvinner som innehar den rette kompetanse, betyr imidlertid ikke at kvinner ikke generelt er like kompetente som menn.*"
[11] Public consultation, response letter from Finance Norway, 1999: "*Det blir et reelt problem å få tak i nok kvalifiserte kvinner som er interessert.*"
[12] Public consultation response letter from The Norwegian Confederation of Enterprises, 1999: "*Den tradisjonelle kjønnssegregeringen på arbeidsmarkedet og derved også utdanningsvalgene, spiller derfor også en avgjørende betydning for kvinnerepresentasjonen I slike posisjoner.*"

mechanism reduces the likelihood of women being elected to boards."[13] Thus, they recognized that established male-dominated networks can be a barrier for female candidates. The Confederation has been committed to promoting women in the business sector; it established the Female Future Program, which aims to provide women in the business sector with relevant qualifications to serve on boards and in management, as well as to make more women visible in the business world.[14] In conclusion, the Confederation of Norwegian Enterprises chose a critical but constructive approach.

Despite the harsh opposition to gender quotas for corporate boards, no one really protested against the necessity of initiatives to redress male dominance in the corporate sector. To some extent, the national self-image of Norway, often depicted as having one of the most gender-equal societies, constituted an important backdrop for the debate. In addition, the concept of regulating the gender composition of corporate boards did not appear too farfetched in light of policies regulating the gender composition of public boards and committees already was in place. Hence, this represented an institutional policy path. The same, we could argue, applied to the regulation of employee representation on boards for companies with more than fifty employees, which was introduced in 1972 (Hagen, 2015). References to these policy legacies also loomed high in the government's justification of the new regulation of gender quotas for corporate boards. The newness of the idea is mainly represented in the definition of what should be understood as core societal obligations for the boards of big companies: to further gender equality through the inclusion of women board members.

The Decision-making Process: A Divided Debate Leads to Mixed Results

The public debate was primarily concerned with whether to adopt gender quotas for corporate boards or not. Alternative approaches, such as self-regulation through the corporate governance code were not an issue. However, until the Norwegian parliament finally adopted the regulation of gender quotas for corporate boards, there existed considerable uncertainty regarding whether this would actually be a reality. Therefore, let us take a closer look at the first and second round of parliamentary discussions of the proposal to get an idea of what was at stake and how the debate on regulating gender quotas for corporate boards changed on its way to adoption.

---

[13] Public consultation response letter from The Norwegian Confederation of Enterprises, 1999: "It is natural to elect board representatives you know and who others know. This mechanism reduces the likelihood of women being elected to boards."

[14] The Female Future program has included more than 1,700 women and 800 businesses, https://www.nho.no/samarbeid/female-future/ (Accessed September 15, 2020).

In the first round, the proposition was to integrate gender quotas for corporate boards in the Gender Equality Act as an extension of the scope of the regulation of gender quotas for public boards and committees. This proposition was initiated and prepared by the minority coalition government comprised of the Christian Democratic Party, the Liberal Party, and the Center Party. When preparing the revision of the act, which took the form of a public consultation document, the government proposed to expand the functioning sphere of the section in the act that requires all publicly appointed boards, councils, and commissions to be represented by a minimum of 40% of each gender in order to extend its scope and to also apply to company boards.

In the public consultation document, different alternatives were put forward. The first alternative considered was that the functioning sphere of the Gender Equality Act should be expanded to apply to the publicly owned company boards, requiring at least 40% of each gender on the boards. The second alternative was to further include companies where the state was investing, again with at least 40% of each gender on the boards. The third alternative proposed that all kinds of companies—limited companies, foundations, and publicly owned companies, should be met by gender quota requirements; for publicly owned companies, each gender should be represented by at least 40%, and for privately owned companies, each gender should be represented by at least 25% with a gradual upward adjustment For all company types, the gender quota should be regulated through the Gender Equality Act.[15]

The extensive debate and strong opposition to such regulations from the Norwegian business community caused this clause to be withdrawn from the proposal for a new Gender Equality Act. This contributed to many assuming that the battle of the quota supporters was lost. However, the reason given by the government concerned matters of formality and a need for clarification on the legality of regulating gender balance on company boards, as well as on whether the application of the Gender Equality Act could be enacted on company boards (Barne—og familiedepartementet, 2000–2001, p. 4).

The withdrawal of the gender quota proposition could be interpreted as a nice way to say that the issue is not on the political agenda anymore. However, the legality of the gender quotas for corporate boards was sent to be assessed by the legal department of the Ministry of Justice, which concluded that a regula tion of gender balance on company boards would not conflict with other rules and regulations and would be in accordance with Norway's European Economic

---

[15] The alternatives are described in Om lov om endringer i lov 13. Juni 1997 nr. 44 om aksjeselskaper, lov 13. juni 1997 nr. 45 om allmennaksjeselskaper og i enkelte andre lover (likestilling i styrer i statsaksjeselskaper, statsforetak, allmennaksjeselskaper mv.; Barne- og familiedepartementet, 2002–2003, p. 13). A mapping of the consulted organizations and the government's consideration of it are described in Om lov om endringer i likestillingsloven mv. [AU: Please add the closing parenthesis] (plikt til å arbeide for likestilling, skjerping av forbudet mot forskjellsbehandling på grunn av kjønn, forbud mot seksuell trakassering mv.). (Barne- og familiedepartementet, 2000–2001).

Area-commitments. Furthermore, it was maintained that it would be more appropriate to place regulation of gender balance on company boards under the legislation that applies to companies, the Public Limited Companies Act, and other parts of the company legislation relevant for state-owned companies and inter-municipal companies, and later municipal and cooperative companies.

In the second round, a proposal to regulate gender quotas for corporate boards was to be incorporated into company legislation. The transition from gender equality legislation to company legislation was of major significance for the later successful implementation of the ruling. The sanction system and enforcement apparatus attached to the Gender Equality Act[16] was weak, as until recently there were no effective sanctions (Skjeie et al, 2019), while a strong sanction system has been a part of all regulations in company legislation. The implementation has been monitored and enforced by the Norwegian state's business register[17] responsible for initiating a further legal process in eventual cases that violate any regulations in the company legislation. If a company does not comply with the requirements set by the Companies Act, the company will, after warnings and expensive fines, ultimately be dissolved if it does not correct non-compliance in accordance with the regulations. These are powerful means of force that ensure the legislation is complied with, of which there is little need to use, as the consequences of not complying are too harsh.

Another important change from the first to the second round was the increase of the gender balance target from 25% to 40% for all companies included in the new proposal. Several of the actors in support of gender quotas had been skeptical of a 25% gender quota and argued to maintain Norway's "standard formula" of a 40% to 60% gender quota. In addition, the increase from 25% to 40% for all companies included in the gender quotas for corporate boards implied that the Labor Party got to put its stamp on the proposed legislation (Teigen, 2018).

The transition from the Gender Equality Act to company legislation, as well as the increase in the gender quota target, implied a strengthening of the proposal. However, simultaneously, the scope of companies to be covered under the ruling was dramatically diminished from the first round where all types of companies were included to the second round where the proposal narrowed down to include state-owned, inter-municipal, and public limited companies. In the proposal, the ministry's argument for restricting the scope was due to feasibility, as many limited companies are often small and family-owned, and the owners themselves serve on the company board (Barne—og familiedepartementet, 2002–2003, p. 14). This is true for many limited companies, and most public limited companies are larger;

---

[16] The Gender Equality Act is now integrated into legislation addressing other strands of discrimination and is named the Equality and Anti-Discrimination Act.

[17] The Norwegian state's public business register is called Brønnøysundregistrene (no English name is yet applicable) (https://www.brreg.no/) and formally records all companies and organizations, and is set to oversee that they follow rules and regulations.

however, the majority of the 200 biggest Norwegian companies are limited companies. In other words, the choice to limit the scope of the gender quota regulation to companies by organization type instead of by revenue and/or number of employees implies that many of the largest companies escaped the quota ruling. Hence, the comprehensiveness was severely limited.

Gender Quotas for Corporate Boards: Authoritative Legislation with Limited Coverage

In 2003, the Norwegian parliament passed legislation with a gender quota for corporate boards that applied to state-owned, inter-municipal, and public limited companies. The specific stipulations of the law are presented in Table 10.1. According to the new law, each gender is to be represented by a minimum of 40% on boards constituted of ten board members or more. For smaller boards, the number of men and women to be represented are specified in detail (i.e., boards constituted by four members need to be represented by two men and two women, five members at least two men and two women, etc.). The gender balance ruling applies respectively for election of deputy members.[18]

Table 10.1 Policy Measures for Gender Equality on Corporate Boards in Norway

STATE REGULATION	
Public Limited Companies Act (Allmennaksjeloven) 2003	**The Companies Act (Aksjeloven)**
* Public limited companies * Minimum of 40% of each sex on boards (§ 6-11 a) * Deadline: 2006 for newly established companies, 2008 for all companies * Enforcement of non-compliance follows the same principles as any other regulation in companies' legislation (§ 6-9) * Progressive coercion starting with a written request to comply, if not fines may be imposed, and finally the company may be dissolved * Reporting is binding, non-compliance is immediately monitored and sanctions enforced by the business register, which is a delegated responsibility and authority	* State-owned (2003); inter-municipal (2003); municipal (2009); cooperative companies (2007) * Minimum of 40% of each sex (§ 6-11 a) * Enforcement of non-compliance follows the same principles as any other regulation in companies' legislation (§ 6-9) * Progressive coercion starting with a written request to comply, if not fines may be imposed, and finally the company may be dissolved * Reporting is binding, non-compliance is immediately monitored and sanctions enforced by the business register, which is a delegated responsibility and authority

---

[18] The rules regarding representation of both sexes shall apply separately to employee-elected and shareholder-elected representatives in order to ensure independent election processes. The rules do not

The gender balance regulation was to be immediately implemented for state-owned and inter-municipal companies by January 2004. The ruling of gender balance for the boards of public limited companies was formulated as a "threat" provision; if the companies themselves were able to reach the 40% gender target by July 2005, the legislation would not be enacted. The representation of women increased but did not reach the 40% target by 2005. Thus, in December 2005, the government finalized its decision from 2003. The gender quota regulation was mandatory from 2006 for all companies established that year and, from 2008, for the boards of all public limited companies. Regulation of gender representation on corporate boards was later expanded to cooperative companies and municipal companies.

All regulations apply similar sanctions. Hence, as stated in the original proposal to parliament (Barne—og familiedepartementet, 2002–2003), the regulation of gender representation on boards was to be enforced through the general enforcement system for company legislation. The business registry is a means to control and enforce compliance with all rulings. All companies have to record their board members with the business registry: their names, national identity, residence, and gender. If the information provided by the company is not in accordance with the law, an inquiry is opened. Because the procedure had been established prior to the law, there was no need for a separate evaluation of the company fulfillment of the gender quota regulation. Companies not complying received a written request from the business registry and were given formal responsibility to monitor compliance. If the company does not correct the matter, the registry has the authority to issue a fine, and if the company still does not comply, the registry then initiates the dissolution of the company and determines the timeline. According to a representative from the registry in an interview, there have been no instances where the dissolution process was initiated; the non-compliant business instead corrected the infraction.[19]

The 2003 Law in Practice: Easy, Almost Automatic Implementation with Few Ripple Effects

By the date when the gender quota was to be enforced in 2008 women already held 36% of board seats and 40% by 2009. The other types of companies covered by the gender quota in the law had also already fulfilled the 40% target by the dates the enforcement was to start. In comparison, the proportion of women on the boards of limited companies remained stable, however, with a small, moderate increase. This

apply to employee-elected board members in companies where one of the genders are represented by less than 20%.
[19] Senior advisor at the business register, 20 October 2020.

numerical progress, however, produced few ripple effects to executive branches of the companies covered by gender quotas for boards, or to the company boards not covered by gender quota regulations. Moreover, the actual practices pursued by the company leadership did very little to change the dominant gender-biased norms or to expand the pool of women being considered for the newly opened positions on boards. In fact, compliance was quite seamless given the gender composition of boards had been evolving incrementally from the early 2000s onward. Thus, in 2008, by the time the strict and punitive sanctions were to be applied to non-compliant companies, the gender balance regulation had often been met, and in cases where the target had not been met, it was often a question of only recruiting one or two more women.

Moreover, much of the recruitment of women to boards took place as a result of a parallel professionalization of corporate board recruitment, a result of the corporate governance movement (Wulf, 2014), which included the creation of election committees within the firm to recruit new board members. The recruitment of women was easily incorporated into the professionalization of the recruitment processes of board members in general. A 2007 study of these new election committees provides some crucial insight into how firms were able to recruit women to corporate boards through this new process, along with other new members. In the interviews conducted for the study, election committee chairs had few problems with recruiting women and indicated that the recruitment of women to company boards involved only minor changes to their regular routines, except for the recruitment of competent female candidates for company boards, as women were often not part of their primary professional networks (Hetland, 2007). As one chair stated in an interview for the study,

> I perceive that companies that have a nomination committee as well as those that do not have a nomination committee to be very aware that they have the deadline to ensure a gender distribution on the board.... The Nomination Committee perceives this as a framework condition.
>
> (Ibid, 72)

A second committee chair said,

> So I'm really against any quota and think that you should have managed without a quota, but when it's here it's of course okay to live with. It makes the nomination committee's work more demanding, but it can be okay once you have a nomination committee.
>
> (Ibid)

Databases with information about relevant female candidates were infrequently used in the search for female board member candidates; although recruitment firms have been used to some extent, especially to find female board candidates from other Nordic countries (Hageland, 2010; Heidenreich, 2010; 2014; Hetland, 2007). In addition, studies have shown that while the increased representation of women on company boards was a result of the gender quota law as a threat, this process involves relatively few women (Løyning, 2015), thus low policy empowerment. The women who were recruited in this new process were already central actors in Norwegian business life, primarily as owners who were willing to sit on many boards (Seierstad and Opsahl, 2011), although Løyning (2015) shows that the number of women serving on several boards diminished over time.

Another part of the absence of ripple effects comes from the important difference in the patterns of board recruitment, which tend to keep women removed from decision-making on boards even if they are members. The boards of public limited companies are often composed of internal (owners/shareholders) and external (experts) board members. Women are most typically external, with no or only small ownership interests, while men are more often internal board members, with stronger ownership interests. For some companies, board members are often recruited from the company that owns the company. Hence, the recruitment of board members does not necessarily change as a consequence of the introduction of gender quotas for corporate boards; however, when recruited from another company, the board members are more often recruited among all the top executives instead of the CEO (Heidenreich, 2010; 2012).

Some businesses may have also actually changed organizational form to avoid gender quotas. Companies that previously registered as public limited companies were able to re-register as limited companies; although, the consequence of this was they could not be listed on the stock exchange. The number of public limited companies diminished quite dramatically after the introduction of gender quotas for corporate boards, which has been interpreted by some as an expression of a silent protest and an escape from the gender quota regulation (Bøhren and Staubo, 2014). However, it is not clear that this was the case. For example, a 2009 survey given to companies that had changed from public limited companies to limited companies found that only 10% of the companies agreed that they re-registered as a response or protest to the gender quota ruling. The main response was that the rules and regulations applying to public limited companies compared to limited companies were too complicated; after all, there is no reason to choose to register as a public limited company if the company is not planning to be registered on the stock exchange. Another reason for the drop in numbers of public limited companies was the change in the securities trading act in 2007 that lifted the requirement that all security companies had to be registered as a public limited company (Heidenreich and Storvik, 2010). Thus, the argument of silent rebellion may be erroneous; to date, there is no clear evidence that companies left the stock exchange to avoid the requirements of the gender quota ruling.

Thus, we can conclude that gender quotas for corporate boards were implemented more or less automatically without important changes in established recruitment practices. Female board members were mainly found within the same circles as male board members before the implementation of the gender balance regulation and very few women or women's advocates were involved in the process. While there has been a reduction in the number of public limited companies, it is hard to verify whether this was a reaction to the introduction of gender quotas for public limited company boards or whether this was caused by other circumstances.

Given the 2003 law has been now in force for thirteen years, there seems to be some recent shift in the impact of the law with two periods of implementation. In the first ten years, there were indeed few ripple effects and implementation occurred with little involvement from women. Since 2013, there has been a subtle shift away from gender accommodation and the ripple effects from the law may be turning into waves.

2003–2013: Gender Accommodation and Low Policy Empowerment

In the run-up to the legislation, the government was quite cautious in the accounts presented in the proposal sent to parliament about what greater impact could be expected as a result of introducing gender quotas for corporate boards. The ambitions, as accounted for in public documents, were simply to recruit more women to company boards until the 40% target was met (see Barne—og familiedepartementet 2000–2001). The official aim to empower women was, in other words, limited to the inclusion of both men and women in non-executive positions of power in Norwegian business life. The main impression, however, was that the debate was permeated by great hopes that the recruitment of women to boards would spread to the recruitment of women to boards and management in Norwegian businesses and that it would contribute to a cultural change in the substantive empowerment of women, and through this be of a gender transformative nature.

In an interview with one of the key players in implementation, Turid Solvang emphasizes the importance of the introduction of gender quotas for corporate boards:[20]

The debate about and the introduction of the quota law sent shockwaves into Norwegian business, which later spread to business circles across large parts of the world. The regulation of gender quotas for boards has been extremely important in focusing on who has/should have decision-making power in the business community. In countries where women have higher education and participate in

---

[20] See note 2 for Turid Solvang's experience and background.

working life on an equal footing with men, it is meaningless that they should not be represented where the most important strategic decisions are made. Decisions that not only affect stock prices, but ultimately the society in which the companies cooperate.

To be sure, the numbers of women on the boards of public limited companies increased significantly from the early 2000s. The implementation of gender quotas for corporate boards soon led to the fulfillment of at least 40% women on the company boards covered by the regulation. This is a significant change and a change in the gender composition that has not happened for limited company boards not covered by the gender quota ruling. However, the representation of women and men does not randomly vary between 40% and 60% of each gender, as implied by the formulation of the regulation in the 2003 legislation. Most companies fulfill the minimum requirements for women on boards, but very few boards expose a higher share of women. The introduction of gender quotas for corporate boards has not led to more women in executive branches of companies. There have been modest positive developments in women's positions in the business sector, but the changes have not been stronger for companies covered by gender quotas for corporate boards than for those not.

Turid Solvang also maintained that the lack of ripple effects may be seen partly as a reflection of how the new women board members adjusted to their new positions:

It seems to be a zero-sum power game, and the challenges to get more women into top positions seem to be the same, regardless of national borders, culture, industries, etc.… After the introduction of the quota law, the debate on gender balance at the top of the decision pyramid in Norwegian business and industry "died." One of the reasons was that the last thing the new board women wanted to talk about was (their) gender, for fear of becoming known as a "quota woman." Fortunately, the debate has flared up again. Some have also claimed that the new female board candidates "skipped" the leadership role and "slipped" directly into the boardroom. Which may contribute to why there have been few ripple effects.

Thus, the modest, still positive, developments toward gender balance, together with women board members choosing not to be gender equality advocates, points in the direction of accommodation to existing gender relations more than gender transformation. And it may be worth noting that, as Norway was the very first country to introduce gender quotas for corporate boards, central actors felt a not unfounded fear that strong opposition and gender backlash could follow the introduction of the gender quota. However, it appeared the opposition was probably weaker than the media had signaled. Many, even in the business sector, probably found such regulations rather sensible, or even necessary, to make changes happen, although they had been passive bystanders while the public debate rolled, particularly given the actual practice of compliance to the quotas occurred prior to the actual enforcement of the strict penalties and with little change to the gender-biased practices in business. Few new women were recruited outside of women already in business. Women on boards were often far removed from decision-making and leadership arenas, and some companies may have actually changed their status to avoid compliance and, perhaps, most importantly, no new voices were brought into the practice of recruiting and placing women on boards. More-over, intersectional considerations about women from different lower classes or different ethnic groups have been absent from the debate. Gender balance has been the primary concern, emphasizing the right of women with similar backgrounds and competence to men to represent and be represented in decision-making in the business sector.

From 2013 toward the Future: A Transformative Potential?

Recent studies on the situation of gender equality in business show that there are signs of movement away from gender accommodation toward transforma-tion (Teigen et al, 2019; Teigen and Karlsen, 2020). Attitudes to gender equality and gender quota policies in particular, as well as views about the causes of male dominance in top positions, may be in the process of changing as a policy feed-back reaction to the implementation of gender quotas for corporate boards. An analysis based on two comprehensive surveys from 2000 and 2015 of the national elite population within ten sectors of society investigated whether changes in atti-tudes toward quotas corresponded to changes in beliefs about the causes of male dominance (Teigen et al, 2019). The analysis showed that gender quotas for cor-porate boards had a high and increasing level of legitimacy among Norwegian elites, and the increased support of gender quotas for corporate boards was found particularly among male business leaders (Teigen et al, 2019, p. 399). This move-ment away from gender accommodation is also illustrated in the recent, intensified debate on the persistence of men's dominance in business that has generated ambi-tious strategies to promote gender equality within many of the biggest companies (Teigen and Reisel, 2016). Another indication of change is the recent sharpening of the duties applied to public authorities, employers, and social partners in the Equality and Anti-Discrimination Act, which requires companies to investigate and document their own gender equality challenges (Skjeie, Holst, and Teigen, 2019).

To some extent, the debate on gender representation on boards has opened a new discussion of more ethnic diversity in Norwegian business life (Teigen and Midtbøen, 2015). Thus, it appears that interest groups advocating ethnic diversity have perceived gender balance advocates as allies in a common pursuit for diver-sity. Class has been absent in this new development, although present through the regulation of employee representation on the boards of companies with more than fifty employees (Hagen, 2015). Hence, employee representation came forward as an argument for the inclusion of women, not the other way around. Therefore, considerations of intersectionality where women on boards are given a color, sexual orientation, class, or ethnic background are still far from the agenda as far as gender equality on corporate boards is concerned.

Conclusion

When the debate on introducing gender quotas emerged in Norway in the late 1990s, the backdrop was the sharp contrast between the overwhelming male dominance in top positions in the business sector and the dominant image of positive gender development in recent decades in most areas of society. Norway's introduction of gender quotas for corporate boards has been of great importance in different ways. The representation of women has increased in central positions in the business sector, particularly in the boards covered by the gender quota regulation; the introduction of gender quotas for corporate boards stimulated a wider politicization of the lack of gender balance in the business sector, and the Norwegian example has been used in the push for gender quota regulations for corporate boards in many countries of Europe and beyond. Still, the coverage of the gender quota regulation is low in terms of comprehensiveness, and the ripple effects have been limited, with only recent signs of expansion leading to potential real gender transformations. In this sense, the introduction of gender quotas for corporate boards in Norway has not been a complete success.

The main outcome of gender quotas for corporate boards appears to be somewhere between gender accommodation and gender transformation: gender accommodation because of low comprehensiveness and modest, if at all, ripple effects but gender transformation in the sense that there has been a revival of a public debate on men's continued dominance in top positions in the business sector, as well as increased positive attitudes to the importance of gender equality and in favor of gender quota policies. To conclude, the introduction of gender quota policies does not automatically change gender norms, but in the long run, they may prove to be an important element that pushes in the direction of gender transformation.

References

Andersen, Marius L, Janne Kaada Erichsen and Anne Kaurin (2018) *Corporate Governance in Norway.* Kvale Advokatfirma, https://www.kvale.no/wp-content/uploads/2019/03/corporate-governance-2018-norway.pdf (Accessed October 26, 20).
Barne—og familiedepartementet (1999–2000) *Høring: Forslag til endringer i likestillingsloven.* Oslo: Barne—og familiedepartementet.

Barne—og familiedepartementet (2000–2001) *Om lov om endringer i likestillingsloven mv. (plikt til å arbeide for likestilling, skjerping av forbudet mot forskjellsbehandling på grunn av kjønn, forbud mot seksuell trakassering mv.).* Oslo: Barne—og familiedepartementet, https://www.regjeringen.no/contentassets/d495493b08ef4fd c9f46412c524f2466/no/pdfa/otp200020010077000dddpdfa.pdf (Accessed September 17, 2020).

Barne—og familiedepartementet (2002–2003) *Om lov om endringer i lov 13. Juni 1997 nr. 44 om aksjeselskaper, lov 13. juni 1997 nr. 45 om allmennaksjeselskaper og i enkelte andre lover (likestilling i styrer i statsaksjeselskaper, statsforetak, allmennaksjeselskaper mv).* Oslo: Barne—og familiedepartemetet. https://www.regjeringen.no/ contentassets/d91a84242b8347c5a39ed0061558dcf0/no/pdfs/otp2002200300970 00dddpdfs.pdf (Accessed September 17, 2020).

Bøhren, Øyvind and Siv Staubo (2014) "Does Mandatory Gender Balance work? Changing Organizational Form to Avoid Board Upheaval," *Journal of Corporate Finance*, 28, pp. 152–168.

Cvijanovic, Anette (2009) *Rettferdig og rimelig? Om kjønnskvotering i styrene i allmennaksjeselskap.* Master-dissertation i politikk og samfunnsendring. Fakultet for samfunnsvitenskap, Høgskolen i Bodø.

De Wulf, Hans (2014) "Do Gender Quotas Contribute to Better Corporate Governance?" in Marc De Vos and Phillippe Culliford (eds) *Gender Quotas for Company Boards.* Cambridge: Intersentia.

Ellingsæter, Anne-Lise (2014) "Nordic Earner–carer Models—Why Stability and Instability?" *Journal of Social Policy*, 43 (3), pp. 555–574.

Ellingsæter, Anne-Lise and Leira Arnlaug (2006) *Politicising Parenthood in Scandinavia: Gender Relations in Welfare States.* Bristol: The Policy Press.

Engeli, Isabell and Amy Mazur (2018) "Taking Implementation Seriously Is Assessing Success: The Politics of Gender Equality Policy," European Journal of Politics and Gender, 1 (1–2), pp. 111–129.

Gulbrandsen Trygve (2019) *Elites In an Egalitarian Society: Support for the Nordic Model.* Palgrave Macmillan. https://www.palgrave.com/gp/book/9783319959832 (Accessed September 17, 2020).

Hageland, Øyvind Wessel (2010) *Rekruttering til ASA-styrer via hodejegerfirmaer. En kvalitativ studie på bakgrunn av lovregulert kjønnskvotering til ASA-styrene.* Masteroppgave. Institutt for sosiologi og samfunnsgeografi, Universitet i Oslo.

Hagen, Inger Marie (2015) "Participation and Co-determination: Why Some Arrangements Fail and Others Prevail," in Fredrik Engelstad and Anniken Hagelund (eds) *Cooperation and Conflict the Nordic Way. Work, Welfare and Institutional Change in Scandinavia.* De Gruyter Open, pp. 77–95. https://www.degruyter.com/view/books/ 9783110436891/9783110436891006/9783110436891-006.xml. (Accessed September 17, 2020).

Heidenreich, Vibeke (2010) "Rekruttering til ASA-styrer etter innføringen av kvoteringsregelen," *Magma*, 7.

Heidenreich, Vibeke (2012) "'Det er en kabal som skal gå opp'. Styredannelser i lys av eiersammensetning og krav til kjønnsbalanse," *Søkelys på arbeidslivet*, 29 (4), pp. 310–328.

Heidenreich, Vibeke (2014) *Kjønnskvotering i selskapsstyrer og rekrutteringseffekter.* Phd Dissertation. Institutt for sosiologi og samfunnsgeografi, Universitetet i Oslo.

Heidenreich, Vibeke and Aagoth Storvik (2010) "Rekrutteringsmønstre, erfaringer og holdninger til styrearbeid blant ASA-selskapenes styrepresenentanter," Rapport 2010 (11). Oslo: Institutt for Samfunnsforskning.

Hernes, Helga (1987) *Welfare State and Women Power. Essays in State Feminism*. Oslo: Norwegian University Press.

Hetland, Aslak (2007) *Betydningen av kjønn og nettverk ved styrerekruttering. En kvalitativ studie av rekrutteringsprosesser til styrer i allmennaksjeselskaper*. Master-disseration. Institutt for sosiologi og samfunnsgeografi, Universitetet i Oslo.

Hughes, Melanie M, Pamela Paxton and Mona Lena Krook (2017) "Gender Quotas for Legislatures and Corporate Boards," *Annual Review of Sociology*, 43, https://doi.org/10.1146/annurev-soc-060116-053324 (Accessed September 17, 2020).

Leira, Arnlaug (2012) "Omsorgens institusjoner, omsorgens kjønn," in Anne Lise Ellingsæter and Karin Widerberg (eds) *Velferdsstatens familier—Nye sosiologiske perspektiver*. Oslo: Gyldendal Akademisk, pp. 76–93.

Løyning, Trond (2015) "Næringslivseliter og makt," in Mari Teigen (ed.) *Virkninger av kjønnskvotering i norsk næringsliv*. Oslo: Gyldendal Akademisk, pp. 139–159.

Seierstad, Cathrine and Opsahl, Tore (2011) "For the Few Not the Many? The Effects of Affirmative Action on Presence, Prominence, and Social Capital of Female Directors in Norway," *Scandinavian Journal of Management*, 27 (1), pp. 44–54.

Skjeie, Hege, Cathrine Holst, and Mar Teigen (2019) "Splendid Isolation. On How a Non-member Is Affected by—and affects—EU Gender Equality Policy," in Moira Dustin, Nuno Ferreira, and Susan Millns (eds) *Gender and Queer Perspectives on Brexit*. London: Palgrave, pp. 439–461.

Skjeie, Hege, Cathrine Holst, and Mari Teigen (2017) "Benevolent Contestations. Mainstreaming, Judicialization, Europeanization in the Norwegian Gender+ Equality Debate," in Heather McRae and Elaine Weiner (eds.) *Towards Gendering Institutionalism*. London: Rowman & Littlefield International, pp. 121–141.

Sørensen, Siri Øyslebø (2011) "Statsfeminismens møte med næringslivet. Bakgrunnen og gjennombruddet for kjønnskvotering i bedriftsstyrer som politisk reform," *Tidsskrift for kjønnsforskning*, 35 (2), pp. 102–119.

Teigen, Mari (2002) "Kvotering til styreverv—Mellom offentlig og privat handlefrihet," *Tidsskrift for samfunnsforskning*, 43 (1), pp. 73–104.

Teigen, Mari (2003) *Kvotering og kontrovers: Om likestilling som politikk*. Oslo: Unipax.

Teigen, Mari (2015) "The Making of Gender Quotas for Corporate Boards in Norway," in Fredrik Engelstad and Anniken Hagelund (eds) *Cooperation and Conflict the Nordic Way. Work, Welfare and Institutional Change in Scandinavia*. De Gruyter Open, https://www.degruyter.com/view/books/9783110436891/9783110436891007/9783110436891-007.xml (Accessed 17 September 17, 2020).

Teigen, Mari (2018) "The 'Natural' Prolongation of the Norwegian Gender Equality Policy Institution," in Eléonore Lépinard and Ruth Rubio-Marin (eds) *Transforming Gender Citizenship: The Irresistible Rise of Gender Quotas in Europe*. Cambridge: Cambridge University Press, pp. 341–365.

Teigen, Mari and Liza Reisel (2016) Kjønnsbalanse på toppen? Sektorvariasjon i næringsliv, akademia, offentlig sektor og organisasjonsliv. ISF-report, 2017:11, https://samfunnsforskning.brage.unit.no/samfunnsforskning-xmlui/handle/11250/2473133 (Accessed September 17, 2020).

Teigen, Mari and Hege Skjeie (2017) "The Nordic Gender Equality Model," in Knutsen Oddbjørn (ed.) *The Nordic Models in Political Science. Challenged but Still Viable?* Oslo: Fagbokforlaget.

Teigen, Mari, Hege Skjeie and Rune Karlsen (2019) "Framing and Feedback: Increased Support for Gender Quotas among Elites," *European Journal of Politics and Gender*,

2 (3), pp. 399–423, https://doi.org/10.1332/251510819X15639713867651 (Accessed September 17, 2020).

Teigen, Mari and Rune Karlsen (2020) "Influencing Elite Opinion on Gender Equality through Framing: A Survey Experiment of Elite Support for Corporate Board Gender Quotas". *Politics & Gender*. Vol. 16: 3, pp. 792–815. DOI: https://doi.org/10.1017/S1743923X19000060

Teigen, Mari og Arnfinn H. Midtbøen (2015) "Kunnskap om kjønnsbalanse," in Mari Teigen (ed.) *Virkninger av kjønnskvotering i norsk næringsliv*. Oslo: Gyldendal Akademisk.

Walby, Sylvia (2009) *Globalization and Inequalities: Complexity and Contested Modernities*. London: SAGE Publications.

11

A "Success Story" beyond Numbers

Business Resistance Trumps Timid Feminist Demands in France

Soline Blanchard and Marion Rabier

Introduction

In a little over ten years, France has gone from being a laggard to a leader in the feminization of corporate boards at both European and global levels; the percentage of women board members in the largest listed companies has increased from 10.2% in 2009 to 45% by mid-2020 according to data collected by the European Institute for Gender Equality (EIGE).[1] This result is all the more surprising given that female representation on boards had been stagnating below 10% before 2009, and vertical segregation remains high at the pinnacle of power in French companies, with women accounting for only 5.4% of CEOs and 20.4% of executives in 2020. This dramatic evolution is usually credited to the 2011 law on gender-balanced representation on corporate boards, which introduced a target of 40% women members by 2017 and made France the second country to adopt such a quota after Norway. As the former Minister of the Family, Childhood and Women's Rights stated (Rossignol, 2016), "The law has proved effective. … France is now the leader in Europe while the country was among the poorest performers." However, as this chapter argues, an in-depth look into the policy implementation, evaluation, and outcomes of what is a mostly state-driven approach to gender equality on corporate boards questions the narrative of France as a success story in gender equality in the corporate world.

Going beyond the numerical increase in women's share of corporate boards shows that the adoption and implementation of gender quotas have fallen short of challenging the established gender norms that keep women out of positions of

---

[1] The EIGE reporting focuses on the first fifty companies of the primary blue-chip index of each country. The French official stock market is Euronext Paris; major stock indexes include the CAC 40 (made of the forty largest listed companies) and the SBF 120 (made of the 120 largest ones).

Soline Blanchard and Marion Rabier, *A "Success Story" beyond Numbers*. In: *Gender Equality and Policy Implementation in the Corporate World*. Edited by Isabelle Engeli and Amy G. Mazur, Oxford University Press.
© Oxford University Press (2022). DOI: 10.1093/oso/9780198865216.003.0011

significant influence and power. When women business leaders have called for gender equality measures at the corporate board level, these calls have been quite timid, showing deference to established gender norms rather than challenging the gender-biased status quo. And when feminist activists in business and femocrats in women's policy agencies have sought to make a symbolic policy more authoritative, the powerful (male) gatekeepers have been able to block these efforts through their apathy toward any meaningful policies that would seriously strike down long-established gender hierarchies.

After an overview of vertical segregation in the French business context, the chapter traces the process of how female access to corporate boards has been placed on the political and business agenda by a coalition of actors speaking for women, including some feminist voices. Next, it analyzes the decision-making process and its outputs arguing that the rather consensual adoption of legislative gender quotas carried out under a right-wing government has diluted the potential to seriously challenge dominant economic gender norms. The chapter then highlights how women's policy agencies and businesswomen networks have taken a front-line position in the implementation process and tried to overcome the law's shortcomings in terms of monitoring and evaluation in the context of a left-wing government. Finally, it assesses the impacts of legislative quotas revealing the policy's mixed results and the persistence of gendered patterns in the corporate world, despite a broad societal acceptance of parity across all arenas of French society.

Persistent Vertical Segregation in Line with EU Average

Comparisons between European countries in terms of work/care gender configurations have classified France in a moderate position with a "modified male breadwinner model" (Lewis, 1992; Chang, 2000). The combination of family life and full-time work for women has been promoted through an effective family policy (Hantrais and Letablier, 1996) and a policy framework on equal pay and equal employment, or *égalité professionnelle* (Laufer, 2014), supported by active state feminism (Revillard, 2016) including women's rights ministries and a highly developed women's policy administration. Nevertheless, gender inequalities are still blatant and located within the average of the EU-28, and progress has recently slowed down (OECD, 2017).

Corporate vertical segregation persists, despite impressive changes in board representation at the turn of the 2010s. In terms of occupational categories, women are more likely to be clerical workers or unskilled workers than men, and less likely to be managers (INSEE, 2020). However, their proportion among managers has increased constantly since 1990, from 30% to around 40%. Women also represent one-third of senior managers and executives, a figure that perfectly matches the EU-28 average (Eurostat, 2020). One-third of self-employed individuals and salaried company managers are women, and these figures have stagnated over the past fifteen years (INSEE, 2015). Women account for 40% of the self-employed but only 25% of managers of limited liability companies and 17% of managers of public limited companies and simplified joint-stock companies. They are better represented in personnel (29% vs. 16%) and healthcare service (25% vs. 11%). Only 15% of the independent businesses with more than twenty employees are women. The overall gender pay gap is 31% but depends on the type of business: it is higher in businesses of fifty persons or more (34%).

Women's positions at the top of the largest listed companies display a mixed picture as Table 11.1 shows. On the one hand, the figures are poor regarding senior management and executive positions; in the first half of 2020, women only accounted for 5.4% of CEOs, and France was at the bottom among EU-28 members (average 7.9%) and represented 20.4% of executives, which is about the European average (19.3%). On the other, the presence of women on corporate boards has increased since 2003 and the pace has dramatically sped up in the past years, from 12.3% in 2010 to 45% in 2020, compared with 29.2% at the EU-28 level. The same trend has been observed in Euronext companies, reaching between 31%

Table 11.1 Percentage Share of Women on Boards in the Largest Listed Companies in France, 2004–2020

| | EU-28 board members | FRANCE | | | | |
		Board members	President	CEO	Executives	Non-executives
2004	9	5.3	1.9	—	—	—
2005	9.8	5.9	4.1	—	—	—
2006	9.7	7.3	4	—	—	—
2007	10.4	7.6	4	—	—	—
2008	10.8	8.8	0	—	—	—
2009	11	9.3	0	—	—	—
2010	11.9	10.2	0	—	—	—
2011	13.7	12.3	2.8	—	—	—
2012	15.8	21.6	2.7	0	8.4	27.8
2013	17.8	25.1	5.6	0	11.3	32.4
2014	20.2	29.7	8.6	0	11.4	35
2015	22.7	32.4	5.6	0	13.1	38.2
2016	23.9	35.6	2.8	2.9	14.9	43.9
2017	25.3	41.2	5.7	2.9	15.2	46.2
2018	26.7	43.4	2.9	2.8	17	46.6
2019	28.8	43.9	2.8	5.6	19.7	48
2020	29.2	45.3	2.8	5.4	20.4	47.8

Source: EIGE Database. Data for October each year, except for 2020 [April]

and 39.5% in 2017, depending on the estimates (AFECA, 2017; Gouvernance & Structures, 2017). The rise has also been notable in public companies and institutions, reaching nearly 40% (Montalcino et al, 2017). The number of women in board subcommittees has increased in all private firms: more than 60% of new appointees were women in 2016 and 80% in 2017 (AFECA, 2017). It is the same for board committee chairs: for instance, between 2013 and 2017, the percentage of women chairs almost quadrupled in audit committees of SBF 120 companies, and more than doubled in appointments committees (Deloitte, 2017; Ethics & Boards, 2017). Nevertheless, female board chairs are still very rare (2.7% vs. 7.8% in EU-28 in 2020), and no significant progress has been observed over time. Moreover, the gender wage gap between female and male board members is more than 10% (Deloitte, 2015).

A Deferential but Effective Mobilization to Get Corporate Quotas on the Agenda

State actors and feminist groups representing women in business joined forces to put power-sharing and gender quotas for corporate boards on the agenda starting in the mid-2000s under the right-wing presidency of Jacques Chirac (2002–2007) and then Nicolas Sarkozy (2007–2012). The first impetus came from feminist politicians and femocrats in a context of renewed institutionalization of the women's cause in the state (Revillard, 2016). The collaboration between conservative MP Marie-Jo Zimmermann, also head of both the Observatoire de la Parité (2002–2010)—a bureaucratic advisory board created in 1995 and dedicated to the promotion of gender parity in political representation—and the Parliamentary Delegation on Women's Rights (2002–2012), and the senior official Brigitte Grésy, former head (1998–2004) of the Service des Droits des Femmes et à l'Égalité—the permanent administrative agency dedicated to driving forward gender equality policies since the 1980s—, a member of the Ministry of Parity (2003–2006) and a gender equality expert (2006–2012), was particularly important for this issue. Following the adoption of a 50–50 gender quota called "parity" for elected offices, the same coalition introduced the principles of parity on corporate boards. A broad acceptance of the principles of parity—or "parity grammar" (Bereni and Revillard, 2007)—spread from the political arena into the business world, which drew the attention of the media and the general public to the issue of gender equality at the corporate level, a controversial issue according to Grésy (2009). For her part, Zimmermann (cited in AFP News, 2009) stated, "It is not a feminist demand. We just want women [in business] to have equal access. And parity laws in politics have proven to be effective." They also built on European efforts that had promoted gender balance in decision-making over the past two decades (Jacquot, 2015) and used the supranational EU level to support and legitimate their action, as well as the Norwegian model for gender quotas on corporate boards. For instance, on May 19, 2009, the Conseil Économique et Social (Economic and Social Council) organized a symposium dedicated to comparing Norwegian and French gender equality policies, including "equal access for women and men to professional responsibilities."[2]

At the same time, professional and businesswomen's groups began to multiply, reflecting the (relative) feminization of higher education and executive positions, as well as the growing interest of companies in gender diversity. Among these, the following can be mentioned for their activism and visibility: Grandes Écoles au Féminin, bringing together managers who graduate from the elite training schools, the French section of the European Professional Women's Network, and the Women's Forum, nicknamed "Women's Davos." Different as these networks were, they structured themselves around the common cause of women's access to economic power and played a crucial role in gaining corporate attention, producing expertise, and organizing key events. An emblematic illustration was the first release of the McKinsey biannual studies entitled *Women Matter*, which was commissioned for the 2007 Women's Forum meeting in Deauville. At first, only a few of these groups advocated for authoritative gender quotas; most argued for soft law measures and a persuasion strategy in line with the principles of French republican universalism (Lépinard and Mazur, 2009). However, in 2009, businesswomen's groups started to endorse massively the idea that gender quotas were a "necessary evil" since they could only reflect the "cruel absence of progress." Véronique Morali (cited in Renault, 2010), an influential figure involved in multiple business and women's networks, declared, "I support the law all the more given that I was initially against gender quotas. Then I joined in because otherwise nothing will happen."

During the same period, the Deputy Minister for Women's Rights commissioned a report on corporate gender equality, including the *Confidence Barometer for Women Managers* driven by the main women's networks (Grésy, 2009). This report made the issue more visible and contributed to building a stable coalition of women brought together by the original leaders of the parity movement, including politicians, civil servants, business leaders, and managers, as well as journalists, to push for the quota legislation (Blanchard, Boni-Le Goff, and Rabier, 2013). The public discussions on gender quotas on corporate boards, however, were far less widespread than those on political parity (Bereni and Lépinard, 2004) and focused on only a portion of the more feminist demands. For example, the use of positive discrimination was widely contested even among the women leaders on the grounds that merit alone should be taken into consideration and not gender, that

---

[2] Since then, Norway has regularly served as a touchstone for French corporate equality policies, as evidenced by the 2013 symposium held in the Senate and entitled, The Norwegian Model, or the promotion of the Norwegian lesson during the Tour de France of gender equality in 2017.

there was a lack of qualified women, and that quotas were counterproductive for women's interests.

On the right, MEDEF (Mouvement des Entreprises de France)—the main employer organization—and right-wing MPs appealed to the sacrosanct principle of corporate autonomy and argued that the framework of a legislated quota would not take into account the specificity of companies, that the state should not intervene in private business affairs and that financial penalties would harm business. On the left, some feminist groups and political leaders argued that gender quotas were narrow and elitist, and ineffective in addressing overall gender inequalities in the workplace because of the focus on a very small number of women at the top.

In response to these criticisms, the women's coalition opted to defend quotas using the business case argument. They first sought to show a positive correlation between greater gender balance on boards and business profits, using the tools developed in the USA by women's groups such as Catalyst and aimed to prove that women's quotas were a good deal for companies in economic terms.[3] The arguments of social justice and equality, therefore, were relegated to the background for pragmatic and strategic purposes, and the economic argument was placed front and center. Businesswomen at the top were framed in terms of added value through taking advantage of feminine management qualities, which were complementary to masculine qualities. During this period, the world economic and financial turmoil gave more fuel to the business case and the issue was reframed in terms of a "testosterone crisis" (Vittori, 2009), which warranted a change in governance; women and gender quotas were thus praised as remedies to the economic emergency.

The French media also framed the issue in these essentialist terms. A press review carried out using the Europresse database between March 2009 and December 2012 revealed that over thirty-five articles in the print media cited the following quote attributed in France to Christine Lagarde, then Minister of the Economy, "If Lehman Brothers had been Lehman Sisters, we would not be where we are today."

The Dilution of Legislation through Low-profile and Consensual Decision-making under a Right-wing Majority

Following an initial period of limited support for a legislative quota, certain right-wing politicians saw the advantage of a quota, as long as it was not too coercive; the actual adoption of the 2011 law turned out to be swift with little controversy or

---

[3] References were made to the 2004 and 2007 Catalyst reports entitled *The Bottom Line: Connecting Corporate Performance and Gender Diversity* and to the 2005 *Catalyst Census of Women Board Directors of Fortune 500*.

debate, given that the law lost much of its authority in the parliamentary process. The first attempt to introduce a gender quota for boards dated back to 2006 when Zimmerman had managed to insert in the first draft of a law on equal pay a 20% target of the underrepresented sex on corporate and supervisory boards. However, the law was thrown out by a Constitutional Council decision that the equal pay law violated equality principles.

In July 2008, Zimmerman jumped into constitutional reform to overcome the formal barrier and introduced an amendment to Article 1 of the Constitution, "The law promotes equal access of women and men to electoral mandates and elective functions, as well as to professional and social responsibilities." In March 2009, she tabled the first bill on gender quotas, which failed to be examined due to lack of political support. A few months later, she finally found a powerful ally, Jean-François Copé, the conservative party president in the National Assembly. In his words (Copé cited in Basini, 2010), "[I am] convinced that modernity is measured by the position society gives to women and that shock therapy is necessary to break the gridlock."

The bill divided conservative MPs, and only 106 out of 313 voted for it. Rather than any opposition to the principle of quotas, the MPs who voted against the bill did so to express their disapproval of Copé's aspirations to lead the party. In any case, a new bill was introduced in December 2009, with a strict 50–50 gender parity goal for board directors for all listed companies and state institutions. In order to stem the coming wave of regulation, AFEP (Association Française des Entreprises Privées)—a very select club of corporate leaders—and MEDEF responded by adopting a recommendation on women's presence on boards in their joint corporate governance code dedicated to listed companies. It was clearly a counter-strategy to prevent regulation given that a similar provision had been strongly rejected in 2005 when the first female president of MEDEF, Laurence Parisot, had tried to put the subject on the table. Despite the efforts of big business, the bill was amended and passed in the Senate in October 2010, then adopted in a second reading in the National Assembly in January 2011. The decision process was quick and even surprised the promoters of gender quotas. As Grésy (2015) stated, "I was thinking: one more report that goes in the closet. 40% women will never catch on. And then: poof! In 2009, with the wave of a magic wand … this law was adopted very, very quickly."

At the same time, it was not surprising the bill sailed through parliament given that the final law was stripped of any content that would authoritatively promote 50–50 parity on corporate boards; provisions linked to more general principles of gender equality were progressively removed in the process. In the first bill, companies had been required to submit a complete evaluation of gender inequalities in their annual activity report. Several amendments from socialist MPs were also dismissed, such as financial penalties for businesses that refused to engage in collective bargaining on the issue or a 10% increase in employer contributions for extensive use of part-time work. Marie-Hélène des Esgaulx (2010)—the conservative MP who spoke in the name of the Law Commission in the Senate—thus explained that "penalizing companies financially would be pain-free for decision-makers and ineffective" and that women's presence in top positions was sufficient to promote gender equality at work, by creating a "virtuous circle": female board members were expected to pay attention to gender balance in corporate boards and benefit from promotions in their own companies.

Discussions on the level of the quota led to the rejection of strict gender parity in favor of a less restrictive objective. MPs quickly latched on to a 40% target in the debates. While Grésy (2009) claimed that she "promoted 40 because it appeared just right," a reference to the Norwegian model was used to justify the lower level and to make the compromise, beyond Grésy's assessment. The range of companies required to comply with the quota was also circumscribed by employer organizations. The initial discussions mentioned only listed companies and firms with more than 1,000 workers. Other proposals were put forward but finally rejected, such as extending the same rules to chambers of commerce, technical centers, and competitiveness clusters of individual businesses (submitted by conservative MPs and Grandes Écoles au Féminin); or limiting the combination of several board mandates in order to make room for women (submitted by socialist and centrist MPs). In the end, the most restrictive proposals for sanctions were rejected in the course of the debates, notably under the pressure of the business group AFEP. For example, the socialist group had proposed that board decisions be declared null and void in the event that gender quotas were not met in the boardrooms; but Zimmermann herself rejected this proposal (Commission des Lois de l'Assemblée Nationale, 2009), considering it an "excessive punishment" that would expose companies to "legal uncertainty and risks."

The Adoption of a Timid State-driven Approach: Authority Instruments without Meaningful Sanctions and Monitoring

In terms of the GEPP categorization for policy instruments, the French approach is mostly a state-driven one with a focus on gender quotas (Table 11.2). The law is situated on the high level of the comprehensiveness continuum, with mandatory targets applied to a large number of private and state-owned companies. It can also be described as light coercion: while the regulation is binding, monitoring and control procedures are not defined, and non-compliance is lightly sanctioned.

On the self-regulation side, the AFEP-MEDEF attempted to halt the quota bill by adopting a recommendation in their 2010 corporate governance code. It urged boards to "reassess their gender balance" to reach and maintain over 20% female corporate board members by 2013 and 40% by 2016—i.e., the objectives under discussion in the bill, give or take a year. The signatory members were required to indicate objectives, modalities, and results in their annual report in accordance

Table 11.2 Policy Measures for Gender Equality on Corporate Boards in France

SELF-REGULATION	
Corporate Governance Code of Listed Corporations 2010[a] * Listed companies * Minimum of 40% women * Deadline: intermediate in 2013, final in 2016 * Comply-or-explain *Annual report to include targets, modalities, and results	**Corporate Governance Code of Listed Corporations 2016[a]** * Listed companies * Gender is clustered with diversity (nationality, international experience, and knowledge)

STATE REGULATION	
Law n° 2011-103 of January 27, 2011 * State-owned and large private companies with more than 500 employees and sales in excess of fifty million euros over three successive accounting periods * Minimum of 40% for the underrepresented sex * Deadline: 20% in 2014, 40% in 2017 * Boards to deliberate annually on equal pay and equal employment policy * New board nominations to be declared null and void in the event of a breach of the parity obligations; board members' attendance fees to be suspended	
Law n° 2014-873 of August 4, 2014 * Companies with more than 250 employees * Minimum of 40% for the underrepresented sex * Deadline: 2020	**Law n° 2019-486 of May 22, 2019** * Board decisions to be declared null and void in the event of a breach of the parity obligations

Joint Code of the Association Française des Entreprises Privées (AFEP) et Mouvement des Entreprises de France (MEDEF), often referred to as the AFEP-MEDEF Code.

with the comply-or-explain principle of the code. After the legislative quota was passed, no more recommendations were included in the 2015 code; and in 2016, quantitative objectives disappeared, boards only being asked to "consider the desirable diversity balance," including gender, nationality, international experience, and knowledge. Thus, these self-regulatory efforts were strategies to pre-empt the quite authoritative regulation more than any concerted effort to promote gender equality on boards. On the state regulation side, the text of the 2011 law on Balanced Representation of Women and Men on Corporate and Supervisory Boards and Professional Gender Equality was relatively short, with only eight articles. It modified the French Commercial Code—the reference document with regard to the composition of boards of directors. Both private and state-owned firms were concerned, in the name of equal treatment between the public and private sectors.

The law introduced two thresholds for gender quotas: 20% by January 1, 2014, and 40% by January 1, 2017, covering corporate and supervisory boards of all listed companies and firms that combined more than 500 employees and sales in excess of 50 million euros over three successive accounting periods (approximately 2,000 firms). When corporate or supervisory boards were made up of less than eight board members, the gap between the number of female and male members could not be higher than two. Two types of sanctions were designed: new appointments would be declared null and void if they did not respect the parity objective, and board member attendance fees would be suspended (but they would be reinstated with retroactive effect once the board was properly composed). Article 7 stated that a report on women's access to corporate boards should be made before December 31, 2015, including "the efforts made or planned by the state" to achieve the 40% target, without specifying by whom the report should be made. Article 8 mentioned that boards should deliberate annually on company policy on professional gender equality and equal pay.

This seminal law was supplemented by various texts. In 2014, a new law on Real Equality between Women and Men slightly modified the scope of the 2011 law, the threshold of 500 workers being lowered to 250, with effect from January 2020. In 2018, the law "for the freedom to choose one's professional future" reaffirmed that boards had to deliberate annually on gender equality issues and also urged boards to report annually on the (gender) diversity policies they applied to themselves and the gender balance in the top 10% positions. And in 2019, the law "relating to business growth and transformation" significantly increased the sanctions with board decisions to be declared null and void in the event that gender quotas were not met in the boardrooms, a proposal that had been rejected only a few years earlier. Beyond these general provisions, the formal policy statements were unclear about implementation as well as evaluation procedures and failed to mention any specific monitoring process. These gray areas were a result of the speed of the adoption process; the authorities that had been approached for reporting and monitoring did not have time to give their consent, including the Autorité des Marchés Financiers (Financial Markets Authority), statutory auditors, and the Contrôle Général Économique et Financier (General Economic and Financial Auditing Agency). The lawmakers, therefore, decided not to let the window of opportunity close, even if it meant postponing the question of application and evaluation, as confirmed by Grésy (2015), "The law was rushed through because there was a political opportunity. … But then, it is true that we took it and did not say: 'You have to do this, you have to do that.' It is so unusual."

There was also no reporting system on the gendered composition of boards in place prior to the law. The lead-up to the law's adoption had given rise to several private initiatives in the 2000s, but they were limited and sometimes provided divergent results. Moreover, the gender dimension had only been recently introduced in national statistics and had not yet been extended to numbers on corporate governance. Finally, the scope of implementation of the law was expanded to more companies and administrations and the rules turned out to be more complex than expected, including a multitude of criteria. As a result, it became increasingly unclear which organizations were actually affected and what reporting and control procedures were in place for each of them.

A "Design by Doing" Implementation Process Driven by Women's Policy Agencies and Businesswomen Networks

In response to the absence of clear provisions about implementation and monitoring, women's policy agencies and businesswomen's groups, some of whose members were already involved in the adoption process, quickly positioned themselves to oversee the implementation and assess the progress of the policy instruments that had been adopted.[4] During the presidency of the socialist François Hollande (2012–2017), the state feminist network included the ministerial offices in charge of gender equality—and, in particular, the Ministry of Women's Rights headed by the feminist activist Najat Vallaud-Belkacem (2012–2014); the Service des Droits des Femmes et à l'Égalité; the Haut Conseil à l'Égalité entre les Femmes et les Hommes, which replaced the Observatoire de la Parité in 2013 and benefited from a strong expertise in monitoring political parity and an extension of its field of competence to the economic world; and the Conseil Supérieur de l'Égalité Professionnelle—a consultative public body created in 1983 to promote gender equality at work—, which regained visibility under the direction of Grésy (2013–2019).

The business feminist networks included established groups and new structures such as the Fédération Femmes Administrateurs, which brought together five professional women's groups to promote women lawyers, barristers, chartered accountants, high-level officials, and judicial officers on corporate and public boards (2011), and Financi'Elles, a grouping of eleven networks in the banking, finance, and insurance sectors, aiming to promote gender diversity (2010). The implementation and follow-up objectives of these groups emerged along the way and their mobilization followed the timing of the law in two phases.

2011–2014: Counting Women and Supporting Businesses and Appointees

During the first phase, feminist lobbies gave priority to establishing a picture of gender inequality on corporate boards and supporting target businesses and female candidates. Femocrats observed that their own institutions and the public

---

[4] If the AFEP-MEDEF code and the 2011 law came into force almost at the same time, mobilizations focused on the latter because of its authoritative scope.

authorities more generally lacked the resources to monitor legal implementation on their own and decided to establish partnerships with private agents, mainly businesswomen's networks and consultants. In 2013, the Ministry of Women's Rights called in the consulting firm Ethics & Boards to create the yearly Ranking of Women Representation within SBF 120 companies, presented as both a reporting tool—establishing a first collection of "reliable" figures—and a monitoring tool— benchmarking results with an eye on the legal objectives (Blanchard, 2018). It also aimed to foster a fruitful competition among companies—relying on a "name and celebrate" (as opposed to name and shame) strategy (Felstiner, Abel and Sarat, 1980)—and to broaden the dynamics for gender equality—including indicators about executive bodies and top management positions, and inviting businesses to join a network facilitated by the Service des Droits des Femmes et à l'Égalité.

In 2014, the Ministry, the Fédération Femmes Administrateurs, other women's networks, and the Institut Français des Administrateurs—the main professional organization of French board members—launched a web platform to "put forward the existing pools of women" and to "facilitate the matching" between candidates and corporations.[5] The initiative also included Viviane de Beaufort, an academic expert who had designed specific training courses for female candidates in her business school in association with women's networks and consulting firms as early as 2011.

Gender equality consulting firms led by entrepreneurs from the movement (Blanchard, 2019), conventional consulting firms or headhunters, and academics also developed new services, including benchmarking, talent pools, recruitment advice, or mentoring programs for nominees. In parallel, from 2014, AFEP and MEDEF began to follow up the application of the 2010 corporate governance code—presented as an "anticipation of the 2011 legislative reform"—in CAC 40 and SBF 120 companies, and periodically stated a satisfactory evolution of gender balance on boards despite a few "deviations" from the comply-or-explain principle.

From 2015: Broadening the Scope and Monitoring the Law

A second phase of implementation began when the socialist Ministry of Social Affairs, Health and Women's Rights Marisol Touraine asked the Haut Conseil à l'Égalité entre les Femmes et les Hommes and the Conseil Supérieur de l'Égalité Professionnelle to carry out the mid-term evaluation enshrined in the 2011 law. Their conclusions urged a wider application of (the spirit of) the text and the search for relevant monitoring and control systems. The mid-term evaluation report pointed out that big listed companies had easily achieved the target of 20%

[5] http//administratrices.femmes.gouv.fr (Accessed November 24, 2014).

women by 2014, which was far from being the case in smaller organizations, particularly in non-listed companies. Assuming that these had poor legal knowledge, they called for more institutional communication. And in 2017, the Deputy Minister for Women's Rights organized a specific training for the ten most backward businesses of the SBF 120 and used the "name and shame" strategy for those that declined the invitation.

Another conclusion was that the sharing of seats on boards was not synonymous with the sharing of power, women still being underrepresented in key positions on boards and in senior management. As the evaluators stated (Bousquet et al, 2016, p. 7), "While the law appears to be followed to the letter in a number of companies, the intention of the reform is not always respected." This triggered the creation of new indicators beyond the legal scope, analyzing the representation of women in board committee chairs, executive bodies, and (top) management positions. For instance, the Financi'Elles/Ethics & Boards Index was initiated in 2016. The next year, the Ethics & Boards group and the Institut du Capitalisme Responsable—a corporate think tank founded by an entrepreneur of the movement—launched the Zimmermann Index at the National Assembly (Ethics & Boards and ICR, 2017), which proposed to "maintain the momentum generated in 2011 and extend it to all levels of the company."

Finally, the evaluators noticed that their task was a challenging exercise since they had to juggle various and partial public/private data focused on large-listed companies, while the situation of non-listed ones and public organizations was still "terra quasi incognita" (Bousquet et al, 2016, p. 105). They observed major difficulties in identifying the organizations subject to the laws, getting access to the gendered composition of governing bodies, and committing relevant authorities to reporting, monitoring, and control processes. However, as Delphine Chauffaut from the Ministry of Social Affairs, Health and Women's Rights noted (2015), "We want[ed] a more systematic system of measurement and control, because deadlines [we]re coming up and we [would] have to start applying the sanctions prescribed by law." To address the emergency, the evaluators suggested not focusing on audits and sanctions—which had actually been indefinitely postponed—but on monitoring, defined as carrying out an exhaustive and detailed inventory, providing advice to companies, and alerting them in cases of non-compliance. Priority was given to methodical and uniform data collection, to introduce more accurate indicators in the existing reporting systems of public and private agents. As confirmed by Marine Darnault from the Service des Droits des Femmes et à l'Égalité (2015), femocrats approached several bodies, including the Institut National de la Statistique et des Études Économiques (National Institute for Statistics and Economic Research), the Autorité des Marchés Financiers and the Contrôle Général Économique et Financier. More recently, new avenues were discussed, such as Infogreffe—the French companies register—or the Directorate-General of Firms in the Ministry of the Economy and Finance (Grésy, Arcier, and Ressot, 2019).

From 2019: Promoting the Quota Strategy

Under the center-right presidency of Emmanuel Macron (since 2017), the Deputy Minister for Gender Equality Marlène Schiappa commissioned a prospective report on women's access to leadership positions from the Haut Conseil à l'Égalité entre les Femmes et les Hommes (Grésy, Arcier, and Ressot, 2019) that confirmed the strategy of the femocrats and their businesswomen allies to advance gender equality through the motto, "No quotas, no results." The Haut Conseil à l'Égalité entre les Femmes et les Hommes recommended "enhancing obligations" and extending quotas in two ways: to more companies (all listed companies and partnerships limited by shares with sales in excess of fifty million euros, with a target of 40% female board members by 2024); and to executive and management committees with a target of 40% women by 2024 in listed companies and firms combining more than 250 workers with sales in excess of fifty million euros. This proposal had the support of Schiappa and the French Minister for the Economy, Bruno Le Maire, and was adopted with some adaptations in the December 2021 Law to accelerate economic and professional equality: companies with more than 1,000 employees should reach and maintain over 30% female executive managers and female members of executive and management committees by 2027, and 40% by 2030, on pain of a financial penalty (maximum 1% of the wage bill).

Taking up a provision introduced by the 2014 law relating to real gender equality, the Haut Conseil à l'Égalité entre les Femmes et les Hommes also recommended making public financing of innovation conditional on compliance with gender parity rules (or *éga-conditionnalité*) in governance and decision-making bodies and/or in partnerships for companies and investment funds, with a target of 50% by 2026. It paved the way for an original incentive based on the premise that money means power and was justified in the name of overall consistency of policymaking and the exemplary role of the state. Once again, AFEP and MEDEF tried to promote a parallel alternative self-regulatory solution to stem the coming wave of regulation; in 2019, AFEP released a *Vademecum of Feminization*, including good practices, and a new version of the AFEP-MEDEF code was announced with recommendations on gender balance in executive positions.

The Limits of a Deferential Process: Gender Accommodation over Transformation

The various assessments carried out by public and/or private actors have drawn up a mixed review of the 2011 law and its amendments, and indeed, the general impact of the quotas on gender transformation is limited to gender accommodation.

Descriptive and substantive empowerment is high but reflects the interests of a "happy few." Women's groups have played a key role in the entire policy process, from pre-adoption to implementation, through data collection and monitoring, lobbying political and business leaders, and advocacy among female managers. They have also received ongoing and publicly repeated support from the authorities. For instance, during the 2013 symposium on the glass ceiling in Paris, the Minister for Women's Rights called for considering women's networks as "gender equality bridgeheads in business" (Vallaud-Belkacem, 2013). And in some of the biggest companies, women's networks are indeed recognized and established as think tanks for gender equality (Pochic, 2019) but also business issues (Aubé, 2016).

Moreover, cooperation and politicization have increased in these groups during the implementation process. In addition to the creation of network federations, joint initiatives have emerged. For instance, a gender equality consultant organized the meeting of 200 presidents of businesswomen's networks in 2017, which gave birth to the Pulvériser le Plafond de Verre (Smashing the Glass Ceiling) project calling for a self-organized "movement" and "absolute sisterhood" (Gagliardi, 2017). In 2018, several of the most influential networks launched a new manifesto in favor of parity (BPW France, Administration Moderne, Femmes Administrateurs, and Financi'Elles, 2018), "No women, no debate!"

Thus, women's interests have been represented in the post-adoption phase but exclusively at the elite level. White women with the most prestigious curricula and careers have expressed their views and influenced the whole policy process. They have imposed a broad vision of women's access to the top, constantly repeating that administrators were just the tip of the iceberg. And most of the implementation tools have responded with a twofold diagnosis on the glass ceiling, namely women's internal barriers and managerial rules penalizing female careers. Therefore, the defense of the specific interests of a few women has led to the overshadowing of any intersectional perspective; only single attributes are considered as sources of inequality (age, geographical origins, and nationality) without situating each element in a larger and complex gendered power structure. Moreover, any demand for attention to "ordinary women workers" made by women politicians, femocrats, and trade unionists has not resonated with the businesswomen-dominated networks and hence has been left behind.

Varying Quantitative Results, Poor Qualitative Parity, and Persistence of the Glass Ceiling

While implementation has been quite successful on a numerical level, these gains have been eclipsed by the absence of significant qualitative progress. To be sure, the aggregate increases since the adoption of the law are dramatic; 102 of SBF 120 businesses complied with the law in 2017 and 110 in 2019 (Ethics & Boards, 2017; Convictions RH, 2020). A closer look, however, shows quite disparate situations by the type and size of structures. The overall objective of 40% has not been reached, for example, by Euronext[6] businesses, with the smallest firms lagging furthest behind: 34.8% for the "big caps," 30.6% for the "mid caps," and 28.3% for the "small caps" in 2017 (AFECA, 2017). The figures are even further from the mark for non-listed companies; the first exploratory survey estimated 14% female board members (Bouaiss and De Beaufort, 2015) and a more recent one 24% (Roth-Fichet, 2019). The unclear and varying scope of application of the law over time—which made it hard for firms to understand whether and how they were concerned—and the lack of heavy penalties are some of the reasons for these poor results.

Significant differences exist in the profile of female board members as well, depending on the size of the company (Allemand and Brullebaut, 2014; Bender, Dang, and Scotto, 2016) with different situations emerging for smaller and larger firms, although with the same outcome; women board members have no real independent power on the board. In the smallest companies, "token women" are appointed because of their gender and family connections; and in the biggest companies, women board members are often foreigners or are independent with no prior relationship with the firms. More generally, studies have shown that the composition of board committees is still dictated by gender stereotypes with women members still having little access to the key and prestigious committees like strategic and investment positions or the presidencies of commissions. Instead, women board members are found more often than men in committees on ethics, governance, or risk; however, they seem to be fairly represented in audit, appointments, and compensation committees (AFECA, 2017; Deloitte, 2017; Labrador Maverick, Ethics & Boards, and EY, 2019). Women are also still highly underrepresented in top management and executive positions (AFECA, 2017; Ethics & Boards, 2017; Convictions RH, 2020), be it as chairs of the boards, as CEOs, or in the highest positions: around 20% of executive committees and a quarter of the top 100 managers in SBF 120 companies in 2019. In other words, as asserted in the final evaluation of the 2011 law (Roth-Fichet, 2019, p. 23), "The expected trickle-down effect from parity in corporate boards to executive positions is not happening." Lastly, most companies do not comply with their legal obligation to enter into collective negotiations about gender equality on boards (Gouvernance & Structures, 2017): 55% of CAC 40 companies did so in 2017, but only 36% of big caps, excluding CAC 40, 29% of mid caps, and 20% of small caps; and the figures have changed very slowly in the past few years.

---

[6] The French official stock market is Euronext Paris, where companies are classified into three sub-funds according to the level of market capitalization: segment A (more than one billion euros: "big caps"); segment B (150 million to one billion euros: "mid caps"); and segment C (less than 150 million euros: "small caps").

No Real Gender Norm Change, Backed Up by Men's Strategies to Keep Power and Gender Stereotypes

On the one hand, gender quotas have widened professional opportunities for women. They have played a part in countering biases about women's inability and men's skills in the exercise of power and launched the discussion on the composition and role of corporate boards, and the opening of access to all. Debates on a sufficient pool of female candidates and women's skills have led to the growing professionalization of all administrators and given birth to initiatives aiming to establish occupational standards, proper training, and formalized recruitment processes. For instance, SciencePo Executive Education and the Institut Français des Administrateurs created a certificate dedicated to the practice of the position in 2010. The implementation of the parity legislation has also made ambitious women no longer taboo. Growing egalitarian demands, soft law instruments, and binding laws have forced the largest organizations to set up dedicated programs. The promotion of women's careers is now endorsed as one of their concerns and it is widely publicized; and many economic and political leaders, including the current French president (Macron in Tumler, 2017), promote the idea that "the future lies with women."

On the other hand, the apparent widespread acceptance of parity quotas on the part of male decision-makers and gatekeepers, and the framing of the issue, have failed to challenge gender norms. Many business leaders have dragged their feet in implementing gender quotas in their companies. Some have shown official support yet have blamed women for the persistent inequalities, arguing that the available pool of women fell short or that female candidates would abuse their strong position on the market and be too demanding. Others have developed "bypass strategies" (Achin et al, 2007), reflecting their reluctance to give way to women and get rid of the boy's club. In many cases, they have opted for the creation of new positions rather than the replacement of men (Ferrary, 2016; AFECA, 2017); and they have also developed various attempts to sidestep the law such as changing legal status, the decrease in membership of the board, the shifting of power to other formal or informal committees (Bousquet et al, 2016), or corporate evasion with the transfer of headquarters to neighboring countries where regulations are more flexible (Ferrary, 2019).

The focus on the business case argument has eclipsed an in-depth reflection on structural inequalities in the workplace. Career standards have not been called into question and still rely on meritocracy and the traditional male model of the hyper-available worker. New management tools (such as teleworking or flexible working hours) called for by women to facilitate a better work-life balance are selective and perfectly fit with extended hours and full commitment. Moreover, they do not challenge the gendered distribution of domestic tasks, even more so since male managers who show new aspirations are scarce and stigmatized (OECD, 2020). The implementation of gender quotas has come along with discourses and practices that have strengthened gender stereotypes as well. Both male and female leaders have praised the complementary qualities of women throughout the process. As a consequence, not only are female board members assigned to specific positions, but they are also cherry-picked on the basis of their willingness to assume a specific gender identity and contribution. To give just one example, the slogan of the Fédération Femmes Administrateurs is, "Parity for a different management."[7] To conclude, the strategy of gender equality from the top designed by the public authorities has largely failed. No link between women's access to top management positions and the promotion of gender equality has been proven to date (Marry et al, 2017; Pochic, 2018).

An Increasingly Positive Public Attitude toward Corporate Gender Quotas, but No Priority

Isolating the impact of gender quotas policy on public opinion is a difficult task since it is part of a wider public gender equality policy and it takes place in a period of renewed feminist activism, as evidenced by the recent mobilizations around #balancetonporc, the French version of the #MeToo movement (Cousin et al, 2019). What has emerged is that this policy has received widespread media coverage and has had some impact on public opinion. By putting forward the good results of the laws and female role models, the media has helped to legitimate both gender quotas and women's careers and ambitions.

Numerous surveys conducted by professional and businesswomen networks among managers have revealed a strong and stable perception of unequal treatment: a rather low but increasingly positive assessment of business leader attitudes toward female managers and strong support for women's groups and gender quotas as a good management practice. However, men show more skepticism toward support for gender equality (Financi'Elles, 2011, 2014, and 2017; Grandes Écoles au Féminin, 2012). Other public opinion surveys suggest a strong and stable, if not increased, perception of gender inequalities in the workplace, a dominant shared conception that men are not better managers than women, and a decline of the male breadwinner/female caregiver model (TNS/LinkedIn, 2012; IFOP/FJJ, 2017; ANDRH, 2019). In any case, female access to top positions is outranked by equal pay and work-life balance in terms of priorities (Make.org, 2020).

---

[7] www.federation-femmes-administrateurs.com (Accessed July 25, 2020).

Conclusion

In the final analysis, the French policy to promote gender equality on corporate boards, a mostly state-driven approach supported by femocrats and business-women, can be qualified as both a symbolic and a concrete reform (Revillard, 2016) with impacts limited to gender accommodation. Gender quotas have had undeniable and direct positive effects on the quantitative feminization of corporate boards. The ambitious goal of the 2011 legislation of 40% women has been reached on time in the largest companies, and the momentum is set in other businesses, as well as in the public service. The relatively early adoption of the law has also strengthened France as a world leader for quotas and gender equality "à la française through parity" (Mazur et al, 2020, p. 45). The policy process is associated with high levels of descriptive and substantive empowerment but limited to certain women's groups. The arguments and support for gender quotas thus reflect the interests of a happy few, namely white women who have graduated from the most prestigious schools and who have made their careers in the largest companies or the senior public service. While the collective voice of elite white women has been heard in the decision-making process, it has been silenced with the adoption of symbolic policies by the right-wing legislature and business. Nonetheless, the groups who represent the "happy few" have been crucial in making symbolic policies more concrete in implementation and evaluation in partnership and alliance with the activist coalition of femocrats under a left-wing government.

Furthermore, a closer look at the impact of these policies questions the numerical success story. The situation in the smallest and non-listed companies is still largely a mystery and the existing data suggest low compliance with the law. The letter of the law is not respected; women still face the glass ceiling in corporate boards and executive positions. More generally, the French policy has had a rather low impact on changing the dominant framing of gender relations in firms. Gender quotas have widened professional opportunities for women and legitimated their ambitions and the topic has been largely covered by the media, participating in the broad denunciation of women's experience of discrimination at work. Still, the deferential approach promoted by businesswomen has failed to challenge gender norms; male gatekeepers have developed bypass strategies to retain power without any in-depth reflection on structural inequalities and stereotypes in the workplace. These mixed results directly stem from the balance of power and the choices articulated throughout the policy process. The coalition of women's interests has been able to push for female access to board positions, but it has faced subtle yet strong resistance in elected offices—leading to light coercion and no procedures controlling legislative quotas—and in the business arena—driving the circumscribed application of the spirit of the law. The limits are also in the strategy deployed; the framing is entangled in the gender-biased economic rationale, which emphasizes the business case argument and gender complementarity and a quantitative approach to inequalities, which overshadows qualitative analysis and has undermined gender transformation.

The latest prospective report of the Haut Conseil à l'Égalité entre les Femmes et les Hommes (Grésy, Arcier, and Ressot, 2019) seems to open up a new phase in the strategy of femocrats and their businesswomen allies, with the ambition "to build a genuine culture of gender equality in companies" through various proposals such as carrying out qualitative studies on women board members qualitative follow-through, rather than a single number-based analysis, training recruiters about gender biases, making public financing conditional on compliance with gender parity rules, or extending quotas to real power sites (executive positions), which has been taken-up in a new law adopted at the end of 2021. At the same time, the other proposals have been thus far ignored. Only time will tell whether these new developing policy efforts are able to actually call into question the gendered structure of power-sharing and prove more effective than previous attempts.

Interviews

Delphine Chauffaut, Advisor in Charge of Professional Equality, Ministry of Social Affairs, Health and Women's Rights, 2015.

Marine Darnault, Head of the Office of Professional Equality, Services des Droits des Femmes et à l'Égalité, 2015.

Brigitte Grésy, Gender Equality Expert at the General Inspectorate for Social Affairs and then Head of the Conseil Supérieur de l'Égalité Professionnelle, 2009 and 2015.

References

Achin, Catherine, Lucie Bargel, Delphine Dulong, and Éric Fassin (eds) (2007) *Sexe, Genre et Politique*. Paris: Economica.

AFECA (2017) *La place des administratrices dans les conseils et leurs comités des sociétés cotées sur Euronext (compartiments A, B, C) Paris et Alternext Paris*. http://www.femmes-experts-comptables.com/wp-content/uploads/2017/06/TELESCOP_AFECA_2017V2.pdf (Accessed July 28, 2020).

AFP News (2009) "Proposition de loi pour des quotas de femmes à la direction des entreprises," March 4.

Allemand, Isabelle and Bénédicte Brullebaut (2014) "Le capital humain des femmes récemment nommées dans les conseils d'administration des sociétés françaises cotées à Paris," *Management International*, 8 (3), pp. 20–31.

ANDRH (2019) *Enquête flash: parité dans les instances de gouvernance*. https://www.andrh.fr/uploads/files/attachments/617681f6a9b18789402386.pdf (Accessed July 28, 2020).

Aubé, Claire (2016) "Réseaux féminins, une force d'accélération," *L'Express*, February 19, p. 46.

Basini, Bruna (2010) "Parité: Il faut un électrochoc," *Le Journal du Dimanche*, January 18.

Bender, Anne-Françoise, Rey Dang, and Marie-José Scotto (2016) "Les profils des femmes membres des conseils d'administration en France," *Travail, genre et sociétés*, 35, pp. 67–85.

Bereni, Laure and Éléonore Lépinard (2004) "'Les femmes ne sont pas une catégorie.' Les stratégies de légitimation de la parité en France," *Revue française de science politique*, 54 (1), pp. 71–98.

Bereni, Laure and Anne Revillard (2007) "Des quotas à la parité: 'féminisme d'État' et représentation politique (1974-2007)," *Genèses*, 67 (2), pp. 5–23.

Blanchard, Soline (2018) "Le benchmarking au service de l'égalité? Sociogenèse du Palmarès de la féminisation des instances dirigeantes du SBF120," *Gouvernement et action publique*, 7 (4), pp. 39–61.

Blanchard, Soline (2019) "The Market for Gender-equality Expertise: Providing Services to Public and Private Organisations in France," *European Journal of Politics and Gender*, 2 (1), pp. 93–111.

Blanchard, Soline, Isabel Boni-Le Goff, and Marion Rabier (2013) "A Privileged Fight? Women's Movements for Equal Access to Corporate Leadership and Management Positions," *Sociétés contemporaines*, 89, pp. 101–130.

Bouaiss, Karima and Viviane De Beaufort (2015) *Application de la loi relative à la représentation équilibrée F-H au sein des conseils: État des lieux pour les entreprises en deçà du SBF120*. Cergy-Pontoise: CEDE-ESSEC.

Bousquet, Danielle, Brigitte Grésy, Réjane Sénac, Sébastien Point, and Caroline Ressot (2016) *Vers un égal accès des femmes et des hommes aux responsabilités professionnelles: la part des femmes dans les conseils d'administration et de surveillance*. Paris: HCE/CSEP.

BPW France, Administration Moderne, Femmes Administrateurs and Financi'Elles (2018) *Une nouvelle action publique en faveur de la parité: pas de femmes, pas de débat!*, 8 March. http://www.bpw.fr/files/4115/2102/9963/08_03_2018_-_Manifeste_signe_par_les_4_reseaux.pdf (Accessed July 28, 2020).

Chang, Mariko Lin (2000) "The Evolution of Sex Segregation Regimes," *American Journal of Sociology*, 105 (6), pp. 1658–1701.

Commission des Lois de l'Assemblée Nationale (2009) *Compte rendu n°29 du 22 décembre*. https://www.assemblee-nationale.fr/13/cr-cloi/09-10/c0910029.asp#P9_1328 (Accessed July 28, 2020).

Convictions RH (2020) *7ᵉ Edition du palmarès de la féminisation des instances dirigeantes du SBF120*. https://www.convictionsrh.com/fr/news/palmares-2020-de-la-feminisation-des-instances-dirigeantes-sbf-120 (Accessed July 28, 2020).

Cousin, Olivier, Julie Landour, Pauline Delage, Sabine Fortino, and Marion Paoletti (2019) "#MeToo, #Travail?" *La Nouvelle Revue du Travail*, 15. http://journals.openedition.org/nrt/6021 (Accessed July 28, 2020).

Deloitte (2015) *Structure de gouvernance des sociétés cotées. Radiographie*. https://www2.deloitte.fr/documents/deloitte_etude-gouvernance-entreprises_presse.pdf (Accessed July 28, 2020).

Deloitte (2017) *Féminisation des organes de Gouvernance*. http://vdb-gender-mixite.com/wp-content/uploads/2017/03/Mixite%CC%81-des-organes-de-gouvernance-au-01-Mars-2017-200317-v-def.pdf (Accessed July 28, 2020).

Des Esgaulx, Marie-Hélène (2010) *Rapport sur la proposition de loi relative à la représentation équilibrée des femmes et des hommes au sein des conseils d'administration et de surveillance et à l'égalité professionnelle.* Paris: Commission des Lois du Sénat.

EIGE (2020) *Gender Statistics Database: Women and Men in Decision Making.* https://eige.europa.eu/gender-statistics/dgs (Accessed July 28, 2020).

Ethics & Boards (2017) *Palmarès de la féminisation des entreprises du SBF120: Synthèse qualitative.* https://www.ethicsandboards.com/studies/318-publication-du-palmares-2017-de-la-feminisation-des-instances-dirigeantes-des-entreprises-du-sbf120 (Accessed July 28, 2020).

Ethics & Boards and ICR (2017) "Launch of the Zimmermann Index," *Press Release*, January 30.

Eurostat (2020) *Employment and Activity by Sex and Age: Annual Data*, 2019. https://ec.europa.eu/eurostat/en/web/products-datasets/-/LFSI_EMP_A (Accessed July 28, 2020).

Felstiner, William L.F., Richard L. Abel, and Austin Sarat (1980) "The Emergence and Transformation of Disputes: Naming, Blaming, Claiming," *Law and Society Review*, 15 (3/4), pp. 631–654.

Ferrary, Michel (2016) *Observatoire Skema de la féminisation des entreprises.* https://www.skema-bs.fr/facultes-et-recherche/recherche/observatoire-de-la-feminisation (Accessed July 28, 2020).

Ferrary, Michel (2019) *Observatoire Skema de la féminisation des entreprises: Les évadés sociaux du CAC40 qui s'expatrient pour éviter les quotas de femmes dans les conseils d'administration.* https://www.skema-bs.fr/facultes-et-recherche/recherche/observatoire-de-la-feminisation (Accessed July 28, 2020).

Financi'Elles (2011, 2014, and 2017) *Baromètre de la confiance des cadres au sein secteur banque, finance et assurance.* https://financielles.org/nos-initiatives (Accessed July 28, 2020).

Gagliardi, Emmanuelle (2017) *Appel #PPV. Pulvériser le plafond de verre*, September 25. https://fr.linkedin.com/pulse/l-appel-ppv-emmanuelle-gagliardi (Accessed July 28, 2020).

Gouvernance & Structures (2017) *Les administratrices des sociétés cotées sur Euronext Paris.* http://g-et-s.com/docdech/rfin%20juin2017.pdf (Accessed July 28, 2020).

Grandes Écoles au Féminin (2012) *Quels dirigeants, quelles dirigeantes pour demain?* https://www.grandesecolesaufeminin.fr/pdf/Presentation-5eme-Etude-GEF-21022012.pdf (Accessed July 28, 2020).

Grésy, Brigitte (2009) *Rapport préparatoire à la concertation avec les partenaires sociaux sur l'égalité professionnelle entre les femmes et les hommes.* Paris: IGAS.

Grésy, Brigitte, Agnès Arcier, and Caroline Ressot (2019) *Accès des femmes aux responsabilités et rôle levier des financements publics: Des nouveaux champs pour la parité.* Paris: HCE.

Hantrais, Linda and Marie-Thérèse Letablier (1996) *Familles, travail et politiques familiales en Europe.* Paris: CEE/PUF.

IFOP/FJJ (2017) *Les inégalités femmes/hommes dans la société française et les nouveaux enjeux pour la condition des femmes.* https://www.ifop.com/wp-content/uploads/2018/03/3886-1-study_file.pdf (Accessed July 28, 2020).

INSEE (2015) "Indépendants et dirigeants salariés d'entreprise: un tiers de femmes," *INSEE Première*, 1563.

INSEE (2020) "Une photographie du marché du travail en 2019," *INSEE Première*, 1793.

Jacquot, Sophie (2015) *Transformations in EU Gender Equality Policy: From Emergence to Dismantling*. London: Palgrave MacMillan.

Labrador Maverick, Ethics & Boards, and EY (2019) *Panorama de la gouvernance: Gouvernance et responsabilité 2019*. https://assets.ey.com/content/dam/ey-sites/ey-com/fr_fr/topics/assurance/ey-panorama-de-la-gouvernance-2019.pdf (Accessed July 28, 2020).

Laufer, Jacqueline (2014) *L'égalité professionnelle*. Paris: La Découverte.

Lépinard, Éléonore and Amy G. Mazur (2009) "Republican Universalism Faces the Feminist Challenge: The Continuing Struggle for Gender Equality," in Sylvain Brouard, Andrew M. Appleton, and Amy G. Mazur (eds) *The French Fifth Republic at Fifty: Beyond Stereotypes*. New York: Palgrave Macmillan, pp. 247–266.

Lewis, Jane (1992) "Gender and the Development of Welfare Regimes," *Journal of European Social Policy*, 2 (3), pp. 159–173.

Make.org (2020) *Consultation citoyenne. Comment assurer l'égalité femmes-hommes dans l'économie?* https://make.org/FR/consultation/egalite-femmes-hommes/results (Accessed July 28, 2020).

Marry, Catherine, Laure Bereni, Alban Jacquemart, Sophie Pochic, and Anne Revillard (2017) *Le plafond de verre et l'État: La construction de genre dans la fonction publique*. Paris: Armand Colin.

Mazur, Amy G., Éléonore Lépinard, Anja Durovic, Catherine Achin, and Sandrine Lévêque (2020) "Party Penalties for Parity: Less than Meets the Eye," *French Politics*, 18, pp. 28–49.

Montalcino, Caroline, Élisabeth Roure, Isabelle Amaglio-Terisse, and Fabienne Helvin (2017) *La parité dans les conseils d'administration et les conseils de surveillance des établissements publics et des entreprises de la sphère publique*. Paris: CGEFI.

OECD (2017) *The Pursuit of Gender Equality: An Uphill Battle*. https://read.oecd-ilibrary.org/social-issues-migration-health/the-pursuit-of-gender-equality_9789264281318-en (Accessed January 10, 2021).

OECD (2020) *Trends in parental leave policies since 1970*. https://www.oecd.org/els/family/PF2_5_Trends_in_leave_entitlements_around_childbirth.pdf (Accessed January 10, 2021).

Pochic, Sophie (2018) "Féminisme de marché et égalité élitiste?," in Margaret Maruani (ed.) *Je travaille donc je suis: perspectives féministes*. Paris: La Découverte, pp. 42–52.

Pochic, Sophie (eds) (2019) "L'égalité est-elle négociable? Enquête sur la qualité et la mise en œuvre d'accords et de plans égalité femmes-hommes élaborés en 2014-2015," *Document d'études DARES*, 231–232.

Renault, Enguérand (2010) "Plus de femmes dans les conseils d'administration," *Le Figaro*, May 29, p. 28.

Revillard, Anne (2016) *La cause des femmes dans l'État: Une comparaison France—Québec*. Grenoble: PUG.

Rossignol, Laurence (2016) "Closing speech," 4th *Awards Ceremony of the Ranking of Women Representation within SBF120 Companies*. Paris, November 14.

Roth-Fichet, Denis (2019) *Rapport sur la féminisation des instances de gouvernance et de direction des entreprises*. Paris: Secrétariat d'État chargé de l'égalité entre les femmes et les hommes et de la lutte contre les discriminations.

TNS/LinkedIn (2012) *Le succès professionnel, les réseaux sociaux et les femmes.* https://fr.slideshare.net/LinkedInFrance/linkedin-les-femmes-et-le-succs-professionnel-oct12 (Accessed July 28, 2020).

Tumler, Alice (2017) "Interview du Président de la République," *TraceTV*, December 4.

Vallaud-Belkacem, Najat (2013) "Closing speech," *Symposium on the Glass Ceiling*, Paris, April 9. https://www.dailymotion.com/video/xyvs1r (Accessed July 28, 2020).

Vittori, Jean-Marc (2009) "Messieurs les banquiers, embauchez des banquières!," *Les Échos*, March, 6, p. 14.

12

Opportunities for Equality in Times of Crisis

The Transformative Potential of Corporate Quotas in Belgium

Hannelore Roos and Patrizia Zanoni

Introduction

On July 28, 2011, the Belgian gender board quota law came into effect, which stipulates that the boards of directors of listed companies, autonomous public undertakings and the National Lottery may not have more than two-thirds of their members of the same sex. This chapter discusses this unexpected government intervention legally granting women access to Belgian corporate boards. Although Belgium has strong equal legal work rights (World Bank Group, 2020), inequality in leadership positions such as on corporate boards has remained persistent. At the time of the economic crisis in 2008, 53% of the listed companies did not have a single woman on their board of directors, and 27% counted only one woman. Moreover, Belgium's governance code made no reference to gender diversity.

At the time of the adoption of the law, women held only 11% of seats on boards registered on the BEL 20, the twenty largest publicly listed companies for the Euronext Brussels stock market, and scored well below the European average of 14%. The introduction of this hard law with sanctions in case of non-compliance was a bold political step that drastically reshaped the gender composition of corporate boards. While Belgium had been clearly lagging behind, the implementation of the law increased women's representation on corporate boards to 36.5% in 2020. In what follows, we analyze the specific historical context in which the law was adopted, its impact on board composition, and board member recruitment practices, as well how the new reform fostered the emergence of a public narrative surrounding women in corporate leadership positions and Belgian society.

Belgium's adoption of gender board quota legislation for listed companies was surprising, as it broke both with the country's corporatist tradition and the more

Hannelore Roos and Patrizia Zanoni, *Opportunities for Equality in Times of Crisis*. In: *Gender Equality and Policy Implementation in the Corporate World*. Edited by Isabelle Engeli and Amy G. Mazur, Oxford University Press.
© Oxford University Press (2022). DOI: 10.1093/oso/9780198865216.003.0012

recent, widely supported neoliberal idea that the state should refrain from intervening in the functioning of the market economy. We interpret the gender quota
law as resulting from four conditions that serendipitously came together at the
time of its adoption. First, the economic crisis of 2008 had created a sense of urgency that traditional company governance structures needed modernization and
opened up an opportunity for gender equality advocates to put the longstanding
underrepresentation of women in leadership roles on the agenda. Second, the European Union provided a strong supra-national narrative championing gender
equality in leadership positions, including corporate boards, as a way to foster
equality and a condition of good governance. Third, the existence of a gender
quota on federal parliamentary election lists since the 1990s provided symbolic
legitimacy to the adoption of the quota for corporate boards and at the same time
ensured a more gender-balanced composition of the parliament that adopted the
law. Finally, and crucially, after the elections to the Federal Parliament in Belgium
on June 13, 2010, a left caretaker government (2010–2011) took the initiative to
propose quota reform despite political resistance to state intervention in business
governance.[1]

The chapter is structured as follows. After discussing Belgium's incomplete gender equality and the absence of female leaders on boards of directors, we elaborate
on the Belgian corporate governance system as a specific type of the so-called continental European "blockholder" system and how the economic crisis provided an
opportunity for quotas to be placed on the political agenda. Further, we discuss
how in the Belgian context the introduction of gender quotas in politics paved the
way for quota legislation for corporate boards and trace the processes leading to
the adoption of the 2011 law. We show how the economic crisis of 2008 accelerated the shift from soft to hard law since all trust in the proper functioning of a
corporate governance approach was lost. Next, we present the features of the Belgian legislation and its impact on corporate boards during the implementation
phase, up to January 1, 2020, in which corporate boards transitioned from male
bastions to a more gender diverse composition. We then discuss the outcomes of
Belgium's gender board quota legislation in terms of empowerment and gender
transformation at the gatekeeper and societal levels. We conclude the chapter by
summarizing the key institutional factors that made gender board quota legislation a possible reality. More specifically, for Belgium, the European context and
the local path dependency for quota legislation, as well as the pressure of an economic crisis combined with a political impasse, proved to be fertile ground for the
initial steps toward inclusive change and sowing the seeds for meaningful gender
transformation.

---

[1] Especially opposition was felt from the Flemish-Nationalist New Flemish Alliance (N-VA), the
largest party in Flanders and the country as a whole in 2020.

Incomplete Gender Equality and the Absence of Women Leaders on Corporate Boards

In Belgium, three federal laws provide the legal basis for the fight against discrimination at work. First, the law of July 30, 1981, amended by the law of May 10, 2007, punishes certain acts inspired by racism or xenophobia.[2] This law prohibits discrimination based on nationality, so-called race, skin color, origin, or national or ethnic origin. Second, the law of May 10, 2007,[3] to combat certain forms of discrimination, prohibits discrimination based on age, sexual orientation, marital status, birth, ability, religion or belief, political affiliation, language, current or future health, disability, physical or genetic trait, or social origin. Finally, the law of May 10, 2007,[4] on combating discrimination between women and men prohibits any form of discrimination based on sex. The notion of discrimination contained in the law is meant to cover gender reassignment, gender identity, and gender expression. This strong legal framework to combat discrimination, however, does not grant women and other historically underrepresented groups access to the highest decision-making positions and bodies in companies. For example, vertical gender segregation has been a persistent reality in publicly listed companies, as Table 12.1 shows. Despite the feminization of the boardroom since 2011 to comply with the board quota, high-ranking positions of power and influence are still primarily held by men. In 2020, only 5.9% of CEOs and chairpersons were women (EIGE, 2020). The slow uptake of women representation among those key roles indicates that change toward gender equality is today only starting.

As indicated by Table 12.1, the increase of women in boards of directors of listed companies has been significant. At the time the law was passed, 102 out of 118 corporate boards had to make changes in the gender composition of their boards. At the end of 2017, compliance to the quota law had led to a representation of 30.7% women directors, more than five percentage points above the average in the EU 28 of 25.3% (EIGE, 2020). Until 2014, there had not been a single woman CEO of the twenty largest listed companies. However, at the end of 2017, Belgium was ranked around the European average with 5.9%.

Similar to other continental western European countries, such as Germany and Austria, Belgium historically has a conservative welfare regime grounded in the male breadwinner model and is culturally strongly influenced by the Catholic tradition. This model is characterized by a gendered division of roles between a male breadwinner and a female caregiver (Celis and Meier, 2007; OECD, 2017) and

---

[2] http://www.ejustice.just.fgov.be/cgi_loi/change_lg.pl?language=nl&la=N&table_name=wet&cn=1981073035
[3] http://www.ejustice.just.fgov.be/cgi_loi/change_lg.pl?language=nl&la=N&table_name=wet&cn=2007051035
[4] http://www.ejustice.just.fgov.be/cgi_loi/change_lg.pl?language=nl&la=N&table_name=wet&cn=2007051036

Table 12.1 Percentage Share of Women on Boards in the Largest Listed Companies in Belgium, 2004–2020

	EU-28 board members	BELGIUM				
		Board members	President	CEO	Executives	Non-executives
2004	9	6.8	0	—	—	—
2005	9.8	6.2	0	—	—	—
2006	9.7	5.8	0	—	—	—
2007	10.4	6.4	0	—	—	—
2008	10.8	7.2	0	—	—	—
2009	11	7.6	0	—	—	—
2010	11.9	10.5	0	—	—	—
2011	13.7	10.9	0	—	—	—
2012	15.8	12.9	0	0	9.6	14.1
2013	17.8	16.7	0	0	11.8	18.4
2014	20.2	22.4	11.1	5.6	13.3	23.9
2015	22.7	26	11.1	5.6	15.2	27.4
2016	23.9	28.6	11.8	5.9	17.1	30.6
2017	25.3	30.7	5.9	5.9	13.4	33.5
2018	26.7	32	6.3	6.3	14.4	34.9
2019	28.8	35.9	5.9	11.8	14.8	38.6
2020	29.2	36.5	5.9	5.9	13.7	39.8

Source: EIGE Database. Data for October each year, except for 2020 [April].

institutions that protect the "family wage" and social protection not only for the male worker but also for his dependents. From the 1970s onward, this model has gradually evolved toward a one-and-a-half breadwinner model, characterized by formal equal legal rights between men and women, a steady and substantial increase of women's participation in the labor market (although often in part-time jobs), and individualized social rights for workers. This evolution cannot be understood without the economic and institutional integration of Belgium in the European Union. Since its origins in the mid-1950s, the integrated EU market stimulated a growing demand for (female) labor. To promote women's access to the labor market, EU legislation was passed that required member states to equalize female and male workers' rights (Lemeire and Zanoni, 2021; Schonard, 2020).

As a result of this specific historical evolution, women's equality in the economic sphere in Belgium today is advanced, yet remains incomplete. On the one hand, Belgium has a gender pay gap of 6.1%, which is among the lowest in the EU (Van Hove, 2015) and ranks fifth in the domain of work of the European Gender Equality Index 2019 (EIGE, 2019), which measures the extent to which women and men can benefit from equal access to employment and good working conditions. On the other hand, the female employment rate (ages 20–64) of 65.5% is the lowest among its neighboring countries (Eurostat, 2018) and 40.5% of women workers work part-time, a percentage among the highest in the EU (Eurostat, 2018). This reflects persistent large differences in time spent on care and household work between men and women, despite convergence over the longer run (EIGE, 2019; RoSa vzw, 2016). Moreover, the labor market remains highly gender segregated, with women concentrated in sectors such as education, healthcare, and social work (40.1% in 2017, EIGE, 2019), and almost absent from industry and construction activities at 8% (Eurostat, 2018). The incomplete character of gender equality in the economic sphere is reflected in Belgium's 54th place in the Global Gender Gap Index 2020 rankings regarding the category Economic Participation and Opportunity and the fact that the country did not make any progress in closing this gender gap since 2006 (World Economic Forum, 2018; 2020).

Belgian companies have been traditionally independent of the stock market, as their activities have largely been financed by reference shareholders, such as (noble) families, holdings, and foreign groups. Usually, the sons of the CEOs were prepared for a seat on the board, and only in exceptional cases, in the absence of a son, a daughter was given access to the boardroom. Michèle Sioen, one of the best-known women CEOs of a Belgian listed family company declared in the press a few years ago: "If I had a brother, I wouldn't be here" (Desmet and Smedts 2014, p. 26), and "I have been extremely lucky not to have a brother" (Lauwers and De Cat, 2018, p. 10). The Belgian governance regime is a specific type of the continental European "blockholder" system (Bratton and McCahery, 1999), which is characterized by a high degree of ownership concentration among families and upper-class circles with kin-like close ties (Daems, 1998; De Preter, 2016; Renneboog, 1997; 2000; Van Veen and Marsman, 2008). Despite management's increasing professionalization (De Preter, 2016), until the turn of the century, professional managers who were not family members were excluded from strategic decision-making in many Belgian firms (Daems, 1998). The blockholder model allows a tight-knit group of long-term directors to closely monitor managers, yet also entails a risk of self-dealing, a dividend of privileged position (Becht, Bolton, and Röell, 2003), and some vulnerability to loyalty claims that favor shareholders for whom a director is appointed (Laster and Zeberkiewicz, 2014/2015). This governance system, based on close-knit networks almost exclusively made up of men, might explain the strong underrepresentation of women on boards until recent years, despite the progression of women in education and the labor market.

Under Belgian law, companies are headed by a unitary board of directors or a single-tier system of administration, and executive and non-executive members sit on the same board. Executive directors, also referred to as "inside directors" are those who also fulfill a management function within the company. In contrast, non-executive directors come from outside the company. Some can be considered to be "independent" when they comply with the criteria of independence as laid down in the Code on Corporate Governance. Corporate boards of Belgian listed companies are mostly composed of outside, non-executive directors, and a separation of roles of the CEO and chairperson of the board is nowadays common practice (Levrau, 2017).

The 2008 Crisis as an Opportunity to Put a Corporate Gender Quota on the Political Agenda

In this institutional context, the lack of women directors among corporate boards was long a non-issue for listed companies. A single reference code for Belgian listed companies, which was published for the first time in December 2004 (the so-called Code Lippens), did not address gender diversity. It rather referred to cognitive diversity: "The composition [of the board of directors] is determined on the basis of the necessary diversity and complementarity in terms of skills, experience and knowledge" (Corporate Governance Committee 2004, p. 14). This Corporate Governance Code was based on the principle of "comply-or-explain" and thus allowed for the possibility to divert from the rules laid out in the Code. No consequences or sanctions in case of non-compliance were provided.

Only in the wake of the 2008 economic crisis, explicit references to diversity and gender diversity were introduced into the new Belgian Corporate Governance Code of 2009 as a principle of board composition. This reads as follows: "In converting values and strategies into key policies, the board of directors take into account corporate social responsibility, gender diversity and diversity in general" (Corporate Governance Code 2009, p. 11). In addition, the Code recommended disclosing the list of the members of the board in the corporate governance statement and stipulated the creation of specialized committees within the board, such as an audit, remuneration, and nomination committee.

It should be noted that the comply-or-explain rule of the Corporate Governance Code was poorly followed by companies. Proponents of the gender board quota used this lack of effectiveness as an argument to demonstrate that self-governance and a corporate governance approach would not enhance gender diversity on corporate boards in the Belgian context. Meanwhile, opponents to the gender board quota argued that the comply-or-explain approach did not receive a fair chance given it was only anchored in the law as late as 2010, just one year before the quota legislation was passed. One of the architects of the Belgian Corporate Governance Code of 2009, a very senior man, commented in a personal interview (December 12, 2014):

> I always found it better that companies arrange it their way, through a rule of comply-or-explain. Now I think we were wrong. It wasn't strong enough. There was little interest in putting women on boards of directors. That quota law was actually a necessary evil. I am not for laws. Laws are very, how should I say …

limiting. But in this case, in order to face the macho behavior of people on the board, mostly men, in order to admit women, it had to be a law. Yes, I thought it was a pity, because I had expected that more companies would do something themselves [self-regulate], and I have always been in favor of self-regulation. But I felt that the business community did nothing and I actually welcomed the quota law because otherwise nothing would have changed. … I warned the business community that legislation would follow if they did not make changes themselves. They never took it seriously.

Although the idea of board quota had been discussed in feminist circles almost ten years earlier, only in 2009, the report "Women at the Top" published by the Belgian Institute for the Equality of Women and Men drew, for the first time, explicit attention to the lack of women in decision-making positions. This evidence stimulated a wide public debate regarding board quotas. The monitoring of the persistent absence of women on boards of directors was important as it provided ammunition to some women politicians to lobby for change. The Deputy Prime Minister and Minister for Employment and Equal Opportunities in the legislature of 2008–2011, Joëlle Milquet (cdH),[5] referred to the "Women at the Top" report to underscore the importance of a quota system for the boards of listed companies. In November 2009, she announced to be working on a gender board quota law in the federal government (the Institute for the Equality of Women and Men 2013, GVA November 18, 2009). The Minister also announced that imposing quotas for women in the executive committees of these companies would be considered. To pass her proposal, she convened all women MPs for a debate. Being aware of the pushback from affected businesses, she mentioned the French proposal of the "Union pour un Mouvement Populaire", Union for a Popular Movement (UMP), the party of president Sarkozy that had imposed 40% gender diversity in French listed corporate boards. The Federation of Enterprises in Belgium (VBO) responded immediately in the press stating that "We do not believe in a forced 'one size fits all approach'" and pleaded for giving self-regulation a chance (Broeckmeyer, 2009, p. 6).

In the preceding parliamentary debates discussing gender board quotas, direct references were made to the financial crisis as the failure of male-dominated businesses. The global economic crisis of 2008 had cast sufficient doubts about the effectiveness of existing corporate governance, showing the failure of softer comply-or-explain rules (de Cabo, Gimeno, and Nieto, 2012). Facing a heavy bill for the state, politicians came to regard the gender board composition as vital to prevent future crises. The final gender board quota act was based on draft bills prepared by male and female members of the various left and center political parties

---

[5] The Humanist Democratic Centre or Centre démocrate humaniste (cdH) is a Christian-democratic French-speaking political party in Belgium.

across the regional language divide, including Colette Burgeon (PS), Bruno Tuybens (sp.a), Joseph George (cdH), Catherine Fonck (cdH), Sonja Becq (CD&V), Muriel Gerkens (Ecolo-Groen!), and Eva Brems (Ecolo-Groen!).

Studies tend to associate gender diversity with good corporate governance, an aspect that gained further attention globally in the wake of the financial crisis (de Cabo et al, 2012). The economic crisis of 2008 fostered a positive public discourse of gender diversity and even led to the formulation of the Lehman Sisters hypothesis, namely the claim that the financial crisis would have been less severe if the Lehman Brothers had been Lehman Sisters (Morris, 2009; Staveren, 2014). Or in the words of IMF director Christine Lagarde: "If Lehman Brothers had been 'Lehman Sisters,' today's economic crisis clearly would look quite different" (Dealbook, 2010). Similarly, EU Commissioner Michel Barnier suggested that having more women on boards of banks would end the kind of "group-think" that had exacerbated the crisis (Treanor, 2011).

The seeds of the Belgian board gender quota law were planted, however, far before the financial crisis occurred. For example, within the Advisory committee on equal opportunities for women and men, Sabine de Bethune, a member of the Flemish Christian Democratic Party, had brought up the topic of "a balanced presence of women and men on the boards of directors" already in 1998 (Senate, commission bulletin of October 10, 1998). Almost a decade later, on February 28, 2007, Sabine de Bethune submitted for the first time a board gender quota proposal in the Belgian Senate, called the "Bill to promote the equal representation of women and men on the boards of governmental economic enterprises and of companies that have made a public appeal to savings" (Legislative document No 3-2088/1). This proposal stated that:

> With regard to economic decision-making, a quota system has already been worked out for a number of economic public companies. [References to bills of 2002, 2004 and 2006].... Just as government companies and public institutions play an exemplary role in the field of corporate governance, it is also recommended that comparable standards and rules are in place for companies that have made an appeal to the savings from the public.... The so-called "companies that have made a public appeal to savings" are companies whose shares or other securities are distributed among the public. It is therefore logical to subject these companies to the same gender diversity. They also have great social relevance.

The proposal also stated that the Corporate Governance Code of 2004 did not mention gender diversity or gender. The quota legislation of Norway inspired de Bethune (personal interview de Bethune May 10, 2019). She actively worked on establishing broader political support by formulating a recommendation to the advisory committee on equal opportunities in the Senate. Once de Bethune had gained political support from her party, CD&V, and its chairwoman Marianne Theyssen (May 15, 2008–June 23, 2010), rapid progress was made (Ibid).

Simultaneously, a similar proposal was submitted by Colette Burgeon from the French-speaking socialist party (PS) on October 19, 2006 (DOC 51 2714/001) and again on July 13, 2007 (DOC 52 0048/001) in the Chamber of Representatives (Lower House), the "Legal proposal amending the law of March 21, 1991, concerning the reform of certain economic public companies and amendment of the Code of companies, in order to guarantee that women have a seat in the autonomous decision-making bodies of governmental economic enterprises and listed companies." Together with male and female colleagues from her party, she resubmitted this proposal again on September 24, 2010 (DOC 53 0211/001) in the Chamber of Representatives (Lower House). Only the later proposal made it to the Parliament, where it was heavily debated. On March 15, 2011, the proposal was adopted in the Lower House.

Quota proposals, which had long been neglected, gained attention thanks to the opening of a political window of opportunity. The political party, Open VLD,[6] which has always been a fierce opponent of quota legislation, withdrew from the coalition government. An alternative parliamentary majority was formed (including the Christian-Democrats, Socialists, and the Greens), which was much more favorable to the principle of a corporate quota. This caretaker government lasted from April 2010 to December 2011. This long period allowed it to gain the support of the House's Committee with responsibility for commercial and economic problems in March 2011. However, the political resistance was strong and the opponents left no procedural stone unturned for delaying the legislative process. For example, opponents (Open VLD, N-VA,[7] and MR[8]) demanded advice from the Council of State in the plenary session of March 31, 2011. The Council rendered an opinion on April 26, 2011, and criticized the proposed sanction for non-compliance. According to the Council of State, the sanction of the nullity of the decisions of the boards of directors was a bridge too far and could endanger the continuity and proper functioning of the corporation. The quota advocates amended the bill to abide by the requirements laid out by the Council. The initial version of the bill entailed the nullification of all resolutions adopted by a board of directors non-compliant with the legal gender quota. The amended text that replaced the nullification of the decisions of the board of directors with "the nullification of appointments until a person belonging to the underrepresented sex is appointed" and "the suspension of all the financial and other benefits of all directors," was adopted by the Committee on June 1, 2011, and adopted by the House at

---

[6] Open Vlaamse Liberalen en Democraten (VLD)/Open Flemish Liberals and Democrats is a Flemish liberal party.
[7] Nieuw-Vlaamse Alliantie/New Flemish Alliance is a Flemish nationalist party.
[8] Mouvement Réformateur/Reformist Movement is a Francophone liberal party in Belgium.

its plenary session of June 16, 2011. That happened with seventy-one votes in favor (CD&V, sp.a, Greens, PS, and cdH), fifty-four against (N-VA, Vlaams Belang,[9] Open VLD, LDD,[10] Laurent Louis, and the MR MPs François-Xavier de Donnea and Denis Ducarme), and sixteen abstentions (MPs from the MR[11] and Gwendolyn Rutten from Open VLD). At that time, there were 39% women MPs in the House.[12]

The text adopted by the House was discussed on June 22, 2011, by the Senate's Finance and Economic Affairs Committee and finally approved after a vote in the Senate on June 30, 2011. The votes mostly followed the party line with thirty-six votes in favor (sp.a, Ecolo, Groen!, CD&V, and cdH), twenty-two votes against (Open VLD, N-VA, and Vlaams Belang), and eight abstentions.[13] At that time, there were 40.8% women senators[14]. What is remarkable is that one female MP, Gwendolyn Rutten, belonging to Open VLD, who is said to have sympathy for the cause of gender equality as a liberal principle, had abstained from voting, thereby going against the party line.

Belgium strengthened the position of women in electoral politics through the introduction of a legally binding quota law in 1994, the Smet-Tobback Act. This forced parties to include a minimum of one-third of the candidates of the opposite sex (in practice meaning women) on their electoral lists. While there were only 15.8% women MPs in 1995, this percentage had risen to more than one-third at the time when the gender board quota was voted in 2011 (Institute for the Equality of Women and Men, 2019).

Decision-making Process: Parliamentary Debate on the Gender Quota Law

The analysis of the preparatory work, the preceding parliamentary debates,[15] and the plenary discussions in the Senate[16] leading to the adoption of the law of July

---

[9] Vlaams Belang/Flemish Interest is a Flemish nationalist party.
[10] Libertair, Direct, Democratisch/LDD (Libertarian, Direct, Democratic) is a minor Flemish liberal party.
[11] The point of view of the MR as expressed by Senator Richard Miller in the Senate (June 30, 2011) was. "We have often resolutely stood up for equal rights for men and women. But the text before us, which wants to put government and private companies under one hat with the same regulations, is a real attack on private rights. The MR considers it is legally open to criticism and is not fit for purpose. This text conflicts with the economic interests of our country, our region and companies in the Walloon region. The MR abstained in the commission and it could stay that way."
[12] https://igvm-iefh.belgium.be/nl/activiteiten/politiek/cijfers
[13] http://www.senaat.be/www/?MIval=/consulteren/publicatie2&BLOKNR=34&COLL=H&LEG=5&NR=28&SUF=&VOLGNR=&LANG=nl
[14] https://igvm-iefh.belgium.be/nl/activiteiten/politiek/cijfers
[15] http://www.dekamer.be/FLWB/pdf/53/0211/53K0211004.pdf
[16] http://www.senaat.be/www/?MIval=/publications/viewTBlokDoc&DATUM=%2706/30/2011%27&TYP=handeen&VOLGNR=1&LANG=nl#P262_84344

28, 2011, shows that the political landscape was from the very start sharply divided between the advocates of quotas and the other opposing parties. While quotas regulating public companies are less controversial as these are considered to act as role models, the composition of the board of private businesses is much more sensitive. It touches upon the hierarchy between the right to equality and the right of freedom of association of shareholders. The social-democratic (PS and sp.a) and Christian-democratic (cdH and CD&V) French and Dutch speaking political parties, as well as the Greens actively support legally binding board quotas in order to tackle the corporate glass ceiling restricting women from participating in economic decision-making bodies (Marghem and Uyttersprot Doc. 53-0211/004). The case of Norway proved to be influential. Professor Mari Teigen from the Oslo-based Institute for Social Research was invited to present Norway's gender board quota law and its impact in detail to the Federal Parliament.

In addition to the leading example of Norway (Huse and Brogi, 2013), proponents drew on the business case for diversity, stating that women—and "outsiders" in general—are refreshing boards with new perspectives, which would lead to better corporate performance. References were made to the positive effects of political quotas, the slow pace of self-governance, the stance that companies and their boards should reflect society, and that limiting sovereign powers are justified in light of ensuring adequate gender representation. References were made to the work the European Union was undertaking to release a database on women and men in decision-making bodies. Also, the fact that EU Commissioner Viviane Reding pleaded in the European Parliament (July 14, 2010) in favor of gender board quotas was an argument to be more proactive.

The opposing right-wing parties, Open VLD, N-VA, VB, LDD, and MR built their defense against statutory quotas around the principles of freedom of association and the rights of the shareholders, which, they held, should not be overruled by politics. They argued that the gender board quota law was paternalistic, a threat to the separation between the public and the private sectors, and the freedom of choice of shareholders. They also referred to criticism expressed by the business world, indicating that quotas are a form of state interference insulting for self-made women and are not the right tool to enhance gender equality.

As an alternative, they pleaded for keeping a corporate governance approach based on the comply-or-explain principle, referring to the law of April 6, 2010, that made it compulsory for listed companies to publish an annual corporate governance declaration, legally anchoring the 2009 Belgian Code of Corporate Governance. The proponents of the gender board quota stated, however, that not businesses but the legislator "is the guardian of civilization" and that "the right of equality is superior to the freedom of association" (Senate, plenary session June 30, 2011).

Outputs: Belgium Opts for Full Coercion to Increase Women's Presence on Boards

As Table 12.2 shows below, a brief period of self-regulation (2009–2011) preceded the gender board quota law.

The law of July 28, 2011, to guarantee the presence of women on the decision-making bodies of autonomous public undertakings, listed companies, and the National Lottery, prescribes that at least one-third of board members be of the underrepresented sex. The quota applies to Belgian publicly listed companies progressively according to size, with deadlines ranging from six to eight years, up to 2019. The largest listed companies, most of which are in the BEL 20, had to comply by January 1, 2017. Companies "whose free float is less than 50% and to

Table 12.2 Policy Measures for Gender Equality on Corporate Boards in Belgium

---

SELF-REGULATION

Belgian Code on Corporate Governance
* Publicly listed companies

Code 2004
* Cognitive diversity (complementary skills, experience, and knowledge)
No recommendation on expiring mandates
No goals or targets
No timeframe
No minimum annual increases
No incentives to stimulate compliance
Comply-or-explain
No sanction in case of non-compliance

Code 2009
* Cognitive + gender diversity recommended (complementary skills, experience, and knowledge)
No definition of gender diversity
Comply-or-explain

Code 2020
* Principle 3: The board shall have an effective and balanced board: "The composition of the board should be determined to gather sufficient expertise in the company's areas of activity as well as sufficient diversity of skills, background, age and gender."

STATE REGULATION

Gender Board Quota Law of July 28, 2011
* Autonomous public undertakings, listed companies, and the National Lottery
* At least one-third of the board members be of "another sex"
* Deadlines ranged from six to nine years progressively according to firm size; state-owned companies had to comply by 2012
* Sanctions for non-compliance: nullification of appointments and suspension of compensations, rewards, or advantages of all board members

---

listed companies that, on a consolidated basis, satisfy at least two of the following three criteria: an average workforce of fewer than 250 employees during the fiscal year concerned; total assets of less than or equal to 43,000,000 euros; net annual turnover of less than or equal to 50,000,000 euros" had to comply by January 1, 2019 (Lambrecht, 2014, p. 106; Article 7, §2, Law 28 July 2011 in Belgisch Staatsblad, 2011, September 14). The sanction for non-compliance is the nullification of appointments until a person belonging to the underrepresented sex is appointed. In addition, all rewards, advantages, and compensations relating to the position of director are suspended until the quota is met (Lambrecht, 2014; Belgisch Staatsblad, 2011, September 14). Companies seem to have largely complied with the regulation and no sanctions have been reported as of now. It remains, however, unclear whether and how the sanctions will be enforced (Lambrecht, 2014). The legislator did not specify who is in charge of assessing and executing sanctions and how the law will be evaluated in the Belgian Parliament in 2023. Reflecting how MPs looked to France as an example, this state-driven approach where there is full coercion with monetary sanctions affecting the compensations paid to board members was similar to the French quota law adopted the same year. Like the French law, Belgium can be situated rather high on the comprehensiveness continuum.

Implementation and Evaluation in Practice: Significant Uptake and Interest by a Wide Range of Actors

The Institute for the Equality of Women and Men acts as a watchdog. In 2018, it named for example twenty-two companies that were still not compliant with the law. That led to last-minute changes in boards, as well as to firm statements of companies explaining to the public how they were working toward compliance. The need to appoint more women has cascaded into a significant change in recruitment practices that have expanded beyond informal recruitment from directors' own social networks. The media has started to pay more attention to women in leadership and the presence or absence of women leaders has been more publicized than in the past. In the last years, to make the female talent pool more visible to male networks facilitating compliance, several organizations have taken some initiative. For example, the organization Women on Board has compiled an extensive database of female professionals with board potential (www.womenonboard.be/access-pool). Also, GUBERNA, the National Institute for Directors, has created a database for male and female candidate directors to bundle the supply side, making especially the underrepresented group of female candidates known to the demand side who are looking to diversify the gender composition of their board (www.guberna.be/databases). These bottom-up initiatives are important in enlarging the pool from which directors are drawn beyond established predominantly male networks.

GUBERNA, the National Institute of Directors, serves also as the reference for director training. In recent years, it witnessed a remarkable growth in women attending its programs. In addition, GUBERNA and its partners were the first to launch the Belgian Mentoring Program at Board Level in 2011. A 2013–2014 mentoring program followed the 2011–2012 edition. Inspired by the FTSE-100 Cross-Company Mentoring Executive Program, the GUBERNA program offers a mentee, a qualified and talented man or woman, the opportunity to be mentored by an experienced board chair or director (male/female) during eighteen months. The main objective is to transform the qualities, behaviors, and thought processes of the mentee that are key as a manager or director in early years, into those that are ingredients of being an effective and confident director, as well as to provide the mentee an experienced view on life in the boardroom. About forty-four pairs have participated in the first two editions. GUBERNA and its partners strongly believe that the added value of this program is also in the change it enables in corporate boardrooms by involving powerful male captains of industry as mentors (Levrau, 2017).

Statistics systematically show the underrepresentation of women in senior management positions, too. Besides, warnings have been voiced that the push to increase female non-executive directors on boards may cannibalize the female executive pipeline (EWOB, 2016). Therefore, it can be argued that gender diversity on boards should be embedded in a much more comprehensive policy on diversity within the whole corporation, enabling women to get to the C-level. The well-known studies of McKinsey reveal that women continue to face barriers on their way to the top and summarize various "best practices" to encourage companies to take further actions (McKinsey, 2012; 2010). In Belgium, the Institute for the Equality of Women and Men (2018) reiterates the importance of protecting and strengthening systems for flexible parental leave and career breaks and encourages fathers to make use of such policies, which should become more common and integrated into the business world. It also advocates that gender quotas be imposed for the executive management committees of listed companies and autonomous public companies because it advocates that it is the most efficient way to achieve actual results in the short term regarding gender equality in the corporate world.

The first generation of post-quota female directors is today providing new role models of women who occupy visible economic decision making positions, with whom other women can identify. The significant consequence of the gender board quota law cannot be underestimated in the quest for realizing gender equality given that research has demonstrated the positive and motivating impact female role models have had upon other women (Pande et al, 2011; Lockwood, 2006). For example, Dominique Leroy, a member of Women on Board, was selected by a headhunter and became the first woman CEO of a BEL 20 company, Proximus Group, formerly Belgacom (2014–2019), an autonomous public-sector company. She was continually praised in the press as a role model for breaking through the glass ceiling, being self-made, multilingual (Dutch and French), and combining her career with motherhood. The media portrayed her as "the best candidate," pointing at the selection procedure and her capabilities to perform professionally. They emphasized that she had not been selected because of positive discrimination and described her as being "exceptional" throughout: "She does not even seem to be a bitch" [sic] (Vandenberghe, 2019, p. 9). It should be noted however that Dominique Leroy received significantly lower remuneration compared to her male predecessor. Effective November 1, 2020, she was appointed as a board member for Deutsche Telekom's Europe segment.

Given the multiple barriers experienced by women in business contexts, progress in gender equality will crucially depend on additional conditions next to the presence of role models. Although the introduction of binding gender board quota "imposes" commitment on the leadership, this commitment needs to be further supported within companies by programs for women and collective enablers, such as key performance indicators and HR processes (Women Matter reports from McKinsey & Company 2010, 2012, 2013). These insights are in line with the scientific literature suggesting that equality is most effectively achieved through policies establishing organizational responsibility for diversity (Kalev et al, 2006). While the gender board quota act does not apply to executive committees, the Institute for the Equality of Women and Men goes beyond the figures of the BEL 20 and the demands of the gender quota law and calculated for all Belgian listed companies that the percentage of women in the executive committees has been gradually increasing. The media and the Institute for the Equality of Women and Men have been keeping track of the implementation of the gender quota legislation and drawing attention to the inequality in power positions. This is vital to enhance the empowerment of women directors and to push for the translation of the law into the substantive representation of women in the corporate world. As a result of company compliance with the gender quota legislation, there is today a critical mass of women represented that goes beyond tokenism (Kanter, 1977) and male absolute dominance on corporate boards—in numerical terms—is effectively being reduced through the law. In 2008, women represented only 7.4% of the members of the executive committees of listed companies, while in 2017 that number had risen to 18%. Remarkably, two-thirds of the executive committees of listed companies in 2017 had no or only one woman. Yet, an important evolution in the executive committees of public-sector companies can be observed, where the percentage of women has dramatically risen from 8.3% in 2016 to 20% in 2017 (Institute for the Equality of Women and Men, 2018).

Despite the numerical increase in women directors, the most powerful directors remain male. Since the introduction of the gender board quota law, the media is more attentive toward the gender of power and tends to carefully track the number of directorships among men and women directors. Among the twenty most powerful directors, only four are women, featuring on the 7th, 14th, 17th, and 19th positions (Sephiha, 2018). Also, women rarely hold the position of chairperson of the board. There were only five (4.3%) companies in 2017 with a corporate board chaired by a woman (Institute for the Equality of Women and Men, 2018).

Notwithstanding its limitations, Belgium's gender board quota legislation can be described as transformative on various levels. The feminization of corporate boards goes against traditional and long-held norms about masculine and feminine roles and the male breadwinner model. In addition, the gender board quota is transforming corporate governance practices, since it deinstitutionalizes informal recruitment practices and creates a market for the training, recruitment, and selection of board directors in general. This shift in practices, resulting from the need to comply with the quota legislation, has also the potential to generate a shift of attitudes toward women in the corporate world as it presents women to be trustworthy and competent decision-makers. We observe that Belgium's mandatory quota thus acts as a lever for cultural change.

Direct Impacts

Longitudinal data available for the BEL 20 companies since 2003 demonstrates that the number of women directors increased from 6% in 2003 to 36.5% in 2020, or from twenty-eight women directors in 2003 to seventy-three in 2020. We thus clearly observe a change in the direction intended by the gender board quota law. However, two reservations are in place; it is unclear what the evaluation of this law, planned for 2023, will entail. Moreover, it remains unclear how sanctions can be enforced in case of non-compliance. Usually, a growing economy is mentioned to be a significant factor for favoring the adoption of feminist policies (Jenson et al, 1988). In our case, it rather was the economic crisis of 2008 that weakened the corporate world's power to resist government interference, as it undermined the legitimacy of traditional governance in the hands of almost exclusively male networks of directors. Hence, the economic crisis offered valuable arguments to change male-dominated leadership, turning the gender board quota proposal into a legitimate policy. The business case for gender equality gained strength at that time and received tremendous political support. The resistance from opposing business leaders had no teeth as they simultaneously tried to regain confidence in the eyes of the government and society at large.

Policy Empowerment

A Belgian Christian Democratic women's movement affiliated with the political party CD&V, Vrouw&Maatschappij, lobbied in favor of the gender board quota law. It is the largest political women's movement in the country and is known for striving for equal representation of men and women in all political institutions as well as in other sectors such as juridical institutions, the business world, and civil society. It strives to empower women in socioeconomic vulnerable positions and to amplify the voices of all women by addressing their concerns in the political debate. In the framework of this vision, more than a decade ago, gender quota for publicly listed companies became a topic of discussion that led to one of the various policy instruments they promote to strengthen the position of women in society at large (www.vrouwenmaatschappij.be).

The gender board quota law, while it was still debated, gave a push to organizations to cater to the needs of women in economic organizations. Gender quota has been criticized for speaking only to white upper-middle-class elites; the bottom of the corporate hierarchy is indeed more socioculturally diverse than its boardrooms. Nevertheless, thanks to the imperative and urgency of the law, corporate gender equality gained significance as, for example, shown in award ceremonies celebrating change agents within and beyond listed companies (since 2010 Wo.Men@Work awards are handed out by the social enterprise JUMP http://jump.eu.com/news).

Gender Transformation at the Gatekeeper Level

Whereas the Belgian corporate leadership traditionally recruited individuals informally within close-knit, homogeneous, male-dominated networks, it today increasingly engages with inclusive selection practices, through formalized board practices, mediated by a nomination committee who in order to meet their demand more than ever tends to consult external brokers, resulting in more women on boards. Non-inclusive recruitment practices were legitimized based on prerequisites such as "social fit" or "chemistry" (Coverdill and Finlay, 1998). These practices were legitimized as a way to maximize trust and social cohesion within the male-dominated corporate leader networks, as these are understood to be essential conditions for good board governance. Women's exclusion was hereby justified by referring to their lack of management experience and absence from existing corporate networks.

Driven by the increased demand for women board members, external brokers such as executive search firms, headhunters, and top women's associations emerge constituting a market of "professional" board directors, whose profiles are now formally defined by board nomination committees. These external brokers generate outside peer pressure as they take up a governing role as the board gender quota law enables the expansion of the pool of gatekeepers to corporate boards.

In other national contexts where company shares tend to be more dispersed among the public, external mediators such as headhunters are important gatekeepers excluding or including women on boards (Doldor et al, 2016). In the Belgian context, these mediators, on the contrary, have appeared only recently due to the increased demand for women directors. Social networks are not completely excluded, yet recruitment and selection are done more closely in function of the diverse competences required by the firm as well as in compliance with the gender quota.

Gender Transformation at Societal Level

Preceding the first deadline of 2017 for the gender quota, media articles were rather skeptical about the law, featuring leading women who were openly opposed to gender quotas. Such is the remarkable case of two female CEOs who both steered gender-balanced boards, even exceeding the gender board quota rules before there was even a discussion about gender board quota, but who were strictly against state interference within businesses. The two rather pointed out the responsibilities of the state in enabling the careers of women, instead of outsourcing such tasks to the corporate world. Influential newspapers featured articles written by leading women lawyers such as "Thanks, but No: Thanks" (Wyckaert and Janssens, 2011) or published extensive interviews of leading businesswomen including statements such as, "Quotas are an insult to women" (De Cort, 2016a), "Top women reject more quotas" (Eckert and Vanhecke, 2016) and "Top women prefer not to be seen as women" (Ibid).

The media as a watchdog meticulously followed the increasing number of women directors and covered how business procrastinated, with headlines such as "Thirty boards of directors without a woman" (De Cort, 2016b) and "Resistance to women's quotas until the last day" (Eckert and De Cort, 2016). That several companies waited until the very last moment to comply with the law can be seen as an indication that voluntary measures would have never produced significant results.

In the months preceding the first deadline of 2017, when the largest companies had to install their gender-balanced board of directors, the media featured also positive and encouraging news of the impact of the gender board quota legislation—even in more conservative news outlets such as De Tijd, a leading Belgian newspaper covering the financial markets, business, and economics, which is also considered the main information source for Belgian managers. Already in 2015, this newspaper held a survey among shareholders asking what their view was regarding women directors. The results were predominantly positive. The newspaper had to conclude that, "The feminization of governance is an irreversible phenomenon" (Sephiha et al, 2016). Conspicuously, while headlines earlier featured opinion pieces against gender quota and token women, after the first deadline had passed, headlines highlighted the bright side of gender board quotas; for example, "Stock exchange companies embrace female directors" (Vanbrussel, 2017) and "The more female top managers, the higher the stock price," which praised gender quotas leading to higher returns; "[M]ore women in top management leads to higher stock prices, more profit and a lower debt ratio" (Van Hamme, 2017, p. 28).

Nevertheless, a mandatory quota remains contentious, and their controversial nature was still a topic of debate in the public domain, such as featured in the article: "What Do Boards Need? Young People!" (Serrure and Haeck, 2018), as opposed to (quota) women. The article presents an interview with a woman director, described as a "power woman" since she serves on several corporate boards and is known for opposing quotas, drawing upon the argument that these are insulting toward women. Instead, fiscal advantages to outsourcing household chores (to other women) is mentioned as a remedy to advance women's careers.

Conclusion

As in many other countries, also in Belgium, businesses did not work toward women's equal representation on their boards of directors on a voluntary basis without any binding sanctions. The gender quota law of July 28, 2011, has definitely accelerated the process of change resulting in more gender-balanced outcomes, as well as a more positive public debate on women in leadership positions. In the Belgian context, the gender board quota was necessary to disrupt vicious circles of recruitment practices within "old boys networks." The financial crisis of 2008 offered valuable arguments in favor of gender diversity. This drive for change materialized during the political crisis of 2011, which proved to be an opportunity to translate earlier formulated gender equality proposals into hard law.

With the introduction of gender quota for corporate boards, the state actively reshaped a labor market for corporate leaders, thereby disrupting the reproductive role of boards. With the increased demand for women directors, the state facilitates a shift in power from (male) incumbents, who were exclusively in control of board appointments, to external, professional intermediaries who have a governing role in mediating the board director recruitment processes. Despite its obvious positive effects, the current gender board quota legislation has not feminized management in male-dominated sectors and businesses. While the gender board quota does not have large redistributive effects between men and women, due to the small group it directly affects, it is a highly visible and symbolic measure. Additionally, it opened public discussions about the lack of opportunities and recognition for women in various domains such as science, sports, arts, music, and academia. At the same time, the quota regulation remains contested even after its implementation and is still subjected to criticism in Belgium, not least from the corporate world. It should be noted that the public debate and reporting have been limited to gender. Race, ethnicity, age, or other demographic characteristics of board members are usually not disclosed and have not been made the object of discussion. This well shows that there is a long road ahead of us before the public is fully represented on the boards of publicly listed companies.

References

Becht, Marco, Patrick Bolton, and Ailsa Röell (2003) "Corporate Governance and Control" in G.M. Constantinides, Harris, and R.M. Stulz (eds) *Handbook of the Economics of Finance*. Amsterdam: Elsevier, pp. 1–109.

Belgisch Staatsblad (2011) *Law of 28 July 2011*, http://www.ejustice.just.fgov.be/cgi_loi/change_lg.pl?language=nl&la=N&table_name=wet&cn=2011072814 (Accessed June 17, 2019).

Bratton, William and Joseph McCahery (1999) *Comparative Corporate Governance and the Theory of the Firm: The Case against Global Cross Reference*. http://scholarship.law.upenn.edu/faculty_scholarship/832 (Accessed June 17, 2019).

Broeckmeyer, Ivan (2009) "One Third of Women in Top Large Companies l Minister Milquet Wants Quotas for Boards of Directors of Listed and Public Companies l VBO Opposes Imposed Numbers," *De Tijd*, November 19, 2009, p. 6.

Celis, Karen, and Petra Meier (2007) "State Feminism and Women's Movements in Belgium: Complex Patterns in a Multilevel System," in J. Outshoorn and J. Kantola (eds) *Changing State Feminism*. London: Palgrave Macmillan, pp. 62–81.

Corporate Governance Code (2004) *Belgian Corporate Governance Code 2004*, http://www.ecgi.org/codes/documents/bel_code_dec2004_nl.pdf (Accessed June 22, 2017).

Corporate Governance Code (2009) *The 2009 Belgian Code on Corporate Governance*, http://www.corporategovernancecommittee.be/sites/default/files/generated/files/page/corporategovukcode2009.pdf (Accessed June 17, 2019)

Coverdill, James E., & William Finlay (1998) Fit and skill in employee selection: Insights from a study of headhunters. *Qualitative Sociology*, 21(2), 105-127.

Daems, Herman (1998) *The Paradox of Belgian Capitalism*. Brussels: Lannoo.

Dealbook (2010) "Lagarde: What If It Had Been Lehman Sisters?", *New York Times*, 11 May 2010, https://dealbook.nytimes.com/2010/05/11/lagarde-what-if-it-had-been-lehman-sisters/.

De Cabo, Ruth Mateos, Ricardo Gimeno and Maria Nieto (2012) "Gender Diversity on European Banks' Boards of Directors," *Journal of Business Ethics*, 109 (2), pp. 145–162.

De Cort, Goele (2016a) "Quota Are an Insult to Women," *De Standaard*, March 2, p. 28.

De Cort, Goele (2016b) "Thirty Boards of Directors without a Woman," *De Standaard*, January, 26, p. 26.

De Preter, René (2016) *The Invisible Hand above Belgium*. Antwerp: Garant.

Desmet, Lieven and Sjoukje Smedts (2014) "If I Had a Brother, I Wouldn't Be Here," *De Morgen*, March, 8, p. 26.

Doldor, Elena, Ruth Sealy, and Susan Vinnicombe (2016) "Accidental activists: Headhunters as marginal diversity actors in institutional change towards more women on boards," *Human Resource Management Journal* 26 (3), pp. 285–303.

Eckert, Maxie and Goele De Cort (2016) "Resistance to Women's Quotas until the Last Day," *De Standaard*, December, 30, p. 8.

Eckert, Maxie and Nikolas Vanhecke (2016) "Top Women Reject More Quota," *De Standaard*, May, 13, p. 1.

EIGE (2019) *Gender Equality Index*, https://eige.europa.eu/gender-equality-index/2019/domain/time/BE (Accessed March 3, 2020).

EIGE (2020) *Gender Statistics Database*, http://eige.europa.eu/gender-statistics/dgs/indicator/wmidm_bus_bus__wmid_comp_compbm/datatable (Accessed November 10, 2020).

Eurostat (2018) *Employment—Annual Statistics*, https://ec.europa.eu/eurostat/statistics-explained/index.php?title=Employment_-_annual_statistics (Accessed September 10, 2020).

EWOB (2016) Gender Diversity on European Boards, http://www.femmes-experts-comptables.com/wp-content/uploads/2016/07/EWoB-qualitative-WEB-2.pdf (accessed January 27, 2022).

Guberna (2011) *Investigation of the BEL 20 Companies Regarding Their Compliance With the Belgian Corporate Governance Code 2009, Financial Year 2010*, http://www.guberna.be/sites/default/files/pubs/NL%20Monitoring%202011_DEF.pdf (Accessed June 17, 2019).

Guberna (2016) *Good Governance at Flemish Public Organizations*, https://www.guberna.be/sites/default/files/pubs/Rapport%20Deugdelijk%20Bestuur%20Vlaamse%20Publieke%20Organisaties.pdf (Accessed June 17, 2019).

GVA (2009) *Joëlle Milquet wil quota voor vrouwen in raden van bestuur, Gazet van Antwerpen, 18 November*, https://www.gva.be/cnt/eid47095/extern-joelle-milquet-wil-quota-voor-vrouwen-in-raden-van-bestuur (Acccessed October 30, 2020).

Huse, Morton and Mari Brogi (2013) "Introduction," in S. Machold, M. Huse, K. Hansen, and M. Brogi (eds) *Getting Women on to Corporate Boards: A Snowball Starting in Norway*. Cheltenham: Edward Elgar Publishing, pp. 1–8.

Institute for the Equality of Women and Men (2009) *Women at the Top 2008*, https://igvm-iefh.belgium.be/sites/default/files/downloads/33%20-%20Vrouwen%20aan%20de%20top_NL.pdf (Accessed December 20, 2019).

Institute for the Equality of Women and Men (2013) *Women at the Top 2012*, https://igvm-iefh.belgium.be/sites/default/files/downloads/65%20-%20Vrouwen-aan-de-Top-NL.pdf (Accessed December 20, 2019).

Institute for the Equality of Women and Men (2018) *Third Balance of the Law of 28 July 2011 Regarding Gender Board Quota*, https://igvm-iefh.belgium.be/sites/default/files/derde_balans_26.11.2018.pdf (Accessed June 17, 2019).

Institute for the Equality of Women and Men (2019) *Figures*, https://igvm-iefh.belgium.be/nl/activiteiten/politiek/cijfers (Accessed June 17, 2019).

Jenson, Jane, Elisabeth Hagen, Ceallaigh Reddy (eds) (1988) *Feminization of the Labour Force: Paradoxes and Promises*. Cambridge: Polity Press.

Kalev, Alexandra, Frank Dobbin, and Erin Kelly, (2006) "Best Practices or Best Guesses? Assessing the Efficacy of Corporate Affirmative Action and Diversity Policies," *American Sociological Review*, 71, pp. 589–617.

Kanter, Rosabeth (1977) *Men and women of the corporation*. New York: Basic Books.

Lambrecht, Philippe (2014) "The Law of 28 July 2011 to Guarantee the Presence of Women on the Decision-making Bodies of Autonomous Public Undertakings, Listed Companies and the National Lottery," in M. De Vos, and Ph. Culliford (eds) *Gender Quotas for Company Boards*. Cambridge: Intersentia, pp. 83–108.

Laster, Travis and John Mark Zeberkiewicz (2014/2015) "The Rights and Duties of Blockholder Directors," *Business Law*, 70, p. 33.

Lauwers, Bert and Kurt De Cat (2018) "Being Put With Your Feet on the Ground Every Now and Then, That Helps," *Trends*, January 11, p. 10.

Lemeire, Veronika and Patrizia Zanoni (2021) "Beyond methodological nationalism in explanations of gender equality: The impact of EU policies on gender provisions in national collective agreements in Belgium (1957-2020)" European Journal of Industrial Relations, DOI: 10.1177/09596801211027400

Levrau, Abigail (2017) "Belgium: Male/female United in the Boardroom," in C. Seierstad, P. Gabaldon, and H. Mensi-Klarbach (eds) *Gender Diversity in the Boardroom. Volume 1: The Use of Different Quota Regulations.* Cham: Palgrave, pp. 155–175.

Lockwood, Penelope (2006) "Someone Like Me Can Be Successful: Do College Students Need Same-gender Role Models?" *Psychology of Women Quarterly*, 30 (2), pp. 36–46.

McKinsey & Company (2010) *Women Matter 2010. Women at the Top of Corporations*, http://www.mckinsey.com/global-themes/women-matter (Accessed June 19, 2019).

McKinsey & Company (2012) *Women Matter 2012. Making the Breakthrough*, http://www.mckinsey.com/global-themes/women-matter (Accessed June 19, 2019).

McKinsey & Company (2013) *Women Matter 2013. Gender Diversity in Top Management*, http://www.mckinsey.com/global-themes/women-matter (Accessed June 19, 2019).

Morris, Nigel (2009) "Harriet Harman: 'If only it had been Lehman Sisters'." *The Independent* 4, p. 4–5.

OECD (2017) *How Do Partners in Couple Families Share Paid Work?* https://www.oecd.org/gender/data/how-do-partners-in-couple-families-share-paid-work.htm (Accessed June 17, 2019).

Pande, Rohini and Deanna Ford (2011) *Gender Quotas and Female Leadership: A Review*, http://www.tinyurl.com/yxhp8v6z (Accessed June 17, 2019).

Renneboog, Luc (1997) "Shareholding Concentration and Pyramidal Ownership Structures in Belgium," in M. Balling, E. Hennessy, and R. O'Brien (eds) *Corporate Governance, Financial Markets and Global Convergence.* Dordrecht: Kluwer Academic Publishers, pp. 263–300.

Renneboog, Luc (2000) "Ownership, Managerial Control and the Governance of Companies Listed on the Brussels Stock Exchange," *Journal of Banking & Finance*, vol. 24, pp. 1959–1995.

RoSa vzw (2016) *Labor Participation in Belgium*, https://rosavzw.be/site/kwesties/arbeidsparticipatie/in-vlaanderen (Accessed June 17, 2019).

Schonard, Martina (2020) *Equality between Men and Women*, https://www.europarl.europa.eu/factsheets/en/sheet/59/equality-between-men-and-women   (Accessed January 7, 2021).

Sephiha, Michael (2018) "Glass Ceiling about to Burst," *De Tijd*, June 23, p. 6.

Sephiha, Michael, Thomas Roelens and Maarten Lambrechts (2016) "The Feminization of Governance Is an Irreversible Phenomenon," *De Tijd*, June 11, p. 16.

Serrure, Ben and Pieter Haeck (2018) "What Do Boards Need? Young People!" *De Tijd*, June 23, p. 23.

Treanor, Jill (2011) "EU calls for women to make up one-third of bank directors", *The Guardian*, June 21, https://www.theguardian.com/business/2011/jun/21/eu-women-bank-directors.

Van Staveren, Irene (2014) 'The Lehman sisters hypothesis." *Cambridge Journal of Economics* 38(5), pp. 995–1014.

Van Hamme, Kris (2017) "The More Female Top Managers, the Higher the Stock Price," *De Tijd*, May 26, p. 28.

Van Hove, Hildegard (2015) *Country Fact Sheet Belgium. Some Facts about the Gender Pay Gap in Belgium*, http://www.genderpaygap.eu/documents/Factsheet_Belgium. pdf (Accessed June 18, 2019).

Van Veen, Kees and Ilse Marsman (2008) "How International Are Executive Boards of European MNCs? Nationality Diversity in 15 European Countries," *European Management Journal*, 26 (3), pp. 188–198.

Vanbrussel, Emmanuel (2017) "Stock Exchange Companies Embrace Female Directors," *De Tijd*, April, 8, p. 14.

Vandenberghe, Hanne (2019) "Representation of Women in the News: Balancing between Career and Family Life," *Media and Communication*, 7 (1), pp. 4–12.

Vanhecke, Nikolas and Eckert, Maxie (2016) "Top Women Prefer Not to Be Seen as Women," *De Standaard*, May, 14, p. 18.

World Bank Group (2020) *Women, Business and the Law 2020*, https://openknowledge. worldbank.org/bitstream/handle/10986/32639/9781464815324.pdf (Accessed January 5, 2020).

World Economic Forum (2018) *The Global Gender Gap Report 2018*, http://www3. weforum.org/docs/WEF_GGGR_2018.pdf (Accessed June 17, 2019).

World Economic Forum (2020) *Global Gender Gap Report*, http://www3.weforum.org/ docs/WEF_GGGR_2020.pdf (Accessed January 5, 2020).

Wyckaert, Marieke and Deborah Janssens (2011) "Thanks, but No: Thanks," *De Standaard*, May 25, p. 54.

Track 2. Mixed Approach: Self-regulation Stumbles Slowly into Legislated Quotas

13

Early to Act, Late to Achieve

Poor Implementation Limits Transformative Change in Spain

Emanuela Lombardo and Tània Verge

Introduction

Spain developed a mixed approach to corporate board quotas by adopting in 2006 a corporate governance code that strived for gender balance in boards, and in 2007, it was one of the first European countries to regulate by law a minimum presence of 40% for the underrepresented sex on the corporate boards of publicly traded firms (IBEX 35) and state-owned companies. However, in 2020, with 27.4% women on the boards of the largest listed companies, Spain ranked last after Portugal among the European Union countries with legislated quotas—33.7% average—and was even outperformed by most of the member states applying only self-regulation codes—29.3% average (EIGE, 2020). How did an early bird regulator country become a latecomer in terms of outcomes?

Such a puzzle is explained by lax oversight of the implementation of statutory quotas and continued opposition from the business sector. Gender equality regulation has been gradually weakened through lowering the target from 40% to 30%, extending the deadline from 2015 to 2020, diluting the gender diversity requisite into diversity of knowledge and experience, and watering down the requirements for companies to comply or explain. Unsurprisingly, such a policy shift has further reinforced non-compliance patterns and entailed a very slow feminization of corporate boards, which stands in sharp contrast with the strong quotas applied to the political field and the impressive results achieved (Verge and Lombardo, 2018), with 47% women serving as MPs in the lower house after the April 2019 general elections.

We argue that the contentious politics underpinning the policy has been pivotal in preventing the effective implementation of Spain's corporate gender quotas and in gradually weakening both the self-regulation code and the legislative framework

Emanuela Lombardo and Tània Verge, *Early to Act, Late to Achieve*. In: *Gender Equality and Policy Implementation in the Corporate World*. Edited by Isabelle Engeli and Amy G. Mazur, Oxford University Press. © Oxford University Press (2022). DOI: 10.1093/oso/9780198865216.003.0013

across time (Verge and Lombardo, 2019). This chapter investigates the dynamics of resistance and alliance that change and opposition actors have articulated throughout the whole policy process and draws implications for descriptive and substantive empowerment of businesswomen.[1] Our results show that the strong opposition of the business community in the adoption phase, including businesswomen themselves and the main conservative political party, was determinant to water down the design of positive action measures, which has been detrimental to effective implementation. Nonetheless, there are signs of potential transformation. The resulting relatively marginal feminization of corporate boards coupled with a gradual dismantling of the regulatory framework have broadened the support coalition in favor of gender quotas, now encompassing insider allies from within the policy sector, namely businesswomen. Policy learning about the failure of policies in delivering equality results, facilitated by the development of new alliances and platforms, has empowered businesswomen, especially from small and medium-sized companies, moving them to publicly support a regulatory approach to gender quotas.

After a brief contextualization of gender equality in the Spanish corporate world, we discuss how the issue of women's presence in corporate boards entered the political agenda and review the arguments that were put forward in favor and against gender quotas. We then examine the policy instruments adopted and their enactment and monitoring in practice, moving thereafter to an assessment of women's empowerment and gender transformation.

Gender Equality in the Corporate World: Women-Unfriendly Firms in a Changing Care Context

In the past two decades, women's presence as top managers has remained rather stable around 33% (INE, 2019). Vertical segregation is acute in publicly listed companies, as Table 13.1 shows. Although moderate progress has been observed over time, in 2020 women only represented 27.4% of board members and just 7.8% of presidents, and 2.9% of CEOs (EIGE, 2020).

Spanish firms are not particularly women-friendly. They tend to recruit board members through families' and friends' networks and show high rates of localism, endogamy, and concentration of ownership along with a low degree of rotation of

---

[1] Acknowledgment: we wish to thank interviewees for sharing their time and ideas with us and editors for their helpful and constructive guidance. The empirical analysis builds on process-tracing and content analysis of policy documents. We also examine the monitoring reports of the self-regulation and legislative frameworks produced by public and private actors. Three semi-structured interviews, including two businesswomen and one key policymaker, allowed us to clarify implementation dynamics. Lastly, to capture the position of businesswomen, the target group expected to benefit most from gender quotas, we look at press interviews, blogs and op-eds.

Table 13.1 Percentage Share of Women on Boards in the Largest Listed Companies in Spain, 2004–2020

	EU-28 Board members	SPAIN				
		Board members	President	CEO	Executives	Non-executives
2004	9	4.2	1.9	—	—	—
2005	9.8	4.3	3.9	—	—	—
2006	9.7	4.5	4.1	—	—	—
2007	10.4	6.2	0	—	—	—
2008	10.8	8.7	0	—	—	—
2009	11	9.5	2.9	—	—	—
2010	11.9	10.5	2.9	—	—	—
2011	13.7	11.1	0	—	—	—
2012	15.8	12.3	2.9	2.9	5.7	13.9
2013	17.8	14.8	6.1	3.0	9.1	16.9
2014	20.2	16.9	9.1	3.0	9.6	19.6
2015	22.7	18.7	8.8	2.9	10.6	21.7
2016	23.9	20.0	8.8	2.9	11.5	23.7
2017	25.3	22.0	8.8	2.9	13.2	25.6
2018	26.7	23.7	6.1	2.9	14.7	27.7
2019	28.8	26.4	7.5	2.9	16.2	30.4
2020	29.2	27.4	7.8	2.9	16.3	31.5

Source: EIGE Database. Data for October each year, except for 2020 [April].

board posts (Mateos, Gimeno, and Escot, 2010). About 70% of female board members in publicly listed companies are independent members with no significant shareholding and about a fourth are proprietary, that is, they are shareholders or represent shareholders—usually the female heirs of family-owned companies (Atrevia-IESE, 2020, p. 13). Men's overrepresentation in corporate boards is also explained by their long tenure. Data from 2015 indicates that male board members serve on average 7.6 years, whereas women serve 4.8 years (de la Fuente Sanz, 2015, p. 39). While the average female employee already earns 15.1% less than the average male employee (EU average, 16.3%) (Eurostat, 2016), the gender pay gap widens even more in corporate boards, especially among all executive members or internal directors (35.6%) and independent members (33.2%). Women's share of company remuneration is also systematically lower than the share that we would expect to correspond to them given their presence in the board (male board members in the top publicly listed companies earned 93.6% of the total company's remuneration despite them being only 84.9% of the board members, while women only earned 6.4% of the total remuneration despite them being 15.1% of the board members) (Conde-Ruiz and Hoya, 2015, pp. 12–14). Furthermore, women have fewer voting rights than men in all board member types except for proprietary members—33.3% vs. 55.6% in the case of executive female board members, and

21.8% vs. 31.6% in the case of independent board members (Conde-Ruiz and Hoya, 2015, p. 17).

The work-life balance context has not enabled the dismantlement of the structural obstacles that women face as managers of firms. In Spain's conservative-familialist welfare model female activity rates are mainly sustained by informal family help, with grandmothers being the main childcare providers (León, 2007, p. 74). The government-funded family benefits only represent 1.5% of the GDP, as compared to the EU average of 2.76%, and the insufficient public infrastructure entails that just 38.1% for children under three are enrolled in formal childcare and 44% of children between three and six are only enrolled part-time (Mills et al., 2014).

The traditional male breadwinner care model in Spain is nonetheless gradually shifting toward greater redistribution of gender roles in care between working parents. Maternity leave in Spain is sixteen weeks (fully paid), as compared to the EU average of 21.8 weeks, and paid paternity leave has been extended to twelve weeks in 2020 (of which the first four will be compulsory) with a further four-week extension in place from 2021 onward.

Getting Political and Corporate Attention: A Progressive Approach Resisted by the Business Sector and Conservative Political Actors

The issue of women's presence on corporate boards was put on the agenda with no prior public debate under the initiative of the Spanish Socialist Workers' Party (PSOE) government elected in 2004 at the time when the National Securities Market Commission (CNMV) elaborated a new industry self-regulation instrument. The expert group that updated the code included four women: three out of the six members proposed by the PSOE government and one out of the eight members proposed by the private sector. The measures on gender diversity included in the initial draft of the Unified Good Governance Code (CNMV, 2006a) aligned with the Draft Equality Law the PSOE government was preparing at the time. Recommendation 15 of the so-called Conthe Code required listed companies with few or no women on their board to explain the underlying reasons and undertake actions aimed at correcting the gap. It also introduced the requirement to reflect on the potential gender biases underpinning recruitment processes and indicate the share of women in candidates' shortlists in the annual reports submitted to the CNMV.

Publicly listed company opposition led to a substantial reformulation of Recommendation 15. Whereas in the first draft, gender diversity was argued not only in terms of corporate social responsibility but also in terms of the implicit biases faced by women in recruitment processes, including old boy networks, reference to the latter disappeared from the final draft (CNMV, 2006b, p. 3). The very same tone of the recommendation was also softened to make it sound less imperative and the requirement to provide data on the sex distribution of personnel across all company levels and on the changes enacted to comply with gender diversity in the yearly report of corporate governance was lifted (Fagan, González, and Gómez, 2012).

In parallel to the discussion of the Conthe Code, the Ministry of Labor and Social Affairs, particularly the Secretariat-General for Equality Policies—led at the time by the feminist sociologist Soledad Murillo—drafted the Equality Law. This bill was part of a broader gender equality program to promote substantial gender reforms, encompassing gender quotas for the political and economic fields, a progressive revision of sexual and reproductive rights, marriage equality, and the furthering of care services. Although no specific stimulus was acknowledged, the Norwegian legislation adopted in 2003 may have partially inspired the adoption of statutory corporate gender quotas (González and Martínez, 2012, p. 172).

The bill triggered a heated public debate before and after its adoption. The PSOE government invoked women's talent as an asset for company competitiveness, but gender quotas were primarily justified on grounds of justice and equality, with the Minister of Labor defending in Parliament the need to remove the obstacles hindering women's access to corporate boards. Conversely, the main opposition party, the conservative Popular Party (PP), rejected legally binding provisions— "no quotas" and "no deadlines—to respect company" freedom (Congreso de los Diputados, 2006, p. 11470).

Business sector actors met the draft law with resistance. The largest Spanish employer organizations, the Spanish Confederation of Business Organizations (Confederación Española de Organizaciones Empresariales, CEOE) and the Spanish Confederation of Small and Medium Size Businesses (Confederación Española de la Pequeña y Mediana Empresa, CEPYME) argued that quotas infringed upon meritocracy and company competitive interests (CES, 2006). Businessmen did not want to lose their privileges concerning salaries and informal networks (Interview, September 17, 2019). There were no debates on reporting instruments. The women representatives of these organizations attributed women's underrepresentation in corporate boards to supply factors, namely gender differences in qualifications and willingness to join corporate boards, and emphasized that businesswomen did not want to be treated as "quota tokens" (CES, 2006, p. 17). Independent businesswomen's organizations were also against statutory quotas (CM, 2006). Indeed, a survey sampling 400 senior executive women found that around half of them rejected quotas in 2007 because they believed their merits would be put into question (Adecco, 2010).

Alternatively, they supported the introduction of state incentives for those firms showing good performance on women's representation and the adoption of gender action plans in companies, as stated by the president of the businesswomen's organization Omega (CM, 2006). Corporate gender quotas were only defended in public debates by femocrats of the statewide women's agency (Instituto de la Mujer), left-wing parties, and feminist organizations unrelated to the economic field, such as the Women Lawyers Association, Themis, and the Federation of Progressive Women. These organizations emphasized the constitutionality of quotas and the need for legally binding measures to remove the barriers women face in selection processes (CM, 2006). Lack of support from within the business sector inevitably led to the adoption of a more diluted measure. The initial bill (Anteproyecto de Ley Orgánica de Igualdad entre Mujeres y Hombres, March 2, 2006) provided a rather strong formulation of corporate gender quotas; it fixed a four-year period to attain a minimum of 40% of corporate members of either sex; companies were required to incorporate at least 10% of women every year to reach this minimum share, and the expiring mandate of male board members was to be used to appoint women. In sharp contrast, the final draft of the law stretched the deadline to eight years, did not establish annual goals, and only recommended companies to consider expiring mandates to recruit female board members. Act 3/2007 only introduced reporting instruments for state-owned companies, with private company monitoring thus resting only on the annual reports required by the Conthe self-regulatory code. CEOE's threat to leave the negotiation table, which included other important equality measures such as the extension of paternity leave, moved the government to reform its original quota proposal (Interview, September 17, 2019).

Continued business resistance brought about an even softer governmental approach, especially from 2011 onward when the electoral victory of the conservative PP ousted the policy promoter from the government, the PSOE. The approach was further weakened through legislation that lowered the target of women on boards from 40% to 30% and extended the deadline from 2015 to 2020. The new self-regulation code also diluted both parity goals and reporting requirements, as explained in the next section.

Outputs: A Mixed Approach of Regulation, Self-regulation, and Intermediate Coercion

The regulatory approach adopted in Spain has two phases (Table 13.2). The first phase saw a mix between self-regulation and state-driven legislation. Self-regulation was established in 2006 through the aforementioned Conthe Code, whose Recommendation 15 on gender diversity required publicly listed firms with few or no women on their board to introduce voluntary corrective measures. Through the "comply-or-explain" principle, listed companies had to either comply with the Code or justify any failure to do so, in accordance with Article 116 of the Securities Market Law (de Anca, 2008, p. 97), making reporting mandatory and assigning the monitoring to the CNMV.

State-driven legislation was adopted in 2007 through the Equality Law, giving publicly listed firms (Article 75) eight years to achieve gender balance, defined

Table 13.2 Policy Measures for Gender Equality on Corporate Boards in Spain

SELF-REGULATION	
Unified Good Governance Code of Listed Companies 2006[a]	**Unified Good Governance Code of Listed Companies 2015[b]**
* Listed companies * Minimum of 40% women * Comply-or-explain * Annual report to reflect on the gender biases underpinning recruitment processes and to indicate the share of women in candidate shortlists *Sex-disaggregated data requirement lifted	* Listed companies * Gender clustered with other diversity issues (knowledge and experience) * Minimum of 30% women * Verify-and-inform replaces comply-or-explain * Deadline: 2020

Unified Good Governance Code of Listed Companies 2020[c]
* Listed companies
* Gender clustered with other diversity issues (knowledge and experience)
* Minimum of 40% for the underrepresented sex
* Comply-or-explain
* Deadline: 2022

STATE REGULATION	
Organic law 3/2007 of March 22, 2007	**Law 31/2014 of December 3, 2014**
*State-owned and large private companies * Minimum of 40% women * Deadline: eight-year phase-in period (2015) * No minimum annual increases * Recommendation to use the expiration of male board members' mandate to appoint women *Prioritized in public tendering	* Listed companies * Target defined by companies * No deadline * No minimum annual increase * No recommendation on expiring mandates * Comply-or-explain

[a] Often referred to as "Conthe Code," [b] often referred to as "Rodríguez Code," [c] often referred to as "Albella Code"

as a minimum of 40% and a maximum of 60% for either sex. This law also required the government to observe the principle of gender balanced presence in the appointments of company boards where the state enjoys capital participation (Article 54). Monitoring is carried out in this case by the Ministry of Economy. As well, the Equality Law established that companies with over 250 employees and public administrations should adopt a gender action plan (Article 45), but monitoring mechanisms have only been set up for state-owned companies, which report to the Court of Auditors.

The assessment of the type of regulatory approach found in Spain in this initial phase suggests that it fell in between the high and intermediate positions of the comprehensiveness continuum; a specific target was set, but coverage was limited to the largest companies. Despite being a statutory measure, no sanction for non-compliance was established. Rather, the Equality Law defined a positive incentive for companies championing gender diversity, namely priority status for government contracts. All combined, Spain presents an intermediate coercion level.

Yet, from 2008 onward, the approach shifted toward a light coercion level. The central government adopted further laws and soft policies allowing companies to set their own targets of gender diversity. This second phase started with the PSOE government, which in the face of strong resistance from the business community against the statutory quota, gradually reinstated self-regulation. Measures such as the program Objective 15 were launched to instill a cultural change in companies and to help the latter find highly qualified women directors for their boards—it included a directory of female directors and actions to facilitate contact between these women and companies (González and Martínez, 2012).

Despite companies' disregard of the parity goal set by the Equality Law for 2015, with the PP government (2011–2018) the regulatory approach became even softer. The new law on capital firms (Act 31/2014, *Ley de Sociedades de Capital*) ignored the statutory quotas and instead recommended companies to adopt measures to increase women's presence in their boards, which is perplexing since the Equality Law is higher in rank—it is an organic law; Act 31/2014 leaves to company selection committees the definition of guidelines and the setting up of targets for the underrepresented sex. Firms shall report on their progress, following the principle of comply-or-explain. The move toward further self-regulation was coupled with the adoption of a new Unified Good Governance Code in 2015, known as the Rodríguez Code, which reflected business demands for minimal regulation. Its Recommendation 14 lowered the gender equality target to 30% women and extended the deadline until 2020 (CNMV, 2015). Furthermore, the requirement of transparency about the reasons and measures adopted by companies with few or no women on their boards was partially eliminated. Besides, gender diversity goals were clustered with other diversity issues (knowledge and experience).

Simultaneously, the framing of women's underrepresentation shifted back from demand to supply arguments, pointing at women's lack of training rather than at male dominance and gendered logic, in line with the business community's liberal and individually-centered ideology. Accordingly, the statewide Equal Opportunities Plan (2013–2016) promoted by the PP government established a "framework of collaboration" with companies that volunteer to meet a gender-balanced representation in their boards. This plan included measures such as women's training in management skills, the creation of networks of women in managerial positions, mentoring programs, and the exchange of best practices. The Objective 15 program was substituted in 2013 by the Promociona Project, a project managed by the central government women's agency, coordinated by the Spanish CEOE, and initially financed through the European Economic Area Norwegian Grants, and from 2016 onward, through the European Social Fund. It aimed at strengthening women's leadership skills and facilitating highly qualified women managers' access to decision-making positions in companies through mentoring and coaching. Between 2013 and 2017, according to official data, over 400 female executives and directors of 250 companies participated in this project.

Some businesswomen felt more empowered after the training (Interview, September 14, 2019). In 2015, the participants of the first two editions of this project created the Spanish Association of Female Executives and Board Members (Asociación Española de Ejecutivas y Consejeras, EJE&CON) intending to provide mentoring to female directors as well as engaging men in organizational change.[2,3] Additionally, the statewide women's agency set up a training program to develop the executive skills of women occupying intermediate-level decision-making positions.[4] The PP government also set up the initiative More Women, Better Companies, a public-private collaboration framework through which companies voluntarily subscribe to an agreement to increase in four years women's presence on boards and more generally on executive positions (Ministerio de Sanidad, Servicios Sociales e Igualdad, 2015, p. 30).

Implementation and Evaluation Practice: Poor Implementation of Statutory Quotas and Non-Compliance with the Gender Diversity Recommendation

While in 2006 three-fourths of the IBEX 35 companies had all-male boards, in 2016 just one firm did so. This notwithstanding, gender parity remains an elusive goal. Women's presence on the boards of the publicly listed companies augmented from 4.2% to 6.2% between 2004 and 2007, and from 2007 onward, the average annual increase was 1.7 percentage points. Unsurprisingly, the minimum target of 40% women on boards prescribed in the Equality Law failed to meet the deadline. In 2015, there were only 18.7% women among corporate members of the publicly listed companies (see Table 13.1). Only one out of the thirty-five publicly listed companies of IBEX 35 met the 40% target of the Equality Law, and five of them reached at least the 30% target of the 2015 Code (del Val Tolosana, 2015, pp. 32–33).

Failure to reach gender balance has increasingly caught up media attention, particularly due to the numerous reports produced by relevant private actors in this policy field like consultancy firms, business schools, and businesswomen's groups (see Atrevia-IESE, 2020; Observatori Dona, Empresa i Economia, 2016; ESADE, 2017; Informa, 2020; Talengo-APD, 2018). These reports, which use naming and

---

[2] The Comisión Nacional del Mercado de Valores is a supervisory agency ascribed to the Ministry of Economy. Its members are appointed by the central government.
[3] For more information, see: https://ejecon.org/ (Accessed May 5, 2018).
[4] Further information about this program can be found at: https://proyectopromociona.com/

shaming by issuing rankings of companies' performance, have had a remarkable coverage in both the generalist and economic press and tend to be issued on dates close to Women's International Day when more public attention is devoted to gender equality issues.

In 2020, just 12.9% of companies subject to Article 75 of the Equality Law had at least 40% women on their boards (Informa, 2020, p. 2). In 2020, women represented 27.4% of corporate members in publicly listed companies, a share below the EU 28 average (29.2%). In listed companies above 500 million euro revenue, boardrooms included 19.7% women, and in companies under that amount, female board members represented 16.7% (CNMV, 2018, p. 50). Given that the Equality Law provided incentives but defined no sanction, companies got away with non-compliance. Businesswomen that advocate quotas put it clearly: "The 'flexiquota' of the Equality Law, as we call it, didn't work. It only works if it's a hard quota with sanctions that hurt, that is, financial sanctions" (Interview, September 14, 2019).

State-owned firms or companies with state participation present a better performance, reaching 36.3% women in their corporate boards in 2018, as can be seen in Figure 13.1.

According to the Court of Auditors monitoring reports, in the period 2009–2013 only 15% of such companies complied with the statutory principle of gender balance on their boards while around thirty companies (over 20% of these companies) had all-male boardrooms (Tribunal de Cuentas, 2015, p. 53). These reports also monitored the approval of gender action plans by state-owned companies.

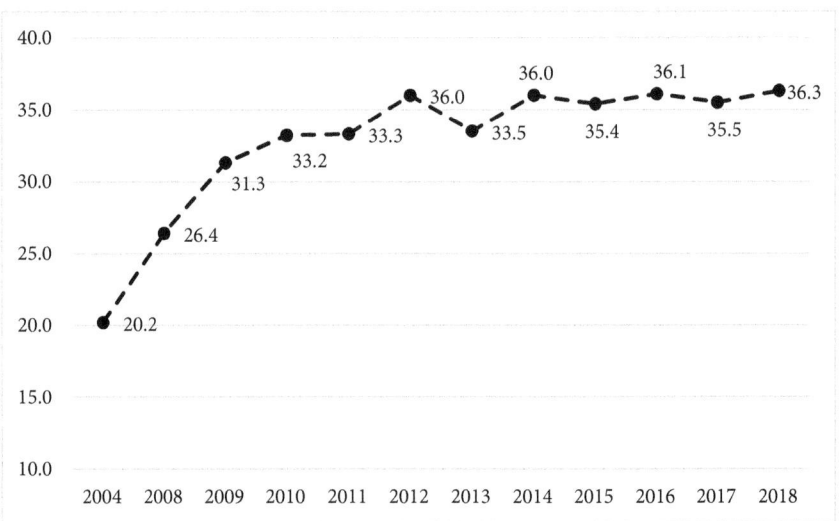

Fig. 13.1 Percentage Share of Women on Boards in Companies with State Participation in Spain, 2004–2018

Source: Own elaboration based on the reports of the Ministry of Finance (Ministerio de Economía y Hacienda) on the application of gender equality policies, years 2008–2016.

Out of the 206 companies that integrate the public business sector, fifty-three of them had adopted by 2013 a gender action plan—twenty-nine were obliged to do so because they employed over 250 workers, and the remaining twenty-four had voluntarily adopted such measures (Tribunal de Cuentas, 2015, p. 84). However, even after the adoption of 6/2019 Decree by the PSOE government establishing a public register of equality plans, by 2020, no register had been created and no supervisory body monitors the effective implementation of such plans yet.

The softer self-regulatory measures were also poorly implemented, as shown in the monitoring work of the CNMV, which reflects upon the annual reports publicly listed companies must submit in accordance with the comply-or-explain tool. The recommendation about gender diversity in board appointments is among the least followed recommendations of both the 2006 and the 2015 Code (CNMV, 2011). For example, in 2018, 66.4% of publicly listed companies complied with the gender diversity recommendation, nineteen percentage points less than the average compliance of the remaining recommendations of the Code (CNMV, 2018, p. 95).

All monitoring reports on the Conthe Code also highlight that "in most cases, the appointments and remunerations' committee does not report to the board of directors on gender diversity issues" (see e.g., CNMV, 2011, p. 71; CNMV, 2013, p. 62). Firms also get away with not explaining the reasons behind the non-compliance with the gender diversity recommendation (Velasco Gámez et al, 2010, p. 108). Companies simply state that there are no women or just a few women on the board and in the explanation box they claim that mechanisms for selecting board members have absolutely no biases that prevent the selection of women.[5] This systematic practice indicates light oversight (Tobías Oliarte, 2018, pp. 121–125). Indeed, it was not until 2018 that the CNMV started publishing an annual report on the presence of women board members in each of all the publicly listed companies, thereby deploying the "naming" strategy (CNMV, 2018).

The results of the Promociona Project on business cultural change are not impressive either. A survey of the female directors of the companies that have participated in this project reveals that only 15% of them confirm that their company must propose a minimum of female applicants when there is a vacancy and that in 14% of these companies, all-male boards are still found (ESADE, 2017, pp. 14–15). Likewise, a recent survey of Spanish firms with over 150 employees notes that only 23% of them allocate part of their budget to diversity, and 70% do not use indicators to assess their progress in this area (Talengo-APD, 2018).

[5] See the annual corporate governance report submitted by VIDACAIXA (2010), https://www.vidacaixa.es/uploads/files/07-informe-de-gobierno-corporativo-y-control-interno.pdf (Accessed April27, 2018);MAPFRE (2012), https://www.mapfre.com/corporativo-es/images/informe-anual-de-gobierno-corporativo-2012_tcm884-139133.pdf (Accessed April 27, 2018); and INDITEX (2012), http://static.inditex.com/annual_report/es/Desempeno/FGradodeseguimientodelasrecomend acionesdeGobiernoCorporativo.html (Accessed April 27, 2018).

Assessing Empowerment and Gender Transformation

Low Policy Empowerment

When considering policy implementation in relation to descriptive representation, lack of compliance with both the self-regulatory and statutory approaches and the lowering of the target for women's representation in corporate boards has resulted in a rather low level of women's empowerment. In terms of intersectionality, the voices represented were primarily those of white upper and middle-class women, and the diversity recommendation of the various self-regulation codes have explicitly targeted diversity of knowledge and experience, not of sociodemographic backgrounds other than gender. Furthermore, the increase in the share of female board members has been fundamentally stirred by the recommendation to increase the presence of independent board members (González and Martínez, 2012, p. 189). For example, while in 2006 42.3% of the twenty-six female board members were independent (CNMV, 2007), in 2020 this is the case of 75% of the ninety-three female board members (Atrevia-IESE, 2020, p. 27). Women's access to corporate boards has also occurred as family members. Also, the fact that one-fourth of female board members are foreign born (Atrevia-IESE, 2020, p. 33) suggests foreign companies are performing much better than Spanish ones, which may depend on the stronger regulatory frameworks of their countries of origin.

Moreover, newly appointed women are mostly assigned to less powerful positions as non-executive (independent) directors. These women are often accused of tokenism, although they typically have higher qualifications than their male peers in terms of financial educational background and international experience (González and Martínez, 2012, pp. 192–196). Consequently, decision-making positions remain male strongholds. Women's presence in 2020 as presidents (7.8%) or CEOs (2.9%) and in executive board positions (16.3%) is very low (see Table 13.1).

As regards substantive empowerment, on the one hand, no significant changes have been observed in work-life balance policies besides the already mentioned extension of paternity leave. Quite the contrary, the fiscal retrenchment enacted in Spain as a result of the global financial crisis has brought remarkable setbacks in social policy, such as cuts on the state support provided to people that care for a dependent relative, and reduced family subsidies (Lombardo, 2017). On the other hand, the new regulatory framework establishing corporate board quotas and gender action plans did not reach small and medium-sized companies, which represent about 99.9% of Spanish companies. Regional equality laws that sought to encourage smaller companies to adopt a gender action plan saw this provision appealed by the PP government before the Constitutional Court and subsequently suspended on the grounds that the unity of markets and the statewide legislation was infringed. Upon ousting the PP in 2018 through a no-confidence vote, the PSOE government sought to institute a hard quota, but the calling of new elections meant that the government could only legislate by decree, which can only include a few measures. Other more pressing priorities were prioritized, like making it mandatory for all companies with more than fifty employees to adopt a gender action plan by 2022 and publishing the registry of average salaries, a measure aimed at combating the gender pay gap (Interview, September 17, 2019).

Gender Accommodation and the Awakening of Businesswomen

The assessment of policy impact, societal, and gatekeeper change shows that gender accommodation describes in the Spanish case the effects of the implementation of the corporate gender quota framework. While the enacted policies have led to some change, traditional gender relations in the corporate world have been accommodated rather than transformed. Policy impact of the regulations aimed at feminizing corporate boards has been unquestionably low. In 2007, publicly traded firms and state-owned enterprises were given eight years to reach at least 40% women, but in 2015 women's descriptive representation achieved a scant 17% on the boards of publicly traded companies and 36.2% in state-owned firms. Positive incentives have not been able to stimulate organizational change and the absence of sanctions for non-compliance has rendered the Equality Law ineffective in this matter, especially in the private sector, wherein the leading business organizations keep vocally opposing gender quotas.

Despite the unsatisfactory outcomes, the central government furthered self-regulation, particularly from 2011 onward, in line with the neoliberal ideology of the PP, which weakened the gender equality target and extended the deadline to reach it. Spain thus took a step backward in the efforts aimed at promoting gender diversity on corporate boards. Leaving the solution of this issue to time and company voluntarism has clearly not worked. Companies have gotten away with non-compliance and with a lack of explanation for their poor performance. In January 2020 women's representation in boards of the publicly listed companies only reached 26.4%, thereby failing to reach the lowered target of 30% by 2020, not least because Act 31/2014 did not establish any monitoring of implementation (Interview, September 17, 2019).

Against this background of slow progress, in 2020, the CNMV sought to accelerate the feminization of boards. The new self-regulatory code adopted in June 2020 strengthened Recommendation 14 with the promotion of measures to increase the recruitment of women executives and included in Recommendation 15 the requisite of a minimum of 40% board members for the underrepresented sex to be met in 2022, which will be supervised with the "comply-or-explain" principle rather than with the "verify-and-inform" principle. In the public consultation period of the new draft, these two changes were the most disputed ones of the revised code (Osborne Clarke, 2020). After receiving multiple requests for a delay in the implementation of the 40% target, a two-year extension was granted, up to 2022. Business elites justified their request upon the alleged difficulty to capture talented female board members due to the COVID-19 crisis (Vélez, 2020).

Transformation at the societal level is relatively low. Over a decade after the introduction of quotas, most Spanish citizens still hold the opinion that capacities and merit should be the only recruitment criteria used by companies, as can be seen in Table 13.3. Yet, female citizens and left-wing voters (PSOE and Podemos) are more supportive of establishing a minimum presence for women than men and right-wing voters (PP and Ciudadanos).

This notwithstanding, recent signs of transformation among businesswomen have been observed. Surveys to senior executive women from small, medium, and big size companies conducted yearly by the human resources consulting firm Adecco on the effects on women employees of the implementation of Act 3/2007 reflect a substantial attitudinal change; while half of the senior executive women rejected quotas in 2007 (Adecco, 2010), the percentage had decreased to 32% in 2017 (Adecco, 2017). Besides, businesswomen's organizations from small and medium-size companies do now defend strong gender corporate quotas, as parliamentary debates of regional equality laws show.[6] For example, businesswomen from PIMEC (Petita i Mitjana Empresa de Catalunya) publicly advocate for statutory gender corporate quotas the only measure to effectively increase women's presence (Pietra, 2017). As one businesswoman claims: "Until 2017 businesswomen were against quotas, now you can talk about it, even the IBEX-35 businesswomen support them'"(Interview, September 14, 2019).

For its part, Isotes, a platform created in 2012 by a group of independent professional women to lobby for the attainment of the 30% target in 2020, has joined

Table 13.3 Views on Rationale for Women's Presence in Companies (in %)

Women's presence in companies should respond to...?	Men	Women	PP	Ciudadanos	PSOE	Podemos
Capacities and merit exclusively	66	51	66	67	49	54
Capacities and merit but reserving a minimum representation for women	34	49	33	31	49	45

Source: Metroscopia (2016).

[6] In the hearings before the Equality Committee of the Catalan Parliament during the drafting of the Catalan Equality Law businesswomen urged for the introduction of measures to make parity effective in corporate boards: https://www.parlament.cat/web/canal-parlament/sequencia/index.html?p_cp1=7420346 (Accessed June 15, 2019).

the public debate on gender quotas through the publication of studies, public presentations, and a platform for people to join the initiative.[7] Other businesswomen have engaged in concerted lobby activities to support a greater presence of women on companies' boards. For instance, in Barcelona, a network of businesswomen's organizations from different sectors has created the Association 50to50, aimed at achieving parity in boards and business associations. Its most outstanding initiative has been the presentation of women candidate lists to the elections of the Chamber of Commerce of Barcelona.[8]

In their public claims, businesswomen are recasting the prevailing notion of equality of opportunity within the business sector, challenging the myth that quotas undermine the quality of candidates, and demanding gender justice in the distribution of power (Interview, April 5, 2018). Years of poor implementation of equality measures in the business world and a period of massive feminist mobilizations (Jones, 2018) have contributed to enhancing businesswomen's awareness and empowering them to speak up. As the Director of the Observatori Dona, Empresa i Economia (2016), Anna Mercadé claimed that inequality in the business world is the result of "multifactorial obstacles" underpinning a "patriarchal society" (Sheleader, 2019).

Alliances between businesswomen and European and national women lawyers' associations have been established (Interview, September 14, 2019). Non-affiliated female shareholders have set up the initiative Parity in Action (Paridad en Acción), the Spanish branch of the action Women Shareholders Demand Gender Equality found in eleven European countries. This initiative was funded through the PROGRESS Program by former European Commissioner for Justice and Fundamental Rights, Viviane Reding, who drafted the directive bill on gender quotas in corporate boards. Businesswomen participating in this project strategically use the EU not only as a material but also as a legitimacy resource for their demands about gender equality in boards: "Viviane Reding supports us, she gave us 500.000 euros" (Interview September 14, 2019). Members of this project buy actions or ask shareholders that are sympathetic with the cause of equality to transfer them their right to participate in the board meeting of publicly listed companies. During the meetings, they provide data on the percentage of women on the board and ask for explanations, with the goal of putting gender equality on the companies' agendas and obliging them to discuss it with shareholders. Questions asked to the board of directors include: "How were board members appointed? How many women will be recruited in the next five years?" Activist speeches open as follows: "Do not misunderstand me, I didn't come here as a gender activist; I am here to protect my

[7] See http://www.isotes.org (accessed April 27, 2018).
[8] This organization groups together economic operators from all sectors of activity. See the website of this initiative: https://www.50a50.org/es/donde-hacemos-lobby (Accessed July 22, 2020).

own investment."[9] Making the business case for gender equality is thus used as a strategic framing to persuade businessmen of the legitimacy of quotas.

Even the statewide businesswomen's organizations aligned with the interests of big companies and with the Spanish Employer Association CEOE, which have traditionally advocated for measures addressing "supply"—lack of qualified aspirant women and the need to further work-life balance measures—rather than "demand"—gender biases of corporate selectorates (Bujaldón, 2017), like the Spanish Federation of Female Executives and Directives (FEDEPE), now sustain that companies "should be forced to commit with feminism's goals" and that quotas are "a necessary lever" to accelerate change, as claimed by its president, Ana Bujaldón (El Periódico, 2019). Some women CEOs from the largest corporations, like the president of the Banco Santander, Ana Botín, have also defended quotas as a means to overcome structural discrimination against women (Botín, 2018). However, most businesswomen from listed companies are still reluctant to fully support quotas in public, either due to a generational factor that makes them particularly conservative (Interview, September 14, 2019) or because they are a "captive of the organization [the CEOE] they represent" (Interview, September 17, 2019).

Conclusion

Spain has adopted a mixed approach to address the low presence of women in corporate boards, both regulatory, through legislated corporate gender quotas, and self-regulatory, through good governance corporate codes. The political will of the PSOE government and the role of state feminism were key factors in promoting progressive reforms. Yet, opposition by the business sector and the conservative PP led to an intermediate level of coercion, due to the absence of sanctions for non-compliance behavior in the Equality Law. Sustained resistance to gender quotas and lack of insider allies from within the business sector entailed that from 2008 onward, Spain progressively backslid into soft measures. As a result, gender quotas on corporate boards have been poorly implemented and their impact has been very moderate.

Policy empowerment has been equally low, both in descriptive and substantive terms. Intersectional interests represented were those of white upper-middle-class women. An overall assessment of policy impact along with societal and gatekeeper attitudinal change indicates that, rather than transforming traditional gender relations in the corporate world, the measures implemented have yielded "gender accommodation," maintaining male dominance in Spanish firms. However, the

---

[9] See http://www.paridad.eu/blog (accessed 27 April 2018).

poor results delivered by an increasing voluntarist approach have brought about a remarkable attitudinal change among businesswomen. Whereas male business elites and right-wing parties keep vocally opposing these quotas, disillusion with policy failure has triggered policy learning among businesswomen, favored by the multiplication of women's fora, especially at the initiative of businesswomen from small and medium-sized companies. While at the time of adoption of the Equality Law businesswomen had believed in the possibility of achieving equal representation in boards without regulation, policy learning has yielded an interest realignment that aims at reformulating and strengthening the regulatory framework. From opposing corporate gender quotas in the adoption phase and the early implementation phase, the majority of businesswomen now publicly defend them and have launched concerted lobby efforts to increase women's presence in boardrooms. Signs of gender transformation have finally emerged in the Spanish corporate world.

References

Adecco (2010) *IV encuesta Adecco a mujeres directivas*, https://www.adeccogroup.es/wp-content/uploads/notas-de-prensa/233.pdf (Accessed June 10, 2019).

Adecco (2017) *VII encuesta Adecco a mujeres directivas*, http://www.impulsando.es/impulsandodigital/el-782-de-las-directivas-espanolas-cree-que-sigue-habiendo-discriminacion-salarial-por-genero (Accessed May 5, 2018).

Atrevia-IESE (2020) *Mujeres en los consejos del IBEX-35*, https://landings.atrevia.com/wp-content/uploads/2020/03/Informe_Mujeres2020.pdf (Accessed June 8, 2020).

Botín, Ana (2018) "Por qué me considero feminista y tú también deberías," *El País*, August 19, https://elpais.com/economia/2018/08/19/actualidad/1534709488_687720.html (Accessed August 19, 2018).

Bujaldón, Ana (2017) "Interview with Ana Bujaldón," *Blog Canal CEO*, http://canalceo.com/entrevista-ana-bujaldon-fedepe/ (Accessed June 15, 2019).

CES (2006) *Dictamen sobre el anteproyecto de ley orgánica de igualdad entre mujeres y hombres*. Dictamen 8/2006. Madrid: Consejo Económico y Social.

CNMV (2006a) *Proyecto de Código Unificado de Recomendaciones sobre Buen Gobierno de las Sociedades Cotizadas*. January 18, 2006. Madrid/Barcelona: Comisión Nacional del Mercado de Valores.

CNMV (2006b) *Informe del Grupo Especial de Trabajo sobre Buen Gobierno de las Sociedades Cotizadas. Código Unificado de Buen Gobierno*. May 16, 2006. Madrid/Barcelona: Comisión Nacional del Mercado de Valores.

CNMV (2007) *Informe anual de Gobierno Corporativo de las compañías del IBEX-35. Ejercicio 2007*. Madrid/Barcelona: Comisión Nacional del Mercado de Valores.

CNMV (2011) *Informe anual de Gobierno Corporativo de las compañías del IBEX-35. Ejercicio 2011*. Madrid/Barcelona: Comisión Nacional del Mercado de Valores.

CNMV (2013) *Informe anual de Gobierno Corporativo de las compañías del IBEX-35. Ejercicio 2013*. Madrid/Barcelona: Comisión Nacional del Mercado de Valores.

CNMV (2015) *Código de buen gobierno de las sociedades cotizadas*. Madrid/Barcelona: Comisión Nacional del Mercado de Valores.

CNMV (2018) *Informe de Gobierno Corporativo de las entidades emisoras de valores admitidos a negociación en mercados secundarios oficiales. Ejercicio 2018*. Madrid/Barcelona: Comisión Nacional del Mercado de Valores.

CNMV (2020) *Código de buen gobierno de las sociedades cotizadas*. Madrid/Barcelona: Comisión Nacional del Mercado de Valores.

Comisión Mixta de los derechos de la Mujer y de la Igualdad de oportunidades (CM) (2006) "Comparecencias para informar en materia de igualdad efectiva entre mujeres y hombres," Sesiones 16-17-18. *Diario de Sesiones de las Cortes Generales*, 76-78-79. October 16, 24, 25.

Conde-Ruiz, José Ignacio and Carmen Hoya (2015) "Gender (in) Equality Act and large Spanish Corporations," *Policy Papers 2015/03, FEDEA*, https://ideas.repec.org/p/fda/fdapop/2015-03.html (Accessed July 1, 2020).

Congreso de los Diputados (2006) *Diario de sesiones del Congreso de los Diputados*, Núm. 225, December 21.

de Anca, Celia (2008) "Women on Corporate Boards of Directors in Spanish Listed Companies," in Susan Vinnicombe, Val Singh, Ronald J. Burke, Diana Bilimoria, and Morten Huse (eds) *Women on Corporate Boards of Directors*. Northampton, MA: Edward Elgar Publishing, pp. 96–107.

De la Fuente Sanz, Luis (2015) *Informe: Evolución de indicadores de buen gobierno de las empresas del IBEX 35 durante el ejercicio 2015*. Madrid: Fundación 1º de Mayo.

del Val Tolosana, Paloma (2015) *Ibex 35: Presencia femenina en los consejos e impacto del Código CNMV de 2015*, Asociación Española de Ejecutivas y Consejeras, EJE&CON, https://ejecon.org/wp-content/uploads/2016/01/docu-igualdad-de-genero-en-empresas-del-ibex.pdf (Accessed May 5, 2018).

EIGE (European Institute for Gender Equality) (2020) *Database on Women and Men in Decision Making*, https://eige.europa.eu/lt/gender-statistics/dgs/browse/wmidm (Accessed July 1, 2020).

El Periódico (2019) "Interview with Ana Bujaldón," *El Periódico*, March 23, https://byzness.elperiodico.com/es/noticias/economicos/20190323/mujeres-excelentes-igualdad-estereotipos-7361427 (Accessed July 1, 2020).

ESADE (2017) *II ESADE Gender Monitor. Equilibrio de género en las empresas*, http://itemsweb.esade.edu/wi/Prensa/ESADE_Gender_Monitor_2017.pdf (Accessed July 1, 2020).

Eurostat (2016) *Eurostat Labour Force Survey. Gender Pay Gap in Unadjusted Form*, https://ec.europa.eu/eurostat/tgm/table.do?tab=table&init=1&language=en&pcode=sdg_05_20&plugin=1 (Accessed July 1, 2020).

Fagan, Colette, Maria C. González, and Silvia Gómez (2012) *Women on Corporate Boards and in Top Management*. London: Palgrave Macmillan UK.

González, Maria C. and Lara Martínez (2012) "Spain on the Norwegian Pathway: Towards a Gender-Balanced Presence of Women on Corporate Boards," in Colette Fagan, Maria C. González, and Silvia Gómez (eds) *Women on Corporate Boards and in Top Management*. Basingstoke: Palgrave, pp. 169–197.

INE (2019) *Encuesta de población activa*, https://www.ine.es/ss/Satellite?L=es_ES&c=INEPublicacion_C&cid=1259924822888&p=1254735110672&pagename=ProductosYServicios%2FPYSLayout&param1=PYSDetalleGratuitas (Accessed July 1, 2020).

Informa (2020) *Presencia de las mujeres en la empresa española*, https://cdn.informa. es/sites/5c1a2fd74c7cb3612da076ea/content_entry5c5021510fa1c000c25b51f0/ 5e60dd402c76cd00b1dd529d/files/Mujeres_empresa2020_v1.pdf?1583406400 (Accessed June 7, 2020).

Jones, Sam (2018) "More than 5m Join Spain's 'Feminist Strike,' Unions Say," *The Guardian*, March 8, https://www.theguardian.com/world/2018/mar/08/spanish-women-give-up-work-for-a-day-in-first-feminist-strike (Accessed June 16, 2019).

León, Margarita (2007) "Towards the Individualization of Social Rights: Hidden Familialistic Practices in Spanish Social Policy," *South European Society and Politics*, 7 (3), pp. 53–80.

Lombardo, Emanuela (2017) "The Spanish Gender Regime in the EU Context: Changes and Struggles in the Wake of Austerity Policies," *Gender, Work & Organization*, 24 (1), pp. 20–33.

Mateos, Ruth, Ricardo Gimeno, and Lorenzo Escot (2010) "Discriminación en consejos de administración: análisis e implicaciones económicas," *Revista de Economía Aplicada*, 53 (XVIII), pp. 131–162.

Metroscopia (2016) *Actitudes y percepciones sobre la desigualdad de género en España*, http://metroscopia.org/discriminacion-positiva-pero-no/ (Accessed May 5, 2018).

Mills, Melinda, et al (2014) *Use of Childcare in the EU Member States and Progress towards the Barcelona Targets*. Santa Monica, CA: Rand.

Ministerio de Economía y Hacienda (2008) *Informe sobre la aplicación de políticas de igualdad. Ejercicio 2008*. Madrid: Ministerio de Economía y Hacienda.

Ministerio de Economía y Hacienda (2009) *Informe sobre la aplicación de políticas de igualdad. Ejercicio 2009*. Madrid: Ministerio de Economía y Hacienda.

Ministerio de Economía y Hacienda (2010) *Informe sobre la aplicación de políticas de igualdad. Ejercicio 2010*. Madrid: Ministerio de Economía y Hacienda.

Ministerio de Economía y Hacienda (2011) *Informe sobre la aplicación de políticas de igualdad. Ejercicio 2011*. Madrid: Ministerio de Economía y Hacienda.

Ministerio de Hacienda (2018) *Informe sobre la aplicación de políticas de igualdad. Ejercicio 2018*. Madrid: Ministerio de Hacienda.

Ministerio de Hacienda y Administraciones Públicas (2012) *Informe sobre la aplicación de políticas de igualdad. Ejercicio 2012*. Madrid: Ministerio de Hacienda y Administraciones Públicas.

Ministerio de Hacienda y Administraciones Públicas (2013) *Informe sobre la aplicación de políticas de igualdad. Ejercicio 2013*. Madrid: Ministerio de Hacienda y Administraciones Públicas.

Ministerio de Hacienda y Administraciones Públicas (2014) *Informe sobre la aplicación de políticas de igualdad. Ejercicio 2014*. Madrid: Ministerio de Hacienda y Administraciones Públicas.

Ministerio de Hacienda y Administraciones Públicas (2015) *Informe sobre la aplicación de políticas de igualdad. Ejercicio 2015*. Madrid: Ministerio de Hacienda y Administraciones Públicas.

Ministerio de Hacienda y Función Pública (2016) *Informe sobre la aplicación de políticas de igualdad. Ejercicio 2016*. Madrid: Ministerio de Hacienda y Función Pública.

Ministerio de Sanidad, Servicios Sociales e Igualdad (2015) *Informe intermedio de ejecución del Plan Estratégico de Igualdad de Oportunidades 2014–2016*. Madrid: Ministerio de Sanidad, Servicios Sociales e Igualdad.

Observatori Dona, Empresa i Economia (2016) *Dones en els consells d'administració de les empreses a Catalunya*, http://www.donaempresaeconomia.org/wp-content/uploads/2017/04/2016-12-Estudi-dones-conselleres_IV.pdf (Accessed July 1, 2020).

Osborne Clarke (2020) "Propuesta de modificación del Código de buen gobierno de las sociedades cotizadas," *Insights*, https://www.osborneclarke.com/es/insights/proposal-amend-good-governance-code-listed-companies/ (Accessed July 1, 2020).

Pietra, Iolanda (2017) "Llei de quotes per a la igualtat de gènere," *Blog PIME al dia*, https://www.pimealdia.org/llei-de-quotes-per-a-la-igualtat-de-genere (Accessed June 15, 2019).

Sheleader (2019) *Interview with Anna Mercadé*, March 21, http://beta.sheleader.eu/web/es/post/entrevista-anna-mercade-no-se-puede-detectar-solo-un-obstaculopara-avanzar-en-igualdad-la (Accessed March 26, 2019).

Talengo-APD (2018) *Diversidad e inclusión. El punto de vista del CEO*, https://www.apd.es/wp-content/uploads/sites/2/2018/01/estudio-de-diversidad-talengo-2018.pdf (Accessed May 5, 2018).

Tobías Olarte, Eva (2018) *Equilibrio de género en los consejos de administración de las empresas*. Cizur Menor: Thomson Reuters Aranzadi.

Tribunal de Cuentas (2015) *Informe de fiscalización de la ejecución de las distintas medidas destinadas a la racionalización y reordenación del sector público empresarial estatal no financiero, adoptadas en los ejercicios 2012 y 2013*. Madrid: Tribunal de Cuentas.

Velasco Gámez, M. del Mar, Raquel Puentes Poyatos, and Juan Vilar Hernández (2010) "El Código Unificado de Buen Gobierno: su nivel de seguimiento por empresas socialmente responsables," *Revista de Estudios Empresariales*, 2, pp. 99–113.

Vélez, Antonio (2020) "La CNMV aplaza dos años la recomendación de que las cotizadas alcancen un 40% de consejeras," elDiario.es, June 2, https://www.eldiario.es/economia/CNMV-recomendacion-cotizadas-alcancen-mujeres_0_1033796852.html (Accessed July 1, 2020).

Verge, Tània, and Emanuela Lombardo (2018) "Gender Quotas in Spain," in Eléonore Lépinardand Ruth Rubio-Marín (eds) *Transforming Gender Citizenship: The Irresistible Rise of Gender Quotas in Europe*. Cambridge: Cambridge University Press, pp. 126–155.

Verge, Tània, and Emanuela Lombardo (2019) "The Contentious Politics of Policy Failure: The Case of Corporate Board Gender Quotas in Spain," *Public Policy and Administration*, Epub, May 29. DOI: 10.1177/0952076719852407.

14

Mobilizing for Quotas Against All Odds

The Long Road to Corporate Equality in Germany

Petra Ahrens and Alexandra Scheele

Introduction

Despite strong horizontal and vertical labor-market segregation, women in the workforce, and blatant underrepresentation of women in economic decision-making positions, the issue of women on corporate boards remained off of the political agenda until the mid-1990s in Germany. While gender-equality laws for public administration were introduced in 1994 and 2001, legislating gender equality in private business was fiercely contested. Despite several legislative proposals since 2001, only the 2013 grand coalition of the Christian Conservative Party (CDU) and the Social Democrats (SPD) adopted a corporate gender-equality law. While the Equal Participation of Women and Men in Leadership Positions in the Private and Public Sectors Act was adopted in May 2015 and came into force on January 1, 2016, the majority of companies are not covered under the law, so the overall approach to gender equality on boards has been mixed. Why did it—despite a 1998 draft law—take so long to adopt a corporate quota law in Germany? Why was the law's coverage so limited? What have its results been in practice? One major factor, as we explain, was that two deeply entrenched blocks with opposing positions on the issue, with only minor shifts over the years, made any compromise virtually impossible. Given the many speed bumps in the road to a corporate-quota law that significantly slowed down the process and diluted the eventual content of the law, the outcome of 2015 led to uneven results in terms of actual gender equality in the corporate world in Germany.

After providing an overview of gendered labor market segregation and pertinent legislation, we analyze the "long road" to the corporate-quota law due to the stalemate between business and women's interests that produced an only moderately authoritative law. The formal content and instruments provided by the law are examined in the next section followed by the analysis of the practice of putting the law into action after 2016. In the last part of the chapter, we assess the mixed

Petra Ahrens and Alexandra Scheele, *Mobilizing for Quotas Against All Odds*. In: *Gender Equality and Policy Implementation in the Corporate World*. Edited by Isabelle Engeli and Amy G. Mazur, Oxford University Press.
© Oxford University Press (2022). DOI: 10.1093/oso/9780198865216.003.0014

results of the quota legislation. While the corporate world has complied with the minimal requirements of the law, it has proved neither effective in increasing the number of women on supervisory boards, nor tackling gender inequalities on the labor market in a broader sense.

Persistent Gender Inequality in the German Corporate World

Germany is the largest European Union (EU) economy. Characterized as a conservative and strongly "corporatist" welfare state (Esping-Andersen, 1990) with a strong male breadwinner model (Lewis, 2001), Germany's traditional family structures have changed only slowly since reunification in 1990 (Lang, 2017). Despite significant welfare and labor-market reforms, the conservative foundation of the West German welfare state continued to shape gender-equality policies after unification. The former Federal Republic of Germany only partly modernized into a second-earner model (Leitner, 2013), and the ideological framing of mothers as the main caretakers, unavailable for the labor market persists (Peukert, 2012). Building on its legacy, the former German Democratic Republic, however, featured an adult-worker model with equal labor-market integration for men and women (Lewis, 2001; Auth et al., 2015).

The persistent gender-biased norms maintained the vertical and horizontal segregation of Germany's labor market in terms of gender, including on corporate boards. Until 2010, women's share on boards stagnated below 15%, while the EU average increased steadily as shown by Table 14.1. Women are also underrepresented in public- and private-sector leadership positions, and even more on the executive and supervisory boards of larger companies.

In 2018, the share of women at the top management level in 15,500[1] companies in Germany was 36%. The size of the company impacts women's chances of being in a leadership position; in the smallest companies (up to nine employees), women have a share of 44% of corporate boards, in the largest companies (>500 employees) only 28% (Kohaut and Möller, 2019). In 2018, only 9% women sat on executive boards and 26.9% on supervisory boards in Germany's top 200 private companies (not counting the financial sector) (Holst and Wrohlich, 2019, p. 19). Government-owned companies had a share of 17.9% of women on their executive boards and 30.6% on supervisory boards, and for boards in public administration, women member's share ranged from 13% to 35% in regional state authorities and was at 33% in federal authorities (BMFSFJ, 2017).

---

[1] Since 1993, the Germany Institute for Labour Market Research (IAB) carries out an annual representative survey (IAB Betriebspanel) of 15,500 companies in different sectors and of different sizes; thus, the label 15,500. Since 2004, these companies have been asked about women in management positions (Kohaut and Möller, 2019).

Table 14.1 Percentage Share of Women on Boards in the Largest Listed Companies in Germany, 2004–2020

	EU-28 Board members	GERMANY				
		Board members	President	CEO	Executives	Non-executives
2004	9	11.7	0.0	—	—	—
2005	9.8	12.2	0.0	—	—	—
2006	9.7	11.2	0.0	—	—	—
2007	10.4	11.3	0.0	—	—	—
2008	10.8	13.3	0.0	—	—	—
2009	11	12.9	0.0	—	—	—
2010	11.9	12.6	0.0	—	—	—
2011	13.7	15.2	0.0	—	—	—
2012	15.8	17.9	0.0	0.0	7.2	17.9
2013	17.8	21.5	0.0	0.0	7.9	21.5
2014	20.2	24.4	3.3	0.0	7.0	24.4
2015	22.7	26.1	3.3	0.0	8.4	26.1
2016	23.9	29.5	3.3	0.0	10.6	29.5
2017	25.3	31.9	3.3	0.0	13.4	31.9
2018	26.7	33.8	3.3	0.0	13.8	33.8
2019	28.8	35.6	3.4	3.4	14.2	35.6
2020	29.2	36.1	3.4	3.4	14.5	36.1

Source: EIGE Database.

Moreover, Germany regulates different company types[2] (independent of turnover and employee numbers) through different laws, which impedes a simple quota solution. The 736,000 corporations that are either stock corporations (Aktiengesellschaften/AG)[3] or private limited companies (Gesellschaften mit beschränkter Haftung/GmbH) are regulated differently, the former through the 1965 Stock Corporation Act (SCA; Aktiengesetz) and the latter through the 1892 Limited Liability Companies Act (ACLL; GmbH-Gesetz). SCA companies have a two-tier board system with a separate executive and supervisory board (the latter electing the former), whereas GmbHs are only obliged to have boards under certain conditions. Board rules are connected with laws originating from institutionalized wage bargaining between trade unions and employer associations (Waas, 2014, pp. 135–137). Two co-determination acts regulate work councils and supervisory boards. The Coal and Steel Co-determination Act of 1951 and its supplementary Act of 1956 regulate employee representation on supervisory boards of

---

[2] Germany had 3,483,691 corporations in 2018—2,146,043 sole proprietors; 395,415 business partnerships, 736,279 incorporated companies, 205,954 unspecified companies. Sources: https://www.destatis.de/DE/Themen/Branchen-Unternehmen/Unternehmen/Unternehmensregister/Tabellen/unternehmen-rechtsformen-wz08.html?view=main%5BPrint%5D.

[3] Only AGs can be listed and traded on the stock exchange.

corporate groups and enterprises with more than 1,000 employees. The 1976 Co-determination Act law stipulates equal representation of workers and shareholder representatives in all incorporated firms in commerce, trade, and services with more than 2,000 employees. Trade union members, usually representing workers, are elected for almost half of the supervisory board (12–20 members) regardless of their legal type (Müller-Jentsch, 1997; Waas, 2014).

The Works Constitution Act (first adopted in 1952 and heavily reformed in 1972), in turn, allows the election of four-year-term works councils on the initiative of employees (supported by trade unions) in companies with more than five employees. In 2001, the act was amended again, including Section 15 on a gender quota: "The gender that accounts for a minority of staff shall at least be represented according to its relative numerical strength whenever the works council consist of three or more members" (BMAS, 2018). With this reform, the state for the first time intervened in private companies to improve women's representation in works councils, a relevant actor in operational procedures. While law introduced gender equality principles into business decision-making structures through works councils, but not the decision-making boards, it was limited, given that women are still underrepresented in works councils; only in enterprises with fewer than 30% women employees does their share exceed that among all employees. In this multi-tiered system, the number of employees becomes important; about 9,880 incorporated companies have 250 or more employees (around 530,852 up to 9, another 195,000 about 10 to 249). Regardless of their number, however, no firm is obliged to have a works council. Hence, the majority (those with the highest percentage of women employees) is not obliged to have worker representatives, who could potentially elect women, on the supervisory board.[4]

Promoting corporate gender quotas was not a salient issue for German politics and its core actors until the mid-1990s (Müller, 2019; Ferree, 2012; Lang, 2017). The main actors involved in the German board-quota debate originally split into three blocks: opponents (employers' associations, CDU/CSU, the liberal Party Freie Demokratische Partei (FDP), conservative newspapers), proponents (SPD, Left Party, Greens, women's organizations and associations, liberal newspapers), and indifferent (trade unions, single companies). The proponent position remained relatively stable over time with changes happening on the side of opponents and indifferent actors who slowly changed their position, a crucial shift that paved the way to adopting the Equal Participation of Women and Men in Leadership Positions in the Private and Public Sectors Act in 2015.

---

[4] Source:https://www.destatis.de/DE/Themen/Branchen-Unternehmen/Unternehmen/ Unternehmensregister/Tabellen/unternehmen-rechtsformen-wz08.html?view=main%5BPrint%5D

1990 to 2001: Constitutional Change and a Toothless Paper Tiger

With the East German legacy featuring gender equality more prominently, German unification opened a window of opportunity (Ferree, 2012; Lang, 2017). The unification treaty from August 31, 1990, contained two paragraphs in Article 31, which asked the legislator to revise the German Basic Law regarding equal opportunities for women and men, as well as the improvement of the reconciliation of paid work and family duties. When the constitutional commission was founded on January 16, 2002, a women's alliance across all party groups pressured it to include state responsibility for equal opportunities in the new constitution. They were successful, and the revised 1994 constitution obliged the state to actively promote equality by adding the clause "promoting equality between women and men to Article 3" (Schultz, 2003). In addition, women's organizations from East and West Germany jointly organized a women's strike in Germany on International Women's Day, March 8, 1994. More than one million women demonstrated for equal pay and against violence against women, but the women's strike did not receive much attention (Schmollack, 2014). Women also organized themselves within the political parties to demand party quotas and an equal representation of women in politics as well as in federal bodies. The first German quota law prescribing 40% women in all federal bodies was the Appointments to Federal Bodies Act (Bundesgremienbesetzungsgesetz) adopted in 1994. SPD-Green governed German states (Bundesländer) adopted equality laws for public administration, stipulating preferential treatment of women when underrepresented on the next management level up (Berghahn, 2012). Moreover, the Green Party and the SPD adopted voluntary party quotas in the mid-1980s (Ahrens et al., 2020).

Interestingly, corporate equality only slowly gained attention; as late as 1996, an association of companies, trade unions, academia, and ministries—TOTAL E-QUALITY Deutschland e.V.—started awarding prizes to private and public (universities, administrations, associations) organizations for successfully implementing gender equality in human-resource and organization policies.[5] Gaining a positive reputation over time and still active today, the award continuously reminded political parties of corporate gender-equality issues.

The first SPD-Green coalition (1998–2002) formulated the goal of "decisively advancing women's equality in work and society" in their coalition agreement and proposed legislating corporate board quotas as one important element (Müller, 2019). Christine Bergmann, the then-new SPD Minister for Family, Senior Citizens, Women, and Youth pursued an ambitious gender-equality agenda that included tackling inequalities in the corporate world and public administration.

---

[5] Details on the award procedure and winners is available at https://www.total-e-quality.de/ (accessed September 4, 2020).

Building on her previous innovative practices as a Berlin senator, in 1999 she summoned a "consensus group"—unusual for German politics back then—with government, academic, and social partner representatives to collect input and forge broad support for a corporate-equality law. The discussions fed into an all-women expert group designing a draft law (Interview (INT)-1; Pfarr, 2001).

The main target of the draft law was to fundamentally transform gender relations in the corporate world, with board quotas as one element (INT-1). The minister and the consensus group contended that voluntary regulations were too slow in effecting substantial change and ineffective in avoiding indirect discrimination and transforming gendered patterns. CDU, FDP, and major employer associations like the Confederation of German Employers Associations (BDA) and the Federation of German Industries (BDI) opposed the law, stating that "only merit matters" for leadership positions and concordantly claiming a lack of qualified women. The opposing camps entered a long-term stalemate circulating around three legal debates.

The first concerns "freedom of property" where opponents saw a quota law endangering (individual) property and earning prospects, proponents pointed to the limitation of property rights arising from social considerations—a position supported by an earlier court judgment on co-determination (Waas, 2014, pp. 141–142). In the second debate, opponents claimed, on one hand, that a quota law violates "freedom of association" by constraining a company's internal organization and limiting the possibilities of trade unions and employer associations to propose preferred candidates. Supporters, on the other hand, emphasized that co-determination was not a constitutional right but simply a legal right that thus allowed legislators to regulate companies (Waas, 2014, pp. 142–144). Third, when it came to the constitutional "equality before the law," opponents rejected that any discrimination of women on boards existed and legal positive measures would be too excessive, yet proponents insisted on the extended constitutional mandate to promote actual gender equality with a quota law as a proportional measure, since voluntary agreements had proven insufficient (Waas, 2014, pp. 144–146).

The power relations around the three legal debates developed to the disadvantage of the proposed law. Employer associations and companies steadily opposed strict regulation by referring to company autonomy and property rights. This coincided with high unemployment rates, pressuring the SPD-Green government to prioritize the Federal Equality Act and the Works Constitution Act, which were of bigger importance to the SPD party leadership and trade unions. The biggest umbrella women's organization, the National Council of German Women's Organizations (DFR), upheld strong ties to the Women's Ministry and started a nationwide campaign on the proposed law to secure a minimal degree of consent—any kind of legislated quota. Yet, the campaign failed, due to lacking broader civil-society and cross-party support (including the Green coalition partner), weak trade union interest in promoting corporate gender equality, and a still stable societal support of the dominating West German male breadwinner model (INT-1). Then chancellor Gerhard Schröder, with strong ties to the corporate lobby and famous for labeling gender-equality policy as "Gedöns" (useless hoo-ha), yielded to pressure from quota opponents, not least due to their disappointment with other new laws such as the Works Constitution Act (INT-1; Pfarr, 2001). In 2001, thanks to their strong connection with the chancellor, corporate opposition succeeded in turning the proposed law into a paper tiger, the Voluntary Agreement between the Federal Government and the Umbrella Organizations of the Private Economy on Promoting Equal Opportunities for Women and Men in the Private Economy (Vereinbarung zur Förderung der Chancengleichheit von Frauen und Männern in der Privatwirtschaft). Despite new legislation promoting gender equality in the public sector, private economy legislation was thus stopped halfway and would only produce paper reports and, hence, did not transform any numbers or structural inequalities. Still, the agreement signed by government actors as well as employer association representatives did contain the later oft-mobilized argument for the quota law; the potential of qualified women should be better used to meet the challenges of global competition (Müller, 2019).

2001 to 2008: Feeding the Paper Tiger and a Superficial Public Debate

With the failed proposal replaced by a voluntary agreement, public corporate-equality debates faded away. Although the German Women Lawyers Association (Deutscher Juristinnenbund, or djb, intentionally styled in lowercase) dissected each obligatory evaluation report (Bundesregierung Deutschland, 2003; 2006) and showed that the agreement was the expected paper tiger, especially since the share of women remained low (Brader and Lewerenz, 2006), they created only short-term media attention for the continuing underrepresentation of women on boards. Given their close ties to the corporate world, the 2005 CDU-SPD coalition opposed a law, prioritizing family policies instead of pursuing a broader gender-equality policy (Henninger and von Wahl, 2014; Lang, 2017). Its Women's Minister, Ursula von der Leyen, claimed: "It's illusionary to believe laws to be cure-alls," and "the era of quotas is long gone" (Schuler, Schwarze, and Caspari, 2015). Concomitantly, the unpopular effects of social security system changes adopted by SPD-Greens in 2002 and 2003 (Wunsch, 2005) caused public uproar and suppressed any other labor market issues.

In the following years, quota opponents maintained their opposition to a law, yet shifted slowly from opposing any regulation to discussing which rules could reconcile ensuring company autonomy in selecting board members with the broad diversity of companies (both in terms of size, and whether the sector is female or male dominated). Supporters switched their focus from guaranteeing equal representation and transforming gendered patterns as fundamental goals, to emphasizing the overly slow voluntary change and how economic performance would improve through corporate equality, the latter being accepted by some employer associations (Hericks, 2011).

The 2003 Norwegian quota law (re)activated quota advocates in parties and women's organizations. In 2005, Green Party members initiated an online platform registering women available for supervisory boards: Women on Boards (aufsichtsraetinnen.de). The platform and related events resulted in the creation of the association, FidAR e.V.—Frauen in die Aufsichtsräte ([Bring] Women into Supervisory Boards), with many women entrepreneurs as members. They capitalized on the poor performance of the voluntary agreement, which had brought no change in numbers, to call for the introduction of a quota law similar to the Norwegian one (FidAR, 2016). In 2007, FidAR received broad media coverage in response to a statement of the president of the government commission on the German Corporate Governance Code, who had declared, "You know, ladies, supervisory boards are not coffee-klatch gossip!" (Gerhard Cromme cited in FidAR 2016, p. 8; translation by authors). Shortly after, the Green Party (in parliamentary opposition at the time) submitted a motion for quotas for listed companies in 2007 (DS 16/5279), followed up by a public hearing in the law committee of the Bundestag in 2008. The CDU-SPD government, supported by the FDP, used its majority to reject the proposal.

2008 to 2015: Igniting Public Debates and Forging a Minimal Compromise

Evaluation reports (Bundesregierung Deutschland, 2008; 2011; 2013) proved that the voluntary agreement was the suspected paper tiger (Henninger and von Wahl, 2014). Frustrated by the gridlock and the stagnation in numbers, the djb founded in 2009 the Alliance of Female Shareholders, which demanded a 40% corporate board quota. They received broad media attention by attending annual shareholder meetings of listed companies—after buying stocks—and asking about the underrepresentation of women on their boards.

In 2008, the association, Success Factor WOMEN (Erfolgsfaktor FRAU), formed a cross-party and societal-group alliance and issued the Nuremberg Resolution that pledged a 40% board-quota law similar to Norway's. With this combined civil society mobilization and the SPD no longer in government, the Greens and the Left party relaunched the parliamentary debate. In 2010, Deutsche Telekom voluntarily adopted a 30% quota for women in management; others followed with 15–22% self-imposed obligations (Henninger and von Wahl, 2014). These mobilizations of parties and companies coincided with voices from women's organizations blaming the economic and financial crisis on the homogenously male and un-diverse leadership of companies. As a result, public opinion started to lean toward board-quota support. Calls by women's organizations and gender experts to end risk-driven, male-dominated economic behavior and counter it by bringing women onto boards were taken on in newspapers and public debates, though it should be noted that this argument was based on essentialist gender stereotypes (Annesley and Scheele, 2011). From 2010 onward, the public debate only concentrated on executive and supervisory board positions, although vertical segregation existed across all sectors and employment positions. According to a ministerial representative, it was deemed more promising to mobilize around the absence of women in highly visible positions than to challenge gender inequality caused by the structure of the labor market (INT-3).

The 2008 Nuremberg Resolution led women MPs of all parties to launch a coalition with leading women's organizations: the Association of German Female Entrepreneurs, djb, European Business and Professional Women, European Women's Management Development, FidAR, and the German Rural Women's Association. In June 2011, this coalition petitioned parliament to pass a draft bill by the Green Party for "the gender-equitable occupation of supervisory boards"—40% for supervisory boards of companies with more than 500 employees (DS 17/3296). Shortly after and accompanied by huge media attention, the coalition signed the Berlin Declaration, containing a similar proposal, and presented it to the Minister of Women's Affairs. More than 22,500 people and organizations signed the declaration, among them many well-known women politicians (including the then-Vice-President of the EU Commision Vivian Reding), professors, journalists, sportswomen, and women from the cultural sector. Major (liberal) newspapers like *Süddeutsche Zeitung* and *Die Zeit* published articles in favor of quotas. The EU's proposed board-quota directive in 2012 (immediately threatened with a veto by the German government) added to broader mobilization and media attention, but employers' associations still opposed any proposal pointing to company autonomy rights.

Quota law activists received positive public attention in the media and from the parliamentary opposition (SPD, Greens, Left), while considerable decreases in unemployment and constant complaints of a shortage of qualified women due to their unequal opportunities made the blatant underrepresentation of women on boards appear unjustifiable even for the CDU/FDP government (Henninger and von Wahl, 2014; 2018; Lang, 2017). The government started approaching major opponents, including the thirty largest companies that make up Germany's DAX stock index, to tackle women's underrepresentation by means of their choice and thus avoid legislation. In March 2011, the companies promised to set targets for women's representation below board level in the context of implementing the German Governance Code from 2010 and its diversity recommendations, and most DAX companies also adopted supervisory board targets: twenty-one set it at 20–30%, and seven at 30% or more (Waas, 2014, p. 132). With the election of the 2013 CDU-SPD coalition, the government finally committed to adopting a corporate-board quota law and the two SPD-led ministries, Justice and Women's Affairs, started drafting it soon after the election.

The Self-regulatory Approach: Evasive Actions on the Long Road to a Corporate Gender Quota

Aside from government-led legislation, the German political system offers its political actors additional access points for legislative proposals and flexibility in proposing alternative regulations. The decision-making process for the corporate gender quota presents an illuminating case when it comes to evasive actions. It included several failed legislative proposals with content similar to public and political discussions. Despite being part of the SPD-Green coalition agreement, then-Chancellor Gerhard Schröder stopped the first attempt, the 2001 Equality Act for the Private Economy. The voluntary agreement replacing the draft law was a complete implementation failure (Bundesregierung Deutschland, 2003; 2006; 2008; 2011; 2013). The 2009 CDU-FDP coalition agreement only stipulated self-regulation, which entailed voluntary monitoring and company initiative. The then-CDU Women's Affairs Minister, Kristina Schröder, labeled it a "flexi-quota" and made it immediately clear she had no ambition to propose a law (Henninger and von Wahl, 2014). This complied with the company-friendly CDU-FDP position aiming to limit regulatory approaches in gender equality. They argued that due to the different shares of women among employees it would be unjustified to apply the same targets to different companies as they would have different chances to recruit women board members. Though they had no chance of success due to their low number of seats, the Green Party symbolically countered the government's inactivity by tabling a draft Act on Gender-Equal Occupation of Supervisory Boards in October 2010. They proposed embedding a 40% minimum quota for each sex in existing corporate laws, the 2004 One-Third Participation Act, and the 1976 Co-determination Act; quota failure would result in nullifying all board decisions (Waas, 2014, p. 138).

Surprisingly, the then-CDU Minister for Employment, Ursula von der Leyen, reacted to the Green initiative in early 2011 and suggested a 30% board quota. In the aftermath of the economic crisis, she framed enhanced women's representation as a tool of improving corporate decision-making and limiting the hazardous male corporate culture (Henninger and von Wahl, 2014; Kappert, 2011). The Minister's change of mind was also underpinned by a study commissioned by the Ministry for Women's and Family Affairs on women and leadership (Wippermann, 2010), plus the fact that even the Corporate Governance Codex in 2009 included a recommendation on diversity in supervisory boards (INT-3). The latter argued that a quantifiable measure (quota) could be more effective than vague regulation to reach the goal within a reasonable timeframe (INT-3). At this time, Chancellor Angela Merkel rejected the proposal under pressure from employer associations. In October 2012, the SPD, supported by the Greens, submitted a quota law to parliament, and shortly afterward the SPD-Greens government of the most populous Bundesland, North Rhine-Westphalia, submitted a similar one to the Federal Council (representation of the sixteen Bundesländer) (Henninger and von Wahl, 2014; Lang, 2017). Both proposals foresaw a phased system and sanctions: initially a 30% quota for supervisory and a 20% quota for executive boards, both increased to 40% after five years; quota failure would leave seats unfilled, with board decisions invalid after a one-year waiting period (Waas, 2014, pp. 138–139). Both were turned down by the CDU-FDP majority, pressured by employers' associations, and unsure of public support (Henninger and von Wahl, 2014).

2013's CDU-SPD coalition, however, agreed upon introducing a board-quota law, not least because SPD leadership feared that party members would otherwise reject government participation (Waas, 2014, p. 141). Also, women's organizations and civil-society actors pressed the government to honor its promise to turn to legislation if the voluntary agreement remained ineffective. In public debates and media coverage, board quotas were defended as the only effective measure to tackle the significant underrepresentation of women in decision-making positions. Companies and employer associations lobbied the government to forego legislation. The government ultimately reconciled the contrary positions in a law legislating some quota but not covering the full scope.

In January 2015, Minister for Women's Affairs, Manuela Schwesig, and Minister for Justice, Heiko Maas, (both SPD) presented a draft law already approved by the cabinet to be passed by parliament and the Federal Council. The draft law contained the different logics from the actors involved; the Justice Ministry, for instance, excluded executive boards, because they are often family-based and small, so obligations were said to conflict with property rights, which were considered constitutionally higher (INT-2). When it came to setting the quota percentage, Schwesig insisted on reaching critical mass, which she considered 30%, although both ministries were pressured hard to adopt a lower target (INT-2). Also, a clear immediate target with an acceptable horizon to reach it successfully was considered more appropriate than the Norwegian fixed-date solution (INT-2). Overall, the draft to a large extent resembled the 2000 legislative proposal by Christine Bergman. Although the majority of men CDU MPs[6] and employer associations mobilized against it, on May 1, 2015 parliament finally adopted the Equal Participation of Women and Men in Leadership Positions in the Private and Public Sectors Act. Immediately in force yet requiring compliance only from January 1, 2016, onward, the law was a disappointing end of the long road for advocates of authoritative quotas.

---

[6] CDU women MPs were part of the cross-party alliance supporting the law.

From Self-regulation to a Mixed Approach

Thus, in 2016, Germany moved from a self-regulation approach to a multi-tiered mixed approach to gender equality on corporate boards, the general contours of which are presented in Table 14.2.

From January 1, 2016, on, publicly traded companies with more than 2,000 employees (currently 106 companies) had to comply with a 30% quota for the underrepresented sex on their supervisory board. These companies must fill vacant board positions with the underrepresented sex until they reach the minimum of 30%. The regulation is less constraining for companies with a smaller workforce. If

Table 14.2 Measures for Gender Equality on Corporate Boards in Germany

SELF-REGULATION	
Voluntary Agreement 2001[a]	**German Corporate Governance Code 2010**
* Improve the reconciliation of work and family life through effective policies at company level	* Listed companies
	* To consider diversity and women's representation in corporate boards
* Companies to develop effective equal opportunities and family-friendly employment measures	* To set targets for diversity and women's representation on boards
* Companies to identify good practices	
* Further education should be improved	
* Evaluation of company measures every two years (five reports between 2003 and 2013)	

STATE REGULATION	
Act on Equal Participation of Women and Men in Leadership Positions of March 6, 2015[b]	**Federal Act on Gender Equality of April 24, 2015[c]**
* Publicly traded companies with more than 2,000 employees: 30% quota for the underrepresented sex on their supervisory board	* Government and government agencies
	* 50% of women
	* Deadline: 30% in 2015, 50% in 2018
* Companies with less than 2,000 employees but more than 500 to set their own targets for the underrepresented sex on the supervisory board, the executive board, and the two management levels below the executive board (self-regulation within the legislation)	* Each agency to design an Equality Plan for four years in each case
	* Federal Government to submit every four years a report to the German Bundestag on the situation of women and men in the agencies

[a] Voluntary agreement between the Federal Government and the Umbrella Organizations of the Private Economy on Promoting Equal Opportunities for Women and Men in the Private Economy; [b] Act on Equal Participation of Women and Men in Leadership Positions in the Public and Private Sector, also referred to as "FüPoG I"; [c] Act on Equality between Women and Men in the Federal Administration and Federal Enterprises and Courts also referred to as "BgleiG."

they are listed on the stock exchange or subject to public-private co-determination, companies with fewer than 2,000 but more than 500 employees are not subject to the obligatory 30% quota. Instead, they were required to set their own targets for the underrepresented sex on their supervisory board, executive board, and the two management levels below the executive board. Any target below the status quo at the time the law entered into force was forbidden. Thus, these companies could set a target equal to, or higher than, the status quo, or—if the share of women was already higher than 30%—they could adopt a lower target, as long as it was higher than 30%. Targets had to be set by September 30, 2015, with June 30, 2017, as the deadline to reach the target.[7] All other types of companies followed the self-regulatory path; companies decide if quotas would be followed at all and the level of the quota target to be pursued.

All in all, the quota legislation only applies to the supervisory boards of some companies, not to their executive boards or other leadership positions; these are self-regulated (if at all). Therefore, the law is unambitious, neglecting the structural and intersectional problems women face in entering decision-making positions (the career disadvantages for part-time employees, care breaks, not to mention male chauvinism, etc.). In terms of the GEPP indicators, the law can be placed between intermediate and high comprehensiveness: only supervisory boards, certain company types and sizes, a specific target (30%), and the strict empty-seat sanction mechanism (INT-2). The latter stipulates that any board election is invalid when the 30% quota is not met, as the vacant position cannot be filled by the board's decision-making procedures, and majorities could be affected. It is automatically implemented via a court procedure. For the self-set targets, there is a potential sanction mechanism connected to the obligatory annual corporate governance statement companies have to submit. Failing to deliver that annual declaration can mean fines to the business. In recurring or more egregious cases of non-compliance, the individuals responsible for the decision can be subject to a maximum of three-year imprisonment. Yet, this solely applies to the complete statement; companies simply have to mention that they have set targets but do not have to report if and how they go there.

With these important details in mind, Germany has a full coercion strategy within the scope of coverage: restrictive regulation, obligatory monitoring and reporting, and sanctions. The Women's Affairs Ministry enforces the law, monitors it annually, and publishes a report with the support of a data-analysis agency, the Bundesanzeiger Verlag GmbH. The ministry allocated a specific implementation budget in the annual ministerial budget, comprising a new ministerial unit, multi-tiered monitoring, and FidARs Women-on-Board-Index 185 (FidAR, 2018;

---

[7] After 2017, companies have five years to reach the next self-set target.

INT-2).[8] The law obliges companies to report on the quota in their obligatory annual corporate governance declaration to avoid additional and separate reporting
(INT-2). The Bundesanzeiger screens and actually reads every single company report to collect the data (INT-2).[9] Additionally, FidAR receives a ministerial budget
to monitor and rank 160 selected public traded companies, plus twenty-five other
companies subject to the law. They collect data available on the internet, ask companies to confirm the data, and survey them on additional aspects such as the
next board election date. Their monitoring compares targets, changes, supervisory
board elections, and the number of women lacking for shareholder and employee
representatives to reach the 30% quota (FidAR, 2018). Ministerial monitoring is
publicly available (as is the one by FidAR), presented annually in a press conference, in parliament, and via a parliamentary report. This monitoring only concerns
numbers of women and ignores which women (and men) are present in terms of
intersectional considerations such as ethnicity, age, disability, and the like.

Meticulous, but Unambitious Corporate Implementation

Large companies have to implement the law by appointing the "underrepresented
sex"—in other words, women—for every vacant supervisory board seat until the
30% quota is met. The empty-seat sanction is effective and might shift some power
in the supervisory board in favor of employee representatives because they usually fulfill the quota (Hansch, Haag, and Rode, 2016; INT-2).[10] Criticizing the fact
that if employee representatives raise women's share to 30% (or over), the shareholders could simply forego their duty in appointing women; some experts argued
that each group represented on the supervisory board should meet the 30% quota
(Hansch, Haag, and Rode, 2016). Since board members were allowed to finish their
existing mandate even if the quota was not met, some companies thwarted compliance and postponed women's appointments by holding board elections directly
before the law entered into force (Hansch, Haag, and Rode, 2016).

Many criticized that companies with more than 500 employees (either quoted
on the stock exchange or subject to co-determination) subject to the September
30, 2015 deadline could set a 0% target for women on their various management
levels because this was their status quo (Hansch, Haag, and Rode, 2016). Moreover, though 91.4% of the companies on FidARs 185-Index set targets in 2015,
they did so selectively; only 72.6% set a target for the second management level,

---

[8] The ministry connects with additional actors monitoring implementation (INT-2): the German
Institute for Economic Research with its annual Women's Executive Barometer, the trade union-linked
Hans-Böckler-Foundation, and the Albright Foundation.
[9] An extensive evaluation was published in 2020 (INT-2).
[10] To date, only one company was nearly sanctioned but complied in the end (INT-2).

and some companies even set a 30%-target despite already having a higher percentage of women in the respective management level (FidAR, 2018, p. 8). The SPD secured a quota law revision preventing such practices and introducing an enforceable fine for violations in the 2017 coalition agreement (INT-2). In this way the party successfully pushed the government to adjust the leadership positions act in 2021.

Overall, however, the implementation exhibited no major failures within its quite narrow parameters. The law positively affected the composition of supervisory boards covered by the strict quota but had far less impact on companies who have to set targets themselves (Holst and Wrohlich, 2017; 2018; 2019, Kirsch and Wrohlich, 2020). As Table 14.3 shows, in 2019, the average percentage of women on the executive board of the 105[11] publicly traded companies was 10.3%, and 40.0% for supervisory boards (Kirsch and Wrohlich, 2020, p. 41). All companies

Table 14.3 Gender Breakdown on Executive and Supervisory Boards in German Companies under the 30% Quota on Supervisory Boards

	2016	2017	2018	2019
EXECUTIVE BOARDS				
Count of companies	106	106	104	105
With women on executive boards	26	33	34	42
Percentage share	24.5%	31.4%	32.7%	40%
Count of members	447	495	483	494
Men	416	465	442	443
Women	31	39	41	51
Percentage share of women	6.5%	7.9%	8.5%	10.3%
SUPERVISORY BOARDS				
Count of companies	106	105	104	105
With women on supervisory boards	106	105	104	105
Percentage share	100	100	100	100
Count of members	1,562	1,597	1,511	1,577
Men	1,134	1,116	1,016	1,027
Women	428	481	495	550
Percentage share of women	24.4%	30.1%	32.8%	34.9%
Count of chairpersons	104	105	104	105
Men	100	101	100	99
Women	4	4	4	6
Percentage share of women	3.8%	3.8%	3.8%	5.7%

Source: Holst and Wrohlich (2019, p 21), Kirsch and Wrohlich (2020, p 41).

---

[11] The annually published Women Executive Barometer by the German Institute for Economic Research (Deutsches Institut für Wirtschaftsforschung), authored by Elke Holst and Katharina Wrohlich,

presented in Table 14.3 have at least one woman appointed to the supervisory board, but altogether they have only appointed six chairwomen (5.7%) (Kirsch and Wrohlich, 2020, p. 4).

Moreover, any opposition to quotas being too bureaucratic vanished; companies have not complained about costly measures, and all companies complied with reporting (INT-2). Media reporting on the results is balanced, and critical voices about the underrepresentation of women on executive boards remain.

Regulating Women on Boards in Germany: Stopping Short of Real Transformation?

The impact of corporate-board quotas needs to be measured not only in numbers but particularly also in terms of its broader impact on substantively promoting gender equality. Assessing Germany's 2015 law reveals a mixed picture for inclusive empowerment of actors in the process of implementation and evaluation and gender transformation.

Empowerment

Actors committed to promoting gender equality walked a long road to a corporate-board quota in Germany, in a context where gender equality received growing attention, also by conservative-led governments (Henninger and von Wahl, 2014; 2018; Lang, 2017). The corporate-board quota was one of the core proposals of the 2013 CDU-SPD government and became—despite its limited scope—a success for pro-equality actors, who also gained power by making their voices heard in ministries and receiving resources for independent monitoring. The process started with a relatively low level of civil-society mobilization. The first draft by SPD Minister Bergmann in 2000, which targeted structural labor-market-related inequalities, was predominantly result of an expert forum intending to find solutions with employers' associations but without women's organizations or other parties (INT-1).

The apathy following the draft law's failure and its replacement by the voluntary agreement was gradually tackled by several initiatives aimed at improving gender equality in private companies. The governmental evaluations revealing the inefficacy of the voluntary agreement triggered the creation of several women's groups and associations that continuously mobilized against employers' interests, with the djb and finally FidAR prolifically entering both the corporate world and policy-making processes to push for the quota, also through effective use of the

uses the data provided by the listed companies—the number of these companies varies between 100 and 110.

media. Vice versa, these groups influenced political actors, especially putting the topic on the agenda of the Ministries for Women and Family Affairs and for Justice (INT-3). The constant gap between corporate promises and the actual number of women on their boards led to a diverse and powerful alliance consisting of a cross-party group of women politicians, plus lawyers, academic experts, and civil-society actors (among them also quite conservative ones like the German Rural Women's Association).

Nowadays, those alliances are firmly institutionalized in the political landscape, and FidAR was further empowered by becoming responsible for evaluating the law's implementation. Also, the Ministry for Women's Affairs was empowered to enforce women's interests in the face of Germany's extremely powerful employers' associations. By collaborating with the Justice Ministry, they gained new expertise in law preparation (INT-3; INT-2) and in enforcing sanctions. Nevertheless, how substantive that empowerment is remains to be seen in terms of the reach of the quotas outside the numerical increases. In other words, the fact that companies are not complaining makes observers suspicious. Moreover, other studies continue to criticize corporate quotas as "elite politics" that disregard other key structural problems.

Including Women—Maintaining corporate inequalities

Engeli and Mazur (2018, p. 123) define gender transformation as the "gold benchmark" and "by far the most ambitious" bringing deep "changes in gendered and sexualized norms." Despite the long road to a corporate-board quota and changes in arguments, corporate gender relations have not been fundamentally transformed in Germany; the law, at best, corresponds to a form of "gender accommodation" rather than even "simple transformation."

The Direct Impact of Corporate Gender Quotas

More than three-quarters of the 106 companies subject to the law had 30% or more women supervisory board members at the end of 2018 (Holst and Wrohlich, 2019, pp. 25–26); about five companies had just 50% women on the supervisory board, yet never more than that (FidAR, 2018). Although the overall share of women increased to 8.2%, nineteen of the 106 companies lack a single woman executive board member (FidAR, 2018). Moreover, 64.6% of the 185 companies monitored by FidAR set a 0% target of women for their executive board in 2015; in 2017 this decreased to 45.2% (FidAR, 2018, pp. 7–8). However, the executive boards of the 200 largest German companies—including the 106 companies subject to the law—experienced a standstill or even a decline (except the DAX-30 group) (Holst and Wrohlich, 2017) and only slowly started an increase in the number of women members in 2019 (Kirsch and Wrohlich, 2020, p. 40). As the FidAR 185

Index data illustrated, there was no spillover for the self-set management targets for all management levels—in a significant number of cases, there was even a gender rollback (FidAR, 2018, p. 8). Since 2015, fewer companies set targets for the different management levels and many—despite a higher women's share—actually lowered the target to 30%. Apparently, changing biased structures and promoting women and gender equality in their workforce still seems to be a low priority for a shockingly high percentage of German companies. Sustainable results and transforming gender relations beyond the scope of the law both seem unlikely, as broader economic and organizational structures remain untouched, ignoring horizontal and vertical gender segregation and its intersectional aspects. Moreover, quotas and gender-equality measures in the economic sphere disappeared from the public agenda, only women's organizations demand further legislation. And apart from the smaller adjustments planned for this legislature, the government is quite satisfied with the law (INT-2).

While the law is an important step toward better descriptive representation of a small group of elite women, enhancing women's substantive representation is uncertain. Oehmichen, Rapp, and Wolff (2010), however, found that after male and female shareholders worked together, the former were more likely to support appointing women board members in future cases; disappearing all-male supervisory boards might thus indirectly lead to more women on boards. Regarding intersectionality, we lack publicly available data for boards. The women executive board members displayed on company websites appear quite homogenous: German nationality, white, age range 41 to 62, all with a university degree. A gender-disaggregated analysis by Fehre and Spiegelhalder (2017) of supervisory boards before corporate board quota adoption found that women added to a board's diversity in experience; women predominantly studied business administration, men STEM fields; women gained experience in a variety of companies and were externally appointed, while men were internal candidates with limited experience in other companies. Women had more international experience and fewer board positions than men; women also notably had fewer children than men. The opportunities for gender transformation seem incremental at best; either the limitation to supervisory board positions leaves women's career opportunities inside companies unchanged *or* it leads to the systematic promotion of women (Hansch, Haag, and Rode, 2016, pp. 14–18). Furthermore, the quota initiated public discussions on what makes a good supervisory board member moved forward diversity as an issue, and reduced gender-stereotyped job adverts (Ibid, pp. 15–18).

If we look at supervisory board member remuneration and board committee assignments, the situation seems to be less encouraging (Bozhinow, Koch, and Schank, 2017). Despite being regulated, supervisory boards exhibit a gender pay gap of 36%, presumably because women seldom act as chair or committee members (Ibid, p. 9). Controlling for different committees, chairpersons, and differences between companies, a gender pay gap of 12% remains; a study showed that the "rising share of women was achieved at the cost of having relatively fewer women serving on board committees" and in other core functions (Ibid, pp. 10–11).

Indirectly, board-quota discussions also fostered debates on why public administration and courts do not adhere to gender equality. To this end, the Act on Equality between Women and Men in the Federal Administration and Federal Enterprises and Courts (Federal Act on Gender Equality), as well as the Law on Federal Bodies, were considerably reformed to increase women's share in federal public services leadership positions.[12] Since January 1, 2016, the government must ensure a 30% share, and from 2018 onward a 50% share; extending previous laws, the results are monitored and published as the annual Gender Equality Index. Because of the public reporting obligations, the 2015 law also had surprising indirect effects. If a company sets a target, it must be subject to co-determination, yet, as a 2017 study shows, some companies apparently forego worker co-determination (Bayer and Hoffmann, 2017). Thanks to the quota law and its public reporting mechanism, trade unions can now detect such companies and approach them to adhere to co-determination and extend their supervisory board—also including more women.

Changes at the Decision-maker and Gatekeeper Level

The 2017 CDU-SPD coalition agreement signaled slightly transformed standpoints on corporate quotas. The then-Minister for Women and Family Affairs, Franziska Giffey (SPD), together with the Minister for Justice, planned a law revision fining companies with no targets and those failing to report targets at all (Emmrich, 2018; INT-2). Furthermore, both ministers wanted to extend the law to executive boards and more companies—a compensatory measure that does not consider intersectional aspects nor the policy areas needing change to extend the law's impact. Academia and women's organizations strongly supported these plans (Holst and Wrohlich, 2018; FiDAR, 2018). Meanwhile, the CDU-SPD coalition government agreed in November 2020 on a mandatory women's quota for executive boards of listed companies falling under the parity co-determination act. On June 11, 2021, the Bundestag passed the Zweites Fuehrungspositionengesetz (Second Act on the Proportion of Women in Executive Posts), which came into force on August 11, 2021 shortly before the General Elections.

A survey of 300 supervisory board members and top management shortly after the quota law was enforced showed their prevailing unawareness of company quota targets, with women better informed than men; representatives from bigger companies had more positive attitudes toward quota regulations than those from smaller ones, and the younger generation more in favor than the older (FKI,

---

[12] The law uses the term, "underrepresented sex."

2018, p. 2). The survey indicated clear gender differences; 72% of women appreciate the law, but only 30% men, and women were considerably less satisfied with the status of women in the company (Ibid, p. 5). A small 2017 survey, repeating a 2015 one, of eighty-five supervisory board members of stock exchange listed companies points to slow but important changes in attitudes to the law. While women board members were generally more supportive, the share of male board members with negative positions decreased considerably (there was a similar trend among women), and the stereotype that women are only advancing in their careers due to the quota law was declining in both society and corporate culture (DKI, 2017, pp. 13–14). Common essentializing beliefs, such as women changing discussion culture for the better, also declined (Ibid, pp. 16–17).

Transformation at the Societal Level?
Public discussions around quotas spilled over to other societal fields, particularly the media (Hansch, Haag, and Rode, 2016, p. 15). In 2013, the ProQuote Medien association demanded a 30% women's share in leadership positions of print media editorial boards. Likewise, the ProQuote Regie association demanded a 50% women's share within ten years among publicly contracted directors for TV and movies, and decision-making bodies for publicly subsidized movies. The Ministry for Women's Affairs supports ProQuote's efforts. Finally, in 2013, doctors and medical researchers founded the association ProQuote Medicine, demanding 40% women's representation in all leadership positions in the medical sector by 2018.[13]

Conclusion

The long road to corporate equality in Germany had its (interim) highlight with the corporate-board quota adopted in 2015, obliging the supervisory boards of 106 publicly traded companies with more than 2,000 employees to a 30% quota for the underrepresented sex, sanctioned by an empty-seat mechanism, and requiring self-set targets at different management levels for a broad number of companies with more than 500 but fewer than 2,000 employees. The law was successfully implemented within its scope. In 2019, supervisory boards subject to the strict quota reached a women's share of more than 30%. Nevertheless, companies used strategies like having earlier board elections before the strict quota came into force or setting 0% targets for management levels to undermine an even better implementation. Moreover, spillover effects for executive boards or other top management levels are not detectable, and recent comments from employer associations show that they are far from seeing any benefit in

---

[13] There is no information on whether the target was reached or reformulated.

promoting gender equality (Bund, Heuser, and Nezik, 2019). In August 2021, just before federal elections, the Zweites Führungspositionengesetz (Second Act on the Proportion of Women in Executive Posts) came into force. It requires at least one woman on executive boards with more than three members for the currently seventy listed companies that fall under the co-determination act. For federal companies and companies in public ownership (e.g. health insurance companies, pension and accident insurance institutions, Federal Employment Agency) at least one woman must be represented if the executive board has more than two members. Moreover, companies must justify setting a "zero-per-cent-target" – a type of malpractice on the part of many companies exempted from the strict quota (Ahrens and Scheele 2022). Based on the experiences with the women's quota described in our text, it is certainly appropriate not to set expectations too high regarding implementation. It may well be a long and steep road again.

Notwithstanding this mixed evaluation of the direct effects, the law still shows important features of transforming gender relations in Germany. The process is an impressive account of empowerment and a signal of potentially crucial changes in the economic sphere. Thus, two major factors stood out for the successful policy decision. First, persistent women-led mobilization of diverse women's organizations, cross-party alliances, and trade unions changed the public perception to believe that boards require a quota to prevent future risky male behavior (such as the financial crisis) and to ensure women's qualifications and leadership talents are acknowledged. Second, this mobilization was fruitful not only because of the effects of the financial crisis but also due to Germany's slowly changing male breadwinner model and conservative gender norms in the context of a labor market in desperate need of qualified personnel. In this context, the shift in political and public discourse is quite clear. While in the 1980s and the 1990s the plea for gender quotas was legitimized with existing social inequalities, a lack of justice, and ongoing discrimination, in 2001 the danger of wasting human capital if the potential of high-qualified women was not used became the main argument for quotas in the voluntary agreement (Müller, 2019).

Additionally, the adoption of a board quota in Norway in 2003 was insufficient to trigger a similar one in Germany but critical in keeping up the public discussion and the commitment of women's associations. Also, the final decision to exclude executive boards but set sanctionable strict targets made adoption and implementation a success. Standard explanations such as party ideology were less important in Germany, and the unsupportive SPD leadership and the Green Party's inactivity at some crucial points were actually more of a barrier than backing in the early political discussions. This changed over time, and the implementation's success has been ensured by the SPD ministry since the law's adoption. Whether Germany's labor market will experience more exhaustive gender transformation in the future, particularly regarding intersectional aspects, remains to be seen.

Interviews

Dr. Christine Bergmann, Minister for Family, Senior Citizens, Women, and Youth from 1998 to 2002. Interview on June 14, 2019 (INT-1).

Civil Servant, Ministry for Family, Senior Citizens, Women, and Youth. Interview on June 12, 2019 (INT-2).

Eva Welskop-Deffaa, Head of Department for Gender Equality in the Ministry for Family, Senior Citizens, Women, and Youth from 2006 to 2012. Interview on October 1, 2019 (INT-3).

References

Ahrens, Petra, Katja Chmilewski, Sabine Lang, and Birgit Sauer (2020) *Gender Equality in Politics – Implementing Party Quotas in Germany and Austria*. Cham: Springer.

Ahrens, Petra and Alexandra Scheele (2022) "Game-Changers for Gender Equality in Germany's Labour Market? Corporate Board Quotas, Pay Transparency and Temporary Part-Time Work," German Politics, 31 (1), pp. 157–176.

Annesley, Claire and Alexandra Scheele (2011) "Gender, Capitalism and Economic Crisis: Impact and Responses across Europe," *Journal of Contemporary European Studies*, 19 (3), pp. 335–347.

Auth, Diana, Christina Klenner, and Sigrid Leitner (2015) "Neue Sorgekonflikte: Die Zumutungen des Adult Worker Model," in Susanne Völker and Michèle Amacker (eds) *Prekarisierungen. Arbeit, Sorge und Politik*. Weinheim, Basel: Beltz Juventa, pp. 42–58.

Berghahn, Sabine (2012) "Vereint im Kampf für die Frauenquote in Aufsichtsräten? Eine kommentierende Betrachtung," *gender-politik-online*, http://www.fu-berlin.de/sites/gpo/Aktuelles/berghahnquote.pdf (Accessed September 3, 2020).

Bayer, Walter and Thomas Hoffmann (2017) "Frauenquote: Ja – Mitbestimmung: Nein. GmbH mit Frauenquote ohne Mitbestimmung?" *GmbH-Rundschau*, 108 (9), p 441–448.

BMAS (2018) *Co-Determination 2018. Berlin 2018*, https://www.bmas.de/EN/Services/Publications/a741e-co-determination.html (Accessed September 3, 2020).

BMFSFJ (2017) *Zweiter Gleichstellungsbericht der Bundesregierung*, https://www.bmfsfj.de/blob/jump/122398/zweiter-gleichstellungsbericht-der-bundesregierung-eine-zusammenfassung-data.pdf (Accessed September 3, 2020).

Bozhinow, Viktor, Christopher Koch, and Thorsten Schank (2017) "Has the Push for Equal Gender representation Changed the Role of Women on German Supervisory Boards?" *IZA Discussion Paper Series*, September 2017, http://ftp.iza.org/dp11057.pdf (Accessed September 3, 2020).

Brader, Doris and Julia Lewerenz (2006) "Frauen in Führungspositionen. An der Spitze ist die Luft dünn," *IAB Kurzbericht*, (2), 24 February 2006.

Bund, Kerstin, Uwe Jean Heuser, and Ann-Kathrin Nezik (2019) "Jennifer Morgan: Eine von 31," *Die Zeit*, 16 October, https://www.zeit.de/2019/43/jennifer-morgan-sap-vorstand-aufsichtsrat-dax-fuehrungsposition-frau/komplettansicht (Accessed September 3, 2020).

Bundesregierung Deutschland (2003) *Bilanz 2003 der Vereinbarung zwischen der Bundesregierung und den Spitzenverbänden der Deutschen Wirtschaft zur Förderung der Chancengleichheit von Frauen und Männern in der Privat wirtschaft*, https://www.bmfsfj.de/bmfsfj/service/publikationen/bilanz-2003-der-vereinbarung-zwischen-der-bundesregierung-und-den-spitzenverbaenden-der-deutschen-wirtschaft-zur-foerderung-der-chancengleichheit-von-frauen-und-maennern-in-der-privatwirtschaft/96310 (Accessed September 3, 2020).

Bundesregierung Deutschland (2006*) 2. Bilanz Chancengleichheit—Frauen in Führungspositionen*, https://www.bmfsfj.de/blob/jump/93160/2--bilanz-chancengleichheit-data.pdf (Accessed December 22, 2021).

Bundesregierung Deutschland (2008) *3. Bilanz Chancengleichheit—Europa im Blick.* September 3, 2020, https://www.bmfsfj.de/blob/93172/463cca53fdcf37350fec6acaa 0581613/3--bilanz-chancengleichheit-europa-im-blick-data.pdf (Accessed September 3, 2020).

Bundesregierung Deutschland (2011) *4. Bilanz Chancengleichheit. Erfolgreiche Initiativen unterstützen – Potenziale aufzeigen*, https://www.bmfsfj.de/blob/93178/24922bbdf7a333dccba99f50c4e40595/4-bilanz-chancengleichheit-data.pdf (Accessed September 3, 2020).

Bundesregierung Deutschland (2013) *5. Bilanz Chancengleichheit. Chancengleichheit auf einem guten Weg*, https://www.bmfsfj.de/blob/93182/5582278aaef0ebfb11 f56ac2271ffff4/5--bilanz-chancengleichheit-data.pdf (Accessed September 3, 2020).

DKI Deutsches Kundeninstitut (2017) *Aufsichtsräte in Deutschland 2017*, https://www.hengeler.com/fileadmin/medien/broschueren/Studie_Aufsichtsraete_2017_L (Accessed May 20, 2018).

DS 16/5279 (2007) Deutscher Bundestag 16. Wahlperiode: Quote für Aufsichtsräte börsennotierter Unternehmen einführen. Antrag der Abgeordneten Irmingard Schewe-Gerigk und anderen und der Fraktion BÜNDNIS 90/DIE GRÜNEN.

DS 17/3296 (2011) Deutscher Bundestag 17. Wahlperiode: Entwurf eines Gesetzes zur geschlechtergerechten Besetzung von Aufsichtsräten. Gesetzentwurf der Abgeordneten Renate Künast und anderen und der Fraktion BÜNDNIS 90/DIE GRÜNEN.

Emmrich, Julia (2018) "Die Frauenquote wirkt nach drei Jahren—aber nur langsam," *Morgenpost* April 29, 2018, https://www.morgenpost.de/politik/article214147783/Die-Frauenquote-wirkt-nach-drei-Jahren-so-langsam.html (Accessed September 3, 2020).

Engeli, Isabelle and Amy Mazur (2018) "Taking Implementation Seriously in Assessing Success: The Politics of Gender Equality Policy," *European Journal of Politics and Gender*, 1 (1), pp. 111–129.

Esping-Andersen, Gøsta (1990) *The Three Worlds of Welfare Capitalism.* Princeton, New Jersey: Princeton University Press.

European Institute for Gender Equality (EIGE) (2019) *Gender Equality Index*, http://eige.europa.eu/gender-statistics/gender-equality index/2012/domain/power/2/DE (Accessed September 3, 2020).

Fehre, Kerstin and Rebecca Spiegelhalder (2017) "Same Same, but Different: Eine Analyse des Humankapitals weiblicher und männlicher Aufsichtsräte in Deutschland," *Schmalenbachs Zeitschrift für betriebswirtschaftliche Forschung*, 69 (3), pp. 311–343.

Ferree, Myra Marx (2012) *Varieties of Feminism. German Gender Politics in Global Perspective.* Standford: Stanford University Press.

FidAR (2016) *10 Jahre FidAR e.V.—Erfolgsgeschichte einer Initiative*, https://www.fidar.de/webmedia/user_upload/FidAR_10_Jahre_161109_LR.pdf (Accessed September 3, 2020)

FidAR (2018) *Women-on-Board-Index 185*, https://www.fidar.de/webmedia/documents/wob-index-185/2018-05/180114_Studie_WoB-Index_185_I_end.pdf (Accessed September 3, 2020).

FKI Führungskräfte Institut (2018) "Umfrage zu Frauen in Führungspositionen: Gesetzliche Regelungen besser kommunizieren," *Manager Monitor*, February 1, 2016, http://www.fki-online.de/uploads/media/20160201-manager-monitor-quote.pdf (Accessed September 3, 2020).

Hansch, Julia, Christina Haag, and Manuela Rode (2016) "The Impact of the Quota for Women on Supervisory Boards on German Corporations, especially on Employer Representation and HRM," Paper presented at the 5th European Conference on Politics and Gender (ECPG) University of Lausanne, Switzerland, June 8–10, 2017.

Henninger, Annette and Angelika von Wahl (2014) "Grand Coalition and Multi-Party Competition: Explaining Slowing Reforms in Gender Policy in Germany (2009–13)," *German Politics*, 23 (4), pp. 386–399.

Henninger, Annette and Angelika von Wahl (2018) "This Train Has Left the Station: The German Gender Equality Regime on Course Towards a Social Democratic Model (2013–17)," *German Politics*, 28 (3), pp. 462–481.

Hericks, Katja (2011) *Entkoppelt und institutionalisiert. Gleichstellungspolitik in einem deutschen Konzern*. Wiesbaden: VS Verlag für Sozialwissenschaften.

Holst, Elke and Katharina Wrohlich (2017) "Top Decision-making Bodies in Large Companies: Gender Quota Shows Initial Impact on Supervisory Boards; Executive Board Remains a Male Bastion," *DIW Economic Bulletin*, 1+2, pp. 3–15.

Holst, Elke and Katharina Wrohlich (2018) "Top Decision-making Bodies of Large Businesses: Gender Quota for Supervisory Boards Is Effective—Development Is almost at a Standstill for Executive Boards," *DIW Weekly Report*, 3, pp. 3–31.

Holst, Elke and Katharina Wrohlich (2019) "Increasing Number of Women on Supervisory Boards of Major Companies in Germany; Executive Boards Still Dominated by Men," *DIW Weekly Report* 3, pp. 17–32.

Kappert, Ines (2011) "Kein Gedöhns: Der Ruf nach einer Frauenquote ist ein ökonomischer Imperativ," *tageszeitung*, January 29, 2011, http://www.taz.de/!5127637/ (Accessed September 3, 2020).

Kirsch, Anja and Katharina Wrohlich (2020) "Frauenanteile in Spitzengremien großer Unternehmen steigen—abgesehen von Aufsichtsräten im Finanzsektor," *DIW Wochenbericht*, 4, pp. 38–49.

Kohaut, Susanne and Möller, Iris (2019) "Leider nichts neues auf den Führungsetagen," *IAB Kurzbericht* 23, http://doku.iab.de/kurzber/2019/kb2319.pdf (Accessed September 3, 2020).

Lang, Sabine (2017) "Gender Equality in Post-Unification Germany: Between GDR Legacies and EU-Level Pressures," *German Politics*, 26 (4), pp. 556–573.

Leitner, Sigrid (2013) *Varianten von Familialismus. Eine historisch vergleichende Analyse der Kinderbetreuungs- und Altenpflegepolitiken in kontinentaleuropäischen Wohlfahrtsstaaten*. Berlin: Dunckler und Humblot.

Lewis, Jane (2001) "The Decline of the Male Breadwinner Model. Implications for Work and Care," *Social Politics*, 8 (2), pp. 152–169.

Müller, Katja Karolin (2019) "Women on Corporate Boards in Germany: A Result of Constancy and Change in Gendered Categorizations (1980-2013)," in Isabelle

Berrebi-Hofmann, Olivier Giraud, Léa Renard, and Theresa Wobbe (eds) *Categories in Context: Gender and Work in France and Germany, 1900-Present*. New York, Oxford: Berghahn, pp. 129–154.

Müller-Jentsch, Walther (1997) *Soziologie der Industriellen Beziehungen*. Frankfurt/Main, New York: Campus Verlag.

Oehmichen, Jana, Marc Steffen Rapp, and Michael Wolff (2010) "Der Einfluss der Aufsichtsratszusammensetzung auf die Präsenz von Frauen in Aufsichtsräten," *Schmalenbachs Zeitschrift für betriebswirtschaftliche Forschung*, 62 (5), pp. 503–532.

Peuckert, Rüdiger (2012) *Familienformen im sozialen Wandel*. Wiesbaden: Springer VS.

Pfarr, Heide (ed.) (2001) *Ein Gesetz zur Gleichstellung der Geschlechter in der Privatwirtschaft*. Düsseldorf: Hans-Böckler-Stiftung 57.

Schmollack, Simone (2014) "Gegen das Patriarchat," *Tageszeitung*, March 7, 2014, https://taz.de/Internationaler-Frauentag/!5047026/ (Accessed September 3, 2020).

Schuler, Katharina, Till Schwarze, and Lisa Caspari (2015) "Gleichstellung: 'Nach der Quote ist vor der Quote," *Die Zeit*, March 6, 2015, https://www.zeit.de/politik/deutschland/2015-03/frauenquote-zitate-gleichberechtigung (Accessed September 3, 2020).

Schultz, Ulrike (2003) Ein Quasi-Stürmlein und Waschkörbe voller Eingaben: Die Geschichte von Art. 3 Abs. 2 Grundgesetz. *Frauen und Recht. Reader für die Aktionswochen der kommunalen Gleichstellungsbeauftragten 2003*. Im Auftrag des Ministeriums für Gesundheit, Soziales, Frauen und Familie NRW. Düsseldorf, pp. 54–60.

Waas, Bernd (2014) "Gender Quota in Company Boards: Germany," in Marc De Vos and Philippe Culliford (eds) *Gender Quotas for Company Boards*. Cambridge, Antwerp, Portland: Intersentia, pp. 131–146.

Wippermann, Carsten (2010) *Frauen in Führungspositionen. Barrieren und Brücken. Studie für das BMFSFJ*, https://www.bmfsfj.de/blob/93874/7d4e27d960b7f7d5c52340efc139b662/frauen-in-fuehrungspositionen-deutsch-data.pdf (Accessed September 3, 2020).

Wunsch, Conny (2005) "Labour Market Policy in Germany: Institutions, Instruments and Reforms since Unification," *Discussion Paper 2005–06*. Department of Economics, University of St. Gallen.

15

Implementing Paradox

A Conservative Gender Regime Limits the Transformative Potential of Quotas in Austria

Nora Gresch and Birgit Sauer

Introduction

When examining gender equality policies in the corporate world, Austria presents a paradoxical situation.[1] On the one hand, scholars label the country's marriage-centered gender regime "conservative" (e.g., Lewis and Ostner, 1994, pp. 19–25; Dackweiler, 2003, pp. 194), which implies that authoritative gender equality policies with transformative outcomes would be unlikely (Lépinard, 2014, p. 1). On the other hand, the Austrian Parliament ratified the Equal Treatment Law of Women and Men on Supervisory Boards (Gleichstellungsgesetz von Frauen und Männern im Aufsichtsrat—GFMA-G) in June 2017. The act established a 30% gender quota for supervisory boards for all publicly listed companies and firms with more than 1,000 employees. The law's adoption shifted Austria's approach from a purely self-regulatory one to a mixed approach that includes potentially coercive quota legislation for women on boards (BGBl I Nr. 104/2017). Given the resistance to such state regulation from Austria's influential Chamber of Commerce (Wirtschaftskammer Österreich, WKO), the law's authoritative nature is especially puzzling. Prior to the introduction of the GFMA-G, the powerful representation of the employer group, the WKO, had opted for self-regulation rather than involving the state in regulating gender equality on corporate boards. At the same time, Austrian labor law implementation and evaluation have been impeded by ongoing controversies regarding such gender quotas. So far, the GFMA-G has not received the same level of acceptance as similar policy instruments in France, Belgium, or Slovenia. Moreover, Austria has lacked a broad women's

[1] We would like to thank our interview partners Gabriele Heinisch-Hosek, Heike Mensi-Klarbach, and Bernadette Hawel for sharing their time, knowledge, and for providing us with crucial information for writing this paper, as well as Kathrin Glösel for helping to gather research material.

Nora Gresch and Birgit Sauer, *Implementing Paradox* In: *Gender Equality and Policy Implementation in the Corporate World.* Edited by Isabelle Engeli and Amy G. Mazur, Oxford University Press. © Oxford University Press (2022). DOI: 10.1093/oso/9780198865216.003.0015

lobby behind its quota adoption—like Germany's Women to the Boards network (Frauen in die Aufsichtsräte, FidAR)—to counter business opposition. Therefore, the transformative potential of the GFMA-G has been arguably limited to gender accommodation in the corporate world.

The remainder of this chapter traces the paradoxical disconnect between the GFMA-G's agenda-setting and adoption processes and shows how Austria's purely self-regulatory approach was transposed to a mixed approach, both self-regulation and state regulation, through the gender quota law. Despite resistance from corporate representatives and the Christian-conservative Austrian People's Party (ÖVP), who opposed introducing a coercive, state-driven approach for almost a decade, the law was not completely diluted in its final form. Next, we examine the paradox in action during the GFMA-G's post-adoption phase and show how the law's policy outcomes and impacts are better characterized by gender accommodation rather than transformation. However, it is important to first contextualize policy processes, outputs, and outcomes in the topography of gender equality in the corporate world.

Gender Equality in the Corporate World: The Topography of the Austrian Paradox

According to Mensi-Klarbach (2017, p. 105), the economic "…governance system in post-war Austria is characterized by a very close connection and collaboration between the Austrian economic and political elite." The system has been institutionalized in Austria's consociational corporatist system of social partnership, which refers to practices of "…policy-making and solving potential social conflicts through institutionalized bargaining and compromise in a complex web of advisory boards, commissions, and task forces" (Meyer and Höllerer, 2016). Furthermore, Austria's neo-corporatist structure institutionalizes private sector professional interests as public corporations (Fink, 2006, p. 443), thereby sustaining the country's main political viewpoints. On the one hand, the Chamber of Commerce (WKO) and the Chamber of Agriculture (Landwirtschaftskammer) are closely connected with the ÖVP. On the other hand, the Chamber of Labor (Arbeiterkammer or AK) and the Austrian Trade Union Association (Österreichischer Gewerkschaftsbund or ÖGB) have firmly tied bonds with the Social Democratic Party (SPÖ) (Tálos, 2006, p. 430).

Austria's post-World War II development of its corporate sector was shaped by "the relative weakness of private capital (…) a stock market characterized by major block-holders, and a dominant role of the state" (Mensi-Klarbach, 2017, p. 106), which resulted in a large, state-owned economic sector. Another relevant characteristic "…seems to be [the corporate sector's] clear separation between what is thought of as legitimate for state-owned companies and what is legitimate for privately held companies, with a clear resistance to state interference in private companies" (Gabaldon, et al, 2017, p. 276). Austria's corporate governance comprises a two-tier board system, which clearly differentiates between supervisory and executive boards (Mensi-Klarbach, 2017, p. 109). It is shaped by the Austrian Stock Corporation Act (Aktiengesetz, AktG), the Austrian Stock Exchange Act (Börsegesetz, BörseG), the Austrian Commercial Code (Unternehmensgesetzbuch, UGB), the Austrian Limited Liability Company Law (GmbH-Gesetz, GmbHG), and the Austrian Corporate Governance Code (Österreichischer Corporate Governance Kodex, ÖCGK) (Müller, 2011, p. 17).

Austria's conservative gender regime and welfare state system sustain gender inequality in both economic and social welfare participation (Gresch and Sauer, 2015). Hence, the corporate sector is notably characterized by its high level of female labor force participation, of which a large share is employed part-time (47.7% in 2016; Statistik Austria, 2018). Likewise, Austria has one of the largest gender pay gaps within the EU, as well as a labor market that is strongly segregated both horizontally and vertically. Childcare responsibilities are the primary reason for women's high part-time employment, especially according to Austrian women aged thirty to forty-four years (Statistik Austria, 2018). This is reinforced by the scarce availability of public childcare facilities, especially for children under three years and children living in more rural areas. Drawing on Regina Dackweiler's (2003, pp. 193–196) analysis of Austrian social, marital, family, labor market, and gender equality policies from the mid-1970s until 2000, such policies set institutional incentives for women to balance care activities and part-time work, but not for men.

Horizontal gender segregation in the Austrian labor market is reflected by the high rate of women in the service sector. In 2016, the highest percentage of women was found in the trade sector (17.9%),[2] followed by health and social services (17.6%), and education (11.4%) (Statistik Austria, 2019). Likewise, vertical segregation has led to a high gender pay gap compared to other EU member states—although it decreased from 25.5% in 2006 to 20.1% in 2016 (Statistik Austria, 2018). In 2016, only 3.7% of employed women occupied leadership positions, compared to 8.1% of men. Furthermore, only 7.9% of women who completed tertiary education held leadership positions, in contrast to 21.2% of men with the same academic qualifications (Statistik Austria, 2019).

This pattern of vertical labor market segregation is especially reflected within women's representation in economic decision-making. As of January 2018, women comprised only 8.4 and 18.5% of respective executive and supervisory

---

[2] The referenced terms are translations of the ÖNACE code, which is used by Statistik Austria. This is the national version of the Statistical Classification of Economic Activities in the European Community, NACE Rev. 2 (Nomenclature générale des activités économiques dans les communautés européenes); available under http://www.statistik.at/web_de/klassifikationen/klassifikationsmitteilung/beschreibung/index.html (Accessed June 5, 2018).

Table 15.1 Percentage Share of Women on Boards in the Largest Listed Companies in Austria, 2004–2020

	EU-28 Board members	AUSTRIA				
		Board members	President	CEO	Executives	Non-executives
2004	*9*	6.0	2.1	—	—	—
2005	*9.8*	7.1	2.0	—	—	—
2006	*9.7*	5.9	0	—	—	—
2007	*10.4*	5.0	0	—	—	—
2008	*10.8*	6.4	0	—	—	—
2009	*11*	7.0	0	—	—	—
2010	*11.9*	8.7	0	—	—	—
2011	*13.7*	11.1	0	—	—	—
2012	*15.8*	11.9	0	0	4.7	11.9
2013	*17.8*	12.6	0	0	2.8	12.6
2014	*20.2*	17.1	10.0	0	4.2	17.1
2015	*22.7*	20.0	10.0	0	4.3	20.0
2016	*23.9*	18.1	10.0	5.0	5.4	18.1
2017	*25.3*	19.2	10.0	5.0	4.1	19.2
2018	*26.7*	26.1	15.0	5.0	5.1	26.1
2019	*28.8*	31.3	10.0	5.0	7.5	31.3
2020	*29.2*	29.6	10.0	5.0	6.3	29.6

Source: EIGE Database. Data for October each year, except for 2020 [April]

boards at Austria's top 200 private companies (Seebacher and Wieser, 2018, p. 23). In terms of upper management positions, Austria ranked at the bottom of all EU countries, with 5% of CEOs held by women (see Table 15.1). Moreover, 24% of Austria's top 200 companies (i.e., forty-eight) had no women in their governing bodies (Seebacher and Wieser, 2018, p. 23). In 2018, the service sector had the highest share of women in leadership positions (14.7%) and the lowest in the industry sector (4.6%). Although the number of women on Austrian executive boards remained low compared to other European countries, their 8.4% share has nearly doubled within the past decade (from 4.6% in 2008) (Seebacher and Wieser, 2018, p. 24). Regarding all stock listed companies, women held only 10 of 195 leadership positions (5.1%) in January 2018 (compared to 3.9% in 2017) at the executive level (Seebacher and Wieser, 2018, p. 29-30). Table 15.1 presents the Austrian numbers in comparison to the EU average.

The appearance of gender equality in the corporate world changes after taking state-owned enterprises into account, where the state represents the majority shareholder. As of 2018, the state can assign 289 members—representing fifty-four Austrian enterprises—to respective supervisory boards. The state nominated 126 women for these positions, translating to thirty-four companies with 35% or more female members on their supervisory boards, while fifteen have 25–35% and five still have a percentage of women below 25% (Wieser and Werni, 2020, p. 16).

Understanding this considerable difference between state-owned and private enterprises requires acknowledging the 25% women's quota, mandatory for all supervisory boards by the end of 2013 (increased to 35% by the end of 2018) as a self-binding government commitment. Hence, the 2011 introduction of this quota could be considered an instrument of self-regulation for state-owned companies (Seebacher and Wieser, 2018, p. 21). These numbers indicate that most of the respective companies achieved a 35% women's quota by 2016, in advance of the 2018 deadline (Seebacher and Wieser, 2018, p. 21). Thus, Austria's paradoxical situation can be characterized by the unequal gendered topography of the corporate world, the consistent rise in the female employment rate (Leitner and Kreimer, 2000), as well as the enduring differences between the private and public corporate sector regarding women's participation.

Getting Political and Corporate Attention: Deepening of the Self-regulatory Approach

While the Austrian constitution was amended in 1998 to unambiguously ensure that de facto gender equality measures like quotas could be enforced (Gresch and Sauer, 2018), the issue of gender equality in the corporate world only reached the public agenda following the inauguration of an SPÖ-led government in January 2007.

2007–2009: Approaching the Private Sphere of Corporate Gender Equality Legislation

At the municipal level, the then-opposition Green Party of Vienna claimed a 50% gender quota in 2005 for all companies for which the city of Vienna holds shares (PID, 2006). However, Barbara Prammer was the first member of a governing party to formally raise the issue, stating that women's advancement in leadership positions was not feasible without quotas. Prammer, who was the former Minister of Women and Health and then-representative of the SPÖ Women's Caucus and President of the National Council of Austria, referred to Norway as a positive example and explicitly called for Austria to adopt a corporate board quota (SPÖ-Parlamentsklub, 2007). The following year, then-Minister of Women, Media, and Public Service, Doris Bures—also from the SPÖ—again stressed the need for quotas targeting corporate boards. Like Prammer, she framed Norway's introduction of quota regulation, as well as existing quotas in Austrian public service, as an effective approach to advancing gender equality (SPÖ Pressedienst, 2008a).

Three months after Austria's September 2008 snap federal elections, the newly inaugurated SPÖ Minister of Women and Public Service, Gabriele Heinisch-Hosek, had her first interview with the media. She announced that one of her political goals was to introduce a quota for women on supervisory boards during her term in office. However, Heinisch-Hosek was unexpectedly pushed for a statement about the quota target during the interview and spontaneously referred to her party's internal 40% gender quota as the proposed benchmark (Interview with Heinisch-Hosek, 2019).

Heinisch-Hosek's announcement drew significant media attention and was immediately rejected by ÖVP Minister of Commerce, Reinhold Mitterlehner, who argued that qualification and availability of appropriate candidates are the decisive factors for choosing board members. The immediate and clear public rejection of Heinisch-Hosek's assertion was noteworthy because the SPÖ-ÖVP coalition presented several measures to advance women's participation in corporate leadership positions in its November 2008 government program. It included boosting the percentage of women with executive and supervisory board functions, especially in companies with significant state ownership (Bundesregierung Österreich, 2008). The program also pledged to enforce the de facto self-commitment to an equal distribution of men and women on supervisory boards, as per the Corporate Governance Code. However, quota regulation was omitted from the program as a policy tool because the junior government partner, the ÖVP, rejected introducing such a measure (SPÖ Pressedienst, 2008b). Instead, the ÖVP prioritized implementing capacity and learning instruments, including women's skills training, mentoring projects, and an expert database for women who qualify for supervisory board positions (Mensi-Klarbach, 2017, p. 104; Bundesregierung Österreich, 2008). At this stage, the ÖVP had successfully framed the low representation of women on corporate boards as an issue of a lack of appropriately qualified female candidates.

2009–2012: The Lingering Threat of Quota Implementation

The regulation of female representation on corporate boards became more salient when it was first codified within an amendment to the Corporate Governance Code in 2009 (Österreichischer Arbeitskreis für Corporate Governance, 2009). However, the issue only appeared as a very general rule for reporting measures implemented to advance women on executive and supervisory boards. Additionally, the Austrian Commercial Code (UGB) (BGBl I Nr. 71/2009) was changed accordingly in 2009. These changes required specific publicly listed corporations to declare their measures meant to advance women in their corporate governance report and explicitly include activities to promote women in executive and supervisory boards and other leading positions (Seebacher and Wieser, 2018, pp. 18–19).

Furthermore, passing the National Action Plan (NAP) for the Equal Treatment of Women and Men in the Labor Market was another aspect of the government program aimed to create and implement concrete and specific measures concerning women and men's equal treatment in the labor market (Bundeskanzleramt, 2010). The NAP was coordinated by the Minister of Women and Public Service, Gabriele Heinisch-Hosek, and included recommendations and suggested measures, which resulted from a year-long consultative process with representatives and experts from public administration, science, economy, politics, "social partners," as well as NGOs (Naderer et al, 2011, p. 9). Remarkably, while publicly presenting the results from the NAP in June 2010, Heinisch-Hosek concluded that the corporate gender quota recommendations were highly controversial. Thus, she stated that a mandatory quota was not feasible, in part because of the ÖVP's resistance (Der Standard, 2010). Nevertheless, the NAP recommendations encompassed a self-binding commitment for companies to introduce a successive women's quota for supervisory boards at state-owned enterprises, with a 40% target. Likewise, it called for establishing a database of women candidates for supervisory boards, evaluating the Corporate Governance Code's recommendation for men and women's representation on supervisory boards, as well as agreeing to implement mandatory "payment reports" for companies with more than 1,000 employees from 2011 onward.

As a result of this broad discussion process, representatives from the Chamber of Commerce and the Federation of Austrian Industries (Industriellenverband, IV) both pledged to introduce mandatory "payment reports" (Bundeskanzleramt, 2010, pp. 66–72). Upon amending the Equal Treatment Law (BGBl I 66/2004) in 2011, it became mandatory for companies with more than 1,000 employees to publish their payment reports, which was extended to those with more than 500 employees in 2012. Every employee at these companies has the right to have insight into their employer's payment schemes and can take legal action to request a copy of the payment report if it has not been issued (BMBWF, 2011). Furthermore, in December 2009, then-ÖVP Undersecretary of State within the Ministry of Commerce, Christine Marek, advocated for the development of a specific training program, with the support of the Chamber of Commerce. This included establishing a database to increase the number of women in supervisory board positions (Der Standard, 2009). Like other Austrian gender equality policy developments, these changes coincided with broad EU initiatives put forth in 2010 to enhance women's presence on corporate boards, while Heinisch-Hosek reiterated in February 2011 the need to put NAP policy recommendations on the public agenda (Bundespressedienst, 2011).

Unexpectedly, ÖVP Minister, Reinhold Mitterlehner, then agreed to negotiate a codification of the Corporate Governance Code's voluntary self-commitment, referring to its support from Brussels (APA, 2011; Profil Redaktion, 2011). By then, European ÖVP Member of Parliament, Othmar Karas, had publicly supported a mandatory women's quota for supervisory boards in the private sector (SPÖ-Parlamentsklub, 2010). The following week, Mitterlehner agreed to support a corporate board quota for state-owned enterprises via a Cabinet resolution, arguing that the already-chosen measures were not effective and had not achieved a substantive increase of women in economic decision-making bodies (Profil Redaktion, 2011). He continued that the efficacy of such a women's quota should thus be evaluated in enterprises where the state holds the majority as a test run. In July 2011, the Cabinet adopted a resolution to gradually increase the number of women on supervisory boards at companies where the state is the majority shareowner. The target quota would be 25% until the end of 2013 and 35% until the end of 2018.[3] The resolution additionally entailed monitoring its implementation through an annual progress report for the Cabinet (Mensi-Klarbach, 2017, p. 113). If this corporate board quota was not achieved by the end of 2018, further legal measures would be established (Der Standard, 2011a). However, no clarification was given about what legal measures or sanctions the Cabinet intended to implement. This self-binding quota resolution was described:

> first, as the minimum political consensus to take action in order to increase female representation on boards; second, the concession of the conservative party to implement quotas for corporations predominantly held by the state led to the compromise of not regulating publicly listed corporations in terms of gender quotas.
>
> (Mensi-Klarbach, 2017, p. 119)

The Corporate Governance Code was again changed in 2012 because the number of women on corporate boards remained low.[4] The former regulation was tightened into a C-Rule, meaning enterprises would have to report—but also explain—their non-compliance (Mensi-Klarbach, 2017, p. 112–118). That year, the same language from the C-Rule was applied to the Stock Corporation Act (BGBl I Nr. 35/2012) by a motion from the Federal Chancellery. By applying this vague formulation into legislation, an uncertain legal term was added to the Company Act, namely to "consider the representation of both genders appropriately" (§ 87 AktG) without indicating what "appropriately" could mean. What is more, no legal sanctions were defined (Mensi-Klarbach, 2017, p. 113). Following this vague codification regarding gender equality on corporate boards, the threat of a quota implementation and its associated media coverage subsided.

To summarize the developments during the pre-adoption phase of the GFMA-G, the representatives from the corporate sector and the ÖVP bargained firmly against gender quotas, which were primarily advocated for by the SPÖ Minister of Women's Affairs, EU Members of Parliament, and supported by broad media

---

[3] For a summary of the various reforms to the Austrian corporate governance codes along with other policies addressing gender equality on corporate boards, see Table 15.2.

[4] In their analysis of the press coverage on corporate board quotas between 2006 and 2016 by the two leading Austrian daily newspapers, Mensi-Klarbach et al (2019) show that the highest peak occurred between 2010 and 2012.

coverage that incited a need for action (Mensi-Klarbach et al, 2019).[5] On the one hand, these developments led to an increase and a diversification of self-regulation measures and capacity instruments to enhance women's participation in decision-making processes within the corporate sector. On the other, the decisions led to different self-regulating measures for the private and public corporate sectors. This established the basis for future arguments about a shift from self-regulation to coercive legislation in the private corporate sector.

Decision-making Process: Self-regulation Moves to a Mixed Approach through a Shift in Frames and the Social Partnership Network

The opportunity to introduce a quota regulation in the private sector only arose following a leadership crisis between the governing SPÖ and ÖVP, resulting in a new government program in January 2017 (Bundesregierung Österreich, 2017). The new government program included the introduction of a mandatory 30% quota regulation for supervisory boards at all stock-listed companies as well as companies with more than 1,000 employees as of January 1, 2018, which emulated the German legal model (Bundesregierung Österreich, 2017). The government program further stated that the measure would be implemented during the up-coming June 2017 cabinet meeting. Subsequently, MPs Josef Muchitsch (SPÖ) and Michaela Steinacker (ÖVP) introduced the initiative as a motion (Initiativantrag), which meant it was not subject to the traditional assessment by experts, social partners, or NGOs. It was then sent to the Parliamentary Justice Committee and adopted by Parliament on June 28, 2017, with its support from the ÖVP, SPÖ, and the Green Party (BGBl I Nr. 104/2017).

Hajek and Sauer (2019) identify the major frames that were used by supporters and opponents of the proposed reform. Supporters of the proposed legislation presented four frames. The equality frame was forwarded the most frequently out of the four and was used in support of the bill (Hajek and Sauer, 2019, p. 324). Although women and men are equally qualified, this frame acknowledges that they do not have the same opportunities to hold supervisory board functions because of the deeply-rooted networks established by men, which exclude women and have not changed historically on a voluntary basis (Aslan, 2017, p. 381). Thus, "specific instruments to attain justice" (Aslan, 2017, p. 381) are required for women to have the opportunities to realize their potential on supervisory boards, "which

---

[5] Note that Hajek and Sauer (2019) analyzed the debates by both the National and Federal Council for their conclusions to compare two different policy-making processes relevant to the field of Austrian women's policies. Since our chapter only relates to the decision-making process regarding the corporate board quota, we translated the frames Hajek and Sauer identified from German into English according to the major arguments from the corporate board quota debate.

does not work without the quota" (Fekter, 2017, p. 382). Notably, then-ÖVP Vice-Chancellor and Minister of Justice, Wolfgang Brandstetter, emphasized the law's relevance "for the whole society." He also revealed that the high percentage of women in the judiciary would not have been possible without equal treatment legislation (Brandstetter, 2017, p. 383). Hajek and Sauer (2019, p. 324) identified the lagging behind frame as the second most frequently used frame, which asserts that Austria needs to catch up with other European countries, given that the number of women on Austrian corporate boards is too low and that other countries have made more progress concerning women in leadership positions (Aslan, 2017, p. 381).

The profitability frame or "quota as a success story" (Wurm, 2017, p. 379) arose as frequently as the second frame and used the business case to support the proposed quota by asserting that enterprises have improved their economic profitability in countries that have introduced gender quota regulations or have a good number of women on corporate boards. This frame was especially employed by female SPÖ members, like Gabriele Heinisch-Hosek, who noted that "…quotas deliver better results; quotas also increase the motivation of employees and quotas eventually create a more even and balanced picture in society, as it is now in many areas" (Heinisch-Hosek, 2017, p. 385). Only ÖVP Members of Parliament invoked the last frame—experience—which was key to explaining the party's reversal in its position on governance and gender equality policies in the corporate world. However, employer representatives remained opposed to legislative, state-driven approaches. The ÖVP Members of Parliament stressed that although they had long rejected the quota, they had gained experience or learned that gender equality requires pressure since only "18 percent [of] women [are currently on] Austrian corporate boards" (Steinacker, 2017, p. 374) and voluntary efforts did not lead to more equality. One debate participant and former-ÖVP cabinet minister cited her personal experiences by pointing out that she was one of her party's quota women and that the "quota did not make her worse or even less motivated" (Fekter, 2017, p. 382).

The positions expressed by the opponents of the proposed reform, including Austrian parties—the FPÖ, NEOS, and Team Stronach—can be categorized into three frames, which captured arguments already presented in the longstanding and stalemated Austrian corporate board debate (Hajek and Sauer, 2019, pp. 325–326). The ineffective frame was frequently used to oppose the law but also contained a feminist perspective. It was primarily used by members of the liberal NEOS party during parliamentary debates. NEOS MP, Claudia Angela Gamon, strongly asserted that the quota did not change the structural inequality affecting women in the labor market, women's old-age poverty, or the significant percentage of women with part-time employment. Accordingly, she summarized her position against supporting the "illusive solution of a quota in supervisory boards," because the quota failed to target the fundamental nature of gendered inequality. She added that she would prefer to talk about "real women's politics" (Gamon, 2017, p. 375). Moreover, she explicitly addressed the ÖVP accusation of sacrificing the basic principle of entrepreneurial freedom by approving the law.

This argument was also used by the right-wing populist FPÖ party, who also stressed that law unfairly restricted enterprises, alluding to the second frame, coercion (Stefan, 2017, p. 373). Additionally, former-ÖVP MP, Marcus Franz, who had become an independent, applied the degrading women frame. He argued that introducing the quota law would be harmful to women because there is "nothing worse than being a quota-woman" (Franz, 2017, p. 380), and a person's qualifications should be the only reason to obtain a position.

With the adoption of the 2017 quota law, the policy approach to promoting corporate gender equality in Austria moved from a uniquely self-regulatory approach to an approach that included business self-regulation and state regulation. Table 15.2 provides a summary of the major measures covered by this mixed approach.

During the lingering threat of quota implementation phase, two major policy tools were implemented by the Ministry of Commerce, the Chamber of Commerce, and the Federation of Austrian Industries: capacity and learning instruments. These instruments comprised a training or qualification program for women in leadership positions (Zukunft.Frauen) and a database for women holding or interested in supervisory board positions (Aufsichtsrätinnendatenbank). The Zukunft.Frauen program was established in 2010 and consists of eight half-day seminars for candidates who must be nominated by an enterprise to participate. As of 2019, more than 310 women have completed the training program (Interview with Hawel, 2019). Additionally, the Aufsichtsrätinnendatenbank, which was established in 2011, is restricted to women who are or have been supervisory board members, supervisory board members who have been nominated by the worker's council, and women who have completed recognized qualification programs for executive leadership positions, such as Zukunft.Frauen, the Compact Supervisory Board Competence course, or one of seven other programs (Zukunft.Frauen, 2020). The WKO Women in Commerce unit also provides the same course, which is a half-day module (Interview with Hawel, 2019; Der Standard, 2011b). The Secretary-General for the WKO Women in Business unit, who is responsible for implementing both the qualification programs and the database, further noted that the qualification program is directed toward employed women, while the Compact Supervisory Board Competence course targets women who run their own businesses (Interview with Hawel, 2019).

Upon adopting the 2017 law, enforcement legislation was passed to determine non-compliance sanctions. Following Germany's legal model, board elections would be considered invalid if the quota was not met and the seats would remain open. In terms of law coverage, it has a high and intermediate position along the GEPP comprehensiveness continuum. Although the law explicitly defines which enterprises it applies to—namely all stock-listed companies and those with more

Table 15.2   Policy Measures for Gender Equality on Corporate Boards in Austria

---

SELF-REGULATION

Austrian Corporate Governance Code

2009	2012
* Recommendation to take into account "the diversity of the supervisory board with respect to the international background of the members, the representation of both genders, and the age structure" for new appointments	* Reasonable attention is to be given to "the aspect of diversity of the supervisory board with respect to the representation of both genders and the age structure" * To include information about the gender composition of the boards and management positions and about the measures to promote women to the management board, supervisory board, and top management positions in the corporate governance report *Comply-or-explain

2018
* At least 30% of women and 30% of men on supervisory board unless the supervisory board has fewer than six shareholder representatives
* To include information about the share of women on the supervisory board and in management positions in the corporate governance report
* To include information about the measures to promote women on the management board, supervisory board, and top management positions in the corporate governance report
* Joint-stock companies: to include a description of the diversity concepts (age, gender, educational and professional background), goals, measures, and results
* Comply-or-explain

Coordinated by Austrian Federal Economic Chamber (Women in Business Unit)

"Zukunft.Frauen" 2010	"Aufsichtsrätinnen-Datenbank" 2011
* Training program for women qualifying for leading positions	* Database for women interested in a supervisory board position

---

STATE REGULATION

The Code of Company Regulations 2009	Incorporated Stock Companies Act 2012
* Publicly listed corporations * Recommendation to include the measures taken to advance women on the management board, supervisory board, and top management positions in the corporate governance report	* Publicly listed corporations * Recommendation to take into account "the diversity of the supervisory board with respect to the representation of both genders, and the age structure" for new appointments
Act on Equality between Women and Men in Supervisory boards 2017 * Publicly traded companies and companies with more than 1,000 employees *At least 30% of women and 30% of men on the supervisory board unless the board has fewer than six shareholder representatives or the share of women employees in less than 20% * Empty-seat provision * Applies to new board appointments only	**Sustainability and Diversity Improvement Act 2017** * Publicly traded companies with more than 500 employees. * Declaration that includes the description of the diversity concept related to the management board and supervisory board, including details about age, gender, educational, and professional background as well as the description of the aims of the diversity concept, the implementation, and the results * Comply-or-explain

than 1,000 employees—the GFMA-G paradoxically stipulates two necessary conditions to fall under the scope of the law. First, the supervisory board must consist of at least six employer representatives and three employee representatives. Therefore, if a supervisory board consists of three employee representatives, but less than six for employers, the company is not required to fulfill the quota. Seebacher and Wieser also point out that the number of supervisory board members can be changed at any time by the statutes of an enterprise or by recalling a member (2018, pp. 16–17). Second, at least 20% of company employees must be from the underrepresented sex. Moreover, the law only targets supervisory boards and not executive boards. However, it stipulates a 30% quota for both sexes as well as a sanction mechanism for invalidating board elections and leaving the mandate open if the quota is not fulfilled. Thus, while the GFMA-G initially targeted 200 enterprises, only seventy to eighty of those companies were estimated to meet both conditions required for compliance (Kals et al, 2017, p. 345).

For state-owned enterprises, the quota regulation only applies to supervisory board positions that the state can nominate (Wieser and Fischeneder, 2019, p. 23), and imposes no sanctions. However, the Ministry for Women and the Ministry of Commerce must give an annual progress report to the cabinet about the nominated board members. Given the enforceable sanctions for non-compliance and required reporting, the new law can be seen as fully coercive in terms of the coercion/voluntary continuum for private companies but only moderately coercive for state-owned firms.

The Practice of Paradox in a Mixed Approach: From Self-regulation to Near Complete Coercion

It is important to note that there was no significant change to the position of women on corporate boards until 2018—a year after the law's adoption—although the public sector experienced a significant increase of women on boards (Mensi-Klarbach, 2017, pp. 113). Companies that meet the 2017 law's two necessary conditions must adhere to it; enterprises must appoint women to vacant seats on their supervisory board until the company reaches the 30% quota. Likewise, the quota regulation applies to nominations and elections after December 31, 2017 (Thaler and Laherstorfer, 2017, p. 7). The law's implementation phase is thus ongoing, and enterprises must report their progress in Corporate Governance Reports, as regulated in the Corporate Governance Code (Kals et al, 2017, p. 349). There is no other obligation to report nominations to a ministry or state institution, nor are there limits to when vacant positions must be filled, or any sanctions if a company does not act in accordance with the law (Kals et al, 2017, p. 349). Furthermore, the law stipulates conditions that encourage circumventing its compliance, as described in the previous section. As Wieser and Werni (2020, p. 31) attest, it is hardly possible to obtain the information required for a complete survey of non-stock-listed companies with more than 1,000 employees. Therefore, only legislative authorities could comprehensively monitor the law's implementation process.

Although the implementation process does not legally require a detailed amount of monitoring, the Chamber of Labor "takes an explicit stance on the issue of increasing the proportion of women in leadership positions" (Mensi-Klarbach, 2017, p. 116) by collecting data on and monitoring changes to female representation on supervisory boards. The annually published Frauen.Management.Report ("Women Management Report") has documented the performance of Austria's top 200 and stock-listed companies regarding women's representation for nearly a decade. The report makes the development and leverage of policies on gender equality in the Austrian corporate world visible and accountable and promotes public debates about women's advancement in leadership positions.

The 2020 Frauen.Management.Report states that as of January 2020, only twenty-eight of seventy-four stock-listed companies (38%) actually fall under the scope of the GFMA-G and must therefore implement its quota legislation. The percentage of women on supervisory boards within these twenty-eight enterprises rose significantly following the GFMA-G's enactment, increasing from 22.4% in 2018 to 31.7% in January 2020. Approximately 64% of the companies that fall under the quota regulation have already met the 30% quota (Wieser and Werni, 2020, p. 32). Moreover, no supervisory board mandates have remained open since the law's introduction, and the sanction mechanism has not yet been required. Within the last two years, roughly 36% of newly appointed supervisory board members have been women (Wieser and Werni, 2020, p. 3). Conversely, stock-listed enterprises that were not required to comply with gender quota regulations have only seen the percentage of women on their supervisory boards increase from 11.9% in January 2018 to 15.4% in January 2020 (Wieser and Werni, 2020, p. 2). However, when looking at all stock-listed companies, the share of women on supervisory boards rose from 18% to 24.6% within the same period (Wieser and Werni, 2020, p. 31). The percentage of women on supervisory boards for enterprises on the Austrian Traded Index (ATX) even rose to 31.9% In 2020, 4.2% more than in 2019 (Wieser and Werni, 2020, p. 3). Nevertheless, the share of women on top-200 supervisory boards only increased by approximately 1% between 2019 and 2020 (Wieser and Werni, 2020, p. 3). Because existing research suggests that the unequal treatment of men and women might persist in subtle forms within the distribution of supervisory board positions and tasks (Mensi-Klarbach et al, 2019), the 2020 Frauen.Management.Report analyzed gender distribution within ATX and Prime Market enterprises for the first time. The analysis concerned the most influential board sub-committees, revealing that other than the nominating sub-committees, the sub-committees were below the 30% quota. Furthermore, of the thirty-seven Prime Market enterprises included in the Frauen.Management.Report, only fourteen women (compared to eighty-two men) were sub-committee presidents (Wieser and Werni, 2020, p. 30).

Nevertheless, the supervisory board quota has helped contribute to more than double the number of women listed in the Austrian supervisory database between 2017 (320) to 2019 (679) (Hawel, 2019). Bernadette Hawel also stresses that the WKO Women in Business unit continuously advocates for making use of the publicly accessible database.

Austria's Gender Equality Law for Corporate Boards as a Tool for Gender Transformation?

Assessing Austria's 2017 law in terms of whether women were empowered in the implementation process, as well as if it helped achieve substantive equality and cultural change in the corporate world and society at large, suggests a mixed picture of its potential for transformation and outcomes.

Low Level of Descriptive and Substantive Empowerment

The political actors entrusted to expedite gender equality in Austria's corporate world needed persistence in order to implement mandatory legislation. At the onset of the law's development during 2009 and 2010, there was a relatively high amount of civil society participation. This participation was part of the NAP for the Equal Treatment of Women and Men in the Labor Market, and coordinated and implemented by SPÖ Minister of Women and Public Service, Gabriele Heinisch-Hosek. The potential quota regulations, which arose from the discussion process and the EU initiative on women's presence on corporate boards, received intense media coverage. As a result, the Ministry of Women's Affairs experienced empowerment and public attention by advocating for legislative regulations to promote gender equality against the powerful interests of the ÖVP-supported business sector. Although these negotiations enhanced self-regulation approaches, they also led to an increase and diversification of self-regulation measures. Likewise, representatives from the Federation of Austrian Industries (IV) drew on these negotiations to promote women's participation in economic decision-making processes (Industriellenvereinigung, 2012).

On the one hand, the new self-regulatory tools included the establishment of a database as well as specific training and qualifications programs for women interested in supervisory board positions. These capacity instruments were and still are managed by the Chamber of Commerce and, in turn, WKO Women in Business, who are responsible for their implementation. On the other hand, the government agreed upon a self-binding quota resolution for state-owned enterprises as a test run to determine the efficiency of the quota regulations. Additionally, the Corporate Governance Code became stricter about women on supervisory boards after adopting language to explain the Non-Compliance Rule—which was also applied to the Stock Corporation Act. Here, the non-state expert group, the Austrian Working Group for Corporate Governance, drafted the rule that was also applied to the Austrian Commercial Code through a proposition from the Federal Chancellery (Mensi-Klarbach, 2017, pp. 112–113). Upon asking actors involved in the Working Group for Corporate Governance, Mensi-Klarbach reported that this amendment was mainly due to "international pressure and the ongoing debate at the EU level" (Mensi-Klarbach, 2017, pp. 118) and a request from the SPÖ (Interview with Mensi-Klarbach, 2019). After deepening the self-regulatory approach, the debate about gender equality measures within the corporate world abated. However, the annual report for progress on women's representation on supervisory boards for state-owned companies continuously showed the efficiency of the self-binding quota regulation. This created an opportunity for the SPÖ-led Ministry of Women's Affairs to regularly call for private sector quota regulations. Ultimately, limited empowerment occurred during the implementation and enforcement process—few new actors that spoke for women came forward, and only the more institutionalized political agents and networks were involved. Moreover, there were no efforts to deepen issues about diversity and intersectionality. It was clear, therefore, that upper-class and white women were more likely to be advanced by these regulations.

Gender Transformation

Taking a closer look at the direct and indirect impacts of the 2017 law helps to better understand its quite limited overall gender-transformative potential. Although the adoption of the GFMA-G marks a change to Austria's dominant frames of discourse on gender equality policies within the private corporate sphere, the topography of Austria's structural inequalities in the corporate world remained unchanged (Bundeskanzleramt, 2020a). Moreover, the law's implementation divides enterprises into those who must comply with the law and those who follow the self-regulatory approach.

Increase on a Quantitative Level and Awareness on a Symbolic Level
In their summary of the 2019 monitoring report, Wieser and Fischeneder (2019) assert that businesses covered by the quota law were compliant within a year of implementation. Nevertheless, the authors conclude that political actors must actively monitor regulation compliance at all types of corporations in a transparent and comprehensive manner (Wieser and Fischeneder, 2019, p. 40). At the same time, law experts and evaluation reports criticized the law for not appropriately implementing the legislator's objectives and setting the conditions to circumvent the quota regulations (Wieser and Werni, 2020, p. 12). Looking at

stock-listed companies covered by the law shows that the share of women on supervisory boards rose from 22.4% in 2018 when the law was implemented to 31.7% in January 2020, compared to the respective marginal increase from 11.9% to 15.4% among stock-listed companies that were not covered by the law (Wieser and Werni, 2020, p. 31). Moreover, women only comprised 6.8% of the executive boards in 2020, while executive boards for the 200 most-profitable businesses showed a decline from 8.4% in female managers in 2018 to 8.0% in 2020 (Wieser and Werni, 2020, p. 2). However, the 2019 annual progress report for state-owned companies shows a much more optimistic outlook concerning the average women's share on supervisory boards, which was 43.6% in 2018—although this represented a decrease from 46.7% in the previous year (Bundeskanzleramt, 2019).

With regard to promoting more diverse corporate boards and an intersectional approach, research is limited on data about characteristics like ethnic background, age, disability, and sexual orientation. The women who were newly appointed to supervisory board positions in 2019 are arguably quite homogeneous and come primarily from the German-speaking countries—Austria, Germany, and Switzerland. In terms of qualifications, most new female supervisory board members hold a business degree, followed by law, and then alumnae of technical study programs. Compared to male supervisory board members, female board members are younger and better formally qualified than their colleagues (Wiener and Werni, 2020, p. 33). A survey of twenty-six stock-listed companies showed that non-financial reporting regulations only marginally addressed diversity issues and that they were not considered of significant value (Baumüller, 2019). In a Deloitte online survey that asked 442 people in leadership positions at Austrian enterprises, 93% agreed that having women on a company's leadership team is a competitive advantage, and 59.5% stressed that their business would like to raise the number of women in leading positions in the coming years. While human resources managers strongly supported increasing the share of women in leading positions (73.2%), 25.9% of the management and 31.4% of executive personnel were against such a move. At the same time, 58.4% of all respondents reported that their enterprise did not have quantifiable objectives to enhance women's representation (Wentner et al, 2019). Thus, the law's direct impact has been limited and has yet to affect companies that it does not cover.

Changes in Decision-maker Frames and the Stagnation of Gender Stereotypes
The attitudes of business lobbying group representatives have remained unchanged. They were fundamentally opposed to the mandatory quota regulation, which they saw as unnecessary and coercive. Likewise, the NEOS neoliberal party still perceives private sector quotas as illegitimate and a threat to entrepreneurial freedom but supports the public sector quota (Bernhard, 2019, p. 14). Nonetheless, the ÖVP's change in position was quite remarkable. Considering the monitored, consistently low number of women in economic leadership positions (despite self-regulatory measures), the success of the quota regulation in state-owned

businesses, and the impending breakup of the SPÖ-ÖVP coalition, the Christian-conservative ÖVP shifted from a strict stance against any quota regulation to supporting a mandatory quota with a sanction mechanism for the private sector. This went against the position taken by the Chamber of Commerce and Federations of Austrian Industries during the debate about the 2017 law, which would have been an unthinkable position even ten years earlier. Introducing sanction mechanisms for non-compliance to quota regulations also signified a step toward more accountability to policy decisions meant to advance gender equality, which is an important indicator for assessing an equality-friendly policy development process (Galligan, 2015). Whether this policy shift will have any long-term effect on the conservative Austrian gender regime's potential to be more supportive of gender equality remains to be seen, but recent studies indicate otherwise.

When asked in the Deloitte online survey about the major obstacles faced by women concerning their careers in economic decision-making positions, 68.1% of 442 enterprise leaders mentioned work-life balance, 60.6% cited conservative gender roles and prejudices, and 60.4% referred to societal and political infrastructure, including childcare availability. However, 52.9% perceived women's lack of ambition and self-confidence as major impediments. Accordingly, factors that were seen to have the least impediment on women were business culture (49.8%), leadership personnel behavior (43.2%), and working conditions, such as expected working hours (37.8%) (Wentner et al, 2019). Thus, the respondents, who represented leadership personnel at Austrian companies, still ascribed the responsibility for women's advancement in economic decision-making positions to individual women and the societal level, but not to behavioral and organizational conditions, nor company norms. Similar to the resistance of business gatekeepers to more gender-equal approaches, there has been little evidence of gender norm shifts among political party decision-makers with regard to private businesses. Although the ÖVP and the Greens agreed to raise the gender quota for state-owned businesses to 40% in their new coalition's government program, there is little support for private sector measures aimed at raising the gender quota as well as adjusting the scope of the GFMA-G. (Bundeskanzleramt, 2020b).

Women on Corporate Boards—Toward More Public Support for Meaningful Gender Quotas

Most media coverage has stressed the high gender inequality on corporate boards, the gender pay gap, and also discussed the effectiveness of quota regulations in other European countries. While public support for gender quota regulations seems mixed, the majority of the Austrian population clearly sees them as legitimate in a legal sense because these regulations are enshrined in the Austrian constitution (Gresch and Sauer, 2018). At the same time, until there is a clear link between the economic benefits of having more women on corporate boards, public support for quotas will remain mixed. Thus, further assessment and studies are needed to evaluate if having more women on corporate boards leads to economic changes that could also benefit the greater society.

As a whole, the direct and indirect impacts of Austria's first mandatory quota law on the private sector can be categorized as gender accommodation rather than any significant transformation of Austria's gendered power relations and its gender regime (Gresch and Sauer, 2018, pp. 333–335). The law only affects a very limited number of companies and targets supervisory—not executive—boards, which remained a taboo issue throughout the pre-adoption phase (Heinisch-Hosek, 2019; Mensi-Klarbach et al, 2019). Moreover, the emphasis on implementing a mandatory gender quota target superseded deliberations and initiatives about intersectional and structural inequalities in the corporate world. Compliance with the quota target extended to the wider measure to at least empower women at bigger companies (Baumüller, 2019). The predefined quotas for different sectors—30% for the private sector supervisory boards, 40% for state-owned enterprises, and a 50% target under the Federal Equal Treatment Law for Public Services—also reflects the high and continuous resistance to transforming the conservative gender regime. Furthermore, the law's recent adoption and the lack of associated research make it difficult to predict whether having more women on boards will change Austria's business and decision-making culture (Mensi-Klarbach et al, 2019).

Conclusion

The codification of the 2017 Austrian gender quota law indicates a move from a uniquely self-regulatory approach to a mixed approach in raising the representation of women on corporate boards, including state regulation and business self-regulation. This was an unusual political outcome given the country's form of consociational corporatism, its institutionalized business aversion to state supervision and control, and its defense of a free play of market forces. This form of decision-making explains Austria's limited implementation of gender quotas and continuing emphasis on company self-regulation to comply with the law.

Measures to implement this mixed approach such as data collection and monitoring by an annual report resulted in higher numbers of women on supervisory boards. Because the law exposes ways to circumvent the quota regulation, its impact on affected companies has been limited to a modest increase. Overall, the implementation process of Austria's mixed approach was characterized by a low level of descriptive and substantive empowerment of women. Femocrats, as well as women in social partnership organizations, were only visible at the beginning of the implementation and evaluation process and had a low overall impact in pushing for stricter implementation, enforcement, and oversight to ultimately more concretely promote gender equality. Moreover, the implementation process did not lead to more diverse corporate boards. Although sound research on the composition of corporate boards with respect to ethnic background, disability, age, and sexual orientation is missing, the appointed women can be categorized as a homogeneous group of well-educated, white women from the German-speaking countries of Austria, Germany, and Switzerland.

Ultimately, the mixed approach did not lead to the transformation of gender relations in the corporate world but rather to gender accommodation. The attitudes of the key business gatekeepers toward gender equality, from their vantage point of institutionalized social partners in the consociational fabric of policy-making, remained unchanged; individual women were still blamed for their underrepresentation in the corporate world. Given this resistance, it was even more remarkable that the leaders of the ÖVP shifted to supporting quotas at all. At the same time, the highly voluntary nature of implementation can be interpreted as a form of resistance to gender transformation and, ultimately, any change to the conservative gender regime. Thus, Austria's paradoxical implementation reinforced the country's conservative gender regime (Gresch and Sauer, 2018).

Looking toward the future, it remains to be seen whether the increased number of women on corporate boards enhances economic growth and hence a greater potential to garner more public support for corporate gender equality. There is some hope that the entry of the Green Party in the current government coalition might help to push the implementation of gender quota law toward more concrete and authoritative policy that could harness the transformative potential of these policies. Only time will tell, however, if the paradoxes of the implementation process thus far, only three years out, will lead to positive change for gender equality in the corporate world in the future and break the grips of the conservative regime.

Interviews

Mag.ª Bernadette Hawel, Secretary General for the Austrian Chamber of Commerce service organization, "Women in Business" (Bundesgeschäftsführerin "Frau in der Wirtschaft," Wirtschaftskammer Österreich), May 3, 2019, Vienna.

Gabriele Heinisch-Hosek, Chairwoman of the Social Democratic Party Women's Caucus (since 2009); Federal Minister of Women and Public Affairs (2008–2013); Federal Minister of Education and Women (2013–2016), May 7, 2019, Vienna.

Dr. Heike Mensi-Klarbach, Assistant Professor, Institute for Gender and Diversity in Organizations, Vienna University of Economics and Business, May 8, 2019, Vienna.

References

Allhutter, Doris (2003) *Europäische Chancengleichheit von Frauen und Männern im österreichischen Recht*. Linz: Trauner Verlag.

APA (2011) "Frauenquote: Heinisch-Hosek unternimmt neuen Anlauf," Austria Presse Agentur, February 1.

Aslan, Aygül Berivan (2017) in Nationalrat der Republik Österreich. Stenographisches Protokoll des Nationalrats der Republik Österreich: 188. Sitzung, p. 381, https://www.parlament.gv.at/PAKT/VHG/XXV/NRSITZ/NRSITZ_00189/fname_674441.pdf (Accessed May 27, 2018).

Baumüller, Josef (2019) Nichtfinanzielle Berichterstattung. Eine Evaluierung der Umsetzung des NaDiVeG in börsennotierten Unternehmen, https://www.arbeiterkammer.at/interessenvertretung/wirtschaft/betriebswirtschaft/Nichtfinanzielle_Berichterstattung.pdf (Accessed October 23, 2020).

Bernhard, Michael (2019) in Gleichbehandlungsausschuss. Bericht des Gleichbehandlungsausschusses über das Volksbegehren (433 d.B.) "Frauenvolksbegehren," 513 der Beilagen XXVI.GP., Ausschussbericht NR, Anlage 2, p. 14. https://www.parlament.gv.at/PAKT/VHG/XXVI/I/I_00513/index.shtml (Accessed August 23, 2019).

BGBl I Nr. 66/2004, *Equal Treatment Law* (Gleichbehandlungsgesetz – GlBG).

BGBl I Nr. 71/2009, *Stock Corporation Law Amendment Act 2009* (Aktienrechts-Änderungsgesetz 2009 – AktRÄG 2009).

BGBl I Nr. 35/2012, *2nd Stability Act 2012* (2. Stabilitätsgesetz 2012—2. StabG-2012).

BGBl I Nr. 104/2017, *Equal Treatment Law of Women and Men in Supervisory Boards* (Gleichstellungsgesetz von Frauen und Männern im Aufsichtsrat—GFMA-G).

BMBWF (2011) "Gleichbehandlungsgesetz (für die Privatwirtschaft)," https://bildung.bmbwf.gv.at/frauen/gleichbehandlung/rg/rg_gbg_privat (Accessed April 26, 2018).

Brandstetter, Wolfgang (2017) in Nationalrat der Republik Österreich. Stenographisches Protokoll des Nationalrats der Republik Österreich: 188. Sitzung, p. 383, https://www.parlament.gv.at/PAKT/VHG/XXV/NRSITZ/NRSITZ_00189/fname_674441.pdf (Accessed May 27, 2018).

Bundeskanzleramt (2010) *Nationaler Aktionsplan Gleichstellung von Frauen und Männern am Arbeitsmarkt*. Wien: Bundesministerium für Frauen und Öffentlicher Dienst im Bundeskanzleramt, https://www.bundeskanzleramt.gv.at/nap2010_druck_web_komplett_25928.pdf (Accessed August 23, 2019).

Bundeskanzleramt (2019) "Vortrag an den Ministerrat. Fortschrittsbericht 2019 über die Erhöhung des Frauenanteils in den Aufsichtratsgremien der Unternehmen mit einem Bundesanteil von 50% und darüber in Fortsetzung der Vorbildwirkung des Bundes," https://www.bundeskanzleramt.gv.at/dam/jcr:bce04a1d-cf14-4512-8a4b-4d1a85a4304e/8_7_mrv.pdf (Accessed 30, August 2019).

Bundeskanzleramt (2020a) *Gleichstellung in Zahlen: Gender Index 2019*, https://www.bundeskanzleramt.gv.at/agenda/frauen-und-gleichstellung/gender-mainstreaming-und-budgeting/gender-daten-index.html (Accessed October 30, 2020).

Bundeskanzleramt (2020b) *Aus Verantwortung für Österreich. Regierungsprogramm 2020–2024*, https://www.bundeskanzleramt.gv.at/bundeskanzleramt/die-bundesregierung/regierungsdokumente.html (Accessed October 23, 2020).

Bundesministerium für Gesundheit und Frauen (2016) *Gleichbehandlungsbericht des Bundes 2016*. Wien: Bundesministerium für Gesundheit und Frauen.

Bundesministerium für Gesundheit und Frauen (2017) *Gleichstellung in Zahlen. Gender Index 2017*. Wien: Bundesministerium für Gesundheit und Frauen.

Bundespressedienst (2011) "Heinisch-Hosek: Österreich ist europäischer Nachzügler bei Frauen in Führungspositionen," APA, February 1, https://www.ots.at/presseaussendung/OTS_20110201_OTS0150/heinisch-hosek-oesterreich-ist-europaeischer-nachzuegler-bei-frauen-in-fuehrungspositionen (Accessed June 28, 2019).

Bundesregierung Österreich (2008) "Regierungsprogramm für die XXIV. Gesetzgebungsperiode," http://www.konvent.gv.at/K/DE/INST-K/INST-K_00179/imfname_164994.pdf (Accessed June 28, 2019).

Bundesregierung Österreich (2017) "Für Österreich. Arbeitsprogramm 2017/2018," http://www.oeaab-wien-aps.at/wp-content/uploads/2017/02/170130_Arbeitsprogramm1718.pdf (Accessed June 30, 2019).

Dackweiler, Regina-Maria (2003) *Wohlfahrtsstaatliche Geschlechterpolitik am Beispiel Österreichs*. Opladen: Leske und Budrich.

Der Standard (2009) "Marek setzt auf Weiterbildung," https://www.derstandard.at/story/1259281897598/weibliche-fuehrungskraefte-marek-setzt-auf-weiterbildung (Accessed April 27, 2019).

Der Standard (2010) "Gleichstellung ante portas," June 30, https://derstandard.at/1277337083497/Nationaler-Aktionsplan-Gleichstellung (Accessed April 26, 2018).

Der Standard (2011a) "Aufsichtsräte: Regierung einigt sich auf eine Frauenquote," March 15, https://www.derstandard.at/story/1297820484932/aufsichtsraete-regierung-einigt-sich-auf-eine-frauenquote (Accessed April 27, 2017).

Der Standard (2011b) "Top-Frauen zum Googeln," March 6, https://www.derstandard.at/story/1297819578071/fuehrungskraefteprogramm-top-frauen-zum-googeln (Accessed April 27, 2019).

Dahlerup Drude and Lenita Freidenvall (2005) "Quotas as a 'Fast Track' to Equal Representation for Women," *International Feminist Journal of Politics*, 7 (1), pp. 26–48.

EIGE (2020) *Gender Statistics Database: Women and Men in Decision Making: Business and Finance*, https://eige.europa.eu/gender-statistics/dgs (Accessed October 28, 2020).

Fekter, Maria Theresia (2017) in Nationalrat der Republik Österreich. Stenographisches Protokoll des Nationalrats der Republik Österreich: 188. Sitzung p. 382, https://www.parlament.gv.at/PAKT/VHG/XXV/NRSITZ/NRSITZ_00189/fname_674141.pdf (Accessed May 27, 2018).

Fink, Marcel (2006) "Unternehmerverbände," in Herbert Dachs, et al (ed.) *Politik in Österreich. Das Handbuch*. Wien: Manz, pp. 443–461.

Franz, Marcus (2017) in Nationalrat der Republik Österreich. Stenographisches Protokoll des Nationalrats der Republik Österreich: 188. Sitzung, p. 380, https://www.parlament.gv.at/PAKT/VHG/XXV/NRSITZ/NRSITZ_00189/fname_674441.pdf (Accessed 27 May 27, 2018).

Gabaldon, Patricia, Heike Mensi-Klarbach, and Cathrine Seiterstad (2017) "Austrian Boards—Combining Soft and Hard Law Regulations," in Cathrine Seierstad, Patricia

Gabaldon, and Heike Mensi-Klarbach (eds.) *Gender Diversity in the Boardroom: Multiple Approaches Beyond Quotas*. Cham: Palgrave Macmillan, 261–284.

Galligan, Yvonne (2015) "States of Democracy. An overview," in Yvonne Galligan (ed.) *States of Democracy. Gender and Politics in the European Union*. London: Routledge, pp. 1–14.

Gamon, Claudia Angela (2017) in Nationalrat der Republik Österreich, 188. *Sitzung*, p. 375, https://www.parlament.gv.at/PAKT/VHG/XXV/NRSITZ/NRSITZ_00189/fname_674441.pdf (Accessed May 27, 2018).

Gresch, Nora, and Birgit Sauer (2015) "Topographies of Gender Democracy in Austria," in Yvonne Galligan (ed.) *States of Democracy. Gender and Politics in the European Union*. London: Routledge, pp. 33–49.

Gresch, Nora and Birgit Sauer (2018) "The Austrian Paradox: The Challenges to Transform a Conservative Gender Regime," in Éléonore Lépinard and Ruth Rubio (ed.) *Transforming Gender Citizenship. The Irresistible Rise of Gender Quotas in Europe*. Cambridge: Cambridge University Press, pp. 308–338.

Hajek, Katharina and Birgit Sauer (2019) "Machen Frauen Frauenpolitik? Das Anti-Gesichtsverhüllungsgesetz und die Quote für Aufsichtsräte," in Blaustrumpf ahoi! (ed.) "Sie meinen es politisch!" 100 Jahre Frauenwahlrecht in Österreich. *Geschlechterdemokratie als gesellschaftspolitische Herausforderung*. Wien: Löcker Verlag, pp. 317–328.

Heinisch-Hosek, Gabriele (2017) in Nationalrat der Republik Österreich. Stenographisches Protokoll des Nationalrats der Republik Österreich: 188. Sitzung, p. 385, https://www.parlament.gv.at/PAKT/VHG/XXV/NRSITZ/NRSITZ_00189/fname_674441.pdf (Accessed May 27, 2018).

Industriellenvereinigung (2012) "Frauen in Führungspositionen. Ein Leitfaden für Unternehmen," https://www.womentalkbusiness.info/wp-data/uploads/2013/08/Frauen_Führen_2012-IndustriellenvereinigungÖsterreich.pdf (Accessed October 27, 2020).

Kalss, Susanne, Brameshuber, Elisabeth, and Georg Durtsberger (2017) "Die Quote im Aufsichtsrat für Kapital- und Arbeitnehmervertreter," *Der Gesellschafter*, 6, pp. 344–361.

Köpl, Regina (2005) "Gendering Political Representation: Debates and Controversies in Austria," in Joni Lovenduski and Claudie Baudino (ed.) *State Feminism and Political Representation*. Cambridge: Cambridge University Press, pp. 20–40.

Langan, Mary and Ilona Ostner (1991) "Geschlechterpolitiken im Wohlfahrtsstaat. Aspekte im internationalen Vergleich," *Kritische Justiz*, 3, pp. 302–317.

Leitner, Andrea, and Margareta Kreimer (2000) "Österreich als erfolgreiches Beschäftigungsmodell für Frauen?" *femina politica. Zeitschrift für feministische Politik-Wissenschaft*, 9 (2), pp. 28–38.

Lépinard, Éléonore (2014) *Gender Quotas and Transformative Politics*. RSCAS Policy Paper 2014/06, Robert Schuman Centre for Advanced Studies, European University Institute, Fiesole.

Lépinard, Éléonore and Ruth Rubio Marín (2018) "Conclusion: Assessing the Transformative Potential of Gender Quotas for Gender Equality and Democratic Citizenship," in Éléonore Lépinard and Ruth Rubio Marín (ed.) *Transforming Gender Citizenship. The Irresistible Rise of Gender Quotas in Europe*. Cambridge: Cambridge University Press, pp. 424–458.

Lewis, Jane, and Ilona Ostner (1994) *Gender and the Evolution of European Social Policies*. 2nd edn. Bremen: University of Bremen Centre for Policy Research.

Mensi-Klarbach, Heike (2017) "Gender Diversity in Austrian Boards—Combining Soft and Hard Law Regulations," in Cathrine Seierstad, Patricia Gabaldon, and Heike Mensi-Klarbach (ed.) *Gender Diversity in the Boardroom: Multiple Approaches beyond Quotas*. Cham: Palgrave Macmillan, pp. 103–128.

Mensi-Klarbach, Heike, Stephan Leixnering, and Michael Schiffinger (2019) "The Carrot or the Stick: Self-Regulation for Gender-diverse Boards via Codes of Good Governance," *Journal of Business Ethics*, https://doi.org/10.1007/s10551-019-04336-z (Accessed October 9, 2020).

Meyer, Renate and Markus Höllerer (2016) "Laying a Smoke Screen: Ambiguity and Neutralization as Strategic Responses to Intra-institutional Complexity," *Strategic Organization*, 14 (4), pp. 373–406.

Müller, Carina (2011) *Corporate Governance—A Comparison between Austria and the Netherlands*. Master's Thesis. Universität Graz, https://unipub.uni-graz.at/obvugrhs/download/pdf/217178?originalFilename=true (Accessed October 10, 2020).

Naderer, Ruth, Petra Sauer, and Christina Wieser (2011) *Frauen in Geschäftsführung und Aufsichtsrat. Eine Untersuchung in den Top 200 Unternehmen. Eine empirische Studie*. Wien: Kammer für Arbeiter und Angestellte für Wien.

Nationalrat der Republik Österreich (2017) Stenographisches Protokoll des Nationalrats der Republik Österreich: 188. Sitzung, https://www.parlament.gv.at/PAKT/VHG/XXV/NRSITZ/NRSITZ_00189/fname_674441.pdf (Accessed May 27, 2018).

Österreichischer Arbeitskreis für Corporate Governance (2009) "Österreichischer Corporate Governance Kodex. Fassung Jänner 2009," https://www.corporate-governance.at/uploads/u/corpgov/files/kodex/corporate-governance-kodex-012009.pdf (Accessed October 1, 2020).

PID. Presse- und Informationsdienst der Stadt Wien (2006) "Wiener Grüne repräsentieren Schwerpunkt ihrer politischen Arbeit," APA, October 16, http://www.ots.at/presseaussendung/OTS_20061016_OTS0099/wiener-gruene-praesentieren-schwerpunkt-ihrer-politischen-arbeit (Accessed June 28, 2019).

Profil Redaktion (2011) "'profil': Mitterlehner: 'Frauenquote für Aufsichtsräte in Staatsbetrieben'," APA, February 19, https://www.ots.at/presseaussendung/OTS_20110219_OTS0007/profil-mitterlehner-frauenquote-fuer-aufsichtsraete-in-staatsbetrieben (Accessed June 30, 2019).

Seebacher, Lisa Marie and Christina Wieser (2018) Frauen.Management.Report.2018. Ab 2018: Die Aufsichtsratsquote. Wien: Kammer für Arbeiter und Angestellte für Wien.

SPÖ Pressedienst (2008a) "Frauentag: Bures will Quoten-Diskussion führen," APA, March 7, https://www.ots.at/presseaussendung/OTS_20080307_OTS0241/frauentag-bures-will-quoten-diskussion-fuehren (Accessed June 28, 2019).

SPÖ Pressedienst (2008b) "SK-Dokumentation. ÖVP übernimmt im Wahlkampf SPÖ-Vorschläge," September 1, http://www.ots.at/presseaussendung/OTS_20080901_OTS0270/sk-dokumentation-oevp-uebernimmt-im-wahlkampf-spoe-vorschlaege (Accessed June 28, 2019).

SPÖ-Parlamentsklub (2007) "Prammer will Vergabe öffentlicher Aufträge an Frauenförderung koppeln," APA, March 5, http://www.ots.at/presseaussendung/OTS_20070305_OTS0107/prammer-will-vergabe-oeffentlicher-auftraege-an-frauenfoerderung-koppeln (Accessed 28 June 28, 2019).

SPÖ-Parlamentsklub (2010) "Wurm: ÖVP-Front gegen verpflichtende Quote bröckelt," APA, September 22, https://www.ots.at/presseaussendung/OTS_201009

22_OTS0326/wurm-oevp-front-gegen-verpflichtende-quote-broeckelt   (Accessed June 30, 2019).

Statistik Austria (2014a) Bruttostundenverdienste der Vollzeitbeschäftigten nach Wirtschaftstätigkeit und Geschlecht 2014, http://www.statistik.at/web_de/statistiken/menschen_und_gesellschaft/soziales/personen-einkommen/verdienststruktur/index.html (Accessed May 27, 2018).

Statistik Austria (2014b) *Bruttostundenverdienste der Teilzeitbeschäftigten nach Wirtschaftstätigkeit und Geschlecht 2014*, http://www.statistik.at/web_de/statistiken/menschen_und_gesellschaft/soziales/personen-einkommen/verdienststruktur/index.html (Accessed May 27, 2018).

Statistik Austria (2017) *Unselbständig Erwerbstätige (ILO) nach ÖNACE und Geschlecht*, http://www.statistik.at/web_de/statistiken/menschen_und_gesellschaft/soziales/gender-statistik/erwerbstaetigkeit/index.html (Accessed April 27, 2018).

Statistik Austria (2018) *Internationaler Frauentag 2018: Immer mehr Frauen sind erwerbstätig, oft in Teilzeit; Lohnunterschied trotz Rückgang über dem EU-Durchschnitt*, https://statistik.at/web_de/presse/116346.html (Accessed May 27, 2018).

Statistik Austria (2019) *Statistics Brief. Frauen am Arbeitsmarkt*, http://www.statistik.at/web_de/services/statistics_brief/index.html (Accessed July 10, 2019).

Stefan, Harald (2017) in Nationalrat der Republik Österreich. Stenographisches Protokoll des Nationalrats der Republik Österreich: 188. Sitzung, p. 373, https://www.parlament.gv.at/PAKT/VHG/XXV/NRSITZ/NRSITZ_00189/fname_674441.pdf (Accessed May 27, 2018).

Steinacker, Michaela (2017) in Nationalrat der Republik Österreich. Stenographisches Protokoll des Nationalrats der Republik Österreich: 188. Sitzung, p. 374, https://www.parlament.gv.at/PAKT/VHG/XXV/NRSITZ/NRSITZ_00189/fname_674441.pdf (Accessed May 27 2018).

Tálos, Emmerich (2006) "Sozialpartnerschaft. Austrokorporatismus am Ende?" in Herbert Dachs (ed.) *Politik in Österreich. Das Handbuch*. Wien: Manz, 425–442.

Thaler, Christian and Daniela Laherstorfer (2017) "Geschlechterquote: Neue Verbindlichkeit für die bekannte Gender Diversity," *Aufsichtsrat aktuell*, 6, 6–11.

Wentner, Gundi, Elisa Aichinger, and Gerhard Wagner (2019) *Frauen und Führung. Eine Studie von Deloitte Österreich*, https://www2.deloitte.com/content/dam/Deloitte/at/Documents/consulting/at-deloitte-umfrage-frauen-und-fuehrung-2019.pdf (Accessed October 30, 2020).

Wieser, Christina and Fischeneder, Andreas (2019) *Frauen.Management.Report.2019. Aufsichtsratsquote—Das Jahr danach*. Wien: Kammer für Arbeiter und Angestellte für Wien.

Wieser, Christina and Jakob Wern (2020) *Frauen.Management.Report.2020. Die Aufsichtsratsquote wirkt—was jetzt?* Wien: Kammer für Arbeiter und Angestellte für Wien.

Wurm, Giesela (2017) in Nationalrat der Republik Österreich. Stenographisches Protokoll des Nationalrats der Republik Österreich: 188. Sitzung, p. 379, https://www.parlament.gv.at/PAKT/VHG/XXV/NRSITZ/NRSITZ_00189/fname_674441.pdf (Accessed May 27, 2018).

Zukunft.Frauen (2020) *Aufsichtsrätinnendatenbank-Registrierung*, https://www.zukunft-frauen.at/app/Eingabe.aspx (Accessed October 30, 2020).

APPLYING A COMPARATIVE LENS

16

What Works and Why? The Politics of Corporate Gender Equality by the Numbers

Isabelle Engeli and Amy G. Mazur

Introduction

With the politics, processes, and outcomes of gender equality policy on corporate boards mapped out systematically in fifteen democracies, we now return to the core questions of the book in this last section through a comparative lens: How were policies that addressed gender equality on corporate boards adopted and implemented? Did they achieve any degree of success in promoting women's presence on corporate boards and broader gender transformative impacts that would allow for real and lasting equality in a highly gender equality adverse arena, the closed and private world of corporations? What were the politics of the pursuit of corporate gender equality across the fifteen countries? What worked and did not work and why? What are the lessons to be drawn from these experiences with the pursuit of gender equality in the corporate world?

The corporate world has been highly resistant to gender balance on boards, with the issue only getting political and corporate attention in the late 1990s and early 2000s and policies starting to be put on the books later that decade up until the present. At the same time, as international organizations like the OECD and EIGE assert women's positions in the hallways of power have been the leading area of significant change in recent years in the fight for gender equality and rights, including in the boardroom. Thus, this systematic comparative mapping exercise not only allows for drawing important conclusions about the politics, policy, and outcomes of corporate board gender equality, but also it contributes to answering larger questions about gender equality policy implementation, to further illuminate the "elusive recipe" for successful gender equality policy and the various long and winding roads that lead to promoting gender equality.

Isabelle Engeli and Amy G. Mazur, *What Works and Why? The Politics of Corporate Gender Equality by the Numbers.*
In: *Gender Equality and Policy Implementation in the Corporate World.* Edited by Isabelle Engeli and Amy G. Mazur,
Oxford University Press. © Oxford University Press (2022). DOI: 10.1093/oso/9780198865216.003.0016

The microscope is therefore moved in these last two chapters from the politics of individual countries to a cross-country comparison that investigates the similarities and divergences in the policy responses and outcomes across time and space through the lens of the GEPP approach in terms of process, politics, policy empowerment, and level of transformative change. In this chapter, the comparative lens is applied to the politics of corporate board equality policy in action, the specific mix and ambition of the policy tools and their outcomes with regard to the numerical success of the policy—the increase of women on corporate boards. The argument is made that numerical progress can only be made through combining mandates and recommendations through a trade-off between regulatory ambition, scope, and coerciveness. The more complex issue of whether, how, and why inclusive policy empowerment and gender transformation has been achieved is the focus of the final chapter. Following a comparative analysis of success beyond the numbers, Chapter 17 concludes the book with a discussion of analytical lessons learned, policy recommendations, and an agenda for future research.

In the first part of this chapter, the politics of regulating equality on corporate boards are assessed for the four types of regulatory trajectories and their outputs. The next part identifies three common trends found across all of the fifteen country cases in the politics of policy implementation regardless of regulatory approach or regional placement of a given country. In the third part, we focus on the policy mix for successful numerical outcomes, first analyzing the progress of women's presence on boards across the fifteen country cases and then delving into the details of the particular policy mixes of recommendations and mandates as well as the trade-offs between regulatory ambition, scope, and coerciveness. In the conclusion the major takeaways from the comparative analysis about what works and why are presented for success by the numbers.

Regulation by Design, Regulation by Default

If Norway cleared the way for organized action toward the promotion of equality on corporate boards, it was nevertheless part of a more global movement fueled by increasing attention from selected venues in the corporate world and supranational organizations. The global economic crisis of 2008–2009 opened an additional window of opportunity for launching public discussion around the issue at the domestic level. The debate about the best approach for solving gender inequalities in economic decision-making quickly became heated and often highly controversial. The policy responses adopted have greatly varied as a result.

Four main regulatory trajectories have developed over time, presented in Figure 16.1. All the countries started from an initial state of regulation left entirely to the individual companies. Australia, Canada, Croatia, Hungary, Serbia,

	Self-regulation Approach	State-regulation Approach
Flagship Track	**Self-regulation by Design**	**Quotas by Design**
	Australia, UK, Sweden	Norway, France , Belgium
Alternative Track	**Self-regulation by Default**	**Quotas by Default**
	USA, Canada, Croatia, Serbia, Hungary, Poland	Spain, Germany, Austria

Fig. 16.1 Mapping the Regulatory Tracks

Sweden, the UK, and the USA pursued the self-regulatory pathway over time. Norway was followed by Spain, France, Belgium, Austria, and Germany into the state-regulatory pathway. One main difference distinguishes the pathways: the role of the state. In the self-regulatory pathway, the state has no leading role in the promotion of equality on corporate boards. In the state-regulatory pathways, the state has gradually strengthened its intervention to finally take over the lead.

The evolution of the regulatory trajectories has further revealed additional key variations, this time within each pathway. Among the countries included in this study, we identify four tracks, two tracks for the self-regulatory pathways and two tracks for the state-regulatory pathways. The flagship tracks are the model tracks where actions and initiatives have been organized through one main driver. The alternative tracks are tracks that are not organized by one main policy logic. It is important to remember that our classification is aligned along a continuum; thus, there are some gray areas between the different categories with some cases being more clearly situated in a given approach and track than others.

Within the self-regulatory pathway, Australia, the UK, and Sweden have taken the "flagship track". These three cases have seen a relatively high level of attention to gender balance on corporate boards and have undergone an organized effort to implement self-regulation under corporate leadership. The three countries display a far-reaching regulatory scope together with a high level of organization. Rather than state-based actors, peak business associations, often through corporate governance codes, have made purposeful choices to promote gender balance on boards through comprehensive self-regulation, in other words, "self-regulation by design."

The "alternative track" to self-regulation is more fragmented and less cohesive; "regulation by default" followed in Canada, Croatia, Hungary, Poland, Serbia, and the USA. In these cases, efforts have not been as far-reaching toward solving the issue of gender unbalance on corporate boards. Poland and the USA have seen very timid first steps toward organized self-regulation in only an embryonic stage. In the case of Canada, we see more progress toward "regulation by design" in words but not yet in deeds. In Croatia, Hungary, and Serbia, while attempts have been made in laying foundational work, they have not materialized. In all six countries, regulation has been largely left to companies themselves. State-sponsored regulations have been either non-existent or limited to symbolic reforms with few outputs or effects, leaving businesses to self-regulate by default. Thus, the policies of these countries follow a self-regulatory pathway, but it is due to a void in government action more than deliberative choices on the part of policy actors to self-regulate.

Norway, France, and Belgium are on the flagship track for the state-led approach "quotas by design." The three countries started their regulatory trajectory from the same departure point as the others: no regulation. Norway was the first to switch paths and pioneered the state-led approach. France and Belgium stayed longer on the self-regulatory path, but when they crossed over, there was no turning back. Although in the three countries, corporate leadership did pursue some self-regulation to prevent the authoritative implementation of quotas, the state took over the lead to specifically design a quota system. Finally, Spain, Germany, and Austria are on the alternative track for the state-regulation pathway. Businesses initially controlled the authority over the pursuit of gender equality on their boards only to slowly lose control incrementally in the face of increased political pressure from state and society actors. In response to the piecemeal self-regulation that failed to produce any tangible improvements, policy efforts stumbled and lurched into legislated gender quotas—"quotas by default"—while leaving some of the regulation to the corporate world, through the mixed approach found in Spain, Germany, and Austria where state and corporate interventions have co-evolved over time. Indeed, quotas were neither the only nor favorite route pursued in the three countries. Spain introduced quotas relatively early in 2007 but backpedaled some years later when their regulatory scope was expanded. Business leaders in Austria and Germany were able to firmly stand their ground on the self-regulatory path until relatively recently.

The Politics of Regulating Corporate Equality: Three Commonalities

While there are clear differences in the two policy paths and four tracks taken, there also are striking similarities across the fifteen countries when comparing the politics of policy pre-adoption, adoption, post-adoption, and outcomes in terms of timing, the threat of quotas, and the campaigns and coalitions for corporate gender equality (Seierstad et al. 2017). Exploring these commonalties suggests that the regulatory pathways have evolved over time under high pressure and the threat of state-sponsored quotas and that pro-equality coalition engineering was pivotal in determining the regulatory trajectory in the face of strong opposition from the corporate sector.

Regulating Under Pressure

The timing of the adoption of the first regulatory steps on corporate gender equality in the fifteen countries, as Figure 16.2 shows, share a number of regularities. Action toward equality on corporate boards emerged and developed under pressure and accelerated at moments of critical junctures (Teigen, 2012). The Norwegian case became an important touchstone for both advocates of and opponents to board quotas: for advocates a source of inspiration (Hughes et al, 2017), for opponents a reason to take alternative action. With the notable exception of Spain, the first reaction of policy actors in most of the other countries was to avoid state-sponsored action. Cumulative pressure triggers the start of the regulatory journey. While this initial trend occurred across all fifteen cases, it did not result in converging policy responses.

Norway, Spain, and Sweden were among the first to kick off the regulatory journey in the first decade of the 2000s. Belgium and Austria joined but in a rather underwhelming way with light touches to their code of corporate governance. For others, the first decade of the 2000s was not yet the decade for action. It was the decade for debating the merit of the business case. The timeline accelerated at the end of the decade to see another series of regulatory actions enacted in the early 2010s with France, Belgium, Australia, and the UK. The laggards, such as Germany, were still hesitant where partisans and opponents clashed in a highly, if not overly, ideologically charged debate.

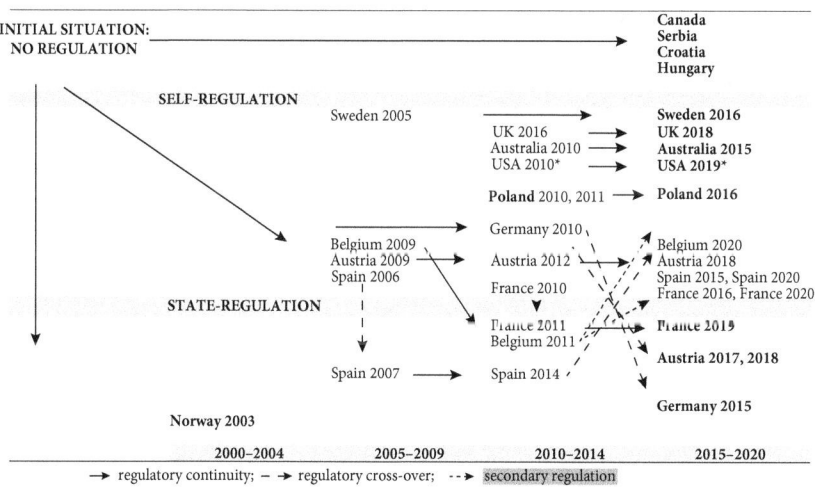

Fig. 16.2 Regulatory Trajectories across Space and Time on Decisions Implemented through January 1, 2020

The emergence of pressure for corporations to do something about the abysmal record of women on their boards rapidly increased. In the early 2000s, across all fifteen countries, women were still largely in the overwhelming minority on corporate boards, or even worse nearly completely absent as in France, Belgium, Spain, Germany, and Austria. With just above 20% of women on corporate boards, Norway was already firmly leading the way when it broke the regulatory omertà (code of silence) and gave an ultimatum to the corporate world: either women reached 40% by 2005 mid-year or quotas would be implemented. The Norwegian shockwave resonated across the Global North. If Norway's breakthrough attracted international attention, it did not become concretely diffused in the first years apart from the Spanish case. Or better said, the quota model stalled, but the debate raged about whether Norway should be admired or abhorred. Another shockwave shook the system with the financial crisis of 2008–2009. The crisis kept the Norwegian window of opportunity open a little longer than expected; business practices and corporate accountability were critically examined. In Belgium, according to Roos and Zanoni in their chapter, the economic crisis, along with Belgian's political crisis, was pivotal in increasing the pressure on companies to take the first self-regulatory steps. As many of the country chapters show, the observation made by French economic minister and later president of the IMF, Christine Lagarde, that the banking crisis could have been averted if the Lehman brothers had been sisters, was used by critics of the gender-biased nature of corporations to argue for more women on corporate boards.

The Threat of Quotas

Another wave of regulations came in the early 2010s when the regulatory pathways were taking shape. The corporate leadership rushed to set up self-regulation that would deter state intervention and neutralize the threat of a quotas-based approach. In the UK, Australia, and Sweden, threats of legislative quotas were cited as a major reason for organized businesses to pursue self-regulation, opting in all three countries for a comply-or-explain approach usually through corporate governance guidelines. In the UK, the threat of quotas was imminent given that the EU, Norway, and France had pursued the legislated quota path that was seemingly being exported to all member states; thus, the consensus through the government-led review processes and business self-regulation through reporting and comply-or-explain approaches in three flagship regulatory countries was a way to pre-empt any European wide movement.

The threat of quotas was also effective in countries that finally implemented them. It pushed peak associations to get organized and launched action toward improving the gender balance on boards. In France and Belgium, business associations adopted governance guidelines on women's presence on boards as an attempt to pre-empt government efforts to adopt legislation or more authoritative rules. It failed in France and Belgium and quotas were enacted in 2011. Even in Norway, the threat of the 40% quota being enforced with all publicly listed companies by 2008, which could lead to company dissolution, actually led those businesses to meet that quota even before the deadline. In Germany and Austria, corporate leadership was at first more successful in maintaining the trajectory onto the self-regulatory pathway. Facing increasing dissatisfaction with the light touch voluntary approach, they nevertheless did the cross-over a few years later.

Interestingly, as Lépinard and Rubio assert in their study of "the irresistible rise of quotas in Europe" (2018), there was no clear connection across the fifteen cases between the presence or absence of a quota for women in political office and the adoption of a quota for women on corporate boards. While in Spain, France, and Belgium political quotas appeared to clear the way for corporate quotas, in Norway, Germany, and Austria there was no political quota; in Croatia, Serbia, and Poland limited political quotas did not lead to any corporate quotas, and in Sweden, the USA, and the UK there were neither political nor corporate quotas.

The Politics of Coalition Engineering: Toward Equality in Hard Times

A clash of visions paced the regulatory trajectories over time (Seierstad et al., 2017; Terjesen and Sealy, 2016) regarding the end-goal of regulatory intervention (to boost economic performance vs. to empower women), the means to reach the end-goal, and the pitfalls to avoid. Initially, at least, domestic debates overwhelmingly weighted in favor of self-regulation. In a similar pattern to the one Elomäki (2018) identifies for the debate at the EU level, it is more often than not through a business case that equality advocates managed to make their voice heard. As Chandler (2016) argues, the way the debates prioritized economic performance over equality certainly contributed to locking in regulatory trajectories.

The corporate world was unanimous in rejecting state intervention across the fifteen cases. They painted the devil on the wall; the pool of qualified women was too small, board appointments should be based on merit only, state intervention atrophies business innovation. The corporate leadership was in a strong position to speak. They were organized in powerful peak associations highly adept at self-regulating. The peak business groups were also highly successful in shaping the initial frame of the debate across the fifteen cases. In Australia and the UK, their success in enshrining the debate into a "supply-side issue" literally closed out for good any discussion on alternative approaches and locked in the regulatory trajectory.

Coalitions and campaigns that articulated the need for change largely struggled in counteracting the powerful discourse of the economic elite. Even in Norway, the model student for corporate quotas, Mari Teigen shows there were virtually no actors that spoke for women directly from business, academia, or the gender equality machinery involved with either the campaign for the 2003 law or its implementation after; rather legislation was adopted through a cross-partisan coalition and pressure and was a part of a larger reform in business governance.

The classic "velvet triangle" (Woodward, 2004) of feminist policy adoption between women's movement actors, women's policy agencies, and women in parliament was rarely in play in the pursuit of gender corporate equality. Advocacy was highly elite-oriented, including women's policy agencies, gender experts, certain women's groups, particularly in the beginning with little buy-in from women business leaders, who were often suspicious of any non-merit-based approaches to promoting women at the corporate level. Grassroots women's movements and trade unions were mostly absent from any of the campaigns, a pattern that will remain for the foreseeable future. In some countries, left-wing trade unions and autonomous feminist groups even opposed the measures for being too weak or too centered on enabling economic elites. Worse, in some countries, there were not even domestic coalitions in favor of actively promoting transformative change.

Andrea Spehar asserts in her chapter on Croatia and Serbia that there were no home-grown "gender champions" inside or outside of government. Rather any advocacy for gender equality on corporate boards was supported and resourced by international NGOs or governments. In Croatia, a handful of women in the chamber of commerce and businesses worked with the Norwegian embassy and UNIFEM, and in Serbia, the 30% Club was launched as a result of the initiative of the Canadian government. The structural weakness of the pro-equality coalition left them even more vulnerable to party competition and strategy.

While party politics do matter, the comparative analysis here shows a somewhat contrasted picture than what has been generally depicted in the scholarship in terms of the importance of left-wing support in successful gender equality policy (Caul, 1999). The promotion of corporate equality has not been driven only by left-wing party coalitions (Terjesen et al, 2015). In some countries, a cross-party consensus was eventually developed. For example, in Austria, the right-wing Christian conservative pro-business party shifted its stance on mandatory quotas from deep opposition to firm support, which Gresch and Sauer observe in their chapter to be "quite remarkable (p. 328)." Similarly, while a coalition government comprised of social and Christian Democrats rejected a proposal for a gender quota by the Green Party in Germany in 2007, by 2011 all parties were showing public support for the quota option, and the final proposal for the 2015 law on quotas was presented by the SPD-CDU coalition government. In France, the first quota law was introduced under a right-wing government in 2011; the expansion of the regulatory scope happened with a left-wing government in 2014, and the strengthening of the sanction mechanism with a center-right coalition in 2019.

For sure, a left-wing majority party in power did matter in some of the countries, but these were more exceptions than the rule. In Spain, the arrival of the right to power after 2008 was instrumental in undermining a quite progressive quotas-based policy. Party indifference or even hostility has been the norm across our four Central and Eastern European cases. In both Hungary and Poland in recent years, starting in 2005 in Hungary and 2010 in Poland, extreme right-wing majority parties have politicized any issues related to women's rights and gender equality as "gender ideology" hence something that should be opposed at all costs. In Serbia and Croatia, the lack of political will and interest in the issue by any of the political parties was a different twist on the cross-partisan consensus in the more established democracies that the meaningful pursuit of gender equality on corporate boards was a good thing.

Success by the Numbers? Policy Response Matters

When comparing regulatory approaches across the fifteen countries, two main takeaways emerge. First, it is clear what does not work in both quantitative aggregate terms and the qualitative assessment of the implementation process: the lack of a comprehensive, large-scale, and organized approach. While incremental progress has been made in the USA, Canada, Hungary, Poland, Croatia, and Serbia, this progress has been slower and smaller. The absence of a clear set of policies coming from either business or the state and any real commitment behind them is an unmistakable recipe for failure. Second, what matters most is not necessarily the fact that self-regulation is more likely to contain a recommendation while state regulation is more likely to rely on a mandate. Both mandates and recommendations have the potential to improve women's numeric presence on corporate boards. The key difference lies in the details of the regulatory approach. Progress by the numbers is far more substantial if driven by a combination of policy instruments that act in conjunction with each other during the implementation process. To better understand these complexities, we first examine the actual progress by the numbers across our fifteen country cases and then turn to a discussion of the details of the mix of regulatory instruments identifying the varieties of recommendations and mandates, and the trade offs that were made between regulatory ambition, scope, and coerciveness on the road to numerical progress.

Progress by the Numbers

The promotion of gender equality at the apex of corporate power is often scrutinized through its numbers typically expressed in the percentage of women's share of seats on boards of directors. Putting an exact and comparable figure on women's representation on corporate boards is a challenging task. The legal status of privately-owned companies varies across systems, the share of women on boards is often an estimate derived from a sample (usually of the largest companies), and the sampling method varies. In addition, as Spehar reminds us in the cases of Croatia and Serbia, these aggregate figures may not be accurate even though they come from official sources. Moreover, interventions to promote women's access to the boards have taken place at varying points in time. The direct effects may not have yet fully taken place in some systems. Last but not least, as we show in Chapter 17, these numbers only show part of the picture of the fight for gender equality on boards. For example, they do not capture issues of the dynamics of intersectional inequalities at stake, particularly since to date, there have been virtually no data collected on women board members from underrepresented groups. Any assessment of progress on the basis of numbers that are not disaggregated by more than just gender should be thus taken with a grain of salt.

With this note of caution in mind, the evolution in the share of women on the boards of listed companies over time displayed in Table 16.1 shows some striking patterns. As expected, women's presence on corporate boards has increased across our sample of countries and the EU. While not a single case in our sample has achieved full gender parity, there has been, on average, a three-fold increase across the sample since 2003, which is in line with the average pace of (numeric) progress across the EU. This is, in itself, already quite remarkable given the relative stagnation in the gender composition of corporate boards prior to the early 2000s. With one exception, all the countries included in the analysis have made progress, including the countries that have not seen any sector-wide promotion of equality on corporate boards. In a similar fashion to national parliaments, the feminization of boards has been happening incrementally no matter what.

The pace of change is nevertheless substantially faster in the systems that have seen organized action on a large scale toward gender balance on corporate boards. The picture is crystal clear regarding what does not work very well. The five cases that have seen the smallest percentage of change are the countries that have not (yet) implemented either a state-regulation approach or a self-regulation approach. Croatia, Hungary, Poland, Canada, and the USA were not all necessarily among the laggards in 2003; the USA was just below Norway. In 2020, they are all firmly at the bottom despite overall incremental progress. Hungary has even fallen slightly behind its 2003 level.

Thus, organized action toward equality matters. This said, a simple numeric assessment does not necessarily give a definitive picture about whether one specific approach is more effective than another. As Lu (2021) argues, "disclosure and quota can be equally effective in shattering the glass ceiling." On the one hand, our state-regulation cases have the highest level of women on boards in 2020. For example, France and Belgium were among the laggards in 2003, but they have registered the largest percentage change over the last seventeen years. On the other hand, the picture gets a bit blurry when one looks at the cases of Norway and

Table 16.1 Percentage Share of Women on Corporate Boards in the Largest Listed Companies by Policy Approach and Track (2003–2020)

	2003	2020	% Change
SELF-REGULATION			
Flagship Track: Self-Regulation by Design			
Australia	8.4[a]	32.1[b]	23.7
UK	15.2	34.7	19.5
Sweden	17.5	38	20.5
Alternative Track: Self-Regulation by Default			
USA	16.9[c] (2004)	28.2[c]	11.3
Canada	11.7[d]	24.5[d] (2018)	12.8
Croatia	13.7 (2007)	26.9	13.2
Serbia	13.5 (2008)	21.7	8.2
Hungary	11.1	9.9	−1.2
Poland	9.1 (2004)	22.9	13.8
STATE-REGULATION			
Flagship Track: Quota By Design			
Norway	20.9	40.4	19.5
France	5.3	45.1	39.8
Belgium	6.0	38.4	32.4
Alternative Track: Quota By Default			
Spain	3.3	29.3	26.0
Germany	9.8	36.3	26.5
Austria	5.6	31.5	25.9
EU 28	**8.5**	**30.0**	**21.5**
Case Studies Average	**10.64**	**30.66**	**20.02**

Source: EIGE Database (Largest listed companies, B2) unless indicated otherwise, [a]ASX 200, Equal Opportunity for Women in the Workplace Agency (2004), [b]ASX 200, AICD (2020), [c]Fortune 100, Deloitte (2021), [d]FP 500, WXN (2018).

Sweden. Norway had the highest percentage of women on boards in 2003 and still holds the second-highest percentage of women on boards across our sample in 2020, right behind France. Nevertheless, Norway has still not reached gender parity on boards. It stands at 40.4% of women in 2020, just above the 40% quota that was enacted in 2003 and implemented from 2006 onward. In contrast to Norway, Sweden opted for the self-regulation approach. Instead of a mandate on representation, Sweden adopted a recommendation. The Swedish self-regulation approach does not seem, numerically speaking, to have been significantly less effective than the Norwegian state-led approach. The rate of change is largely similar between the two cases and the level of women's representation on Swedish boards is only several percentage points below the Norwegian one in 2020.

While neither the UK nor Australia, the two other flagship self-regulation cases, are at the level of representation reached by Sweden or Norway, they display nevertheless a steady pace of progress since 2003: 23.7% percentage change for Australia and 19.5% for the UK. While the progress lags well behind France and Belgium, it is in the same ballpark as the progress made by women on boards in Norway. The overall assessment of the countries with mixed approaches largely confirms the assertion that state-oriented approaches matter. Germany started below half of the countries in 2003 to reach the top half in 2020. While Germany displays one of the strongest rates of change, Spain and Austria are not far behind. Moreover, Germany and Austria both have quite unambitious mandates that have been met.

To sum up, the assessment of progress by the numbers gives us three main takeaways. First, women's access to corporate boards has progressed no matter what. Second, the incremental pace of progress has been slower, and in the case of Hungary, quite fragile with an actual reversal. Third, if we have clear losers, so to speak, we may not yet have a winner. The difference between countries with self-regulation vs. state-regulation approaches is not that pronounced. It may well be, as Htun and Jones have argued (2002) for political quotas, that what matters the most is not necessarily a quota over a more voluntary instrument in the form of a recommendation, but the fact that a quota or a recommendation has been broadly applied across a complete area or sector, which creates a shock to the system of standard operating procedures—short of that, at least bringing the issue into the public spotlight.

In the next section, we argue that this "shock" hypothesis is not the only explanation for the significant difference in numerical performance. The content of policy design matters as well as the extent to which policies once put into place are actionable and sanctionable (Krook et al, 2009; Mateos di Cabo et al, 2019; Franceschet and Piscopo, 2013; Mensi-Klarbach et al, 2021; Mensi-Klarbach and Seierstad, 2020). In a nutshell, a mandate that is not supported by a meaningful sanction is, for example, unlikely to be significantly more effective than a recommendation that is coupled with a sanctionable comply-or-explain mechanism. Right out of the implementation starting gate, actionable policy design is crucial to overcome previous resistance and opposition in order to eventually turn words on paper into concrete action in the form of deeds. In addition, efforts toward equality need to be sustained through time. As the Norwegian example reveals, there must be a goal beyond achieving numeric targets otherwise the system is at risk of running out of fuel. This is where other types of actions aimed at catalyzing and encouraging hortatory instruments may prove useful as the cases of the UK, Australia, the USA, and Canada show.

The Devil Is in the (Policy) Detail

As studies have already pointed out (e.g., Terjesen et al, 2015; Lewellyn and Muller-Kahle, 2020; Mensi-Klarbach et al, 2021; Mensi-Klarbach and Seierstad, 2020), the details of regulation have a clear impact on the pace of progress in the feminization of corporate boards. The analysis of the country cases shows that in what is called in the GEPP approach the "policy mix" has an impact on what works and what does not work on the ground. While policy designs for the promotion of gender balance on boards are never constituted of one single policy instrument across our fifteen cases, they do differ on whether they contain a mandate to include more women on boards rather than a recommendation to do so. Indeed, it appears that both need to be in action if they are to have any effect. It is the specific characteristics of this policy mix that make mandates and recommendations effective (or not) in practice (Mensi-Klarback and Seierstad, 2020; Humbert et al, 2019; Piscopo and Muntean, 2018). As such, the devil is indeed in the policy details.

Varieties of Mandates and Recommendations on the Ground

Among the organized actions toward equality, the difference that has probably been the most commented on in the scholarship is between the approaches that rely on a quota and the ones that rely on a target or a comply-or-explain mechanism. In this chapter, we look at it from a different perspective: the mandate versus the recommendation. A mandate is a classic command-and-control instrument that aims at prescribing a specific behavior. A recommendation is an incentive that aims at nudging toward a specific behavior through encouraging but without imposing it per se. In this perspective, the difference is not so much between a quota or a target but whether this quota or this target is mandatory or just recommended. As such, the mandate is conceptualized to include any binding threshold to reach as well as the binding process to set a target to be achieved. Both mandates and recommendations can be pushed forward by the state and corporate leaders alike.

Table 16.2 reveals two striking differences in the distribution of mandates and recommendations across the cases. First, the ambition of the policy instrument (Mensi-Klarback and Seierstad, 2020) varies across the mandates and the recommendations but also within each category. France, Norway, and Sweden are among the countries setting the bar the highest. Australia, Belgium, Germany, and the UK are among the ones setting the bar at its lowest. The last group does not even set any bar at all; they either recommend taking into account "diversity" or "gender" in unspecific terms, like in the USA, or they do not even attempt to make any recommendation as is the case in Hungary and Serbia. Second, the mixed approach cases tend to exhibit a complex set of intertwined mandates and recommendations that vary quite significantly across types of companies, or even across decisions, as in the case of Spain.

What Works on the Ground: Mixing Encouragement and Sanctions for Equality

Recommendations and mandates are unlikely to have more effective value than the paper they are written on unless they combine with other instruments to help the

Table 16.2 Distribution of Mandates and Recommendations across the Fifteen Cases

MANDATES	RECOMMENDATIONS
Norway 2003, 40% of each sex	—
France 2011, 2014, minimum ratio of each gender cannot be less than 40%	**France 2010**: 20% of women by 2013 and 40% by 2016; **France 2016**, "consider desirable diversity balance"
Belgium 2011, 1/3 "of another sex"	**Belgium 2009**, "board composition on the basis of gender diversity"; Belgium 2020, "sufficient gender diversity"
Spain 2007, at least 40% of women; **Spain 2014**, target-setting	**Spain 2006**: 40% of women; **Spain 2015**: 30% of women; **Spain 2020**: 40% of the underrepresented sex
Germany 2015, minimum of 30% of women and men; target-setting	Germany 2010: "consider women's representation"
	Australia 2011, target-setting (30%)
	UK 2011, 25%; **UK 2016,** 33%
	Sweden 2005, "equal gender distribution"; **Sweden 2016** "gender balance"
	USA 2010, "disclose if has a policy with regard to consideration of diversity"; **USA 2019** "demographic characteristics"
	Poland 2010, to publish gender breakdown; **Poland 2011**, to publish gender breakdown **Poland 2016**, to publish diversity policy

NON-EXISTENT/NOT IMPLEMENTED

Croatia 2011, share of underrepresented gender does not fall below 40% (not implemented)

Serbia, none

Canada 2018, "disclosure relating to diversity" (has not come into force yet)

Hungary, none

process of turning words into deeds. These instruments can be carrots, the positive incentives and rewards for modeling the behavior toward the expectation, or they can be sticks, the sanctions and negative incentives to discourage non-adoption of the expected behavior (Mensi-Klarback et al, 2021.

Across our fifteen cases, where a mandate or a recommendation was formulated, it has rarely come alone. Among the rare exceptions to be found are the case of Poland with the 2010 and 2011 resolutions of the Warsaw Stock Exchange, the case of the Croatian National Policy on Gender equality of 2011, and the Serbian National Strategy for Gender equality from 2016. The Polish resolutions recommended promoting women on corporate boards without any supporting instrument. The result is equivalent to the level of ambition: rather unremarkable. A similar story can be told about the Croatian and Serbian cases. The Croatian policy set a target of a minimum of 40% for the underrepresented sex. The Serbian strategy developed a 30% quota for state-owned company boards. Deprived of any supporting instrument, they were simply not implemented at all, as Spehar explains in her chapter.

The analysis of progress by the numbers revealed that a series of alternative policy mixes tend to produce quite similar levels of performance. Sweden with a recommendation-based policy mix has arrived not far from Norway with its mandate-based mix. Neither the Norwegian nor the Swedish policies came with a stand-alone flagship instrument. Quite the contrary, our comparative analysis shows that mandates and recommendations are more likely to be effective on the ground if they are blended into a mix with additional policy instruments that will support and drive their implementation. Among those, sanctions, monitoring, and reporting, as well as capacity and communication instruments stand out.

Sanctions, if applied on the ground, are powerful tools for inciting companies to comply. The most effective mandates regarding success by the numbers include a range of sanctions. For example, Norway has a progressive system of sanctions that starts with fines and ends with the dissolution of the company. Companies are required to report, and if found in violation are subject to an investigation that could lead to dissolution. The law has been implemented through the business regulatory administration, further showing that the law was serious about businesses meeting the quotas. It is no surprise, as Mari Teigen points out, that businesses met the 40% even before the actual enforcement procedures were implemented.

Germany also imposes a fine for non-compliance with the reporting rule, and Belgium suspends board membership fees. In addition to negative financial incentives, sanctions are targeted at freezing, directly or indirectly, the functioning of boards. In Austria, in cases of non-compliance with the 30% mandate, the election of a new board member(s) can be invalidated until compliance is enforced. France has gone a step further since 2019; non-compliance can result in board decisions being voided. All the countries that have introduced a system of sanctions to ensure compliance have seen major increases in women's access to boards over time. Spain is the only case that has developed a positive direct incentive rather than a system of sanction; compliant companies are given priority when tendering for government contracts. While it is not the only factor in explaining Spain's rather poor performance overall, it seems that a positive incentive cannot fully replace a system of sanctions even if it has had a positive impact on the feminization of the boards for the companies who extensively rely on public tenders (Mateos di Cabo et al, 2019).

The most effective recommendations also include sanctions for non-compliance with comply-or-explain mechanisms or alternative forms of disclosure rules. Those sanctions are not always as developed as the ones supporting the implementation of the mandates. In Australia for example, companies that do not report whether and why they comply with the recommendation can be delisted. More generally, when enforced on the ground, comply-or-explain mechanisms seem to work well even if they may produce a slightly slower pace of progress. That said, the required degree of precision in monitoring and reporting is pivotal. As Blanchard and Rabier explain in the case of France, the ambiguity and lack of specific instructions of how to achieve the 40% quotas or the obligations for smaller enterprises impeded both the quantitative presence of women on boards as well as the quality of their representation, i.e., tokens to respond to the numerical quotas or women who would stay the course and be powerful members of committees. Indeed, in all countries, the lack of specific guidelines for compliance, reporting, and enforcement allowed recalcitrant companies to pursue solutions that limited the "ripple effects from the core quotas" or gender norm changes within the gatekeepers. As Mensi-Klarback and Seierstad (2020) (see also: Mensi-Klarbach et al. 2021; Seierstad et al. 2017) have shown, policy vagueness definitely leaves the door open for businesses to only make symbolic gestures so as to not look bad in the context of mounting public pressure for increasing the presence of women on boards.

Trade-offs Between Regulatory Ambition, Scope, and Coerciveness

The selection and calibration of policy instruments are often the results of (political) decisions on regulatory challenges and dilemmas. The country analyses have emphasized two major trade-offs, the determination of which has an important impact on the capacity of the policy to significantly improve the gender balance on boards. Companies overall have been rather reluctant to embrace measures toward gender equality on boards when not vocally opposed to them. Our analysis shows that there are three main strategies to mitigate the discontent about any potential disruption to company autonomy. These strategies have an impact on the transformative capacity of the regulation.

A first trade-off requires balancing the regulatory scope of policy mix and its degree of coerciveness. The resulting strategy for mitigating discontent from companies is to increase the regulatory scope while downsizing the extent to which the regulation constrains companies to comply or, vice-versa, to increase the coerciveness but to downsize the scope. Figure 16.3 maps out how this trade-off has been handled. Sweden, Australia, and the UK have adopted a rather large scope for their self-regulation but have moderated its coerciveness. All the listed companies are subject to a comply-or-explain instrument but either the level of sanction or the level of monitoring and reporting has been downplayed. Among the mandates, Belgium, Spain in 2014, and France in 2014 have adopted a similar strategy. The case of France illustrates this strategy well. In 2014, the 2011 mandate was extended to a further group of companies and surpassed Norway regarding the regulatory scope. Nevertheless, the coerciveness was largely left untouched until 2019 when France joined Norway in adopting a high level of coercion.

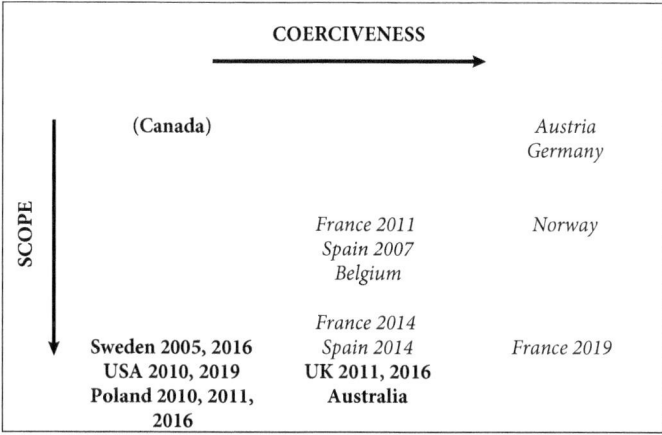

Recommendation, *Mandate*

Fig. 16.3 Policy trade-off between Regulatory Scope and Coerciveness

Austria and Germany adopted an alternative strategy. When the state stepped in to take over the regulatory lead, a rather coercive mandate was introduced. Its appeal was diminished by a limited regulatory scope addressing the supervisory boards of large companies in the most coercive way. This scope reduction has a non-negligible impact, as gender-biased norms are likely to prevail in smaller companies with smaller boards as well, particularly in countries where family ties and patrilineage have historically predominated for board appointments. In the summer of 2021, the current coalition government in Germany agreed to extend the 30% quota to executive boards with the proposed legislation still awaiting parliamentary consideration. This represents a significant shift toward expanding the regulatory scope given that executive boards in corporations hold the decision-making power compared to the supervisory board.

A similar picture emerges from the second trade-off regarding regulatory ambition, scope, and coerciveness, as illustrated in Figures 16.4 and 16.5. Overall, the more ambitious regulation is the less coercive. The third strategy is straightforward. It is easier to formulate an ambitious policy goal than to apply it on the ground. The only exceptions are one more time Norway and France since 2019. The ambition is also modulated by the regulatory scope. Similarly, the higher the ambition is, the lower the scope. In this case, Sweden joins Norway and France in leading the way.

All in all, for countries with better records of success, the policy mixes that reach higher levels of coercion tend to work better as we have seen in Norway, France, and Belgium, but also Sweden. It is not just a matter of sanctions. Sanctions are a last resort, and in some countries, no sanction has ever been applied to date.

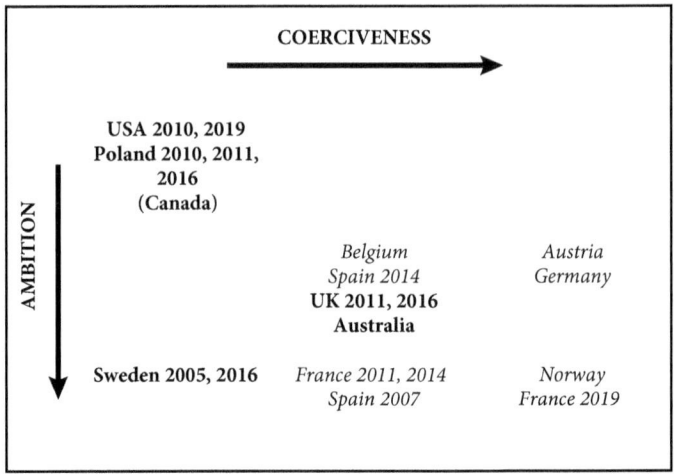

Recommendation, *Mandate*

Fig. 16.4 Policy trade-off between Regulatory Coerciveness and Ambition

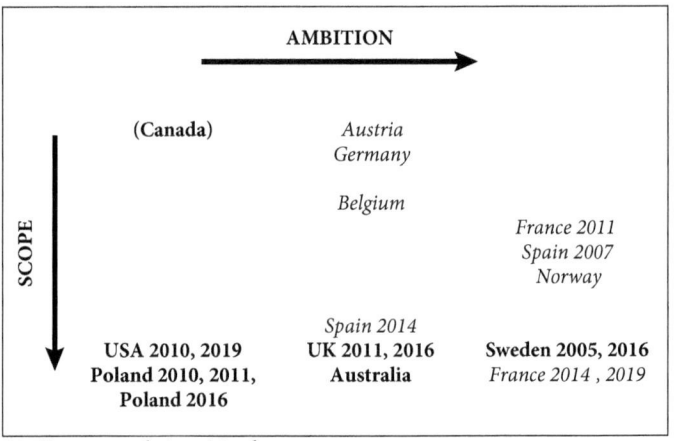

Recommendation, *Mandate*

Fig. 16.5 Policy trade-off between Regulatory Scope and Ambition

Mandatory reporting and monitoring, when detailed and specifically focused on gender, have also proven to be efficient in making equality on boards progress on the ground. The exact configuration of combinations that work may vary. What does not vary is the systematic failure of recommendations and mandates that are not supported by additional instruments as we have seen in the USA, Canada, and Poland.

The Conditional Value of Supporting and Exhorting

If the picture is crystal clear about the necessity to combine the mandate or the recommendation with a system of reporting and monitoring that is actionable through sanctions, it does not mean that less constraining instruments do not have a role to play as well. Quite the contrary, one might argue that encouraging the adoption of good behavior and providing capacity and skills, as well as knowledge and learning, are fundamental to making compliance with the aspiration meaningful in practice. Nevertheless, these need to aim at the right target (the companies) and to be supported by actions that have real teeth to actually make an impactful contribution.

Among the most popular tools, training stands in a preeminent position. Organizations, businesses, recruiting firms, and other pertinent actors have sought to enhance the pool of eligible women for board selection, thus addressing the pipeline issues often raised by business leaders. For example, the Australian Institute for Company Directors ran a course for "preparing women" that is supported by scholarships and a "Chairmen's Mentoring Program." As Newsome and Sheridan explain in their chapter, the entry criteria for the program were so high that it is likely these training programs mostly included women who were senior enough to not need mentoring but simply to just be allowed to join boards. Indeed, as many of the chapters in this book point out, gender imbalance on boards is less often the result of a weak or small pool of candidates than of male-dominated networks and exclusionary recruitment practices. Less frequently, these tools move away from "fixing the women" to address system failures and highlight good practices; although training and knowledge transfer about good practices are offered directly to companies, such as in Sweden. In the UK, the Women in Finance Charter promotes a range of good practices such as diversity champions, diversity targets, and transparency on monitoring performance. The 30% Club, originally launched in the UK and diffused to other countries, specifically aims at promoting business initiatives toward equality.

Comply-or-explain mechanisms, when their implementation comes with resources, are also of use for sharing good practices, celebrating companies that have made progress on the equality front, and scrutinizing the others. In the UK, the Davies and the subsequent Hampton-Alexander Reviews have provided a significant amount of knowledge and skills. But as Milner points out, the annual reports from the Davies Commission also functioned as a reputational incentive to achieve the recommendation, which gathered widespread attention in the media and parliament. Relying on a "traffic light system," companies were ranked according to their annual performance and progress. The companies that had pioneered good practices were mentioned in the reports. In France, the positive aspect of comply-or-explain was also emphasized through the efforts of the Minister for Women's Rights in 2012 to develop a ranking of companies according to their performance on gender balance on boards in order to "name and celebrate" those performing companies. Public disclosure through reporting also allows for "naming-and-shaming." In Sweden, for example, a not-for-profit organization used reports to publish a "red list" of the companies that did not have women on their boards and encouraged boycotts of them.

In countries that have some of the worst performance records by any indicators, capacity and awareness tools have been also developed. For example, in Croatia, the Gender Equality Ombuds, in partnership with the Employers' Association (HUP), launched the "Database of Business Women in Croatia." The Employer Association (HUP) further engaged with the issue and promoted the Croatian chapter of the 30% Club. In Hungary, several initiatives were promoted to enhance networking and mentoring among businesswomen. Those tools largely missed their target, however, because they stood in isolation and were toothless with no real authority. Furthermore, they were not coupled with mandates or recommendations supported by mandatory monitoring and reporting. Promoting training and networking on its own does not work for achieving any level of progress in corporate board gender balance. Thus, developing a systematic monitoring and reporting system is crucial to maintaining pressure on recalcitrant actors whether it be through naming-and-shaming or naming-and-celebrating.

To recap, there is no single line-up of policy instruments that uniquely leads to policy success by the numbers. Nevertheless, the failed cases across the North American countries and the East Central European show that regulatory breadth and depth are crucial to successfully jump over the implementation hurdles triggered by passive resistance when opposition to the promotion of equality on boards is alive and well. Words do not lead to implementation deeds. Actionable policy design does because it mitigates resistance to change at the implementation stage (Verge and Lombardo, 2021).

The Policies that Work

The comparative analysis in this chapter demonstrates that policy implementation clearly matters for the pursuit of gender balance on corporate boards. There are fundamental commonalities in the politics of adoption and implementation shared by all countries regardless of regional location, policy approach, or specific mix. The timing of the adoption of both types of regulation, the way the threat of quotas got highly equality adverse and reluctant business actors to move on corporate board policies, as well as the shared attributes of the coalitions that mobilized around policy adoption and implementation—the absence of autonomous women's groups as well as any significant influence of left-wing majorities, parties, or other actors on the left like trade unions—occurred across quite divergent settings in Western Europe, Central Eastern Europe, and North America. In all cases, the behavior of the state matters. The state has often given the impulsion to start considering the absence of women on corporate boards as a problem to solve. In the state-led approach, the state has taken the matter into its own hands. In the business-led approach, the state has often used the threat of intervention to make the corporate world act. In this sense, the state has moved forward in its role of *guarantor of gender equality* (Franceschet and Piscopo, 2013). At the same time, this does not mean that quotas are the magic bullet for success.

In all of the cases, the simple presence or absence of policy made a difference in getting businesses to change their ways with regard to women on boards. Many of the authors pointed out that increases in women on boards came directly as a result of the policies that were adopted. Germany and Austria are clear examples of the increase in women on boards directly following the adoption of the quota. Moreover, with the threat of quota implementation businesses appeared to pursue corporate gender equality whether the policies were implemented or not. Clearly, in Norway this was the case, as Mari Teigen shows in her chapter, the companies to be covered by the 2003 law hit the 40% target and its enforcement mechanisms were in effect. At the same time, in many other countries, the implementation of monitoring and reporting procedures through disclosure or comply-or-explain mechanisms gave businesses the impetus to take action. When policy implementation was absent, there were minimal results or even a deterioration of the situation as in Hungary. Thus, either directly or indirectly implementation matters at least when taking a look at success by the numbers.

Not only does policy implementation matter, but the particular type of policy mix of instruments makes a difference in the level of numerical success. The successful mix needs to include both carrots and sticks combined, sometimes with higher levels of coercion, expanded scope, and strong policy ambition. While the exact combination of characteristics varies and is complex for the policy mix ingredient for success, the cases of policy failure in the Central Eastern European countries and the two North American countries clearly show that mandates and recommendations must be combined with systems of reporting and monitoring that have meaningful sanctions to back them up. The historical, institutional, and cultural context is no more important in explaining what worked and was successful than the approach and policy mix instruments that played out in a given national setting. The most important ingredient in the recipe for success in corporate gender equality policy implementation, at least by the numbers, is the detail of the policy—the policy mix that combines some combination of specific instruments to support the recommendation or the mandate: the ambition of the policy, its scope, and its degree of coerciveness. Thus, indicating that the elusive recipe for successful gender equality policy, at least in the corporate board room, is complex and goes beyond the dichotomy of state-led vs. business-led. But this is only a part of the comparative story for success given the analytical and theoretical limits of measuring success in numerical terms alone. The next chapter completes our comparative foray through the GEPP framework by looking at the qualitative side of the corporate gender.

References

Baachi, Carol (1999) *Women, Politics and Policies: The Construction of Policy Problems.* London: Sage.

Caul, Miki (1999) "Women's Representation in Parliament: The Role of Political Parties," *Party Politics*, 5 (1), pp. 79–98.

Elomäki, Anna (2018) "Gender Quotas for Corporate Boards: Depoliticizing Gender and the Economy," *NORA-Nordic Journal of Feminist and Gender Research*, 26 (1), https://doi.org/10.1080/08038740.2017.1388282 (Accessed September 1, 2021).

Franceschet, Susan and Jennifer Piscopo (2013) "Equality, Democracy, and the Broadening and Deepening of Gender Quotas," *Politics & Gender*, 9 (3), pp. 310–316.

Htun, Mala and Mark P. Jones (2002) "Engendering the Right to Participate in Decision-making: Electoral Quotas and Women's Leadership in Latin America," in Nikki Craske, and Maxine Molyneux (eds) *Gender and the Politics of Rights and Democracy in Latin America*. Springer, pp. 35–56.

Hughes, Melanie, Pamela Paxton, and Mona Lena Krook (2017) "Gender Quotas for Legislatures and Corporate Boards," *Annual Review of Sociology*, 43 (1), pp. 331–352.

Humbert, Anne Laure, Elisabeth K. Kelan and Kate Clayton-Hathway (2019) "A Rights-based Approach to Board Quotas and How Hard Sanctions Work for Gender Equality," *European Journal of Women's Studies*, 26 (4), pp. 447–468.

Krook, Mona Lena, Joni Lovenduski and Squires Judith (2009) "Gender Quotas and Models of Political Citizenship," *British Journal of Political Science*, 39 (4) pp. 781–803.

Lépinard, Eléonore and Ruth Rubio-Marín (eds) (2018) *Transforming Gender Citizenship: The Irresistible Rise of Gender Quotas in Europe*. Cambridge: Cambridge University Press.

Lewellyn, Krista B. and Maureen I. Muller-Kahle (2020) "The Corporate Board Glass Ceiling. The Role of Empowerment and Culture in Shaping Board Gender Diversity," *Journal of Business Ethics*, 165, pp. 329–346.

Lu, Shirley (2021) "Quota or Disclosure? Evidence from Corporate Board Gender Diversity Policies," PRI Blog, https://www.unpri.org/pri-blog/quota-or-disclosure-evidence-from-corporate-board-gender-diversity-policies/8277.article (Accessed September 20, 2021).

Mateos de Cabo, Ruth, Siri Terjesen, Lorenzo Escot, and Ricardo Gimeno (2019) "Do 'Soft Law' Board Gender Quotas Work? Evidence from a Natural Experiment," *European Management Journal*, 37 (5), pp. 611–624.

Mensi-Klarbach, Heike and Cathrine Seierstad (2020) "Gender Quotas on Corporate Boards: Similarities and Differences in Quota Scenarios," *European Management Review*, 17 (3), pp. 615–631.

Mensi-Klarbach, Heike, Stephan Leixnering and Michael Schiffinger (2021) "The Carrot or the Stick: Self-Regulation for Gender-Diverse Boards via Codes of Good Governance," *Journal of Business Ethics*, 170, pp. 577-593.

Piscopo, Jennifer M. and Susan Clark Muntean (2018) "Corporate Quotas and Symbolic Politics in Advanced Democracies," *Journal of Women, Politics and Policy*, 39 (3), pp. 285–309.

Seierstad, Cathrine, Patricia Gabaldon and Heike Mensi-Klarbach (2017) *Gender Diversity in the Boardroom: Volume 2. Multiple Approaches Beyond Quotas*, Palgrave Macmillan.

Teigen, Mari (2012) "Gender Quotas on Corporate Boards: On the Diffusion of a Distinct National Policy Reform," in F. Engelstad and M. Teigen (ed.) *Firms, Boards and Gender Quotas: Comparative Perspectives* (*Comparative Social Research, Vol. 29*). Bingley: Emerald Group Publishing Limited, pp. 115–146.

Terjesen, Siri and Ruth Sealy (2016) "Board Gender a Multi-theoretical Perspective," *Business Ethics Quarterly*, 26 (1), pp. 23–65.

Terjesen, Siri, Ruth V. Aguilera, and Ruth Lorenz (2015) "Legislating a Woman's Seat on the Board: Institutional Factors Driving Gender Quotas for Boards of Directors," *Journal of Business Ethics*, 128 (2), pp. 233–251.

Verge, Tània and Emanuela Lombardo (2021) "The Contentious Politics of Policy Failure: The Case of Corporate Gender Quotas in Spain," *Public Policy and Administration*, 36(2), pp. 232–251.

Woodward, Alison (2004) "Building Velvet Triangles: Gender and Informal Governance," in Thomas Christiansen and Simona Piattoni (eds) *Informal Governance in the European Union*. London: Edward Elgar, pp. 76–93.

17

The Transformative Power of Public Policy

Looking Back, Looking Ahead

Isabelle Engeli and Amy G. Mazur

Introduction

Zooming out to assess success in terms of the more qualitative and complex GEPP indicators of successful outcomes presents quite a less rosy picture than zooming in on success by the numbers. While women's representation on boards has improved by the numbers, business leadership has largely remained a men's stronghold. Women on boards are concentrated in the least powerful positions, the exclusionary recruitment practices have largely continued, and the gendered norms have been left challenged. Overall, the response of the corporate world is best characterized as a strategic adaptation to new environmental constraints rather than a far-reaching transformation of practices triggered by a change from within. Progress has been made by the numbers on women's access to corporate boards. This progress has not, for the time being at least, cascaded into a cohesive and systematic transformative change toward inclusive equality in economic decision-making.

Thus, the question of what does and does not work covered in the previous chapter in terms of numbers leads to an evaluation that goes beyond numbers of the extent to which policies have engendered inclusive policy empowerment and actually promoted gender transformation and real change in norms and practices in terms of the long road to transformation. A return to the GEPP framework reminds us that one of the core hypotheses is that for policy implementation to be successful, the practice of post-adoption through the policy mix of outputs and tools must be inclusive of the fullest range of actors and voices in an intersectional purview, and, in turn, this is the key to reaching transformative outcomes. In other words, without expanding the inclusivity of the actual practice of a policy, it is unlikely for any policy to attain far-reaching gender transformation.

As the country and comparative analyses show, poor performance on inclusive policy empowerment led to poor performance on gender transformation. Strategic

Isabelle Engeli and Amy G. Mazur, *The Transformative Power of Public Policy*. In: *Gender Equality and Policy Implementation in the Corporate World*. Edited by Isabelle Engeli and Amy G. Mazur, Oxford University Press.

adaptation has superseded, if not prevented transformative outcomes and results. This final chapter delves deeper into the qualitative side of policy success across the fifteen country cases, looking at the past experiences with policy implementation for what has happened and why. A closer look is first taken at the inclusive policy empowerment hypothesis and the near absence of gender transformative outcomes across the fifteen countries. Next, we explore the four major features of the route to strategic adaptation followed at some level in all fifteen countries. We finally come back to the larger lessons learned from these past experiences with tackling gender equality in a historic male bastion of power and their implications for the pursuit of the "elusive recipe" for successful gender equality policy are presented. The book ends with a look toward the future in terms of the road that lies ahead for policy actors and scholars alike through proposing policy recommendations that might tip the scales away from strategic adaptation toward meaningful transformation and an agenda for future research on gender equality policy in action.

Success beyond Numbers? The Limits of the Policy Response

Limited Opportunities for Inclusive Policy Empowerment

The comparative analysis emphasizes what the country chapters recounted already transpired: the necessity for policy to go beyond its paper symbolic records to be implemented and followed through. For that to happen there needs to be a constellation of actors, including businesses, that mobilize around implementation. While the coalition of actors that emerged around post-adoption politics was far from inclusive, where those coalitions included a wider range of actors—e.g., business leaders, women's business groups, femocrats, political parties of the left and right, and policy experts—rather than just one or two of the actors on their own, and that coalition was supported by public opinion and given media attention, there seemed to be more movement toward transformative results.

To be sure, in some countries, the coalitions that lined up behind the demand for corporate equality and the frames that were used by the actors up until the policies were actually put into action continued to be active and to drive the politics and outcomes of evaluation and implementation. For example, in the UK and Australia, the lineup of actors that were adamant in rejecting any state intervention or mandate to argue for voluntary business-led approaches has remained preeminent in the post-adoption stages. Alternative voices advocating a mandate were already marginalized prior to the adoption, and they have remained so post-adoption. As a result, the discourse in the UK and Australia has mostly remained about the business case.

In other countries, post-adoption politics shifted considerably. This shift had a substantial impact on the implementation process. For example, in Germany, major political players had a change of heart such as the then CDU Minister for Employment, Ursula von der Leyen. After a rather unambitious quota was enacted in 2015, a new law was in preparation in the summer of 2021 to push forward the mandate-based approach and increase its actionability. In contrast, when a right-wing populist coalition with an "anti-gender" agenda took over, initial self-regulation fell short in Poland, and emerging attempts got crushed in Hungary. Precious allies have jumped in at post-adoption as well. In Spain, women leaders in business shifted from resistance to alliance, and their involvement in implementation helped to maintain pressure on the successive governments.

The underrepresentation of women in the formal policy process has been the norm rather than the exception overall. Corporate-related regulation has been historically dominated by men, and the struggle over the meaning of the issue of equality on boards has not radically transformed this long-term pattern. The pattern was even more pronounced in countries that opted for self-regulation as this was in the hands of the predominantly male business leaders. As Freidenvall puts it for the Swedish case (p. 99), "Since this was the result of the corporate sector itself, it mainly involved male business leaders not wanting legislative gender quotas on company boards to be introduced."

Despite a context of business lip service or even passive resistance, equality advocates have seized the opportunities provided by the policy. New women's business groups were often created to place pressure on business leaders and to help recruit and mentor women to become more eligible candidates for boards, particularly given that an empty pipeline for women's recruitment onto boards was what the predominantly male business leaders used as an excuse for non-action. In Germany, the Women's Affairs Ministry is in charge of the monitoring and public reporting and has been, so far at least, allocated sufficient resources to make companies accountable. The advocacy coalition that fought for more than fifteen years in favor of state intervention in the promotion of gender balance on boards is now firmly established institutionally. One of the main organizations is now in charge of the evaluation of implementation. In contrast, the Sex Discrimination Commissioner was mostly kept out of the policy process in Australia.

In other countries, equality advocates have not necessarily been formally included in the process. They have grabbed themselves a chair and sat at the table no matter what. Often, they have been able to do that because of the resources that are offered through the implementation process. Among those resources stand reporting and monitoring-related instruments. In Sweden, for example, the Allbright Foundation issues annual reports on progress (and lack of) made by Swedish companies. In Belgium, the Institute for Equality of Women and Men has acted as a "watchdog" to identify and track companies that are not in compliance with the regulation. Among others, the association Isotes that regrouped women professionals in Spain has lobbied government and corporate leadership alike to maintain the pressure on reaching equality. The resilience of equality advocates is not necessarily a given either. In hostile contexts, when there are no policy resources or opportunities to seize, equality advocates have been rather unsuccessful in their attempts as the cases of Hungary, Croatia, Serbia, and more recently Poland attest.

The presence of women in the process should not be taken as evidence of an inclusive process. More often than not, when individual women spoke out or even weighed-in on the process, they were already in a situation of privilege. Women politicians and businesswomen whose voices were heard were overwhelmingly white and from the elite, to the rare exception, such as Maxine Waters in the USA. These corporate equality coalitions have largely failed to speak for more than white women who were already part of the economic elite—as Blanchard and Rabier (Chapter 11) called them, "the happy few." Thus, issues of the intersectionality of inequalities, or even just the fact that women from different ethnic/racial groups, sexual identities, and classes should be promoted, were virtually never raised by advocates of corporate gender equality. As a result, the policy response has remained largely silent on these issues, and implementation, apart from a few exceptions, did not reverse the situation.

Transformative Change Has Remained the Exception

None of the policy responses across the fifteen countries have resulted in any solid gender transformation in the corporate sector either through "simple" gender transformation where policies achieve concrete improvement in closing significant gender gaps, change in the dominant gender norms of gatekeepers, and women being seen as equal partners to men in corporate governance, without reference to issues of intersectionality, much less a more intersectional approach to "complex" gender transformation where the norm is no longer white heteronormativity.

In Norway, Belgium, Sweden, and Germany, the chapter authors assert that there is some potential for transformative change in the future, but it has not happened yet. In Norway, in particular, since 2013, the limited "ripple effects" of the quota law have shifted to real "transformative potential" (Teigen, p. 213) with indications of dominant gender norms shifting on the part of the business elite with additional support for quotas, and even recent emphasis on the importance of board diversity in terms of ethnicity. Rather "gender accommodation" continues to be the rule with some level of policy response and increase in the number of women on boards, but the underlying norms and attitudes of business gatekeepers remain gender-biased, and hence any real transformative change is thwarted. The way in which the frames of the business gatekeepers have continued to be limited to defining the problem as a supply-side issue where qualified women are absent, rather than the need for the male-dominated gatekeepers to change their approach to recruiting women for board leadership positions, are both illustrations of the imperative of gender accommodation over gender transformation.

Gender transformative potential is not as prevalent in Austria, Australia, the UK, and Spain. In Spain, as Lombardo and Verge demonstrate, up until 2008, there was great promise of a policy backed by women's policy agencies and the left-wing party would ferry in a new era of more gender-balanced corporate boards with a real shift in gender norms; however, the arrival of a series of right-wing governments after 2008 effectively "rowed back," in GEPP terms, that transformative movement. Most recently, there has been a feminist backlash to this backtracking in response to the failure with a remarkable awakening of Spanish businesswomen, suggesting that there is still transformative potential to counter the dominant gender norms of the business elite.

"Rowback" has also been on the move in Hungary and Poland in the context of the prevalence of the right-wing "gender ideology" movements, even more pronounced given that movement backward was from a position of "gender accommodation" at best in both countries. "Gender-neutral" outcomes can also be attributed to Canada, the USA, Croatia, and Serbia, with highly weak and piecemeal policies that have little political support and few activists who are genuinely interested in promoting gender equality. Although in Canada, as Joan Grace shows, there has been a recent move to address the poor record of gender balance on boards, and the more feminist province of Quebec adopted a law on a 50% quota on state-run companies.

Therefore, complete gender transformation, either simple or complex, is still a distant goal, which many authors assert will be difficult to achieve due to the gender-biased path dependencies found within the business sector, and how corporate gender equality is still framed as a business case for business performance rather than for equality. Instead, countries across the board have followed the route of strategic adaptation dictated by the powerful, still mostly male, business elite, effectively tamping down what is seen even as an overly ambitious pursuit of transformative change. In the next section, we examine the four features of this situation of stasis and blocked change.

When Strategic Adaptation Thwarts Transformative Aspiration

Keeping the Equality Effort at Bay

The first feature of the route to strategic adaptation is to only follow the strict letter of the law or, in this case, the regulation. Doing the bare minimum allows for compliance while circumscribing broader demands for change that are seen as over-ambitious, thus keeping serious equality efforts at bay. Yes, progress has been made, and the pace of feminization of the boards has accelerated with the increase in global attention and regulatory actions. Nevertheless, even for the most advanced implementation processes, the progressive increase by the numbers has been overwhelmingly limited to the exact object of the regulatory efforts: the boards included in the regulatory scope. Most peak associations have endorsed gender equality among their priorities indeed. By the same token, the attention to gender imbalance on boards has attracted attention to the way the corporate world functions and who should be represented, and why, as Teigen, for example, argues for Norway. It is also true that, as Milner states for the UK, women business leaders have never been as visible as they have been over the recent years. Men are increasingly portrayed as agents of change in Sweden, as Freidenvall reminds us. "Yes, absolutely, I am a feminist," says Canadian Prime Minister Justin Trudeau.[1]

The feature of keeping equality at bay is nicely illustrated in what a (male) chair of a recruitment committee in Norway confided to Mari Teigen: "So I am really against any quota and think you should have managed without a quota, but when it's here it is of course okay to live with it" (Teigen, p. 209). After all, the ambition in most of the regulations was largely numerical. The target group has adapted to the new rule when adaptation was required through encouragement maybe, sanction for sure, and potentially market-based pressure. It remains that behind the flagship metric of the largest companies, women's advancement in leadership has remained largely incremental. Companies have not gone much further than the ambition stated in the mandates and recommendations. There is little substantial variation between the two types of regulatory approaches. The glass ceiling and concrete walls still firmly stand.

Furthermore, regulation that has targeted a certain type of board has not seen comparable improvement in women's representation on the board that were left untargeted when there are no sanctions or monitoring progress has been less steady. The German case provides a telling illustration; the companies that are required to set targets have seen a more moderate feminization than the companies that are mandated to achieve a determined threshold. The differentiation in behaviors between the boards that are regulated and the others has even increased in some cases, including for businesses at the top of the class, where incremental feminization of boards has remained limited at best. Blanchard and Rabier mention a recent estimation of 24% of women only on boards of non-listed companies in France. In Norway, the boards of the limited companies have also seen a much more modest share of women than the board of publicly limited companies: 19% against 43% in 2020 (Teigen, p. 200). The contrast between the regulated and unregulated boards is also very strong in the dual-board systems. As Ahrens and

[1] Carpenter, Julia (2018) "Boss files: Justin Trudeau is a feminist," CNN Business, https://edition.cnn.com/2018/11/12/success/justin-trudeau-feminism/index.html (Accessed September 1, 2021).

Scheele point out, the implementation of the quota law has been "meticulous but unambitious" in Germany. The executive boards are not required to comply with the 30% quota, and so the proportion of women has remained below 10%, and a substantial minority of companies do not have even a single woman on their executive boards.

Smaller companies are often left out from the regulatory scope (with a few notable exceptions such as France since 2014) and their progress seems to be slower. In addition, as Newsome and Sheridan for Australia and Milner for the UK emphasize, public pressure is lower for smaller than for very large companies. As a result, encouragement and exhortation work less effectively for companies of smaller size. In Australia, for example, the companies included in the ASX 100 have reached and overpassed the recommended target of 30% while the companies in the ASX 500 are still lagging significantly behind. Hoard underlines that young American companies also have a harder time putting the feminization of their boards in motion. In 2017, the boards of the top twenty-five Initial Public Offering stagnated at 9.2% against 25.7% for the Fortune 100 (2020 Women on Boards 2019, p. 3). Finally, the sectors that have not been historically gender friendly also lag behind in the feminization of their boards. In Canada, for example, companies in the oil/gas/mining and construction sectors are among the lowest with regard to women on boards (WXN/CCBDC, 2018). In the USA, Hoard points out that despite all the attention to the financial sector triggered by the economic crises and the embryonic intervention of the SEC on diversity reporting, Jane Fraser was the first woman ever to be appointed CEO of a major Wall Street bank as recently as late 2020.

The Gatekeepers Have Remained in Place

The second feature is that the predominantly male gatekeepers have largely remained in place and have failed to radically transform their practices. While more and more women access leadership positions, they tend to be offered positions with the least power. So far, regulatory efforts on corporate boards have not produced much spillover to other leadership positions either. For sure, there has been the almost obligatory incremental progress, but it has remained timid. As such, the apex of economic power has largely remained a men's stronghold, and the regulatory efforts have not (yet?) led to more women across the board. Parity stops at the gates of power (Gresy et al, 2019).

In a pattern reminiscent of the exclusion of women from leadership positions in parliaments, women are more often offered a seat as external or non-executive board members than as internal or executive ones. In France, for example, women who are appointed are more likely to be foreign nationals or have no history with the company. The trend seems to have even increased in Spain. Lombardo and Verge underline that in 2006, 42% of the women board members were outsiders, increasing to 75% in 2020 (p. 269). A different spin seemed to have been taken in Germany through the creation of new seats and the prolongation of board terms all to avoid giving away a man's seat to a woman. In Austria, Gresch and Sauer point out that women are frequently underrepresented on the most powerful and prestigious sub-committees in proportions below the 30% mandate.

The situation is not brighter across the other powerful positions in corporate leadership. Women rarely chair the board they sit on. In France, this disconnect is particularly glaring given women in 2020 made up 45% of board members in the largest companies, but only 3% were in leadership positions. Even in the countries with the longest experience of a substantial number of women on boards, women are highly unlikely to preside over their boards. In Sweden, only 15.4% of the chair-persons were women in 2020 among the largest companies. In Norway, they were just 20%. The situation is not any better regarding CEOs. Only a very small minority of CEOs are women across all the fifteen cases in this study, an overwhelmingly common pattern. In Australia, women led only fourteen of the ASX 200 companies and only twelve of the ASX 500 in 2018 (Workplace Gender Equality Agency, 2020), and in Germany, there are no women CEOs among the largest companies in 2020.[2]

To be sure, it would be unrealistic to expect that leadership that has remained male-dominated for so long would radically change in a few years. Indeed, any given leadership trajectory is built across a lifetime. Bringing in new blood is also completely reliant on the process of appointment renewal. Hoard shows in the USA that one of the points of stagnation for women gaining access to leadership positions has been the lack of renewal. Whereas a handful of pioneer companies have taken the lead in showing the way, these have remained exceptions to the rule. For the time being, the equality endeavor has not substantially rippled over to executive leadership. Newsome and Sheridan emphasize that as long as the feminization of senior executive leadership as a major pathway to boards does not significantly accelerate, it is unlikely that board regulation will have the capacity to dismantle the current structure of gatekeepers, which brings us to the third feature of the strategic adaptation route.

The Exclusionary Pattern of Recruitment Has Not Been Dismantled

The issue of gender imbalance has been pushed to the forefront in the context of the implementation of mandates and recommendations alike, becoming a more explicit consideration in board recruitment. In the Norwegian, French, and Belgium cases, the quota mandate was enacted at the same time as the professionalization of

---

[2] Data for European countries are from EIGE Gender Statistics Database, https://eige.europa.eu/gender-statistics/dgs (Accessed September 20, 2021).

board recruitment was accelerated, which probably contributed to strengthening to some degree the progress on the ground. Despite these best efforts, the actual pool of women available to be recruited to boards has not greatly expanded in any of the countries, subsequently fueling the standard operating procedures of social reproduction and leaving the structure of privileges largely untouched. In addition, if "ambitious women are no longer taboo" (Blanchard and Rabier, p. 234), the focus has strongly remained on training women who often end up being more qualified than their male counterparts on the boards. Abundant examples across the fifteen cases demonstrate that the exclusionary nature of recruitment practices has not really been challenged to the core; lip service has been given to include at best a narrow group of white women that were already in a situation of privilege. Teigen contends, for example, that in Norway, women were recruited within the same networks as men.

Even if women are often more qualified than their male counterparts, Gresch and Sauer highlight the fact that women on Austrian boards are a homogeneous group with a business or a law degree and are predominantly German-speaking. In Spain, Lombardo and Verge emphasize that small companies have largely recruited women from the family that controls the business. In a similar vein, the golden skirt syndrome has serious implications on the capacity of board regulation to achieve transformative change. In Australia, for instance, a limited group of elite women holds seats across multiple boards where women make up 45% of multiple seat holders (Newsome and Sheridan, p. 43). The syndrome also shuts down many of the possibilities for expanding the pool of women and developing fully inclusive practices. Thus, the boundaries of the boys' club have expanded to "add women and stir" without any transformative change to their highly elitist and exclusive nature.

As Milner (p. 80) argues, "race and ethnicity remain intractable areas." In the UK, women board members are still overwhelmingly white.

> ...only 6% of CEOs are female, none of them Women of Color (Kaur, 2020). Only 3% of top positions in FTSE 100 organizations (CEO, finance director, executive board chair) are occupied by people of color, and these are twice as likely to be men as women.
>
> (Green Park, 2020, cited in Milner, p. 60)

In the USA, while women held 19% of the C-suite positions in the financial sector in 2017, Women of Color were only 1% (McKinsey and Company, 2018, cited in Hoard, p. 127). Furthermore, data on intersectionality often do not even exist. Except for the UK, the USA, and Canada, systematic official efforts to collect data on race and ethnicity have yet to be established for all of the countries in this book. Browsing business websites and skimming media coverage of women in business is enough to conclude that corporate boards are mostly composed of white members. But the fact that barely any data is collected is telling about the state of the conversation, which, in most of the cases in this study, has not even begun. Without data, no mentoring is possible and the corporate world can follow the same strategy of looking the other way as it did with white women up until very recently. The intersectional nature of privilege thus remains invisible even if in a handful of countries inclusiveness in business has been gaining some traction.

When "diversity" is mentioned, more often than not it is used as a fuzzy catch-all buzzword implying a range of different notions that have barely anything to do with intersectional approaches to inclusion. In the USA, the most referenced consideration for diversity in disclosure reports is "diversity of experiences (Hoard, p. 121)." In Belgium, "cognitive diversity" was put forward in early attempts at self-regulation (Roos and Zanoni, p. 247). In Austria, "the diversity concept" is mentioned in reporting obligations without any clear definition. As Hoard (p. 121) puts it for the case of the USA, "the issue with allowing corporations to define diversity is that they co-opt diversity to serve their own purpose while avoiding transformative change." Probably as a response to this, Nasdaq Stock Market LLC announced in August 2021 the introduction of a disclosure rule about the "voluntary self-identified gender, racial characteristic, and LGBT+ status" of the company's board and a target of two "diverse" board members per company.[3]

The Gendered Norms Have Remained Unchallenged (for Now)

This overall grim assessment unfortunately does not come as a surprise. Attitudes and practices alike have not kept up with the equality agenda on the ground. The "regulatory shock" seems to have faded away. To be sure, lip service has been paid to add more women on boards. Even in the most conservative settings such as Germany, men board members are less and less likely to have a negative opinion about gender quotas on board (Ahrens and Scheele). A similar situation has been found in Belgium among shareholders (Roos and Zanoni) and in Austria among holders of leadership roles (Gresch and Sauer). Women may be "good for business" after all.

This does not mean, though, that the overall framing of the issue has come that far. Indeed, the issue of women's exclusion from economic leadership still tends, more often than not, to be framed as a "supply-side" problem that needs to be fixed to improve company performance. There has been little attempt over time to consider the "demand-side" and the gendered inequalities in the workplace as a fundamental part of the problem. Freidenvall reminds us that on one hand, in Sweden, women business leaders are still considered through a gendered lens

---

[3] Security Exchange Act Release No. 34-92590 (August 6, 2021). Order approving SR-NASDAQ-2020-081 and SR-NASDAQ-2020-082. https://www.sec.gov/rules/sro/nasdaq/2021/34-92590.pdf (Accessed September 12, 2021).

regarding ambition, skills, resources to lead, and capacity to manage work and care commitments; on the other hand, young men in Sweden still believe that gaining access to business leadership is a matter of merit alone. In Austria, a recent survey among business leaders reveals that a large majority consider that work-life balance is the major barrier to gender equality on boards, closely followed by "women's lack of ambition and self-confidence" (Gresch and Sauer, p. x). In the best cases, initiatives are put in place to "train" women for board membership. In the worse cases, the issue does not even find any champions to support the cause, as Spehar tells us about Croatia and Serbia.

Direct gender stereotypes and discriminations are not systematically called out either. Milner (p. 77) wisely reminds us that "The term of 'chairmen' was not challenged by the Davies review and continues to be routinely used in all communications." In Germany, women board members are, on average, paid less than men. In Belgium, a leading woman figure in business, Dominique Leroy, was greatly lauded in the press but was still paid less than her male counterparts (Roos and Zanoni, p. 372). Despite women on boards having reached a critical mass, the situation remains such that the women board members themselves are often reluctant to deviate from the traditional gender norms, as Teigen contends for the case of Norway and Milner for the case of the UK. "In order to make it to the top, women are coached, mentored and socialized into the existing way of working," says a UK-based interviewee (Milner, p. 79–80). A spillover effect from the dominant norms not being challenged is that women business leaders themselves fail to support and even actively oppose gender quotas. For example, a large share of businesswomen refrained from supporting quota initiatives in Spain until recently (Lombardo and Verge).

The situation may be brighter regarding public attention in the countries where there has been a growing political consensus in favor of regulatory action toward gender equality in leadership. The media has apparently switched sides. In Belgium, the media seized the early outcome of the 2011 quota law to emphasize its merit, at least from a business case perspective; we moved from "Top women prefer not to be seen as women" (Eckert and Vanhecke, 2016, cited in Roos and Zanoni, p. 259) to "The more female top managers, the higher the stock price" (Vanbrussel, 2017, cited in Roos and Zanoni, Ibid.). Blanchard and Rabier (p. 235) highlight a similar effect of media framing in France, "by putting forward the good results of the laws and female role models, the media has helped to legitimate both gender quotas and women's careers and ambitions." In Belgium, Roos and Zanoni also tell us that the current generation of women business leaders has often been portrayed as role models. In Germany, the 30% mandate has even inspired leaders in the media to reflect on their own practices and consider establishing a target for leadership roles (Ahrens and Scheele).

The impact of policy on public opinion is a complex matter for assessment. On the one hand, there have not been large-scale surveys testing attitudes toward equality in economic leadership across a large set of countries and time. On the other, a change in public attitudes may not reflect a change in the regulatory practices so much as a change in the corporate practices under the leadership of pioneer companies as Hoard argues for the US case. Alternatively, a shift in public opinion may actually be the trigger for a change in a company's take on gender equality instead of the other way around. In a nutshell, the jury is still out on policy impact on public opinion.

We zoom in on the three cases where the regulatory trajectory started the earliest to see if the longevity of policy responses has made a difference in the struggle to challenge dominant gender norms: Norway with its quota law in 2003, Spain following with a quota model in 2007, and Sweden where a self-regulatory model was put into place in 2005. An optimistic picture is painted by Mari Teigen and Lenita Freidenvall for societal impact in Norway and Sweden in the long run. Teigen emphasizes that the Norwegian model might be ripe for ripple effects on society more generally through policy feedback. The legitimacy of gender quotas has been on the rise among Norwegian elites, including among men business leaders, and the limited scope of the Norwegian quotas may boost its late popularity given the fact that a large majority of companies were bystanders (Teigen et al, 2019). More importantly, Teigen argues that society has woken up to interrogating the cause of male dominance. Freidenvall makes a similar point about Sweden. She emphasizes that men are gradually part of the solution rather than the problem and that the discussion has moved from whether there is an issue with women's underrepresentation in leadership to how to fix the issue. The picture painted by Lombardo and Verge in Spain is less rosy. A majority of citizens still believe that board appointments are and should be made on the basis of merit only. They nevertheless highlight that the first sign of transformative change might be found among businesswomen who have been increasingly more supportive of a coercive solution.

Lessons Learned and Looking Ahead

With now the full-scale study completed, we return to the point of departure for the book. In the face of persistent gender imbalances and inequality, how and why are the current public policies in action across the globe not up to the task? What can be done to make policy action more resilient on the ground?

The terrain of the corporate boardroom, we knew from the start, was a challenging one. The last major holdout of male power has been put under the gun of policies to actually change the entrenched gender-biased path dependencies of the boardroom. As both the country and comparative analyses have shown, significant, even remarkable, numerical progress has been made since businesses were forced to pay attention to issues of gender balance with quite limited qualitative advances. Still, after fifteen years of policy, we are in the state of strategic adaptation across all of the countries with gender accommodation being achieved in many countries; some of these have lurched back toward little or no movement, and others have moved toward some sort of meaningful progress and even an inkling of transformative change.

Looking Back

Looking at the past policy experiences of the fifteen countries we have learned some valuable lessons.

Lesson 1. Policy Implementation Matters—While there are certainly broader questions about whether improvements in women's rights and reduction in gender-biased norms and hierarchies actually are a direct product of policy efforts, we can say beyond a shadow of a doubt that implementation of corporate board gender equality policy was pivotal in policy progress. Policy implementation matters in terms of numbers as well as keeping opposition at bay and making incremental change in norms and attitudes, albeit not to the level of transformative expectations. But when actionable policy was dutifully implemented, movement was seen, when it was not, nothing happened or, even worse, back-pedaling occurred.

Lesson 2. Complexity, Complexity, Complexity—Confirming past research on the politics of gender equality policy formation, this study shows that simple notions of a single magic bullet, like quotas to solve the gender imbalance problem on boards or mono-causal explanations like the sociopolitical and cultural context being a primary reason for success, did not work at all. Rather, complexity and context specificity were the driving dynamics. The most successful policy responses were complex policy mixes of combinations of recommendations and mandates buttressed by actionable policies with sanctions and solid reporting and monitoring—a bit of training thrown in helped too. The policy experiences in the four Central and Eastern countries arguably went against the grain of complexity, with poor policy performance getting poorer in the face of the rise of anti-gender ideology and illiberal democratic development. At the same time, the abysmal performance of Canada and the USA, from countries with quite different levels of economic and political development, brought back in the rule of complexity at least as far as regional similarities were concerned. The recipes for success in the corporate boardroom were, like so many other gender equality policy areas, comprised of combinations of ingredients working together to overcome the resistance and gender-biased path dependencies.

Lesson 3. Inclusion, Actionable Policy, Public Support, and Persuasion—
Thus, the configurational analytical logic leads us to the third lesson to be

drawn: a well-designed and backed-up policy adapted for the particular place and time, put into place in conjunction with broad-based and inclusive coalitions that bring on board the predominantly male business elite and leads to successful outcomes rather than adopting a one-size-fits-all approach. Without the right policy mix, a broad-based coalition, public support, and the support of powerful men business leaders and their peak business associations, the remarkable progress in numbers and the less remarkable advances in gender transformation would not have been made. Indeed, when these required parts of the puzzle were missing, advances were even more trivial and slow moving.

Lesson 4. Real Change Takes Time—While a tried and true observation for most societal change, this lesson must be included for corporate board equality, particularly given the degree to which entrenched gender norms have been part and parcel of the business world for so long. And this policy is relatively young, taking-off only in the early 2000s when compared to other first-generation gender equality policies like the expansion of women's suffrage and second-generation policies on reproductive and employment rights. Thus, in some ways perhaps the glass is half full rather than half empty. That is, a great deal of movement has happened in a relatively short period of time. Moreover, fundamental change may have been triggered in some of the countries through the process of getting more women into board positions and now with the rising presence of women on boards in critical mass. Only time will tell, of course, as to whether these past developments turn into real pay-offs in the future.

Looking Ahead

No matter what the future brings, this study's findings, in general, provide plenty of fuel for evidence-based recommendations that may facilitate the tide of change that seems to be sweeping across the countries in this study. The following recommendations are even more meaningful given that the absence of evidence-based strategies was a founding principle for the tireless work of the collection of policy scholars who contributed to this book, and for us too, as well as for the launch and maintenance of the GEPP approach and network as a whole. Four recommendations leap out from these collective findings.

Recommendation 1. Look inside Your Country—More than most policy areas, it seems that the solutions and strength to tackle entrenched gender-biased hierarchies and path dependencies come from within a country's boundaries. While to be sure, Norway was a touchstone for many countries, none followed the same path as Norway. Rather, policy mixes, coalitions, and pressure on male leaders came together in different ways within each context. The fact that the EU still has not adopted a policy in this area, and both EU member states and non-member states sojourned on without the EU, further solidifies this recommendation.

Recommendation 2. Good Policy Design Matters—Yes, there are an awful lot of different tools to be considered and used, but policy advocates must think carefully about the right combination of policy tools including mandates, recommendations, and training. And these mechanisms need to be used in a way that actually holds the feet of men business leaders to the fire and provides useful strategies for the handful of policy actors on the side of women.

Recommendation 3. Reach Out to Excluded Women—It is clear that in this policy area, extraordinary effort must be made to go beyond the loyal base of this policy: white privileged women. While it has been slow in coming, the incremental movement to broader inclusion in many of the countries in the book suggests there is hope for the future to turn strategic adaptation into at least simple gender transformation.

Recommendation 4. Talk to the Men and the Men Need to Act—To be sure, it is fundamental that policy mixes have the capacity and sanctions to compel the male business elites to act. But women business leaders and advocacy groups, as well as women's policy actors in the state, must reach out to men leaders to bring them on board the corporate gender equality train that has been steaming ahead—in other words, they must turn male opponents into allies. Persuading men business leaders that the justice case is just as important to make as the business case is crucial for achieving the ultimate prize of gatekeeper frame shifts for achieving true gender transformation. As more women arrive in positions of power on boards, they very well may have more leverage to convince their male counterparts that more needs to be done to empower men as well as women from diverse backgrounds and to move more women of all backgrounds into positions of power. Just as importantly, men need to act and take a leading role in the complex process of identifying, training, and recruiting women for leadership positions, and here the emphasis is on not just bringing women as board members but pushing for their presence at the top.

We would be remiss if we ended the story of corporate board policy implementation without any suggestions for future research. The following three seem to be the most pressing with regards to the larger scholarly interest in the politics of gender equality policy implementation.

Research Agenda Item 1. Keep on Truckin'—First and foremost, policy scholars need to continue tracking and studying the unfolding of future policy actions and responses. Given how quickly policy progress was made on at least a numerical level with more limited qualitative impacts, we need to be attentive to fast-moving shifts and changes and, as we have seen, "shocks to the system." The big question looming is whether we have hit a glass ceiling for women accessing boards, just below gender balance, or will progress reach pure gender balance and quality representation? One observation that is heartening in these challenging times is the extent to which the ball kept rolling even while a global health pandemic raged with many countries making slow but steady progress toward transformative potential and some even seeing the potential for more authoritative policy mixes. Of course, the analyses in this book were only brought up to date at the end of the pandemic; therefore, future studies need to look carefully at the post-pandemic state of affairs for policy responses and outcomes.

Research Agenda Item 2. When do Women Matter and How?—With the cross-country average moving ten percentage points in seventeen years and some countries slowly approaching the 50:50 target, it is time that we end the political, if not analytical, obsession with the number of women on boards. We need to examine a whole series of questions related to issues of substantive and quality representation: Who are the women who get in? How much say do they have in business decisions? For whom do they speak and how long do they stay? Building from the critical mass literature on gender balance in elected office, a major research question to be examined now that so many women have arrived is whether there is a tipping point in their numbers that would allow women board members to actually make a difference, and if so what would that difference be. This research is fine-grained, firm-based, and hence quite costly and time-consuming, an effort that would need funding and infrastructure if it were to be done in the same systematic spirit of this book.

Research Agenda Item 3. What Matters Most? Sector or National/Regional Policy Style?—It is somehow fitting to end our journey into the boardroom with a call to assess the findings and lessons learned in this study in comparison to research on other areas of gender equality policy. The cross-national imperatives of strategic adjustment, numerical progress, and an absence of real transformative change as well as of significant trends in politics or outcomes by regional country grouping all corroborate one of the findings of previous comparative gender policy research, that the policy sector trumps national policy styles in the search for the elusive recipe for gender equality policy success. At the same time, as the cross-sectoral analysis of French policy implementation à la GEPP shows, at least in France there were important commonalities across the wider range of policy implementation cases studied that undermined the argument for sectoral patterns (Mazur and Engeli, 2020).

Whatever the road ahead for following these recommendations and calls for future research, we hope that this comparative study of the past national experiences with policy implementation that tackle the last bastion of male domination and control has provided food for thought for scholars and fuel for advocates alike in different countries, settings, and situations across the globe.

References

Engeli, Isabelle and Amy G. Mazur (2018) "Taking Implementation Seriously in Assessing Success: The Politics of Gender Policy in Practice," *European Journal of Gender and Politics*, 1 (1), pp. 11–29.

Grésy, Brigitte, Agnès Arcier, and Caroline Ressot (2019) *Accès des femmes aux responsabilités et rôle levier des financements publics: Des nouveaux champs pour la parité*. Paris: HCE.

Mazur, Amy G and Isabelle Engeli (2020) "The Search for the Elusive Recipe for Gender Equality Policy: When Implementation Matters," *French Politics*, 13 (1–2), pp. 3-27.

Teigen, Mari, Hege Skjeie, and Rune Karlsen (2019) "Framing and Feedback: Increased Support for Gender Quotas among Elites," *European Journal of Politics and Gender*, 2 (3), 399–423, https://doi.org/10.1332/251510819X15639713867651. (Accessed September 17, 2020).

2020 Women on Boards Gender Diversity Index (2019) *Progress of Women Corporate Director of Russell 3000 Index Companies*.

Workplace Gender Equality Agency (2020) *Australia's Gender Pay Gap Statistics*, https://www.wgea.gov.au/data/fact-sheets/australias-gender-pay-gap-statistics (Accessed August 3, 2020).

WXN/CCBDC (2018) *Annual Report Card 2018: Advancing Diverse Leadership on Canada's Corporate Boards*.

Index